Valentina Vadi
Leicester
2L

OBJECTIVITY IN LAW AND LEGAL REASONING

Legal theorists consider their discipline as an objective endeavour in line with other fields of science. Objectivity in science is generally regarded as a fundamental condition, informing how science should be practiced and how truths may be found. Objective scientists venture to uncover empirical truths about the world and ought to eliminate personal biases, prior commitments and emotional involvement. However, legal theorists are inevitably bound up with a given legal culture. Consequently, their scholarly work derives at least in part from this environment and their subtle interaction with it. This book questions critically, in novel ways and from various perspectives, the possibilities of objectivity of legal theory in the twenty-first century. It transpires that legal theory is unavoidably confronted with varying conceptions of law, underlying ideologies, approaches to legal method, argumentation and discourse and so on, which limit the possibilities of 'objectivity' in law and in legal reasoning. The authors of this book reveal some of these underlying notions and discuss their consequences for legal theory.

European Academy of Legal Theory Series: Volume 10

EUROPEAN ACADEMY OF LEGAL THEORY
MONOGRAPH SERIES

General Editors
Professor Mark Van Hoecke
Professor François Ost

Titles in this Series

Moral Conflict and Legal Reasoning
Scott Veitch

The Harmonisation of European Private Law
edited by Mark Van Hoecke and Francois Ost

On Law and Legal Reasoning
Fernando Atria

Law as Communication
Mark Van Hoecke

Legisprudence
edited by Luc Wintgens

Epistemology and Methodology of Comparative Law
edited by Mark Van Hoecke

Making the Law Explicit.
The Normativity of Legal Argumentation
Matthias Klatt

The Policy of Law
A Legal Theoretical Framework
Mauro Zamboni

Methodologies of Legal Research
Which Kind of Method for What Kind of Discipline?
edited by Mark Van Hoecke

Objectivity in Law and Legal Reasoning

Edited by

Jaakko Husa and Mark Van Hoecke

·HART·
PUBLISHING

OXFORD AND PORTLAND, OREGON
2013

Published in the United Kingdom by Hart Publishing Ltd
16C Worcester Place, Oxford, OX1 2JW
Telephone: +44 (0)1865 517530
Fax: +44 (0)1865 510710
E-mail: mail@hartpub.co.uk
Website: http://www.hartpub.co.uk

Published in North America (US and Canada) by
Hart Publishing
c/o International Specialized Book Services
920 NE 58th Avenue, Suite 300
Portland, OR 97213-3786
USA
Tel: +1 503 287 3093 or toll-free: (1) 800 944 6190
Fax: +1 503 280 8832
E-mail: orders@isbs.com
Website: http://www.isbs.com

© The editors and contributors severally 2013

The editors and contributors have asserted their right under the Copyright,
Designs and Patents Act 1988, to be identified as the authors of this work.

All rights reserved. No part of this publication may be reproduced, stored in a retrieval
system, or transmitted, in any form or by any means, without the prior permission of Hart
Publishing, or as expressly permitted by law or under the terms agreed with the appropriate
reprographic rights organisation. Enquiries concerning reproduction which may not be
covered by the above should be addressed to Hart Publishing Ltd at the address above.

British Library Cataloguing in Publication Data
Data Available

ISBN: 978-1-84946-441-3

Typeset by Compuscript Ltd, Shannon
Printed and bound in Great Britain by
TJ International Ltd, Padstow, Cornwall

Preface

This book contains a selection of papers presented in an earlier version at the 6th Benelux-Scandinavian Symposium on Legal Theory, held in Rovaniemi (Lapland) on 8–10 June 2011. This Conference was organised by Jaakko Husa and Juha Karhu, both Professors at the University of Lapland in Rovaniemi. The general topic of this symposium was 'Objectivity in Legal Theory?'. The first paper in this book by Mark Van Hoecke contains references to the other papers, including summaries, and acts by the same token also as an introduction to the book and to the problems discussed in it.

The preceding Benelux-Scandinavian Symposia on Legal Theory took place in Antwerp in 1983 ('The Utility of Legal Theory'), Uppsala in 1986 ('The Structure of Law'), Amsterdam in 1991 ('Coherence and Conflict in Law'), Turku in 1998 ('Theory of Legislation') and Maastricht in 2002 ('European Legal Integration and Analytical Legal Theory'). The 2011 Symposium focused less on analytical legal theory than the previous symposia. However, the analytic tradition of clarity was continued, alongside with the Benelux–Scandinavian tradition of debating seriously and in a very friendly atmosphere.

We thank Henna Pajulammi and Laura Tarvainen for their help in organising the Symposium, Caroline Laske for revising the English language of the papers.

Contents

Preface v
List of Contributors ix

I. Introduction 1
1. Objectivity in Law and Jurisprudence 3
   Mark Van Hoecke

II. Objectivity of Legal Theory 21
2. Can Legal Theory Be Objective? 23
   Jaap Hage
3. The Impossibility of an Outsider's Perspective 45
   Pauline C Westerman

III. Legal Reasoning 67
4. Objective Legal Reasoning—Objectivity Without Objects ... 69
   Matti Ilmari Niemi
5. Legal Certainty as an Element of Objectivity in Law 85
   Juha Raitio
6. Objective Rules of Argumentation 109
   Bertjan Wolthuis
7. Easy Cases and Objective Interpretation 131
   Niko Soininen

IV. Human Behaviour and its Objective Foundation 151
8. Can Inalienable Rights Provide an Objective Foundation
   for Law and Morality? 153
   Maija Aalto-Heinilä
9. Objectivity and the Law's Assumptions about Human
   Behaviour 171
   Péter Cserne

V. (Legal) Cultures 195

10. Kaleidoscopic Cultural Views and Legal Theory—Dethroning the Objectivity? 197
    Jaakko Husa

11. Translators and Legal Comparatists as Objective Mediators between Cultures? 213
    Caroline Laske

12. Legal Science Challenged by Cultural Paradigms: 'Subjective Objectivity' in Legal Scholarship 229
    Mustapha El Karouni

Index 251

List of Contributors

Maija AALTO-HEINILÄ is a lecturer in Philosophy at the University of Eastern Finland, Department of Law (maija.aalto@uef.fi).

Péter CSERNE is a researcher at Hull University, School of Law (p.cserne@hull.ac.uk). At the time he wrote this paper, he was a researcher at Tilburg University.

Mustapha EL KAROUNI is a researcher at the University of Ghent, Department of Jurisprudence and Legal History (mustapha.elkarouni@ugent.be; mustapha.elkarouni@swing.be).

Jaap HAGE is Professor of Law at the Universities of Maastricht and Hasselt (jaap.hage@maastrichtuniversity.nl).

Jaakko HUSA is Professor of Legal Culture and Legal Linguistics at the University of Lapland, Rovaniemi (jaakko.husa@ulapland.fi).

Caroline LASKE is a researcher at the University of Ghent, Department of Jurisprudence and Legal History (caroline.laske@ugent.be).

Matti Ilmari NIEMI is Professor of Civil Law at the Lappeenranta University of Technology, School of Business (Lappeenranta) (Matti.Niemi@lut.fi).

Juha RAITIO is Professor of European Law at Helsinki University, Faculty of Law (juha.raitio@helsinki.fi).

Niko SOININEN is a researcher at the University of Eastern Finland, Department of Law (niko.soininen@uef.fi).

Mark VAN HOECKE is Research Professor of Legal Theory and Comparative Law at the University of Ghent (mark.vanhoecke@ugent.be).

Pauline WESTERMAN is Professor of Legal Philosophy at the Law Faculty of Groningen University (p.c.westerman@rug.nl).

Bertjan WOLTHUIS is senior lecturer in legal theory at the Law Faculty of the Vrije Universiteit Amsterdam (a.j.wolthuis@vu.nl).

I. Introduction

1

Objectivity in Law and Jurisprudence

MARK VAN HOECKE

I. A NEED FOR CERTAINTIES

PEOPLE NEED CERTAINTIES. This is one of the main functions of religion and of law in any society. They both fulfil this function in two respects: practically and epistemologically.

From a practical point of view, religious rules and rituals and legal rules help in organising one's personal life: not working on Sundays (or Saturdays), following moral rules, participating in collective rituals at important moments in life (birth, transition from childhood to adulthood, marriage, death); traffic rules, rules related to the organisation of work, or to urban planning and so on, all partly organise our lives. They make the world less chaotic for us. This has actually been the main argument in support of strong political power by authors such as Hobbes or Macchiavelli. In their view, the alternative would be chaos with many more disadvantages than having a strong political leader, even a dictator, acting in the interest of his people protecting them against enemies and keeping a stable society within the community he governs.

From an epistemological point of view, religious and legal certainties create a framework which allows us to understand the world, to 'place' things and to provide sense and shape to our lives. A belief in heaven helps to cope with a miserable life if one has a perspective of eternal happiness or a better reincarnation after death. Similarly, believing in the equitable and just character of legal rules, in the neutrality and fairness of judges and the like, creates a more comfortable feeling than if one thinks that corruption and self-interest of law-makers and judges govern legal life. At a more sophisticated level, it creates theories such as Ronald Dworkin's 'one right answer thesis': even if only a superman, a Hercules, is able to find this answer, it is important to believe that such an answer exists and that it is only due to human weakness that we cannot be sure in all cases whether we did find the 'right answer'. The alternative again is chaos. And we do not want chaos, we want an ordered, stable life. Even if we like adventures, we can only move forwards if we may fall back at least on some certainties. Even if we notice that some rules or decisions are arbitrary and unjust, we need to believe that in general, law is just. Moreover, every political or legal system will claim to be just, or at least those in power will make that claim. Along the lines of such epistemological claims (the just legal system, the one right answer to judicial interpretation questions and so on) we may also find the claim to 'objectivity': objectivity of the law, objectivity of the legal actors (especially judges), objectivity of legal doctrine, and even objectivity of jurisprudence. Believing in such objectivity gives us a good feeling. This would contrast with believing that rules are only created to support the powerful against those in a weaker position, or with a belief that all judges are corrupt, that legal scholars just give a personal opinion, not based on sound arguments or, even worse, that they too are corrupt, and/or with a belief that jurisprudential theories have no link with some 'objective reality' but are rather a quite subjective artistic impression of the legal world by some 'scholar' or 'academic'. A good example of this kind of reasoning goes as follows:

> To the extent that we associate law with science, we may hold and convey the hope that objectivity resides in law. Objectivity implies impartiality, and impartiality implies lack of arbitrariness, fairness and justice. Since laws can affect human life in dramatic ways, such as imprisonment and, in some countries, even death through capital punishment, what can justify law if law is not objectively, scientifically, verifiably justifiable?[1]

We need legal certainty indeed.[2]

II. OBJECTIVITY IN LAW

In legislation, 'objectivity'[3] has mainly been translated into the general principle of the 'generality', the general scope of statutory rules and into the equality principle.

Legislation should have a general application and be valid for all those belonging to the same category. Moreover, such categories should not be narrowed down in such a way as to circumvent this broad scope with the aim to advantage or disadvantage certain persons. If, for instance, there are

---

[1] V Grosswald Curran, *Comparative Law: An Introduction* (Durham, Carolina Academic Press, 2002) 3.

[2] See, most notably, on legal certainty Juha Raitio's paper in this volume (ch 5).

[3] Here, we are not entering into the general philosophical debate on 'objectivity' and the varying conceptions related to it. For a good (and concise) overview and critical discussion see G Pavlakos, *Our Knowledge of the Law. Objectivity and Practice in Legal Theory* (Oxford, Hart Publishing, 2007) especially 23–38. See also the references in the first footnote to Peter Cserne's paper in this volume (ch 9).

two family-owned breweries in a small town, one with 38 members of staff, the other one with 75, imposing a local tax on 'all breweries with more than 50 members of staff' would lack 'generality'. Moreover, when it would appear that some members of the family owning the smaller brewery are part of the local government, whereas the other family is not represented, this rule would be considered to be lacking 'objectivity' and as representing an abuse of power, a 'subjective' attack on a competing company. However, the tax rule as worded above would, as such, be perfectly 'objective'. It is the context, which creates the lack of 'objectivity'. In other words, the general scope of the legislative rule is a necessary, but not a sufficient condition for its 'objectivity'.

Whereas emphasising the general scope of a law focuses on its field of application, rather *in abstracto*, the equality principle, on the other hand, looks at this application more concretely from the point of view of the individual citizen.

Making a distinction within the groups to which the rule may apply is as such 'objective'. Allowing extra payment for people working during the night will be considered to be both an 'objective' criterion and not a discrimination. However, if foreigners or nationals of foreign origin would be excluded from such an advantage, it would be considered as a discrimination, even if the distinction is 'objective' in the sense of general, not aimed at disadvantaging some individuals.

This kind of conclusion has led to the distinction between formal and substantive equality. Consumers and professionals may formally be equal when they enter into a contract, but from a substantive point of view they are not. Hence, many legislators, including the European Union, have enacted rules aiming at protecting the consumer in his contractual relationship with the professional supplier of goods or services.

In addition, formal equality is a necessary but not a sufficient condition. The distinction made must be acceptable, otherwise it will be considered to be a discrimination. However, even formal equality may lead to discrimination. If equal situations must be treated equally then unequal situations must be treated differently. Again, criteria outside formal equality will be used to consider the apparently equal treatment as discrimination. Such criteria should be 'objective'. But what does this mean?

What is undoubtedly considered as discrimination in our society may well be (almost) fully accepted in other cultures or may have been accepted in our society in earlier times. A well-known example is the 1979 *Marckx* decision of the European Court of Human Rights which stated explicitly that unequal treatment of children born outside wedlock as compared to 'legitimate' children had been accepted since times immemorial and even at the time of the drafting approval of the European Convention on Human Rights in 1950, but that less than three decades later the general opinion in society had changed and this unequal treatment had to be considered to be an unacceptable discrimination.[4] Obviously, 'objectivity' does not refer to some kind of absolute and eternal truth.

At the level of adjudicating the law, 'objectivity' has been translated into 'neutrality', most notably the neutrality of the judges deciding cases. More recently, actual neutrality has been broadened to the *appearance* of neutrality: when a party in a trial can reasonably fear that a judge is not completely neutral in the case, this judge is burdened with 'lacking neutrality' independently of the question whether he was actually able to decide the case fully 'objectively'. The Belgian 'Spaghetti case' is a rather extreme example of this way of reasoning. In the late nineties and during the investigation in the *Dutroux* case about a paedophile who kidnapped, abused and killed several young girls, the judge in charge of the investigation was invited by the parents of the victims to a 'spaghetti evening', held to raise money to cover the costs of the trial incurred by those parents. The judge received free spaghetti and a pen. This was considered by the Belgian Court of Cassation as sufficient grounds for the accused to doubt the judge's neutrality. As a consequence, the judge was taken off the case and replaced by a different judge.[5] Here 'objectivity' means having no subjective feelings in favour (or to the disadvantage) of one of the parties. However, such feelings can only be proven by external elements, such as comments given by the judge to journalists or having been spotted in the company of a party (or with the lawyer representing them) outside the necessary professional contacts. The elements and criteria taken into account to decide whether or not there is a lack of (apparent) neutrality should once again be 'objective'. These may not depend on the exaggerated fears of one party who may see lack of neutrality everywhere. But what does 'objectivity' mean here?

While the judges neutrality may be a point of discussion before or during a trial and mainly related to the evaluation of facts, discussions on the objectivity of a judicial decision will often relate to the 'objectivity' of the interpretation of a legal text. It is from that perspective that, for instance, Article 164 of the EC Treaty stipulates that the European Court of Justice (ECJ) 'shall ensure that in the interpretation and application of this Treaty the law is observed'. Here, 'the law' becomes a kind of mythical reference to 'truth' and 'objectivity', even more than in the usual reference to 'the aim of the legislator'.

---

[4] ECtHR 13 June 1979, *Paula Marckx v Belgium* (1979) 11 EHHR 330.
[5] Belgian Court of Cassation 14 October 1996, case *Connerotte*, published in many journals, eg *Revue de droit pénal*, 1997, 470.

III. OBJECTIVE, REASONABLE, JUSTIFIED

I am not going to elaborate on the discussion about the meaning of 'objectivity' in general, nor about its use in judicial practice,[6] but I want to point to some conclusions other authors have drawn from such analyses and which show how other (softer) conceptions and approaches are hidden behind apparently strong claims of 'objectivity'.

On the basis of an extensive analysis of Polish judicial decisions, Lidka Rodak came to the conclusion that the concept of 'objectivity' is one readily used by lawyers because of its strong argumentative power. She calls it 'an example of exercising power through words'[7] and adds 'objectivity provides the easiest way to close the discourse and removes personal responsibility from the decisions taken'. The deconstruction of the concept of 'objectivity' finally leads to the statement that objectivity refers to whatever is 'not purely subjective'.[8]

From the discussion above it appears that 'objectivity' in a strong sense is not possible; not in practice, but not even in theory because of a lack of a well-defined frame of reference for testing such 'objectivity'. Eventually, 'subjectivity' is not opposed to 'objectivity' but rather to 'inter-subjectivity'. In this sense, an 'objective' statement is one which is accepted by a large majority of the people concerned or, in most cases, is assuming that such a majority of reasonable people would accept that statement. Hence, 'objectivity' and 'reasonableness' are closely interrelated.

What may be considered to be 'reasonable' is in turn determined by some inter-subjective consensus.

According to John Gardner and Timothy Macklem, '"reasonable" means much the same as "justified"'.[9] These authors also convincingly argue that 'reasonable' means the same as 'rational'.[10] Actually, we are faced with different ways to say that, for instance, a legal decision is 'good', as in our minds we associate 'objective', inter-subjectively supported, 'rational', 'reasonable', 'justified' in relation to a decision, with a *good decision*, and vice versa.

---

[6] See, eg L Rodak, 'Different Conceptions of Objectivity in Legal Discourse' (PhD thesis, Katowice/Ghent University, 2009) who distinguishes three approaches as to objectivity (of law): a metaphysical approach, an epistemological approach and a semantic approach (ch II), where in each approach diverging conceptions of 'objectivity' may be identified. 'Objective' is used in many different senses, such as equating 'objective interpretation' with the 'plain meaning' of the text, eg 'it is reasonable to see the role of the court as being to interpret laws objectively according to the "plain words" used with no particular end in view', N Fennelly, 'Legal Interpretation at the European Court of Justice' (1997) 20 *Fordham International Law Journal* 656–79, at 672.

[7] Rodak, (n 6) 166 (first page of the Conclusion).

[8] Ibid 174 (last page).

[9] J Gardner and T Macklem, 'Reasons', ch 11 in J Coleman and S Shapiro (eds), *The Oxford Handbook of Jurisprudence and Philosophy of Law* (Oxford, Oxford University Press, 2002) 440–75, at 474.

[10] Ibid.

Any of those qualities has a strong argumentative power but 'objective' has probably the strongest. If some statement is 'objective' it does not seem to require further arguments, whereas reference to one of the other concepts may suggest a need for further justification: inter-subjectivity among which subjects and why? rational on the basis of which premises? reasonable in view of which values? justified on the basis of which arguments?

This paper is not about semantic strategies or argumentative power but, in this introductory chapter, it is useful to point to the vagueness and even problematic meaning of the concept of 'objectivity'. It also seems wise to drop any strong (and difficult to uphold) conception of 'objectivity' and to be aware of the inter-changeability of 'objectivity' with other concepts, such as 'inter-subjectivity', depending on the context.

IV. OBJECTIVITY IN LEGAL DOCTRINE

If we agree that 'objective' in a weaker sense bears the same meaning as 'inter-subjective', the core question becomes: inter-subjective within which forum?

It is not accidental that recently the concept of 'community of interpreters' has largely been integrated in legal and jurisprudential language. This is actually the main point of reference in legal doctrine. An interpretation of some legal text will be considered to be 'correct', 'reasonable', 'justified', 'objective', if this interpretation is shared by the large majority of the interpretive community. Even when there are diverging opinions, there will be some consensus on which interpretations may 'reasonably be supported', for which the interpretive community considers that there are sound arguments, independently of the position each of its members takes. This range of 'defendable' interpretations is based on a shared understanding, within that community, of what is acceptable in legal reasoning: which kind of arguments? which values? which hierarchy among those values? and so on. It constitutes the paradigmatical framework of legal doctrine.

The interpretive community is, of course, much broader than the community of legal scholars. It also encompasses all legal practitioners (with some more advanced role for judges, as they have a stronger authoritative position, including when their precedents are not binding) and to some extent politicians (involved in law making) and even the media (commenting on cases with a broader relevance for society). For legal doctrine, this community is demarcated in any case by the borders of the validity of the legal system. The interpretive community for Finnish law is limited to Fins. The interpretive community for canon law is limited to people related to the Roman Catholic Church.

With the exception of international law, there is no fully worldwide interpretive community.

The doctrinal attempts to achieve cross-border harmonisation are a special case. This is a meeting of representatives of different interpretive communities which do not necessarily share the same paradigmatical framework of common views on such matters as law, values, methods, argumentation theories and so on.

Here, the interpretive community will largely be constituted of scholars. However, when they succeed in producing sets of rules which are adopted in legal practice be it, for instance, in the form of a European directive or as an 'optional instrument',[11] the interpretive community will be broadened accordingly.

As long as there is no common paradigmatic framework at this cross-border level, an 'inter-subjective consensus' remains a relative concept. Rather than agreeing on the basis of the same common assumptions, there will be a battle between competing paradigms, a power struggle where a majority may well impose its view on a minority, without there being real consensus. As to private law in Europe, the tension will mainly be between the Common Law and Continental Law. At world level, such diverging and even conflicting basic views will make it difficult to create a genuinely common interpretive community among lawyers from Western, Islamic and African and/or Asian legal traditions. This is already the case in the interpretation of international commercial contracts, but is even more significant in determining the scope of concepts such as 'human rights' and each of those rights separately: 'democracy', 'rule of law' and so on. So, here 'objectivity' even in its weak sense of 'inter-subjectivity' becomes largely impossible, as there is not a sufficiently common framework on the basis of which one may agree that some (interpretation of a) rule or judicial decision is 'reasonable' or 'justified'.

V. OBJECTIVITY IN COMPARATIVE LAW

A major epistemological and methodological problem in comparative law is the question of how to find a 'neutral', 'objective' point of view for comparison, which is not biased by one's own legal system and implicit understandings.

---

[11] V Reding, 'Warum Europa ein optionales Europäisches Vertragsrecht benötigt' (2011) *Zeitschrift für Europäisches Privatrecht* 1–6.

In the last decades most comparative lawyers have assumed that it is possible to use some 'objective' *tertium comparationis*:[12]

> What the comparative lawyer looks at as *tertium comparationis* could be the 'common function' between institutions and rules, the 'common goal' they set out to achieve, the 'problem', the 'factual situations' they are created to solve or the solutions offered.[13]

In particular, the presumed similarity of factual situations assumes the 'objectivity of facts': cases are thought to be the same, only the law would be different. However, it is impossible to determine 'objective' perspectives for comparing cases or legal solutions or for determining criteria for 'similarities' and 'differences':

> Such *'tertia comparationis'* are not objectively 'in the air'; rather they result from a choice about 'what matters', that is, which aspects of the law are relevant for the comparative lawyer, and which aspects of the law might benefit from the additional knowledge which comparison provides. Of course, such 'choices' may be subconscious; they are often influenced by an inherited conceptual and cultural understanding of the law.[14]

There are no 'objective' choices, only subjective ones. This requires clarity about the choices made and the reasons or motives for them.[15] In this way some inter-subjective frame of reference can be build and sheer arbitrariness avoided. Along the same lines of reasoning it has also been noted that in European harmonisation no objective criteria can be found in order to justify the choice as to why the drafters consider the rule they have selected to be the 'better' one.[16]

But there is more: from the nineteenth century, following the successes of positive sciences, lawyers have been looking for 'objective' universal law, a kind of natural law rooted in nature rather than in metaphysics. In the course of the twentieth century this idea of establishing a kind of legal table of Mendeljev valid for all times and places, has increasingly been replaced by a more realistic acceptance of cultural differences. Sometimes this has led to the denial of any possibility of objective comparison and even of

---

[12] First introduced by Ernst Rabel, mainly spread through K Zweigert and H Kötz, *Introduction to Comparative Law*, 3rd edn, translated by T Weir (Oxford, Clarendon Press, 1998) but often criticised as being theoretically weak: see R Michaels, 'The Functional Method of Comparative Law', ch 10 in M Reimann and R Zimmermann (eds), *The Oxford Handbook of Comparative Law* (Oxford, Oxford University Press, 2008) 339–82, especially at 367–69.

[13] E Örücü, 'Developing Comparative Law', ch 2 in E Örücü and D Nelken (eds), *Comparative Law. A Handbook* (Oxford, Hart Publishing, 2007) 43–65, at 48.

[14] N Jansen, 'Comparative Law and Comparative Knowledge', ch 9 in Reimann and Zimmermann *The Oxford Handbook of Comparative Law* (n 12) 305–38, at 314.

[15] Ibid 315.

[16] M Antokolskaia, 'The "Better Law" Approach and the Harmonisation of Family Law' in K Boele-Woelki (ed), *Perspectives for the Unification and the Harmonisation of Family Law in Europe* (Antwerp, Intersentia, 2003) 181.

understanding foreign legal systems. Other comparatists seem to believe that through dialogue all cultural differences may be bridged and in their view the creation of some universal law should only be a matter of time.[17] This tension has been well worded by Vivian Grosswald Curran

> [V]iews as to the presumed nature of law itself influence comparatists in forming their projects and in interpreting their results. For example, if laws either do or should reflect universal human needs and attributes, then comparative law might be a way of discovering objectively verifiable human commonalities. This was the idea of many comparatists in the past. If, on the other hand, human universals are few and far between, and people have culturally determined differences that represent fundamental, distinctive concerns, desires and attributes, then the comparatist's project would focus, rather, on identifying the characteristics of different peoples and different legal cultures, without aspiring to develop a set of universal legal ideals.[18]

VI. OBJECTIVITY IN JURISPRUDENCE

However one may define 'jurisprudence', 'legal theory' or 'legal philosophy', it should be obvious that those disciplines aim at transcending the borders of legal systems, at which legal doctrine inevitably stops. This means that jurisprudence (a term which may be used to cover the three 'disciplines' mentioned) will be faced with varying conceptions of law, ideologies, approaches to legal method and argumentation and so on. There is no sufficiently common paradigmatical framework that may act as a frame of reference for a scholarly community which could reach a high level of inter-subjectivity. This explains why jurisprudence, as conceived and developed in the European tradition, has largely remained a Western product. When non-Western scholars take part in those jurisprudential discussions they will usually (partly or fully) have been educated at a Western university. They may, at least to some extent, have adopted some or most of the paradigmatical assumptions of Western jurisprudents (especially the more rationalist and individualist approach), but that leads to the question to what extent they are still representatives of their original non-Western (legal) culture.

Of course, cultures are not isolated from each other. Modern means of transport and communication have increasingly meant that people around the world are informed about what happens in foreign countries, which makes them aware of differences among cultures and characteristics of

---

[17] A convincing psychological explanation for this tendency among German immigrés in the US, who have been very influential both in the US and in Europe, is offered by Vivian Grosswald Curran in her paper 'Cultural Immersion, Difference and Categories in US Comparative Law' (1998) 46 *American Journal of Comparative Law* 43, 66–78.

[18] V Grosswald Curran, *Comparative Law: An Introduction* (Durham, Carolina Academic Press, 2002) 4.

other cultures. Moreover, through the internet Western views on democracy, rule of law, human rights and the like have influenced large groups in other cultures. Subsequently they claim such Western rights for themselves and hence adopt some Western values and approaches, as the recent demonstrations and revolutions in several Islamic countries have shown. So, one may be cautiously optimistic as to the development of some common scholarly community that may well reach inter-subjective consensus on (most) jurisprudential matters. However, this will inevitably be a slow development, with ups and downs. It is doubtful whether divergences among legal cultures will ever disappear. Moreover, new divergences may develop, as is increasingly shown by the segregation of the Flemish and francophone cultures in Belgium, to such an extent that it became virtually impossible to create a federal government in Belgium.[19] In jurisprudence, it also appears that even within the Western scholarly discussion there are different scientific communities, focusing on different topics, using different methods. That is why almost 30 years ago the first Benelux–Scandinavian symposium on legal theory was organised: we discovered that the Nordic countries and the Benelux countries largely shared a common paradigmatical framework, common interest for the same topics, using similar methods (at that time mainly analytical) and reading the same international languages (at that time, apart from English, also German and French[20]), which meant having access to the same information and being able to built bridges between the larger jurisprudential cultures which until a few decades ago were largely isolated from each other. In June 2011 the sixth Benelux–Scandinavian Symposium on Legal Theory was organised in Rovaniemi, by Jaakko Husa and Juha Karhu. A selection of the papers presented there are published in this volume, sometimes in a thoroughly adapted new version. I will introduce these in the following section.

VII. WHAT DOES THIS VOLUME OFFER?

A. Objectivity of Legal Theory

Jaap Hage starts with the question whether the diversity among the legal systems in the world still allows us to have a neutral terminology by which they may be compared. This is important for legal theory, as theorists,

---

[19] In the years 2010 and 2011 it took more than 500 days before such a government was created.
[20] Meanwhile knowledge of German and French has dramatically decreased in all those countries, but the necessity of reading publications in those languages has decreased to the same extent as, nowadays, English has replaced French and German as lingua franca in jurisprudence. What is really important will be translated and published in English. What proves to be untranslatable may be shown to be very strongly imbedded in a local culture and, hence, to be of limited interest to the more international scholarly debate.

such as HLA Hart claim to say something sensible about the law in general and not only about concrete legal systems. In other words, they implicitly claim that legal theory can be 'objective'. Hage contends that, even when accepting the relativistic criticism on comparability of legal systems and on universality of legal concept and principles, legal theory can be objective at least to some extent. He discusses briefly the changes in classification in exact sciences, due to a change in the theories applied. Whales were originally classified as fish, but were later classified as mammals instead of fish. Pluto was classified as a 'planet' until 2006 when it was considered to be a 'dwarf planet'. The paradigm of those disciplines had changed. This paradigm is based on (inter-subjective) conventions among scientists at a certain moment of time. Hage argues that conventions also play an important role in legal theory, and that the use of these conventions makes it possible that legal theory is objective. The conventions are not objective, but everything that follows from them is. More generally, Hage argues that by distinguishing between 'internal legal concepts' and 'doctrinal concepts', legal theory can objectively demarcate what is governed by the law of a particular jurisdiction.

Pauline Westerman, on the other hand, denies the possibility for legal theorists to take an external 'objective' point of view. The underlying classic distinction is between the internal point of view of legal practice and legal doctrine as opposed to the external point of view of legal theory and legal philosophy. Westerman argues that this distinction overlooks differences between legislators and judges, whereas similarities between legal doctrine and legal theory are not even noticed. She proposes allowing for different concepts of law, depending on the different social practices in which law is understood and used. She shows how both positivist scholars, such as Kelsen or Luhmann, and anti-positivists, such as Fuller or Dworkin, have struggled with reconciling the two perspectives (for example, validity and efficacy). Discussing the metaphor of the legal system as a 'house', often used in explaining the characteristics of a legal system, Westerman points to its limits and pitfalls. She questions the demarcation wall that is erected between normative, practice-oriented insiders and 'neutral' (objective) disinterested outsiders. According to Westerman, it is not the professional position that creates the internal or external perspective, but rather the kind of *question* one may want to answer. Jurisprudence has the task of critically examining the assumptions underlying the specific concepts and their relations in view of the problems experienced in such social practices.

Although Hage and Westerman seem to have opposite views, I think their positions may be reconciled. Hage takes an analytical, scientific approach to legal theory. He tries to find a level of scholarship detached from the concrete rules of specific legal systems, on the one hand, and from culturally determined value systems, on the other. In other words, he tries to demarcate the field of legal theory where 'objective' research may be carried out.

Westerman, for her part, is rather thinking about legal philosophy, which does not claim to be either 'neutral' or 'objective'. This is clearly the case when she writes:

> I have to admit that although an outsider myself, I am not disinterested and neutral at all. I am indignant about certain forms of legislation, about the instrumentalisation of rules, about the loss of legal certainty.

Hage is emphasising the rational aspect of scientific research; Westerman is focusing on the social practices within which they are embedded. Their approaches are complementary, not necessarily opposing.

B. Legal Reasoning

Several papers in this volume discuss some aspect of objectivity in legal reasoning, most notably in judicial decisions.

The most general paper in this group is by **Matti Ilmari Niemi**, who asks whether objective legal reasoning is possible at all.

For Niemi, discussing the objectivity of legal knowledge is a way to outline the relationship between the sentences of legal doctrine and reality, on the one hand, and the nature of legal reasoning, on the other. Here, the fundamental question is: is it possible to combine the perspective of a particular person in the world with an objective view of the same world? Niemi analyses three conceptions of 'objectivity' introduced by Andrei Marmor and a fourth proposed by John Rawls. The first and strongest conception can be called the metaphysical one: objectivity means correspondence between a statement and its object in the discernible world. This conception fits with philosophical naturalism. For Niemi, it is not acceptable in the context of legal doctrine. The second and weaker conception is called the semantic conception of objectivity. A statement is objective if it is a statement about an object, and it is subjective if it is about the subject making the statement. According to Niemi, this conception is not helpful either. The third conception is called the logical conception of objectivity. A statement is objective if it has a determinate truth value. An objective legal statement provides information about the legal order of a society as a fact-based institution. Notwithstanding its attraction, Niemi rejects it as being too strong for law. The fourth and weakest conception introduced by Rawls is called the constructive conception of objectivity. It focuses our attention on the criteria of reasoning instead of presumed entities, objects or truth conditions. For Niemi, this conception is consistent with the nature of legal reasoning: an objective statement is located at a general level and is free from particular interests. If we see 'objectivity' in this way, objective legal reasoning is possible, concludes Niemi. Moreover, he argues, aspiring to objectivity is a necessary element of acceptable conventional legal reasoning.

Juha Raitio discusses the importance of 'legal certainty' as an element of objectivity in law. Legal certainty is linked with predictability and acceptability, with rationality and reasonableness. Democracy requires openness, which implies that judicial decisions must be justified in such a way that considerations relating to moral or social values are revealed. Raitio concludes that even the ECJ is sometimes forced to take moral values into consideration. 'Formal legal certainty' requires avoiding arbitrariness, so that citizens may plan their activities rationally; 'substantive legal certainty' requires acceptability of the decision, based on rational legal reasoning and reasonableness of the outcome. The question is to what extent there are universal 'objective' criteria for the acceptability of judicial decisions, or whether we are faced with a matter of locally varying criteria, depending on the legal community. Raitio distinguishes a third category, which he calls 'factual legal certainty', following Wroblewski's analysis of the concept of 'validity' (systemic, factual and axiological validity). Factual legal validity and factual legal certainty refer to the demand of efficacy in law. It is typical for legal realism, whereas formal legal certainty goes with positivism and substantive legal certainty with natural law theory. Raitio considers that the 'ultra-teleological' interpretation of the law he finds in the case law of the ECJ hampers legal certainty. Court decisions should be context-bound, but one has to keep the coherence of the legal system as a whole, he argues.

Starting from the debate around the acceptability of the argumentation used by the Dutch anti-Islam politician Geert Wilders, **Bertjan Wolthuis** investigates what kind of theoretical framework could be beneficial to a study of this controversy. In other words: how can we determine objective rules of argumentation?

First, the author analyses the approach of Jürgen Habermas, in which objective rules of argumentation are viewed as constitutive of deliberative democratic practices of argumentation. For Habermas, there are four presuppositions in every argumentation. We assume that the one who is arguing is (1) honest; (2) not using force; and that (3) all relevant contributors have access to the debate; and (4) are equal in this respect. Even if we know that this is not always the case, we need such presuppositions to make argumentation for an audience possible at all. For Habermas, these rules of argumentation are 'objective', as they are constitutive rules of a universal game of argumentation, present in all cultures and societies. Wolthuis agrees with this position, but criticises the way some other scholars have tried to operationalise that approach by making a 'Discourse Quality Index' based on the ideal of reaching a genuine consensus. It is not a surprise that researchers have concluded that politicians are not really willing to change their position, even not on the basis of strong, 'better' arguments. According to Wolthuis, Habermas' general notion of argumentation as a game with objective rules cannot be applied directly to specific games of argumentation. Specific practices have particular rules and tactics, that have been created to overcome certain problems in the past, as can be learned from Michel Foucault's studies in the 'history of thought'. Although Habermas and Foucault are often portrayed as rivals, Wolthuis combines Habermas' general notion of argumentation as a game constituted by rules with Foucault's focus on the history of specific games. The rules and tactics of specific games of argumentation can be challenged and changed in the course of the game, within the limits set by the objective rules of argumentation, of which Habermas has given an interpretation. The history of Dutch parliamentary argumentation illustrates this picture of argumentation.

Narrow, literal approaches to the meaning of texts have been regularly criticised, both in philosophy in general (for example by Wittgenstein) and in legal theory. It has been argued that every text requires interpretation, that there are no easy cases and no single right answers. **Niko Soininen** opposes this view and argues that there are indeed some easy cases in which formal logic is the only used form of interference and can be used as the sole justification of the case. He argues that the interpretation of the law adopted in an easy case is the only possible one and, hence, is 'objective'. In order to specify the differences between easy and less easy cases, according to Soininen, one also has to distinguish between hard cases and 'in between' cases. It is only in the easy cases that one right answer, one single 'objective' interpretation exists. The author defines 'easy cases' as those where: (1) similar cases have been solved earlier and there was no ambiguity about the normative or the factual premises; (2) the premises in these cases are similar in all legally relevant aspects; (3) all similar cases have been solved in a similar manner; (4) as a result there can be only one legally relevant interpretation of the law and the facts; and (5) no conflict of interests or interpretations is involved. To support his argument, Soininen analyses several cases related to Finnish water regulations.

Actually, Soininen refers to routine cases where everybody (at least until now) has agreed on the same interpretation. It is this inter-subjective agreement that he calls 'objectivity'.

C. Human Behaviour and its Objective Foundation

Even in a tolerant society, one does not accept cultural relativism. At least some human rights are considered to be universally valid and to be inalienable rights of any person in any culture, independent of social conventions. **Maija Aalto-Heinilä** tries, in her paper, to answer the question whether inalienable rights can provide an objective foundation for law and morality. She focuses on the concept of (inalienable) rights, most notably the will theory of rights (mainly put forward by HLA Hart). If rights are linked to one's own will, there are no inalienable rights and one has to look for another objective foundation of law and morality. The author questions the concept of 'inalienable rights'. For her, it is rather about defining the essence of a human being and about our moral duty to respect humanity in ourselves and in others, related to the entitlement of everyone to be treated as a human being. She concludes that rights need not be taken to be fundamental in moral (or legal) argumentation. She prefers to reserve the term 'right' to those claims only, which may be waived in principle, even if not always in practice. On the other hand, she argues, the idea behind inalienable rights can be expressed without appeals to 'rights' at all. We are rather faced with fundamental prohibitions, which follow from 'objective' facts about humans (for example vulnerability and dependence on each other). Focusing on these fundamental prohibitions and duties would be a more promising direction in search for an objective foundation for morality and law, according to Aalto-Heinilä.

Peter Cserne's paper is on the law's assumptions about human behaviour and the question of objectivity. While the papers in the following chapters discuss the role of law's cultural context and how to grasp it, Cserne focuses on our, often implicit, understanding of reality on which law is based. Not our values, our ideology but our world view in the material sense: how do we see and understand reality? Some presumed rationality of human behaviour, for instance, underlies most of the law. However, this 'model of human nature' may create tensions when confronted with behavioural and social sciences. Lack of objectivity may refer to law's ability to correct (false) assumptions or to correct (wrong) interpretations of correct assumptions or to the acceptance of the dominant theory (whereas there are competing and possibly better theories).

The author concludes that there is an increasing influence of empirical sciences at all levels (in policy making and judicial decisions) but not yet in legal doctrine. He asks: how and to what extent is this increasing awareness and enrichment of legal policy expected to change the doctrinal scaffolding of complex legal systems? How does this incorporation of empirical insights challenge and change the assumptions embedded in fundamental legal concepts and doctrines? His discussion of these questions is primarily explanatory (much of the paper discusses Hart and Honoré's views on the matter as explained and developed in their book on causation), but it also discusses some normative implications for both legal reform and legal doctrine.

Cserne suggests that law's assumptions are both domain-specific (area of law) and system-specific (legal culture).

D. Legal Culture

Jaakko Husa starts from the assumption that twentieth-century Western legal theory is rational, universal and, hence, 'objective'. However, it does not seem difficult to reveal culturally determined assumptions and understandings in those theories, which are probably impossible to eradicate from the way one is carrying out research in legal theory. There is some 'primary epistemology', as Husa calls it, at stake through which, unconsciously, the legal theorist considers the legal system in which he has been educated as 'normal', as the standard. This makes the other legal systems less 'normal'. Hence, the author challenges the possibility of a universally neutral, objective legal theory. He is doing this with the help of a kaleidoscope as a metaphor for law, used to show that there is no single 'right view on law: there is nothing in the legal sphere which would exclude cultural variety. On the other hand, it does not lead to a complete cultural relativism: the different images of law are still limiting other possible ways of grasping law. Husa compares legal theory, which tends to hide or to eliminate cultural pluralism, with comparative law where this pluralism is openly acknowledged. He asks why the unity and conceptual coherence of legal theories leads to such problems with (accepting) legal pluralism. This author distinguishes three archetypes of views on law and related legal theories:

1. A natural image of law, accepting some universally valid set of rules and principles, which may be found in the cosmic sphere, in religion, in rationality and the like. Here, there is no space for cultural pluralism.
2. A positivistic image of law, considering it possible and even desirable to construct a morally neutral descriptive/conceptual theory of law.
3. A socio-legal image of law, such as the ones offered by American or Scandinavian legal realism.

In all cases, Husa shows how such theories are culturally bound, but still claim to have an objective, universal validity.

Finally he words some rules which should show the heuristic benefits of a kaleidoscopic view on law: (1) a certain cultural relativity should be underlined; and one should (2) refuse to rely on conceptual similarities; (3) accept that law is always law-in-context; and (4) accept that 'juridiversity' is common nowadays.

Accepting, but at the same time limiting cultural relativism is also **Caroline Laske**'s concern in her paper 'Translators and Legal Comparatists as Objective Mediators between Cultures?'.

Her aim is to explore the possibility of using linguistic disciplines as cognitive models for comparative law and of adopting some of the linguistic and translation studies methodologies to suggest a more objective basis for research in comparative law, which would also influence legal theory.

Laske first shows how using methods developed by linguistic disciplines reveals how meanings are encoded, including the consideration of the situational and cultural contexts. The linguistic disciplines and translation studies, she argues, are good guides for gaining deep-level and multi-layered understanding of the phenomena that surround us and which have been expressed using language. Contrastive linguistics, corpus linguistics, systemic functional grammar, socio-linguistics, discourse analysis and translations studies, to name just a few, have all developed methodologies that allow for analysis to move away from intuition and onto an altogether more objective and even empirical basis.

Law is institutionalised discourse. Language and law offer some similarities and are closely intertwined: law creates language and language creates law. Both are partly the result of intercultural interaction and borrow/transplant from other systems. Translation studies may offer some methods for a more objective research in comparative law and in legal cultures.

The last chapter, by **Mustapha El Karouni**, analyses the influence of cultural paradigms on legal scholarship. Similarly to Husa, El Karouni starts from the conclusion that Western thinking has relied heavily on rationality since Modern Times. Modern science aims at absolute objectivity, eliminating anything which may be subjective. In practice, however, there is some underlying cultural framework, at least in human and social sciences, which determines research questions, research design, research methods and the whole framework of scientific theories. Hence, El Karouni calls this a 'subjective objectivity' at the opposite of an absolute objectivity or 'objective objectivity'. They are both contrasted with 'subjective subjectivity' to be found, for instance, in primitive societies, which is fully determined by feelings, values and beliefs, on the one hand, and with 'objective subjectivity' on the other, which covers the rationalisation of the first form of subjectivity, for instance through monotheistic religions. Together they offer four ideal types for the relation one may have to reality and truth. Traditional societies are more concerned with belief than with knowledge. World views are strongly oriented towards the past. In a first stage, law is divine or sacred, later it becomes more rationalised in the form of classic natural law. Modern Times are oriented to the future and increasingly focus on knowledge rather than beliefs. In a first stage, this leads to a rational natural law, followed by legal positivism. However, this is not a linear, universal or uniform development. El Karouni asks why Kelsen was far more influential in Europe than in the US and why law and economics became so popular in the US, but not in France. The answer lies in the underlying cultural frameworks. This also explains how a concept such as 'equality' has received such diverging contents over time and place. As a result, objectivity in its absolute form ('objective objectivity') is not possible in law or in jurisprudence. But for El Karouni, this does not lead to a total relativism either. Within a certain culture some values, world views and the like are 'objective'. If he calls this kind of soft objectivity 'subjective objectivity' it does not refer to individual positions but to the assumptions of a certain cultural community. This means that legal theory has to add this cultural dimension to its research, be it in another way than has been argued in comparative law: it is not about the law being put in context, but about theories to be located within their cultural paradigm.

VIII. SOME CONCLUSIONS BY WAY OF INTRODUCTION

Objectivity is not only an important concern of modern Western culture, it also is important for the scholars who contributed to this volume. On the one hand, some epistemological, methodological and cultural relativism has to be accepted, as we have lost both the illusion of absolute objectivity and the monopolies of world views within one and the same territory. Several authors have tried to find some kind of a more realistic, softer form of 'objectivity' and ways to guarantee it. Hage did it for legal theory; Niemi for legal reasoning; Soininen for judicial decisions in 'easy cases'; Aalto-Heinilä for the foundation of law and morality; and Husa, El Karouni and Laske for legal culture; and basically this concern is present in all papers, at least to some extent. One author sees a guarantee for objectivity in emphasising legal certainty and coherence (Raitio). Sometimes there is a strong belief in the objectivity of empirical sciences, which makes the author argue for their increased role in legal doctrine and legal theory (Cserne), but meanwhile we know that absolute objectivity is also an unattainable goal in empirical sciences. So we are often faced with philosophical views rather than with empirical evidence.

However, this volume offers not only a more realistic view on 'objectivity' in law and in jurisprudence, but also some perspectives for research programmes in areas which up to now have been neglected, such as the analysis of the characteristics, contents and influences of cultures on law and legal thinking, the use of methodologies developed in other disciplines, such as translation studies, which appear to come quite close to, for instance, comparative law.

Some authors, on the other hand, have rather challenged false certainties and illusions of objectivity by criticising too rational views on law as a well-ordered system, like a house (Westerman), or when it comes to 'objective' rules of argumentation (Wolthuis). They keep us awake by confronting us with our own understandings of law and legal theory which are inevitably strongly influenced by our own legal education and legal culture.

II. Objectivity of Legal Theory

2

Can Legal Theory Be Objective?

JAAP HAGE*

I. INTRODUCTION

IN 1961, HART published his most famous book, *The Concept of Law*, a title that is both modest in content and pretentious in its presupposition.¹ This presupposition is that it is possible to say something sensible about the law in general, and not only about concrete legal systems. It is a presupposition that is not only made in Hart's work but in most legal theory because legal theorists are interested in the nature of legal phenomena in general and not in the particular way in which these phenomena are implemented in specific legal systems. At least the characteristics of law as such, of the basic concepts of the law, such as 'right', 'obligation', and 'juridical act', and of universal legal phenomena such as legal rules and their mode of operation, would provide a common ground on which such a general theory law can be erected. Or are even these phenomena 'coloured' in the sense that their nature depends on the legal system in which they occur?

Given the diversity of the different legal traditions of the world,² the differences between the legal families in the Western tradition³ and between the legal systems within a single family, it might seem that it is all diversity in the law. Are not the differences so profound that even a neutral terminology by means of which the comparison can be made is lacking?⁴ Hart's presupposition would, therefore, not only seem pretentious but also wrong:

---

* I would like to thank Mark Van Hoecke, Jaakko Husa and Pauline Westerman for their explicit and implicit comments on this paper. They have led to several changes, which I hope are also improvements.
¹ HLA Hart, *The Concept of Law* (Oxford, Clarendon Press, 1961).
² HP Glenn, *Legal Traditions of the World*, 2nd edn (Oxford, Oxford University Press, 2004).
³ K Zweigert and H Kötz, *An Introduction to Comparative Law*, 3rd edn (Oxford, Clarendon Press, 1998) 63–73; J Husa, 'Legal Families' in JM Smits (ed), *Elgar Encyclopedia of Comparative Law* (Northampton, Edward Elgar Publishing, 2006) 382–92.
⁴ See E Örücü, 'Methodology of comparative law' in Smits, *Elgar Encyclopedia* (n 3), 442–54; N Jansen, 'Comparative Law and Comparative Knowledge' in M Reimann and R Zimmerman (eds), *The Oxford Handbook of Comparative Law* (Oxford, Oxford University Press, 2006) 305–38.

the only general thing that can be said about the law is that the law is very diverse.

The same verdict would then also apply to legal theory in general insofar as it aims to tell us something about the law as such. There would be no general things to say; the only noteworthy things about the law would concern the contents of particular legal systems. Objective legal theory in the sense of legal theory that can provide us with knowledge about the law in general, and not merely knowledge about the law of a particular jurisdiction, would be impossible. To the extent that legal theorists aim to provide us with such general knowledge nevertheless, their endeavour must inevitably be fruitless. Moreover, if legal theorists nevertheless provide us with 'knowledge' about the law which claims to be objective, they mislead us—probably without knowing it—because the provided knowledge must be coloured by the contents of a legal system.

Does the above argument why legal theory cannot be objective make sense? This paper hopes to show that there is certainly something to be adduced against its relativist view and that legal theory can be objective at least to some extent. For that purpose, two case studies will be discussed. The first deals with a relatively recent development in legal logic, namely the use of so-called non-monotonic logics to analyse the application of legal rules, and it aims to illustrate the extent to which the operation of legal rules can be neutral with respect to legal systems. The second case study deals with the neutrality of a central legal concept, namely the concept of competence, and gives an insight into how the neutrality of this concept can be maintained and at what cost. Before these two case studies are examined, however, a non-legal example will be studied. This example, on the issue of whether whales are fish, illustrates clearly how necessity and therewith objectivity can be created by conventional means. The two case studies will then illustrate more extensively how a comparable 'objectivity by convention' can be reached in legal theory.

II. OF WHALES AND PLANETS

Question: Are Whales Fish?

Whales live in the ocean, can stay underwater for long periods of time and have strong tails to propel themselves. So do fish. So, are whales fish?

Answer: The short answer: whales are not fish. Whales are mammals, just like you and me. All mammals are endothermic (commonly called warm-blooded), give birth to live young and nurse their young, breathe oxygen from air, and have hair[5]

---

[5] Hart, *The Concept of Law* (n 1).

The 9th edition of Linnaeus' masterwork of classification, the *Systema Natura*, said whales were fish; the 10th edition, published only two years later, said they were not.[6]

These two quotations from the modern source of all reliable knowledge, the worldwide web, give an indication of a discussion that must have taken place some centuries ago (in between the 9th edition of 1756 and the 10th edition of 1758 of the *Systema Natura*?) about the proper classification of whales. Are they fish, because they look like other fish and live in the seas just like other fish? Or are they not fish, because they differ from fish in the following respects:

— Whales move their tails up-and-down, while fish move theirs from side-to-side.
— Whales breathe through their blowholes, which are basically nostrils on the top of their heads. Fish take in oxygen from the water through their gills.
— Whales give birth to live young. Fish lay eggs.
— Whales have smooth skin, while fish have scales.
— Whales are warm-blooded.[7]

Those who are convinced that whales are not fish should also consider that phylogenetically all mammals are fish, and that therefore whales are in a sense both mammals *and* fish.[8]

Present day wisdom is that whales are *not* fish. And yet it can easily been seen that at some moment there must have been a discussion how to classify whales. There are both reasons to stick to what must have been the original classification of whales as fish and reasons, based on acquired insights in biological kinds and their development, why whales are not fish. This discussion must have led to sharpening the criteria for what defines a fish, and *on the basis of these sharpened criteria* it is now obvious that whales and fish belong to different classes.

A similar discussion was conducted much more recently, in 2006, about the nature of planets. In 2003, astronomers discovered a new 'planet' in the Kuiper belt, a region in our solar system extending from the orbit of Neptune to approximately 55 astronomical units[9] from the Sun.[10] This new 'planet' was called Eris, but its discovery almost immediately started a discussion about the nature of planets and whether this 'planet' could still

---

[6] www.robmacdougall.org/blog/2008/12/are-whales-fish/ (last consulted on 17 May 2011).
[7] marinelife.about.com/od/cetaceans/f/arewhalesfish.htm (last consulted on 17 May 2011).
[8] wiki.answers.com/Q/Are_whales_classified_as_fish (last consulted on 17 May 2011).
[9] An astronomical unit is about 149,597,870.7 km (en.wikipedia.org/wiki/Astronomical_unit; last consulted on 17 May 2011).
[10] en.wikipedia.org/wiki/Kuiper_belt (last consulted on 17 May 2011).

be called a planet. The outcome of the discussion was that a new category 'dwarf planet' was introduced, and both Eris and the already recognised planet Pluto would from then on be categorised as dwarf planets and—in the case of Pluto—no longer as a planet.[11]

In both cases there was an initial uncertainty about the classification of objects (whales, satellites of the Sun) and this uncertainty was ended, not by gathering more information about the disputed objects, but by changing or sharpening the convention which defined the boundaries of a category. In doing so, the impossibility of obtaining certainty about the status of whales and planets was turned into certainty by means of conventions.

Obviously, these conventions might have been framed differently and, then, the certainty that whales are not fish and that Pluto and Eris are not planets might have been the certainty that they *are* fish or planets respectively. Does this mean that there is no true answer to the questions whether whales are fish and whether Pluto and Eris are planets? No, there is a true answer, but this answer depends on conventions. Moreover, the conventions as they were actually created were not arbitrary. Their formulations were informed by the most recent scientific information of their ages, and—what is particularly perspicuous in the case of the biological convention—they still stand. And with them, the classification of whales as non-fish and of Pluto and Eris as dwarf planets still stand.

What is the relevance of all this for the objectivity of legal theory? It will be argued that conventions also play an important role in legal theory and that the use of these conventions makes it possible for legal theory to be objective. Admittedly, this objectivity depends on conventions, which might have been different. But first, these conventions do not have to be arbitrary either and, second, the fact that objectivity is based on conventions does not subtract from the fact that it is still objectivity.[12]

III. IS LEGAL LOGIC NEUTRAL?

According to Oliver Wendell Holmes Jr, the life of law has been experience, not logic.[13] As a reminder that legal reasoning cannot and should not be restricted to the application of logical laws to premises, which are exempted from criticism, these words of Holmes remain valuable. As soon as they are misinterpreted as stating that logic is not important for the law, however, they become dangerous, because then they suggest that valid reasoning—for

---

[11] www.gps.caltech.edu/~mbrown/planetlila/ (last consulted on 17 May 2011).
[12] To give an illustration of this point from a completely different subject area: it is by convention that the corners of a rectangle are orthogonal, but given that convention it is objectively the case that all corners of a rectangle are equal.
[13] OW Holmes Jr, *The Common Law* (New York, Dover Publications, 1991) 1.

which logic is the theoretical underpinning—does not play a central role in the law. Argumentation and reasoning are of crucial importance, and it even seems that the standards for legal reasoning are the same in at least the modern Western legal systems. One might therefore claim that where the law obviously differs from system to system, the standards for legal reasoning are everywhere the same.

This claim, that the standards for legal reasoning are—within the modern Western world—universal, is nevertheless false. One only has to look at the differences between the civil law and the common law traditions to see that what counts as a strong argument in the one tradition, for instance the invocation of a precedent, may be much weaker in the other tradition.[14] It is possible, however, to formulate a more modest claim, which has a better chance of surviving comparative criticism, and that is the claim that at least the logic of rule application is universal. Is it not everywhere the case that legal rules have a condition part and a conclusion part, and that if the facts of a case satisfy the conditions of a legal rule, the rule attaches its conclusion as a legal consequence to this case?

This is far from simple, which can be seen from the following example which has, for illustrative purposes, been stripped of all the complications that would characterise more realistic cases. Suppose that a particular jurisdiction, for hygienic reasons, disallows the presence of dogs in shops which sell food. A visually impaired person wants to bring her guide dog into a butcher's shop, and the question arises whether this guide dog may enter the shop. Let us assume, somewhat unrealistically, that the local legislator did not consider guide dogs in drafting the regulation. *At least* four approaches to this case are possible, which might briefly be characterised as the legalistic approach, the interpretive approach, the activist approach, and the deviant logic approach.

A. The Legalistic Approach

The legalistic approach is what Holmes probably wanted to fight when he stated that the life of law was not logic. According to this approach, the content of the law is taken face value, and then applied without making use of the subtle reasoning techniques, which were developed as parts of the lawyer's toolbox. The argument might then run as follows: the rule does not allow dogs in food shops. A butcher's shop is a food shop and a guide dog is a dog, so guide dogs are not allowed in butcher's shops, not in general and therefore also not in this particular case. This argument sounds very 'logical',

---

[14] A brief overview of how the standards for legal reasoning vary from the one jurisdiction to another can be found in JC Hage, 'Legal reasoning' in Smits (n 3) 407–22.

and maybe for that reason legalistic reasoning has been confused with the strict application of logic. Advantages of this style of reasoning are:

— that the step from the formulation of the rule in legislation to the content of the rule is minimal, because the content is precisely what the legislation says it is;
— that the conditions of the rule are given an interpretation, which is in accordance with common parlance (a guide *dog* is obviously a dog); and
— that the logic of rule application is highly similar to the logic that applies to declarative sentences.[15]

The obvious disadvantage of this legalist approach to legal reasoning is that it apparently leaves legal decision makers little choice (although some might consider this to be an advantage, rather than a disadvantage), and that consequently this decision maker cannot accommodate seemingly relevant factors, which are not taken into account in the rule formulation. In our example, this is reflected in the fact that the rule does not distinguish between dogs in general and guide dogs and that the special needs of visually impaired people therefore seem to be ignored.

B. The Interpretive Approach

Lawyers are fond of interpretation, which in part may explain their liberal use of the term. A typical example of *legal* interpretation is when a term is given a meaning other than in its common usage, for instance, because this is in accordance with the purpose of the rule. In our dog example, guide dogs would not be dogs, at least not in the sense of the rule that prohibits the presence of dogs in food shops. This interpretive approach has several advantages, namely:

— that the step from the formulation of the rule in legislation to the content of the rule is minimal;
— that the logic of rule application is very similar to the logic that applies to declarative sentences; and
— that the unusual meaning assigned to 'dog' makes it possible to treat guide dogs different from 'normal' dogs, thereby taking the special needs of visually impaired people into account.

The disadvantage of this approach is that the term 'dogs' in the rule formulation is given a rather unusual meaning, which creates the impression that the rule is bent to make it suit the occasion.

---

[15] We will return to this point later in this section.

C. The Activist Approach

When rules are created by means of legislation, it is natural to assume that the rule has precisely the wording that was also used in the original legislation, the idea that it might differ does not even arise. And yet this is far from obvious. The legislation is not identical to the rule, and neither does it contain the rule. Legislation is a means of creating rules and undoubtedly the formulation used in the legislation is an important factor in determining which rule precisely was created. However, it is not a priori given that the formulation in legislation is the *only* factor that determines the content of the rule that was created.

A legal decision maker who must determine the content of a rule can take a more or less activist stance towards the formulation of the rule in legislation.[16] The more activist the approach, the less authority she assigns to the phrasing of the rule in the legislative texts. In our example, an activist decision maker could decide that the actual rule, which was created excludes guide dogs from its scope of application. The 'real' rule would then be something like: 'With the exception of guide dogs which accompany visually impaired people, it is not allowed that dogs are present in shops in which food tends to be sold.' This activist approach has the advantages:

— that the conditions of the rule are given an interpretation which is in accordance with common usage (a guide *dog* is a dog);
— that the logic of rule application is highly similar to the logic that applies to declarative sentences; and
— that the adapted formulation of the rule makes it possible to treat guide dogs as different from other dogs, thereby taking into account the special needs of visually impaired people.

The disadvantage of this approach is that the rule which is applied and which apparently is taken to be part of the law can no longer borrow its authority—at least to a full degree—from the democratically legitimated legislator. Moreover, the division of powers between state organs is somewhat weakened.

D. The Deviant Logic Approach

Of the four mentioned approaches to legal reasoning, the deviant logic approach is probably the least known to lawyers. This is already an indication that amongst lawyers logic is not seen as something that can be used

---

[16] *Mutatis mutandis* the same can be said about rules created in judicial decisions. Then the ratio decendi plays the role of the rule and the phrasing of the decision has the role of the legislative text.

to influence the outcome of a particular case. Logic is something fixed and if one wants a different conclusion for a legal argument, it is not the logic that can be adapted, but it is the premises that can and possibly should be changed in order to obtain a desired outcome.

And yet, the immutability of logic is not an cast-iron law. In fact, lawyers often use a deviant logic and, more in particular, a non-monotonic logic[17] for the application of legal rules without being aware of doing so. That is, for instance, the case when they make an exception to a rule because application of the rule would be against the rule's purpose. That might be a viable strategy in our dog example. Arguably, the prohibition for dogs is meant for standard cases, where guide dogs are not standard. Therefore, it would be against the purpose of the rule to apply it to a guide dog. Since guide dogs fall under the ordinary scope of the rule (guide dogs are dogs, after all), non-application of the rule can only be realised by making an exception to the rule.

To see clearly what is involved in making exceptions to rules and how this differs from choosing a different rule formulation, it is useful to distinguish between declarative sentences and rule formulations. There need not be a difference in wording between the two but, nevertheless, they fulfil very different functions. The declarative sentence 'Dogs are not allowed in food shops' is *true or false*, depending on what the facts are, and in particular depending on whether dogs are really not allowed in food shops. The rule 'Dogs are not allowed in food shops' is neither true nor false, but rather valid or invalid in a particular jurisdiction. If it is valid, it means that dogs are not allowed in food shops and, indirectly, it also means that the declarative sentence 'Dogs are not allowed in food shops' is true.

Traditional logic was developed to deal with declarative sentences. It deals with the validity of arguments and an argument is considered to be valid if and only if the truth of its premises guarantees the truth of its conclusion.[18] The issue of exceptions does not play a role in logic for declarative sentences, because such sentences do not allow exceptions. A true sentence with an 'exception' would not be a true sentence with an exception, but would be false. Therefore it makes no sense to deal with exceptions in traditional logic, because there are no exceptions, only false sentences.

A valid rule with an exception does make sense, however, and that is only possible because rules do not describe the world but—to some extent—determine its contents. Exceptions to rules are cases in which a rule does not 'work', even though it should work if one only goes by the rule conditions.

---

[17] A non-monotonic logic might informally be described as a logic that allows reasoning with exceptions. A more precise characterisation can be found in JC Hage, *Studies in Legal Logic* (Dordrecht, Springer, 2005) 7–32.

[18] IM Copi and C Cohen, *Introduction to Logic*, 13th edn (New Jersey, Pearson, 2009) 26.

Can Legal Theory Be Objective? 31

An exception to a rule is not an exception clause in the rule conditions, but a type of case to which the rule does not apply even though the rule is applicable according to the rule conditions.

In law it is assumed that such exceptions to the application of a rule are possible and this makes it less certain that traditional logic, which was developed with declarative sentences without exceptions in mind, is also relevant for rule application. The legal 'syllogism', which is used to model the application of a rule to the facts of a case is not automatically the same syllogism that is used to model arguments which consist solely of declarative sentences. In fact, it would be different it were to allow arguments which make an exception to a rule while leaving the rule formulation unaltered.

For instance, one might argue that the rule forbids dogs in food shops and that this rule remains as it is, even though it will not be applied to guide dogs. Then the 'logic' of rule application deviates from an ordinary syllogism, which does not allow exceptions. If the law allows exceptions to rules, for whatever reason, it uses a non-monotonic logic. Notice, however, that even if the law uses a non-monotonic logic that allows exceptions to rules, it is therewith not given under which circumstances such exceptions should be made. This is still an open matter and it is not logic but the law, which must determine in which cases there will be exceptions to rules. The non-monotonic logic only creates the possibility for the law to work with exceptions to rules.

The advantages of allowing exceptions to rules and therefore of using a non-monotonic logic for rule application are:

— that the step from the formulation of the rule in legislation to the content of the rule is minimal;
— that the conditions of the rule are given an interpretation which is in accordance with common usage; and
— that the non-monotonic logic of rule application makes it possible to treat guide dogs different from other dogs, thereby taking the special needs of visually impaired people into account.

The disadvantage of using a non-monotonic logic is that the seeming simplicity of rule application must give way to a more complex logic, which allows for exceptions to rules.

E. Lessons to be Learned

The first lesson to be learned from this case study about a rule that prima facie leads to unattractive results in a number of cases, is that the decision how to deal with such problematic cases is a trade-off between several alternatives. It is possible to accept the unattractive outcome, for instance, in order to limit the role of legal decision makers to applying the law 'as it is'. It is also possible to avoid unattractive outcomes by giving the rule a less traditional interpretation, by weakening the connection between the formulation of the legislation and that of the rule or by allowing an exception to the rule. Which approach is adopted is a matter of the law or legal culture, and it is not a question that can be answered by 'neutral' legal theory.[19] The choice between these different 'solutions' for the problem of unattractive rule outcomes is comparable to the choice of a convention to solve the problem of how to classify 'fish' or 'planets'.

The second lesson to be learned is that if a choice has been made, the 'rest' becomes objective. This rest includes both the possibilities and the implications of a choice. For instance, when the four approaches to seemingly over-inclusive rules[20] have been identified and when it has been established that the choice between these approaches is a matter of law or legal culture, and not of a neutral legal theory, it still seems possible to describe the four approaches in a neutral way. In fact, the earlier part of this section is precisely a brief attempt to do so.

This also holds for the logic of rule application. It is a matter of law or of legal culture whether rules allows of exceptions and under which circumstances exceptions to rules, if any, should be made. However, that relativity does not subtract from the fact that the logic of rule application is fixed, given the choice for a particular model of rules. If it is presupposed that rules do not allow exceptions and that a rule applies if and only if its conditions are satisfied. The implications for this assumption can be described objectively.[21] The same holds if it is presupposed that rules allow the occurrence of exceptions. Which of these two models of rule application is adopted is a matter of convention. One convention may be more adequate than the other, but as conventions they are neither true nor false. Moreover, on the basis of such a convention, it is possible to conduct objective legal theory research, which describes the consequences of the convention that was adopted.[22]

---

[19] It is not necessary that a legal system makes an unconditional choice for one of the mentioned solutions. The choice may be conditional on additional case facts. That does not detract, however, from the fact that if *some* choice has been made, the implications of that choice become objective.

[20] See F Schauer, *Playing by the Rules* (Oxford, Clarendon Press, 1991) 32.

[21] Examples of such descriptions can be found in the works of Tammelo and Weinberger on law and (traditional) logic. See I Tammelo, *Modern Logic in the Service of the Law* (Vienna, Springer Verlag, 1978) and O Weinberger, *Rechtslogik*, 2nd edn (Berlin, Duncker & Humblot, 1989).

[22] Examples of such descriptions can be found in the works of Hage and Sartor on law and non-monotonic logic. See JC Hage, *Reasoning with Rules* (Dordrecht, Kluwer, 1997) and G Sartor, *Legal Reasoning, A Cognitive approach to the Law* (Dordrecht, Springer, 2005).

IV. IS IT POSSIBLE TO HAVE A SET OF NEUTRAL LEGAL CONCEPTS?

The first case study dealt with the issue whether legal theory can provide us with a neutral theory about legal reasoning, and the answer was ambiguous. Many aspects of legal reasoning are determined by the law of a particular jurisdiction, or by a particular legal culture. However, legal theory can describe objectively the possible choices and it can also describe objectively the implications of a choice, for instance, how reasoning with rules that can have exceptions works.

The second case study, which will be conducted in this section, focuses on legal concepts. Legal rules differ from one jurisdiction to another, but these rules are framed by means of legal concepts such as duty, right, obligation, power, competence, juridical act, ownership, contract, license, disposition, crime, misdemeanour and so on. Would it not be possible that these concepts, or at least a number of them, are neutral with respect to the different jurisdictions and would it not be a proper task of legal theory to analyse these concepts?

This section reports on the findings of a conceptual study about juridical acts and, in particular, the role of the concepts of 'power' and 'competence' in this context. To what extent are these concepts influenced by the law of a particular jurisdiction and to what extent are they neutral and the proper object of objective legal theory?

A. Juridical Acts

Juridical acts (*Rechtsgeschäfte, actes juridiques*) are acts, performed by a legal subject with the intention to bring about legal effects, to which the law attaches the intended legal effects for the reason that they were intended.[23] For a juridical act to be definitely valid and to have its intended legal effects, usually several conditions have to be met:

— The actor must have intended to bring about the legal effects by means of his act.
— Sometimes, the performance of the juridical act must satisfy certain requirements of form.
— The intended legal effects should not have a 'wrong' content (conflict with public order, with important demands of morality or with mandatory law).
— The actor must have been allowed to perform this juridical act.

---

[23] The analyses of this section are based on JC Hage, 'A model of juridical acts: parts 1 and 2' (2011) *Artificial Intelligence and Law* 19, 23–73.

— The actor should have possessed both the competence and the capacity to bring about the intended legal effects by means of a juridical act of the performed type. (This will be explained later.)

If one or more of these conditions have not been met, the juridical act in question will either not count as a juridical act at all (in extreme cases), will be considered null and void, or will be avoidable. Sometimes, however, despite the deficiency, the juridical act will be considered definitely valid. This may, for instance, be the case if the actor lacked the relevant intention, but created a justified expectation that he had the relevant intention, or if the performance of the juridical act was forbidden, but avoidability, not nullity, seems the appropriate sanction.

B. Competence

By means of the phenomenon of juridical acts, the law gives legal actors the power[24] to bring about intentional changes in the world of law, the set of facts and things which owe their existence to the law. Because not everybody should be allowed to bring about any change, the demand of competence is used.

If a legal actor is to bring about particular legal effects by means of a particular kind of juridical act, he should have received the competence to do so. This demand has, as its main function, to limit the kinds of juridical acts somebody can perform, or the legal effects somebody can bring about by performing a juridical act of a particular kind.[25] Let us consider some examples.

— Ordinary citizens lack the competence to create statutes, and attempts to do so nevertheless, probably do not even count as juridical acts at all, let alone as the creation of a statute.
— A municipal legislator can create rules, but presumably not rules in which constitutional rights are violated. If this is nevertheless attempted, the result will be legislation that is void, or avoidable.
— Ordinary citizens are competent to contract, but not to create by means of a contract rules that bind other people.
— Judges are competent to take binding decisions in particular cases, but in their role of judge they are not competent to make last wills.
— A public officer has been assigned the task of granting building permits and, therewith, the competence to do so. She will normally not be competent to grant parking permits too.

---

[24] We will return to the term 'power' later.
[25] The related demand of capacity focuses not so much on the content of the juridical act, but on the capability of the actor to form a well-founded intention (will).

Sometimes competences are granted broadly, to be limited by special rules. Typical examples are the competences to contract, and to make rules. These competences are limited by the demands that contracts can only 'bind' the contract parties, and that legislative powers should only be exercised for the purpose for which they were given. Some other competences are limited from the beginning, such as the competence to alienate the goods one owns (and in principle no other goods), and the competence to grant building permits.

Given its function, namely to specify the limits of what legal actors can do by means of juridical acts, it would seem obvious that if some actor transgressed the boundaries of his competence, the resulting 'juridical act' would either be non-existent (for example, an ordinary citizen creates a 'statute') or null and void (for example, a non-owner 'transfers' the ownership of the Empire State Building). While this is often the case, it is not always. For instance, in Dutch administrative law, administrative dispositions which were made ultra vires tend to be avoidable, not null and void from the beginning. The reason why this is the case has to do with legal certainty. The uncertainty whether an administrative disposition is valid is so undesirable that validity is assumed until the disposition has officially been avoided.

Understandable as this may be, it raises the question what this means for the concept of competence. Does the fact that administrative disposition ultra vires are 'only' avoidable mean that the administrative body, which made the disposition was competent after all, or should we give up the idea that competence is a necessary condition for bringing about certain legal effects by means of a certain kind of juridical act?

This dilemma may seem, at first sight, only to be a minor issue in Dutch law, but it has immediate consequences for the central issue of this paper, namely whether legal theory can be objective. The demand that a legal actor needs for every juridical act a special competence might qualify as a result of 'objective' legal theory, as an insight that holds for juridical acts in general, and not only for juridical acts as they happen to be regulated in Dutch law. However, if this insight does not even hold for all parts of Dutch law, we must possibly draw the conclusion that it is not a general and neutral insight from legal theory that juridical acts require the relevant competence. Moreover, if such an 'obvious' insight turns out to be wrong, does it not illustrate that the hope for objective legal theory must be abandoned?

Dutch law seems to be 'inconsistent' by posing, on the one hand, for every juridical act the demand that the actor has the competence to perform this act with this content and allowing, on the other hand, that some juridical acts for which the actor lacked the necessary competence are initially valid nevertheless. How should we deal with this problem? There seem to be two possibilities. On the one hand, we can stick to the demand that a valid juridical act requires the relevant competence. Then ultra vires administrative decisions are by definition non-existent or invalid. If a particular decision is valid nevertheless, there are again two possibilities: either it was not ultra vires after all, or the legal effects are attached to it, not because it was a valid juridical act, but because legal certainty required these effects to be attached to the appearance of a valid decision.

On the other hand, we can drop the demand that valid juridical acts require the relevant competence. Then the seemingly neutral result of legal theory, namely that every juridical act requires a relevant competence, turns out to be at best a characteristic of a particular jurisdiction.

C. Competence and Power

A concept which is closely related to that of competence is the concept of 'power'. In fact, the notions of power and competence are not always sharply distinguished in common usage, so the distinction that will be made between competence and power will have a slightly stipulative nature.

To explain the distinction, it is useful to say a little about the 'world of law'. This world of law consists of those facts and things whose existence depends on the application of legal rules. Typical examples of such things and facts are courts, property rights, legal rules themselves (at least those which were explicitly made), the fact that Obama is the President of the USA, the fact that Judge J is competent to decide the cases presented to her, and the fact that Jones owns Blackacre.

Closely related to things and facts which belong to the world of law are the so-called *internal legal concepts*. These concepts are used for things and facts in the world of law and they include the concepts 'owner', 'president', 'competent' and 'right'. The applicability of these concepts depends on legal rules. If different jurisdictions have different rules for the applicability of internal concepts, the consequence is that these concepts have different scopes of application from one jurisdiction to another. Because the notion of competence will (stipulatively) be used for a special legal status, which is assigned by legal rules to legal actors, being competent is such an internal legal concept, the applicability of which depends on the rules of a particular jurisdiction.

Opposed to the so-called internal legal concepts are *doctrinal concepts*. These concepts are not part of the law itself and their applicability is not defined by legal rules. A doctrinal concept is rather a concept that is used in legal doctrine to characterise legal systems. A typical example is the concept of 'sovereignty', which is to the author's knowledge seldom used as a concept within a legal system, but which is frequently used to characterise legal systems. The same counts for the concepts 'human right' and 'freedom of contract'. It also counts, it is stipulated, for the concept of power.

A person is said to have a legal power if he or she is capable of bringing about legal effects by means of an act aimed at bringing about these effects. This act may be a juridical act, such as an administrative decision, or a last will. It may also be another act, such as moving from one municipality to another, thereby changing the amount of municipal taxes that he must pay. Natural persons have, in general, the power to influence their tax duties, and—as this example illustrates—this power does not necessarily depend on juridical acts.

The presence of a legal power depends on, and is a side-effect—intended or not—of legal rules which attach legal consequences to acts which can be performed intentionally. To the extent that the power can be exercised by means of a juridical act, a legal subject will normally need the competence and the capacity to bring about these legal effects by means of that type of act, but the power does not coincide with this competence or this capacity. Apart from this competence and capacity, the power presupposes the presence of legal rules, which attach the intended legal consequences to a juridical act. The presence of these rules has the side effect that they can be used by a legal actor to bring about legal effects. In a sense these rules create the power, but they do not confer the power, as a misleading expression suggests, because what rules confer is a legal status, such as capacity or competence.

In general, powers are not specifically tied to the law at all. A power is a capability to do, bring something about, or to reach a particular result. For instance, a speed skater may have the power to skate 500 metres in less than 38 seconds, and a politician may have the power to win the elections. A good salesman may have the power to sell this ruin, while most citizens have the power to buy a house. This last example illustrates that some powers may be the result of a particular legal status, but that this is not necessarily the case. Moreover, powers that result from a legal status are not really different from other powers. For every power there must be circumstances which empower somebody to do something: a politician must have influence on the electorate; a speed skater must have exercised enough. In legal cases, these circumstances happen to be legal facts, such as that there are rules which attach legal effects to events, and that somebody has the competence to perform a particular kind of juridical act.

Because 'competence' is an internal legal concept, the law of a particular jurisdiction determines:

— whether it works with this concept;
— when the concept, if it exists, is applicable; and
— what the consequences are, if the concept is or is not applicable in a particular case.

Legal theory can therefore not provide a neutral analysis of what the concept of 'competence' involves in a particular legal system. This does not mean that legal theory cannot say anything in general about competence. The reason is that competence in one jurisdiction will have something in common with competence in other jurisdictions, because otherwise these different 'competences' could not all be denoted by the same term 'competence'. However, these necessary similarities, although they can by and large be listed, cannot be more than approximations of what competence means in the different jurisdictions.

D. Legal Powers

It is different with the notion of power. Although different legal jurisdictions may assign different powers to legal actors, this has no implication for what a power is. In general, it remains true that if somebody actually brought something about, he must have had the power to do so. The main reason why the notion of power does not depend on the contents of the law of a particular jurisdiction is that it is not an internal legal concept. The conditions of applicability of the power concept are not regulated by the law. Where the law has influence on the presence of a power, this is so because it can influence whether the applicability conditions of 'power' are satisfied.

As a consequence, it is possible to say something in general about powers, including legal powers, which are not coloured by the details of specific jurisdictions. Somebody has the power to bring something about if it depends on the will of this person independent of whether she will actually bring it about. In the law things are brought about through the application of legal rules. Some rules attach legal effects to events, independent of whether these effects were intended. For instance, the rule which attaches liability to a tort creates this liability independent of whether the tortfeasor intended to become liable. Even this rule gives legal actors a power, because people can make themselves liable for damages by committing a tort.

The more usual way of bringing about things in the law, however, is through juridical acts. By having rules, which attach legal affects to certain acts, because these acts were performed with the intention to bring these effects about, a legal system recognises juridical acts. By recognising juridical acts, a legal system grants its actors certain powers and because these powers rest on the operation of legal rules, one might call them 'legal powers'. Notice, however, that legal powers are related to the operation of legal rules in general, not only to the operation of rules which attach consequences to the performance of juridical acts. A legal subject will normally have the power to place himself under an obligation, both by contracting and by committing a tort. Only in the first case, the power depends on the presence of a competence.

E. Lessons to be Learned

The above discussion of competences and powers is again an illustration of how and to what extent legal theory can be objective. By distinguishing between internal legal concepts and doctrinal concepts, legal theory can objectively demarcate what is governed by the law of a particular jurisdiction. This includes both the conditions under which a competence is assigned and what the consequences are when somebody attempts to perform a juridical act without having the competence to do so.

An analysis of the notion of 'power' is not typically a task for legal theory, because this notion is not particularly tied to the law and there is no reason to assume that powers in the law are different from powers elsewhere.

What legal theory can do, however, and apparently in an objective way, is to indicate how powers in the law are created as a side effect of rules which attach legal consequences to events, including intentional acts. It can also indicate what this means for the relation between the possibility to perform juridical acts and the power to create legal effects, which is the result from the rules which attach legal consequences to valid juridical acts. Because the validity of legal acts often depends on the competence to perform them (although this is a matter of the rules of a particular jurisdiction), legal theory can also offer an account of how the competence to perform juridical acts relates to the power to bring about certain legal effects.

More generally, we see that in relation to juridical acts, competences and powers, legal theory can help to distinguish between what depends on the contents of law, and what is 'objective' in the sense of independent from the contents of law. In connection with the latter, legal theory can help to gain this objective knowledge. And finally, legal theory can also help to spell out the consequences of the choices that were made by the law of a particular jurisdiction. It may, for instance, point out the consequences for the powers of legal subjects to bring about legal consequences which follow from the choices made in positive law about the role of competence in performing valid juridical acts.

V. CONCLUSION AND REPLY TO SOME POSSIBLE OBJECTIONS

It is obvious that much that can be said about law is about the law of a particular jurisdiction. The question may therefore be raised whether there remains anything to be said about law in general or about particular aspects of it. The examples about whales and planets illustrate that when saying something in general about a category of things, it may be necessary to specify this category by means of a convention which is, in part, of a stipulative nature. Given such a convention, some things become 'true by convention',[26] but the explication of what has become true by convention may, nevertheless, lead to new knowledge.

That such new knowledge by convention is possible can be seen from the case studies on rules, which seemingly lead to unattractive consequences in some cases, and on juridical acts and the role of competences and powers in that context, which I hope offered something new for many readers. In this instance, legal theory can lead to objective knowledge by dividing the subjects into what is relative to a particular jurisdiction (how the law deals with hard cases, what the role of competence is with regard to juridical acts) and into what is objective in the sense of system independent (the distinction between four ways of dealing with hard cases, the logic of rules that allow for exceptions, the notion of a legal power and its relation to the notion of competence). Moreover, the objective part can be described in an objective way, and by combining this objective description to the conventional choices made by a particular jurisdiction, legal theory can also describe objectively where the choices of such a system lead.

A. Toothless Objectivity?

One possible objection against this conventionalist approach to objectivity is that its conventionalism makes objectivity only possible at the cost of downsizing the claim of objectivity to a harmless scope. It may be possible to say something objectively about the law, but only if it has already been presumed that the law has these characteristics which are ascribed to it. Objectivity is only achieved by convention, and such objectivity has no teeth.[27]

This objection has at least a kernel of truth, but it may be questioned whether it is more than a kernel. To see why, it is useful to distinguish between particular knowledge, which is knowledge about concrete things, and general knowledge, which is knowledge about kinds of things. An example of particular knowledge would be that in the Dutch Civil Code the main rule about liability in tort can be found in Article 6:162. Such knowledge may be very useful, but scientific knowledge often aims to be general.[28] An example of such universal knowledge (if it is true) would

---

[26] WV Quine, 'Truth by Convention' in WV Quine, *The Ways of Paradox and Other Essays, Revised and Enlarged Edition* (Cambridge, Harvard University Press, 1976) 77–106.

[27] One might derive this objection from Husa's paper 'Kaleidoscopic Cultural Views and Legal Theory—Dethroning the Objectivity?' ch 10 in this volume, although Husa does not formulate the objection himself.

[28] One might even argue that knowledge can only count as scientific knowledge if it is universal. That would be a convention about science which is very similar to the conventions discussed in this paper.

be that legal systems in the common law tradition attach more value to personal responsibility than systems in the civil law tradition.

If knowledge deals with a kind of 'things', for example, with legal systems in the common law tradition, then it is necessary to set apart the kind with which the knowledge deals, from other kinds which may border on it. In this connection, universal knowledge may play a crucial role. It is attractive to define kinds by means of law-like statements, which are true about these kinds.[29] If such a law does not apply to a particular 'thing' (for example, a legal system), then this might be considered to be a reason why it does not belong to the kind (that is legal systems in the common law tradition). Another example would be that it may be useful to define law as those rules which are enforced by the state. Given this definition, it is a universal and objective truth about the law that it is enforced by the state. Kinds and law-like statements are closely interwoven, even to the extent that it is not merely a 'trick' to define kinds in such a way that particular laws hold true for them.

Such definitions are not true statements but conventions, which are more or less useful for a particular purpose and possibly less or more useful for another purpose. It would be a mistake, however, to see this as a limitation of the possibility to arrive at objective knowledge. It is unavoidable if one wants to achieve universal knowledge and the (physical) sciences are only possible thanks to the use of such conventions.

B. Objectivity from a Perspective?

This leads us to a second objection, which was formulated by Westerman.[30] If conventions are useful, they are useful for some purpose from a particular perspective. The objectivity, which is made possible by these conventions is, therefore, not an objectivity per se, but merely objectivity from a perspective, or—to state it candidly—no objectivity at all.

A reply to this objection should start from a theory about objectivity. As Van Hoecke has pointed out,[31] the term 'objectivity' can be used for different things. One version of objectivity is that reality is described as it is. This version has an underlying ontology, which assumes that there are things and facts about these things which do not depend on the beliefs or acceptance of individual persons. In this connection, a typology of objectivity

---

[29] *Cf* in this connection the discussion about 'projectability' of characteristics in N Goodman, *Fact, Fiction and Forecast*, 3rd edn (Hassocks, Harvester Press, 1979) 72–83.

[30] 'The Impossibility of an Outsider's Perspective', ch 3 in this volume. Although I think that the objection as it is formulated in the main text derives from Westerman's paper, the formulation is that of the present author.

[31] Mark Van Hoecke, 'Objectivity in Law and Jurisprudence', ch 1 in this volume.

developed by Leiter may be helpful. He distinguished between four versions of objectivity or the lack thereof.

Subjectivism assumes that whether a fact exists depends on the view of the cogniser (the person who holds a belief about the fact). This seems the most appropriate view with regard to phenomena, which are considered as merely a matter of taste, such as whether cauliflower is more tasteful than spinach, or whether 'Layla' by Derek & the Dominoes is a better piece of music than Bach's 'Erbarme Dich'.

Minimal objectivism assumes that whether a fact exists depends on views held within the group of cognisers (for example, the officials of a particular legal system). This seems an attractive view with regard to the existence of social phenomena, such as the leaders of informal groups and the existence of customary law or other social rules in the sense used by Hart.[32]

Modest objectivism assumes that whether a fact exists depends on the views which would under appropriate or ideal circumstances (for example, full rationality and maximal knowledge of the facts) be held by the group of cognisers. This is an attractive view with regard to the legal consequences of hard cases, which require some less easy reasoning.

Strong objectivism holds that whether a fact exists does not depend on anyone's views. It is generally adopted with regard to hard 'physical' facts, such as the fact that the North Sea borders on the Belgian shore, or that Mount Everest is the highest mountain.[33]

At least, minimal and strong objectivism allow for the possibility to obtain objective knowledge, because they both assume that there are facts that do not depend on the beliefs or acceptance of the person who holds a view about them. Modest objectivism is a less clear case, because the facts depend on standards of rationality. Only if these standards do not depend solely on the views of the cogniser, will modest objectivism allow for objective knowledge in the sense of the present discussion.

As mentioned earlier, one version of objectivity is that reality is described as it is. This is the version that will be adopted here, with the note that reality is assumed to exist independently of the beliefs and acceptances of the cogniser, but not necessarily independently of the beliefs and acceptances of the members of a group. This form of objectivity is possible if different persons, with different knowledge interests, describe part of reality—for example, the law—from different perspectives. From the one perspective, one set of facts will be relevant; from another perspective a different set of facts will be relevant. Different descriptions will differ, but that does not detract from it that all the descriptions may be true. The point is that the

---

[32] Hart (n 1) 55–57.
[33] Brian Leiter, 'Law and Objectivity' in J Coleman and S Shapiro (eds), *The Oxford Handbook of Jurisprudence and the Philosophy of Law* (Oxford, Oxford University Press, 2002) 969–89.

different knowledge interests make that different aspects of the knowledge object will be described, but that all the descriptions are true of the same object. They are complementary, not in conflict.

The underlying assumption about objectivity is that all the different descriptions from different perspectives must be consistent, because they deal with the same knowledge object. This means that if two descriptions seem to be inconsistent, at least one of them must be false, or that their formulations are ambiguous, and that the descriptions would be consistent if they were disambiguated. This last point is particularly important and it harks back immediately to the main message of this paper. Given the assumption of objectivity, it is not possible that inconsistent descriptions of the same object are all true. If they are true, they cannot deal with the same object. Objects and reality are by convention such that they do not allow true, but inconsistent, descriptions.[34]

So it seems that the view, implicitly adopted in this paper, about the possibility of objectivity is not something which can easily be contested. It is a view, which is, so to speak, true by convention. However, this immediately raises the question whether we should adopt this convention. Let us assume for a while that such fundamental conventions as those about the nature of reality and its relation to descriptions thereof are open to choice, rather than something which just happens to us. Would it be useful to assume that there is no independent reality, but only realities from a particular perspective or knowledge interest? What would a claim to truth amount to according to such an assumption? The very notion of 'truth' seems to presuppose that truth is the same for everybody. The request 'this is my truth, tell me yours'[35] is not really a request, but rather an implicit claim that, on the issue at stake, there is no truth to be had. Subjectivism in the sense of Leiter and truth claims do not fit well together.

The problem with objections such as the one ascribed to Westerman, namely that there is no objectivity at all, is that they collapse under their own weight. As soon as hope is given up on one truth, which is the same for everybody and on a kind of objectivity, which is really objective and not merely objective from a point of view or a particular knowledge interest, the difference between argumentation and persuasion collapses. There is no difference any more between propositions, such as 'Mount Everest is the highest mountain (on Earth)' and 'cauliflower tastes better than spinach'. In fact, there would even no longer be a difference between 'objectivity is

---

[34] Here it is important to realise that the convention does not have to be explicit. In particular 'conventions' about such fundamental issues as the nature of reality and the consistency of true descriptions of reality are seldom made explicit. The Quinean circumscription of such conventions as those parts of our beliefs that are least amenable to revision might be more apt than the term 'convention'. *cf* WVO Quine, 'Two dogmas of empiricism' in WVO Quine, *From a Logical Point of View*, 2nd edn (New York, Harper & Row, 1961) 20–46.

[35] See en.wikipedia.org/wiki/Manic_Street_Preachers (last consulted on 31 October 2011).

always perspective-bound' and '"Layla" by Derek & the Dominoes is a better piece of music than Bach's "Erbarme Dich"'. This paper would not be very different from an attempt to convince the reader of the superiority of paintings by Van Gogh over those of El Lissitzky, and reading it would be little more than an intellectual pastime. At least the author did not intend it to be only that.

3

The Impossibility of an Outsider's Perspective

PAULINE C WESTERMAN*

I. INTRODUCTION

DISCUSSIONS CONCERNING THE nature of law, the relation between rules and principles, as well as about the way to study law are permeated by a vocabulary that suggests a strong and straight dividing line, separating the 'inside' from the 'outside'. The dividing line is to be found in the positivist camp but is equally present in those who argue against legal positivism. It separates actors and activities, principles and perspectives, values and views.

Tempting as it may be to divide the world into 'us' and 'them', it blurs other, equally fruitful if not more relevant distinctions. Differences between legislators and judges are overlooked, whereas similarities between the analysis of legal doctrine and legal theory are not even noticed.[1] In this article, I first explore the assumptions underlying the visual representation of law as a house, the walls of which separate the inside from the outside. Subsequently, I will analyse metaphors by comparing them with syndromes. Both can be understood as a short referral to a cluster of conditions that are thought to hang together and which form the intension of a concept. Consequently, it will be argued that there is not one concept but many different ones, which are all inspired and coloured by the various pursuits of those who think about law. The conclusion is that legal philosophy should analyse and unravel the various inconsistencies underlying these concepts in view of the social practices in which they figure and the aims that are pursued.

---

* With thanks to Jaap Hage who always responds immediately and adequately to my strangest questions at the strangest times of the day, to Dietmar von der Pfordten for his careful reading and stimulating criticism, and to Bert-Jan Wolthuis for his valuable literature suggestions.
[1] I use the term 'legal theory' as a collective term for different disciplines such as legal philosophy, sociology of law, anthropology of law, and law and economics. By 'doctrine', I refer to the study, analysis and classification of positive law.

II. IN AND OUT

Nearly all important theorists of law—positivists and non-positivists alike—have made use of a spatial metaphor of law.[2] Principles, persons, rules and values are either thought to be *within* or *outside* the legal system. The image may be used unconsciously, or it may be used intentionally.

In Luhmann's theory,[3] the metaphor has become the supreme model in which law is conceptualised. Luhmann conceives law as a system that converts input into output. His work can, to a large extent, be understood as the attempt to patrol the boundaries of the system and to understand what happens there. Similarly, in the work of Kelsen, the boundaries function as barriers: they divide the legal official from the lay citizen.[4] In Kelsen's work, and more explicitly in Hart's, the divide also functions to differentiate between *perspectives*. While the legal official is thought to adopt an internal point of view, the sociologist is thought to adopt an external point of view.[5] Accordingly, insiders and outsiders also use different *criteria*. Insiders talk about validity, outsiders about efficacy. Both authors consequently struggle to reconcile the two criteria.[6]

Not only positivists, but also anti-positivists like Fuller and Dworkin cherish this visual scheme. Although Fuller rejects the view of a legal system as a collection of rules and principles and conceives law as an activity, he nevertheless distinguishes the activities of those *within* the system from those living *outside* the system. Consequently, the relevant moral criteria are divided in the same way. Notions of substantive justice are viewed as external morality. The requirements for a proper functioning legal system are called 'internal' morality. The problem then is to establish the relationship between virtues such as generality (internal) and equality (external).[7]

Finally, for Dworkin, the most important part of the debate concerning the status of principles revolves around the question whether they should be assigned a honourable place in the law or whether they are to be seen as

---

[2] See G Lakoff and M Johnson, *Metaphors We Live By* (Chicago, University of Chicago Press, 1980). They call these 'orientational metaphors'.

[3] N Luhmann, *Zweckbegriff und Systemrationalität* (Frankfurt am Main, Suhrkamp, 1973); *Ausdifferenzierung des Rechts: Beiträge zur Rechtssoziologie und Rechtstheorie* (Frankfurt am Main, Suhrkamp, 1981); and *Rechtssystem und Rechtsdogmatik* (Stuttgart, Kohlhammer, 1974).

[4] H Kelsen, *General Theory of Law and State* (trans A Wedberg) (Cambridge Mass, Harvard University Press, 1945) 29–50.

[5] External to law, not external to humanity as such: that something counts as a norm or standard can only be understood from the internal point of view adopted by a human spectator, see HLA Hart, *The Concept of Law*, 2nd edn (Oxford, Oxford University Press, 1994) 56.

[6] See, eg Hart ibid 102.

[7] LL Fuller, *The Morality of Law*, revised edn (New Haven and London, Yale University Press, 1969).

external, informing 'extra-legal preferences'.[8] Not an academic trifle: only if they are to be located inside the law are they thought to be binding.

We see then that the frontier that divides the inside from the outside is used to demarcate binding rules and principles from non-binding ones, but also to differentiate between kinds of actors, between different sets of criteria and even between different sets of values and moralities. The line may be drawn differently (as is clearly seen in the case of equality which, unlike Fuller, Dworkin allows to be central *in* law) but the line is nevertheless drawn. All these writers, their differences notwithstanding, seem to cling to the visual representation of a dividing line separating the inside from the outside.[9]

III. THE HOUSE

Before you think I am about to make fun of the attempts of serious legal theorists who tried to come to terms with legal phenomena, I must immediately admit that I am guilty myself of having made use of the spatial metaphor, which I usually prefer to concretise into the well-known metaphor of law as a house.[10] The temptations of the house metaphor are hard to resist. Students immediately recognise what you are aiming at if you tell them that they are usually working 'inside' the house of the legal system and that you invite them to come out of that house and to adopt an 'external point of view' furnished by legal theory. Apparently, law 'feels' like a house, to which one has become familiarised. And conversely, legal theory 'feels' either like fresh air or, depending on the intellectual temperament of the student, as a bitterly cold wind.

Probably one of the reasons that the metaphor of the house 'feels' right, is that it evokes a number of characteristics that are often attributed to law. I do not say that they *should* be ascribed to law, but merely try to explain the attractiveness of the metaphor by noting that the following properties *are* often seen as crucial to law.

(a) Unity: law, like a house, has many rooms and even wings, but is nevertheless to be regarded as one identifiable house.
(b) Solidity: law, like a house, has foundations, thought to consist of 'rights' or basic 'principles'.

---

[8] 'It could not depend on the judge's own preferences amongst a sea of respectable extra-legal standards' (R Dworkin, *Taking Rights Seriously* (London, Duckworth, 1987) 37).
[9] The question whether there are frontiers that separate the legal system from its surroundings should be distinguished from the question whether it is possible to conceive of legal systems which do not draw the boundaries between appropriate and inappropriate behaviour. This latter question is addressed (and answered negatively) in the interesting article by H Lindahl, 'Boundaries and the Concept of Legal Order' (2011) 2 *Jurisprudence* 73–97.
[10] Lakoff and Johnson, *Metaphors* (n 2) refer here to container-metaphors. They also speak about houses, but then as a metaphor for a theory.

(c) Autonomy: whether law is open to the outside world is a matter of choice, just like the choice to either open or close the window. It is, therefore, perfectly possible to reconcile the idea of a responsive or open system of law without ever being forced to question the solidity of the walls, or for that matter, to question the adequacy of the line that divides 'in' and 'out'.
(d) State-centredness: law, like a house, is tied to the territory on which it stands. Occasionally, one may be aware that there are other houses in the same street, just as one is aware of the legal systems of neighbouring countries.
(e) Systematicity: law, like a house, can only function properly if there is a certain internal ordering with a minimal degree of consistency.
(f) Universality: the idea that different legal systems all share a set of basic properties or a basic structure, that is typical for law, just as there are many different types of houses, that can nevertheless easily be recognised as houses.
(g) Continuity: law, like a house, may survive the ages. In order to survive, maintenance, restoration and a moderate degree of renovation is called for (the flexibility of law, necessary to adapt to changing circumstance) but it still functions as a stronghold against the changing tides of politics and changing morals.

This is quite a list. I should add, therefore, that it is not necessary for users of the image that they share *all* the assumptions that it evokes. To talk about law as a house does not necessarily commit one to thinking that law is autonomous, continuous, universal, systematic and state-centred. I myself, for instance, always doubted and criticised the idea that law should be seen as having (or should be criticised for lacking) 'foundations'. But if the metaphor captures a sufficient number of properties that are usually referred to in discussions concerning a certain phenomenon, I would say that it is a successful one.

IV. METAPHORS AS SYNDROMES

To talk about successful metaphors implies that we have an idea about the function of metaphors. Only then are we able to say whether a metaphor succeeds in carrying out that task. Now, much has been written about metaphors and I am not pretending to even summarise that vast field of inquiry. But it seems to me that, generally, the question what the *point* is of using a metaphor is overlooked. *Why* do people revert to houses when explaining law?

Certainly not in order to find similarities. As Searle correctly pointed out,[11] similarities can help us *understand* the metaphor, they can also help

---

[11] JR Searle, 'Metaphor' in A Ortony (ed), *Metaphor and Thought* (Cambridge, Cambridge University Press, 1979) 92–123.

produce one, but the meaning of metaphors cannot be explained as pointing out similarities between objects as widely differing from each other as houses and legal systems.

What then is the point of using a metaphor? I think that can only be elucidated in a metaphorical way, by comparing metaphors with syndromes. If a person exhibits six out of 10 characteristics of the DSM classification of psychological disorders, one may call him a sufferer of Asperger syndrome. Metaphors function in the same way as syndromes, in the sense that the names of such syndromes suddenly seem *to make sense* of these six characteristics, which were first experienced as unconnected properties. This is one of the reasons for the popularity of such names. ('I always thought that my son was lazy and aggressive, but I now see that he suffers from ADHD!') It makes sense of otherwise disjointed properties by suddenly seeing that these properties are related to each other.[12] The metaphor has the same unifying power. It gives us, in one simple image, an idea of how several unconnected properties hang together.

That is also the reason why syndromes and metaphors are such excellent heuristic devices. The generative power of metaphors and their capacity to develop new perspectives have been noted by several authors.[13] After recognising features 1, 3 and 5 of the DSM list as salient character traits of John, one will go on exploring whether properties 2, 4 and 6 can also be found. The same applies to metaphors. Metaphors frame the relevant questions to be asked. The house metaphor directs the discussion to matters such as the role of principles, ('are they foundations?') or the degree to which law is autonomous ('to what extent is one free to open and close the windows?').

There are drawbacks to this heuristic potential. The selective quality of metaphors obviously implies that a host of *other* questions are not addressed, and are overlooked.[14] The other danger is that one is tempted to push the comparison too far. One stubbornly keeps investigating properties 2, 4 and 6 without any indication that such a search might be fruitful.

These similarities between metaphors and syndromes are all the more remarkable, since in fact they work in opposite directions. Metaphors help to explain that which is unfamiliar by means of an image that is more familiar, that is easily accessible, and which conveys the coherent set of properties *at one glance*. Syndromes explain familiar traits by means

---

[12] See also D Schön, 'Generative Metaphor: A Perspective on Problem-Setting in Social Policy' in Ortony, *Metaphor and Thought* (n 11) 254–83, 264.
[13] Schön, 'Generative Metaphor' ibid; M Black, 'More about Metaphor' in Ortony (n 11) 19–43, 40.
[14] See AJ Wolthuis, *De Formele Kwaliteit van een Politiek Debat* (Den Haag, Boom Juridische uitgevers, 2005) 58–68. He follows Schön here (n 12).

of unfamiliar 'scientific' terms that should be studied before they can be applied. However, the effect of these translations, is roughly the same.

V. NORMATIVE INSIDERS AND DETACHED OUTSIDERS

Because of their heuristic qualities, metaphors are expansive. One is tempted to get carried away with a good metaphor. This is particularly the case with the law–house metaphor. Although there are good reasons to apply the metaphor to the *object* (the legal system), the house metaphor also threatens to dominate the debate on the proper *methods* to be used in order to study law. The house metaphor divides not only legal phenomena from non-legal ones but, as we have seen, it also distinguishes its inhabitants from the outsiders. The insiders are thought to adopt an internal point of view, the outsiders are free to view law from an external perspective.

Again, I am guilty of adopting this scheme myself. In an article on the proper legal methodology,[15] I compared the activity of legal scholars to my mother's frantic reorganisation of drawers and cupboards whenever a new item for the household was bought. I argued that legal scholars, working *in* the house of law, are mainly and primarily busy with restructuring and reorganising legal concepts and categories. They do this with a view to fit in some new development in such a way that the new ordering is practical and coherent with the existing classificatory schemes.

My account was welcomed by those who advocate a proper (normative, practice-oriented) methodology for legal scholars. But it was resisted by those who had grown dissatisfied with legal doctrine over the years. Advocates of a fresh and empirical, non-normative methodology protested at my attempt to lock them in the house of law. They said they preferred 'out of the box thinking'.[16]

Neither of these two opposite camps, however, questioned the demarcation wall itself that is erected between normative, practice-oriented insiders and neutral, disinterested outsiders. The image of the legal inhabitants with their practical and normative concerns is mirrored by the image of non-legal outsiders who are supposed to study law in a way that is truly scientific, empirical and detached. Yet, if I am honest, I have to admit that although an outsider myself, I am not disinterested and neutral at all. I am indignant about certain forms of legislation, about the instrumentalisation of rules,

---

[15] See PC Westerman, 'Open or Autonomous? The Debate on Legal Methodology as a Reflection of the Debate on Law' in M Van Hoecke (ed), *Methodologies of Legal Research: Which Kind of Method for What Kind of Discipline?* (Oxford, Hart Publishing, 2011) 87–110.
[16] J Vranken, 'Methodology of Legal Doctrinal Research: A Comment on Westerman' in Van Hoecke, *Methodologies of Legal Research* (n 15) 111–21; but also J Bell, 'Legal Research and the Distinctiveness of Comparative Law' in Van Hoecke (n 15) 155–76.

about the loss of legal certainty. What does that imply? Can I honestly say that I am normative in a different way? In a way befitting the outsider? Where am I? Standing at the threshold of the house? Uncomfortably hanging out of the window?

VI. WHO BELONGS WHERE?

It is here that the first fissures emerge in the house metaphor. The house may be an appropriate metaphor for the concept of law, but does it capture in an adequate manner the activities that are carried out by insiders and outsiders? The dividing line seems to overlook differences and fails to notice similarities.

Legal scholars, working in the departments of universities, are usually seen as inhabitants of the house of law. Yet they only marginally share the practical concerns of lawyers, judges and legislators. It may be true that they think that they should reconstruct the legal system, its concepts, categories and principles in a way which is useful to those who make use of these items, but this only means that they share *a* concern with practitioners.

But even among the practitioners there are major differences, which are overlooked by gathering them into one big family. The differences between lawyers and notaries are vast, both in professional *habitus* and outlook, the way they define their trade as well as in the virtues they cherish and the principles they adhere to. Judges and legislators not only assume a different professional outlook, but also have a different set of criteria at their disposal. Legislative jurists tend to prioritise effectiveness and efficacy over legal certainty and equality.[17]

Finally, there are many examples of questionable membership. Some seem to include philosophers and historians of law into the household.[18] Others maintain that philosophers, by the fact that they try to answer different questions, hover above the houses in search of their similarities in structure and building-plan, able to discern in an objective way the essential traits of law, of *all* law.[19]

In fact, the only firm position here is occupied by the social scientists. They are unequivocally and always positioned on the outside. They *never* belong to the family. It is here that the divide is at its most poignant. Speaking of law and social sciences, McCrudden, after a nuanced exposition

---

[17] See the various contributions about professional autonomy in (2011) 172 *Rechtsgeleerd Magazijn Themis*, thematic issue no 4.
[18] C McCrudden, 'Legal Research and the Social Sciences' (2006) 122 *Law Quarterly Review* 632–50.
[19] Hage combines this view with conventionalism. See Jaap Hage, 'Can Legal Theory Be Objective?' ch 2 to this volume.

of the ways in which law might benefit from a social science perspective, suddenly betrays himself by repeating that it is *them* and *us,* and that *they* (the social scientists) should also be willing to learn something from *us* lawyers, instead of the one-way traffic to which interdisciplinary research so often boils down.[20]

It seems then that the crude dichotomy between insiders and outsiders, between 'us' and 'them' may meet a psychological need but does not do justice to the variety of pursuits and persons who are somehow involved with law. It does not differentiate between the various insiders, nor between the overwhelming variety of outsiders. By attributing objectivity to outsiders and normativity to insiders it moreover fails to notice that outsiders also have their normative concerns.

VII. TYPES OF QUESTIONS

In order to avoid the caricatures of insiders and outsiders, we should no longer be led astray by the view that the *method* one is supposed to follow should only be informed by the particular features of the *object*. We should also inquire into the aims[21] that are pursued by the various actors, that is, we should keep in mind the different *kinds of questions* that are asked by all those who study and practice law.

In order to clarify what I mean by this, it is useful to refer to the ambiguous position that is occupied by those researchers who engage in comparative law. As inhabitants who regularly walk over to the neighbours, their position is precarious. The question arises: is the comparatist to be regarded as insider or as outsider? Bell responds to this question by saying that the comparatist 'has to present the foreign legal system in a form which is faithful to what it looks like from the inside, even though the comparatist is not his or herself an insider'.[22] Insiders, according to Bell, describe what should be done from a *legal point of view*; they do not make normative statements *all things considered*.[23] Bell's position seems to boil down to saying: 'After all, we house-dwellers are all lawyers'. If we visit the neighbours, we do that in the capacity of fellow-inhabitants. Therefore, we can describe what is going on there from 'within'.

But is this an informative statement? The problem is: it takes for granted that everybody knows what it *means* to reason from a 'legal point of view'. But this is far from clear if we examine the various motives for people to

---

[20] See McCrudden, 'Legal Research' (n 18).
[21] D von der Pfordten, 'What is Law: Aims and Means' (2011) 97 *Archiv fur Rechts- und Sozialphilosophie* 151ff.
[22] Bell, 'Legal Research' (n 16) 168.
[23] Ibid 166.

do comparative research. Let us look at some possible reasons why people study other legal systems:

(a) The legislator who struggles to implement a European directive might want to pay a short visit to other European legal systems, just in order to find out which legal instruments are used there to fulfil the requirements of the directive.
(b) The legal scholar who struggles with the same directive may also study other legal systems in order to find out to what extent the European directive can be made to fit in the national system in a coherent way. His visit should probably last a bit longer, working out not only a particular solution but also the way this solution interacts with other parts of the system.
(c) Still another form of comparative analysis is undertaken by my PhD student[24] who sets out to study goal regulation in both Sweden and the Netherlands in order to assess the effects of this form of regulation on accountability. Her investigation is inspired by the theoretical concern to understand how a certain style of legislation affects different jurisdictions.
(d) Finally, comparative research may be conducted to answer an even broader question, for instance: 'To what extent can goal regulation be seen as privatisation of public law?'

It is clear that these four questions as motives to engage in comparative analysis cannot neatly be parceled out on the basis of the inside/outside dichotomy. Bell may want to differentiate statements that are made 'from the legal point of view' from statements concerning to what should be done '*all things considered*', which is deemed proper to a philosophical, external point of view, but I cannot draw that line in the four examples given. When does my PhD student become a philosopher? When she studies the relation between goal regulation and accountability? Or when she broadens her subject to cover privatisation of public law?

One may reply to this by saying that these questions are not philosophical questions at all, since they are about existing matters of fact and relations, not about *desirable* matters of fact and relations. According to such a view genuine philosophers ask themselves whether privatisation of public law is truly desirable. Apart from the fact that there are reasons to discard this image of philosophy as too narrow, I do not think there is a fundamental difference here. When we ask ourselves whether privatisation of public law is desirable, we need to rely on criteria in the light of which something should be seen as desirable. We may parcel out some criteria as 'legal' and others as 'non-legal' but, again, that is question-begging, for it assumes that

---

[24] ALE Enequist.

we know how to draw the boundaries of a legal system, that separates it from the outside world.

But whatever we do, we certainly do not adopt an 'all things considered' perspective. Also, philosophers have research questions in mind that determine, constrain and limit the kind of things that are considered and philosophers also have criteria in mind that determine how they are considered. These criteria are to a large extent informed by the questions asked and the aims pursued. That means that one's position (inside/outside) and the perspective to be adopted (internal/external) does not depend on the *object* (law) but on the *questions* one may want to answer.[25]

VIII. NOT ENTITIES BUT CONCEPTS

So far, we have seen that the metaphorical line between insiders and outsiders is too crude and does not allow for differentiation on either side. But at the same time, we have also come across very useful qualities of metaphors. Metaphors, like syndromes, make sense of what is already known by the fact that they show how the various features of a certain phenomenon *hang together*. Just as the Asperger syndrome reveals the interdependence between such otherwise disjoint features as making wild gestures, a talent for mathematics and the incapacity to make friends, the house metaphor draws attention to the possibility that autonomy and unity, continuity and solidity hang together. The upside of metaphors is that they unify and show relationships, the downside is that they thereby tend to blur some vital distinctions. Therefore, the question that arises is how we can reap the benefits of metaphors without allowing them to wash away all distinctions.

I think that a possible answer to this question is given by exactly the comparison with syndromes. The comparison of metaphors with syndromes (which in itself is a metaphor for a metaphor) points to the dangers of invoking the metaphor uncritically. All is well as long as the syndrome functions as a short referral to a number of characteristics which may hang together in different combinations. It then functions as a heuristic device. But uncritical use of DSM-classifications may convey the illusion that syndromes not only refer to a set of variable features but stand for an *entity*, a well-defined disease, a disease that you do or do not have, or a disease that no longer allows for a variety in features. In such a capacity syndromes often hinder ongoing research (although they may be useful for other purposes, for example they can be used to prescribe medicine, or to apply for special insurance-money).

---

[25] See also J Hage, 'The Method of a Truly Normative Legal Science' in Van Hoecke (n 15) 19–44, 22.

So what we should keep in mind is what metaphors (and syndromes) stand *for*. Metaphors may *evoke* the image of an entity (house), but it does not mean that law *is* a house or that legal systems should be compared with houses. The metaphor only unifies—in one image—*various different properties*. These properties are to be understood as conditions that should be met in order to qualify as an element of a certain category.[26] Such conditions are commonly regarded as the intension of a concept. Also syndromes are not entities, but concepts. A syndrome just indicates, for example, that if one exhibits six out of 10 listed features, one can be included into the category of Asperger patients. The description of the syndrome forms the intension of a concept whereas all existing Asperger patients form the extension of a concept. In the example adduced by Jaap Hage in this volume, the question whether whales are mammals or fish is determined by conventional criteria that must be met in order to qualify as a member of one of these categories. The criteria specify the conditions that must be met in order to be counted as an instance of such a category. So we might say that metaphors, like syndromes, specify the intension of a concept.[27] And they do that by unifying these conditions in one image or term.[28] The danger is reification: one tends to forget that the image or scientific term does not stand for an entity but for a collection of conditions.

IX. DESCRIPTION OF CONDITIONS

So the intension of a concept specifies the conditions that must be met in order to qualify for membership of the corresponding category. For instance, the concept 'pizza' enumerates the conditions 'made of dough', 'baked in an oven' and 'containing cheese and tomatoes'. If an item fulfills these conditions, it may be considered to belong to the category 'pizza'.

Concepts may say something about the *number* of conditions that should be met, about *the level of abstraction* in which they should be described, about the *status* of these conditions and about their respective *weight*. Finally, they are often accompanied with a paradigmatic or central case as instance of the category.

---

[26] See H Putnam, 'The Meaning of "Meaning"' reprinted in H Putnam, *Mind, Language and Reality: Philosophical Papers*, vol 2 (Cambridge, Cambridge University Press, 1975) 215–71.

[27] Of course, it is possible to entertain a concept of law which sees law as a system. But then, 'law' is still a concept. See J Raz, *The Concept of a Legal System*, 2nd edn (Oxford, Clarendon Press, 1980).

[28] Cp GA Miller, 'Images and Models, Similes and Metaphors' in Ortony (n 11) 201–50, 209. Miller seems to hint at the same connection between metaphors and concepts, but unfortunately does not work out that short reference in the rest of his article.

(a) Number: It may be possible that a concept merely enumerates all the relevant conditions to be fulfilled in order to qualify as member of the category and leaves open the question which combinations of conditions are fulfilled; but it is also possible that it indicates clusters of conditions that must be fulfilled.
(b) Degree of abstraction: It is possible that the concept refers to these conditions in a concrete way (ham, anchovies, olives) or in a more abstract way (topping).
(c) Status: It may be possible that a concept differentiates between necessary conditions to be fulfilled in order to qualify as a member (made of dough) and merely accidental conditions (containing ham).[29]
(d) Weight: It may be possible that a concept prioritises conditions by assigning weight and relevancy to each of them (tomatoes more important than anchovies).

The weight and status of the conditions are often exemplified by a concrete instance that 'stands for' the category as a whole. (The paradigmatic pizza is of course the Marguerita.)

Whereas membership of categories such as mammals and fish is decided by conventional criteria, about which a certain consensus has been established, this is not the case with concepts like 'law' or 'principle', let alone 'justice' or 'the good life'. The extent to which people disagree about the conditions that should be met in order to count as an instance of 'law' can be assessed more precisely once we keep in mind the four dimensions that were distinguished above. In relation to all four dimensions, people might disagree. They may disagree about whether or not the list of conditions is complete; which conditions should be added or discarded; about the degree of abstraction of description; about whether conditions are accidental or necessary; or about the relative importance or weight of each of the conditions. These disagreements will eventually combine in a different choice of paradigmatic case.

Usually, the debates concerning a particular concept exhibit all four kinds of disagreement. For instance, in the Hart–Fuller debate we see that (a) Fuller's set (including Fuller's eight criteria for good lawmaking) comprises many more conditions than Hart's. (b) Hart's description (secondary rules) is more abstract than Fuller's. As to (c) both Hart and Fuller agree that law serves as point of orientation in the mutual adjustment of people's actions, but for Fuller this is a necessary condition and for Hart it is not. Regarding (d) it is not difficult to imagine the two authors would rank the shared criteria differently. Unlike Hart, Fuller favours two paradigmatic cases: customary law as well as contract law.

---

[29] I don't commit myself to the view, expounded by Rey, that concepts should be analysed as a set of necessary conditions that together are sufficient. The colouring of the entire concept is brought about by accidental features as well. See G Rey, 'Concepts and Conceptions, A Reply to Smith, Medin, and Rips' (1985) 19 *Cognition* 297–303.

This fourfold division enables us, I think, to assess more precisely the nature and degree of agreement or disagreement. We might assess whether the disagreement is only about the number of conditions included, about the level of description, about the necessary or accidental status of conditions, or about the way they are prioritised.

X. CONTESTED CONCEPTS

If we allow for a refined assessment concerning the nature and degree of disagreement, there is no need for the a priori assumption that, differences notwithstanding, the users of a particular concept share a common understanding of some basic features of the concept. There have been several attempts to defend that assumption.

Gallie's well-known distinction between concepts and conceptions assumes that although we may disagree on criteria and consequently cherish different conceptions, we can nevertheless be said to share the same concept.[30] The problem with this view is that although the term 'conception' is clear, the term 'concept' is vague. Dworkin does his best to elucidate the distinction metaphorically by comparing concepts with the trunk of the tree on which we all agree, and conceptions with the finer branches on which we no longer agree. But, although we may understand these finer branches and think of conceptions as different combinations of criteria that are assigned different properties and weight, the question remains how that trunk concept should be understood.[31] As the subset of conditions that happen to overlap, no matter the weight that is assigned to them? Or merely as the conditions recognised as necessary by all? I do not think that we can arrive at a defensible choice between these possibilities.

There are quite a few people who believe that a sandwich with a topping of tomatoes and cheese, put in the microwave for five minutes, should be regarded as a pizza. I would object to that view. For me, the paradigmatic pizza is the one I once enjoyed in a Venetian restaurant. Are we all sharing the same concept 'pizza'? I doubt it. We may as well say that people who disagree on such matters cherish different concepts. That does not make disagreement and debate illusionary, as is maintained by Rey.[32] That

---

[30] WB Gallie, 'Essentially Contested Concepts' (1956) 56 *Proceedings of the Aristotelian Society* 167ff.
[31] R Dworkin, *Law's Empire* (Cambridge, Mass, Belknap Press, 1986) 70.
[32] See G Rey, 'Concepts and Stereotypes' (1983) 15 *Cognition* 237–62, 249: 'If the features by which I identify birds have to do with their songs, while those you go by have to do with their feathers, then, since you and I have different sets of properties "in mind", you and I have different concepts associated with "bird". That is—to recall precisely the work concepts are to do in their Stability and Linguistic roles—you and I could not have beliefs and preferences with the same content [bird]; our uses of the word "bird" would be mere homonyms; our agreements and disputes about birds illusory.'

would be the case if the two concepts were to entail mutually exclusive sets of conditions. As long as there is sufficient overlap, there is something to disagree about. What exactly should be regarded as 'sufficient' is difficult to assess. The emergence of new terms, such as 'regulation' or 'governance', seems to indicate that overlap is no longer felt sufficient.

The only way to save the notion of a concept on which we all agree is to decide that the level of abstraction (b) should be very high.[33] If we describe the conditions in a very abstract way, it is easy to view them as necessary conditions and we might then say that these necessary conditions together form the trunk concept. If we say that it is a necessary condition of a pizza that it is 'something to eat', we do not disagree. The price to be paid for such agreement is that concepts tend to become uninformative. There is agreement because there is—literally—nothing to disagree about.

Dworkin's own distinction between so-called 'criterial' (for example, 'bachelor') and 'interpretive' concepts (for example, 'justice')[34] seems to serve the same goal as Gallie's: to maintain the view that underlying the disagreement on conditions, there is a consensus on a certain core meaning. By the term 'criterial concept' Dworkin seems to refer, in the same way as I do, to the conditions and criteria that should be met in order to count as an instance of a category. He mentions 'bachelor' as such a criterial concept. If I understand Dworkin correctly here, the criteria that allow for membership are not only conventional but also shared. Next to this, however, he reserves a special place for what he calls 'interpretive concepts' such as 'justice'. He writes:

> Sharing an interpretive concept does not require any underlying agreement or convergence on either criteria or instances. ... They share the concept because they participate in a social practice of judging acts and institutions just and unjust and because each has opinions ... about what the most basic assumptions of that practice, its point and purpose, should be taken to be.[35]

The problem is: what are these most basic assumptions? Dworkin answers that question by referring to a shared social practice, a practice which in his eyes is incidentally not only inhabited by lawyers but also by philosophers who are all engaged in interpreting law 'in its best light' and with an eye to its underlying purposes.[36]

I think that Dworkin is asserting here the somewhat obvious truth that we cannot sensibly use and debate the concept 'pizza' without ever having eaten one. But that does not resolve matters. We might have difficulty

---

[33] Four levels of abstraction are distinguished in D von der Pfordten, 'About Concepts in Law' in JC Hage and D von der Pfordten (eds), *Concepts in Law*, Law and Philosophy Library, vol 88 (New York, Springer, 2009) 17–33, 28.
[34] R Dworkin, *Justice in Robes* (Harvard, Harvard University Press, 2006) 224–25.
[35] Ibid 224.
[36] Dworkin, *Law's Empire* (n 31) 47.

explaining what a decent pizza is, particularly to someone who never visited a real pizzeria and whose practice of pizza eating consists of eating pizzas bought at the supermarket. His practice of pizza eating is very different from the practice of the Venetian pizza eater. Then I would say that these two pizza eaters entertain different concepts of pizza, stipulating different conditions that reflect the different practices. They only happen to use the same word 'pizza'.

I suspect that the only reason to assume a trunk concept is the desire to prioritise one of these two concepts. Dworkin just wants to defend the view that there is only one genuine, proper pizza. For him that is presumably the original Neapolitan one.[37]

XI. DIFFERENT ROLES AND DIFFERENT TASKS

What applies to 'pizza' equally applies to 'law'. The term stands for a multitude of concepts, which—at least at a certain level of concreteness—are distinct from each other and at best exhibit a certain family resemblance, just as 'game' in Wittgenstein's famous example.[38] The intension of each of these concepts overlaps to some degree with the intension of 'neighbouring' concepts, without there being one necessary element that is shared by all and that can be seen as the core.

The reason for the lack of such a core condition is precisely that concepts are embedded in social practices. Dworkin is quite right in stressing the importance of social practices. Concepts are not only representations, but are used in order to do something and, in the case of 'law,' that activity is collectively undertaken. The categories for which concepts are the gatekeepers are used to order the world with a particular *end in view*.[39] Those ends in view determine to a large extent the level of concreteness in which conditions are described (dimension (b)). The practical uses of concepts, therefore, make it impossible to choose such abstract conditions (like 'something to eat') that one can sensibly speak of a core meaning. But the ends-in-view also determine the other dimensions: the number, status and weight of conditions.

---

[37] That objectivism in taste exists is exemplified by the unforgettable landlord of the British B&B who served me cooked breakfast while exclaiming: 'so here you are, love; the *proper* mushroom!' In fact, the metaphysical existence of 'real' properties forming 'the' concept as distinguished from conceptions, which only flow from perceptions, is presupposed in the criticism expressed by Rey in 'Concepts and Stereotypes' (n 32) 249.

[38] L Wittgenstein, *Philosophical Investigation*, 3rd edn (trans GEM Anscombe) (Upper Saddle River, NJ, Prentice-Hall, 1973).

[39] J Dewey, *Human Nature and Conduct 1922*, vol 14 of JA Boydston (ed), *The Middle Works of John Dewey, 1899–1924* (Carbondale and Edwardsville, Southern Illinois University Press, 1983/1988).

Let me mention just a couple of such social practices, in which the various specific ends-in-view which arise inform the various concepts of law. The ingredients of these concepts—the conditions—are rendered in italics.

Adjudication: Officials like judges, that have to solve concrete cases, are obviously primarily interested in the question: 'how to solve this case'? If judges who do not merely rely, like Solomon, on their own wisdom but on a set of rules, refer to 'law' they refer to a *reservoir* of instruments (rules, contracts, precedents, principles) that enable them to perform this task. These instruments only work when they are supposed to be *valid* and are assumed to have *binding force*. Since they are required to give reasons for their judgment, they see rules as *reasons* for a *fair* solution.

Legislation: Legislative jurists have to implement policies in a legal form. They are confronted with the demands of the minister and of parliament as well as with the demands of the legal system. They are interested in the question: how can law be used to realise policies? When they refer to law, it is as an instrument that can help to steer and regulate society and its members to the ends that are pursued. Law should be *enforced*, *compliance* rates should be maximised, therefore *effectiveness* and *legitimacy* are its prime virtues. Apart from that, new laws should *fit in* the overall legal system. For legislators, rules are not reasons but sign posts. Law is not seen as different from *regulation*.

Academia: In general, legal doctrinal scholars are interested in the question: how can we order the existing legal material? In this respect, the primary concern of academic doctrinal lawyers is pretty much like that of the librarian who is interested in finding a *practical*, and *coherent and consistent* classification of the legal material. However, there are differences in orientation, depending on the kinds of visitors they have in mind. Scholars engaged in administrative law are closer to the perspective of the legislator and for that reason probably more willing to inquire into the effectiveness of law than private lawyers.

Legal theory: What applies to legal scholarship, applies even more to legal theory. I use the term legal theory to encompass positivist as well as non-positivist philosophy of law, logical analysis as well as socio-legal studies. The questions legal theoreticians want to address are very much dependent on the roles and social practices with which they identify. The bulk of legal theory is judge-centered. People like Dworkin see law as a reservoir of rules and principles. The debate on the status of principles ('in' or 'out', legally or morally binding) should be understood in the light of this preoccupation.

It is, however, also possible to identify with the legislator. It is a point of view that I myself adopt and which gives rise to a completely different set of questions: namely, what is the relation between styles of legislation and forms of *control and enforcement*; or: how can traditional values of—judge-centered—law be reconciled with regulatory demands?

Third, legal theory can regard itself as the assistant of legal doctrine.[40] Philosophical and logical analyses of *fundamental concepts* such as 'competence', 'ownership' as well as the way they relate are carried out in order to understand better the nature of the legal material that is organised by the librarian-scholar.

Finally, legal theory can take the point of view of the norm-addressee. Since the time of Ehrlich, sociologists have often taken this perspective.[41] For them, law is primarily the way by means of which people interact, a special or formalised *variety of social rules*. The relationship between social rules and legal rules is studied, not with an eye to the effectiveness of legislator, but with an eye to understand the social *fabric* of society. Here law is seen as a specialised form of *social control*.[42]

These roles are sketched in a crude and unrefined way. It is not my intention to assign people to a predetermined and fixed role. Neither is it my view, that every role or aim is accompanied by one well-defined concept. It is possible that one and the same concept plays a role in addressing different questions. For instance, both the legislative jurist and the sociologist may be interested in effectiveness and both see effectiveness as a necessary condition for the existence of law. Yet, effectiveness in itself is understood differently. For the legislator it is the degree to which laws successfully realise policies. For the sociologist, it is the degree to which laws affect people's daily lives. The same applies to the term 'system'. For the judge the system is a reservoir of reasons that can be given for a particular solution. For Luhmann the term is used to conceptualise the way law interacts with other systems such as economics, politics or morality.

Because of this overlap in images and terms, it seems as if a term has a shared meaning. But there are differences lurking underneath. To see these differences, we should note the obvious fact that conditions are often concepts themselves. As soon as we ask ourselves: what do we understand by 'effectiveness' and inquire into the conditions that are stipulated by that concept, disagreement may arise. The fact that the same words arise is not sufficient reason to assume that the users partake in the same social practice. In order to see that, we should ask which questions these people address and understand concepts as tools to answer these questions.[43]

---

[40] The work of Jaap Hage can partly be understood in this way.
[41] This is one of the reasons why this branch of legal theory is consistently seen as an 'external' perspective.
[42] J Griffiths, 'What is Legal Pluralism?' (1986) 24 *Journal for Legal Pluralism & Unofficial Law* 1.
[43] If we view concepts in this way, it may be clear why people view insects as 'birds' if they learn that the insect-like appearance has been brought about by an accident, and the creature is still capable of giving birth to a bird. The example is adduced in EE Smith, 'Concepts and Categorization' in EE Smith and DN Osherson, *Thinking: An Invitation to Cognitive Science*, vol 3 (Cambridge, Mass, MIT Press, 1995) 26. Smith favours the contrast-model in which categorisation is seen as tracing similarities. The example leads the author to concede that

XII. SHADED CONCEPTS

If we take a look at the terms that are rendered in italics we see that the various concepts of law can be seen as networks of a number of conditions that are assigned more or less weight and which are interrelated to each other. In this scheme, the conditions and concerns of legislators are indicated in light grey, those of the judiciary in dark grey. Common concerns are indicated in white. It should be noted that the weight of the conditions stipulated by the concept, as well as the proximity of the conditions to each other, depend on the specific concerns shared by the participants of the various social practices. The ways in which the conditions and criteria are linked up with the others determine the ways in which they are shaded and understood.

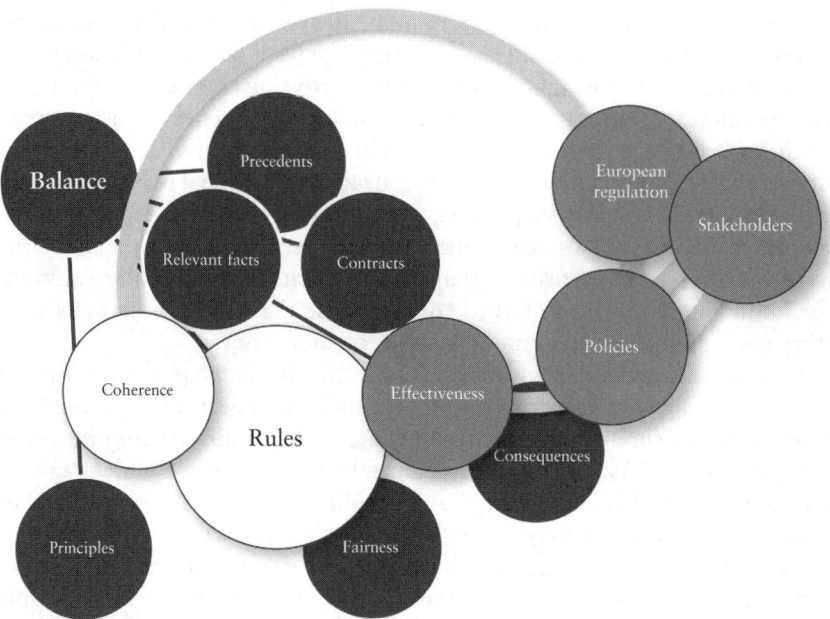

If we analyse the conditions mentioned above (effectiveness, fairness), it looks at first sight as if they are definitely more normative than the conditions of a syndrome such as Asperger ('good at mathematics' or 'inability

---

'sometimes categorization is theory-based rather than similarity based', but he seems to think that that occurs under 'special circumstances'. There is, however, a good reason to assume that categorisation is inherently theory-based. Although it may be true that two items are put in the same category because of their similarity, these two items should, nevertheless, be *judged* to be similar. And that judgment is dependent on the theory and the goals one has in mind.

to understand other people's feelings'). But at a closer look the conditions for Asperger are not so very different.

They share with the legal criteria the fact that they allow for degrees. Just as someone may be *extremely* good at mathematics and have *extreme* difficulty in understanding other people's feelings and can therefore be counted as a paradigmatic example of Asperger syndrome, we may have law, which is *extremely* effective in securing compliance. From the point of view of the legislator, such an effective law is paradigmatic, whereas for the judge it may be an aberration, it may not even be counted as 'law' at all.[44]

One may object that, in the case of Asperger, it is much easier to establish whether the conditions are fulfilled and to what extent. That may indeed be the case. For that reason, legislators are eager to develop tests that enable them to measure effectiveness either *ex ante* (regulatory impact assessment) or *ex post* (evaluation). But we should not forget that in such tests (whether in legislation or in psychology), such an assessment is thoroughly influenced by the selection of what is observed and by which methods. And this selection is inspired by the aims and concerns of the testers.

Still, we might think that there remains a vast difference. We might want to maintain that Asperger is not a normative concept because it is not something people want to realise. There is no 'point or purpose' in Asperger syndrome. That is true. It is regarded as an abnormality. But that does not turn it into a neutral and descriptive concept, on the contrary. Underlying the identification of conditions for Asperger, there are strong normative convictions of how a normal, non-Asperger human being should behave.

If we take these considerations into account, it might be possible to say something more about the so-called objectivity of legal theory. Such objectivity is usually defended by contending that theorists do not share the practical normative concerns of the legal practitioner. In the first instance, we have seen that to be only partly true. As I pointed out earlier, they may have identified with or oriented themselves towards a particular social legal practice. But even if their concerns are 'merely' theoretical, that does not diminish the level of normativity. Legal theorists might be interested in such diverse matters as the relation between law and fundamental values, between law and other forms of social control, or the relation between natural facts and institutional facts. These theoretical interests, *not less than practical concerns*, inevitably colour the concepts that are used, the selection as well as the relative weight that is attributed to the conditions. If there is a difference between the bias resulting from a practical interest and the bias that results from a theoretical interest, it can only be a gradual one.

---

[44] Once, when I told a member of the Dutch Supreme Court that I was interested in the structure of European directives, he remarked: 'But that can hardly be called law at all!'

XIII. LEGAL THEORY ABOUT WHAT?

Concepts are used as tools in order to answer a particular question, either practical or theoretical. The conditions that are stipulated in such a concept are selected in the light of their relevancy for the problem at hand. This means that, *in this respect,* there is no fundamental difference between the concepts used by legal practitioners, legal—doctrinal—academics and legal theorists. There is no dividing line that distinguishes insiders from outsiders. There are only lines demarcating—vaguely—the various social practices and these lines are not parallel to a divide between objective and subjective, or between descriptive and normative.

The question then remains to what extent we may cling to the view that legal theory has a subject or task of its own. I noted above that many legal theorists are inspired by the problems that pertain to a specific legal social practice. But does that imply that legal theory is either the handmaid of the judge or the servant of the legislator or the spokesman of the lay citizen?

On the one hand, I think that legal theorists should not shy away from identifying with the problems of social practices. There is nothing wrong with theorising about the problems that are encountered by legal officials of all sorts who are often unable to spend enough time to reflect on these problems.[45]

On the other hand, we should not identify too readily with the concerns of judges, legislators and citizens. Confining myself now to that branch of legal theory which is my own field, legal philosophy, I think that philosophers should certainly not succumb to the wishes of many practitioners that we supply them with high and noble philosophical foundations. There should be room for a proper philosophical way of inquiring into their problems. This 'proper philosophical way' does not consist of contemplating the house of law from an external point of view and neither do I propose to fly above the houses of law in order to unravel structures and streetplans. When I think of a proper theoretical point of view, I am thinking of that ugly term 'aboutness'. Overzealous identification can be avoided by being aware of the fact that, from a philosophical point of view, we are able to think *about* the tools we use and the tools other people use.

As I argued in this article, the relevant question is not: what 'is' law, nor what is law 'made of'. Such questions assume that law is a definite entity. If

---

[45] Fuller wrote: 'The object of legal philosophy is to give an effective and meaningful direction to the work of lawyers, judges, legislators, and law teachers. If it leaves the activities of these men untouched, if it has no implications for the question of what they do with their working days, then legal philosophy is a failure.' (L Fuller, 'The Needs of American Legal Philosophy' in KI Winston (ed), *The Principles of Social Order: Selected Essays of Lon L Fuller* (Durham, Duke University Press, 1981) 249–50).

we understand 'law' as a concept, the legal philosopher has a different task and, I think, a more important task to carry out. The question then arises: *how can people use these concepts in a coherent and useful way in view of their purposes?*[46] It is the task of legal philosophy to think about the ways people think about their problems. For instance: if legislators repeatedly say that overregulation is brought about by the principle of equality, it is high time to investigate the concepts of equality and overregulation that lead them to think so. If judges complain about the way scientific experts exceed their limits, it is time to explore these judge's assumptions about science and the relation of science to their own expertise.[47]

'Aboutness' does not require a detached point of view, or a bird's eye view. 'Aboutness' does not imply objectivity nor presuppose an objective mind. 'Aboutness' requires a standpoint, sufficiently close to the object of investigation to understand the way problems are experienced and conceptualised, a minimum of logic and analytic power and above all much common sense.

XIV. CONCLUSION

The ways people argue about law are diverse and depend on what they do in life. They may defend clients, issue licenses, work out contracts or study the emergence of international law. These tasks inspire the way law is conceptualised. More precisely: these tasks and aims help selecting the conditions and—often normative—criteria that should be met in order to count as 'law'. The diversity of pursuits implies a diversity of concepts of 'law'. There may be a certain overlap in conditions and criteria. But this overlap should not a priori be understood as agreement about 'the' concept. Shared vocabulary might hide underlying differences about either the number of conditions, the status or the weight of these conditions as well

---

[46] See SK Langer, 'The Pursuit of Meaning in Philosophy' (1929) 26 *The Journal of Philosophy* 379–84. Her article formed the inspiration for this article. See also SK Langer, *Philosophy in a New Key: A Study in the Symbolism of Reason, Rite, and Art* (New York, Penguin Books, 1948).

[47] See I Berlin, 'The Purpose of Philosophy' in H Hardy (ed), *Isaiah Berlin, Concepts and Categories: Philosophical Essays* (London, The Hogarth Press, 1978) para 33: 'The task of philosophy, often a difficult and painful one, is to extricate and bring to light the hidden categories and models in terms of which human beings think (that is, their use of words, images and other symbols), to reveal what is obscure or contradictory in them, to discern the conflicts between them that prevent the construction of more adequate ways of organising and describing and explaining experience (for all description as well as explanation involves some model in terms of which the describing and explaining is done); and then, at a still "higher" level, to examine the nature of this activity itself (epistemology, philosophical logic, linguistic analysis), and to bring to light the concealed models that operate in this second-order, philosophical, activity itself.'

as about the way they should be described. It is up to legal philosophy to analyse implicit assumptions, and to unravel inconsistencies. In order to be critical, legal philosophy should not be too submissive; but in order to be relevant, it should not be too remote from the daily concerns of the various legal practices that are studied.

III. Legal Reasoning

4

Objective Legal Reasoning—Objectivity Without Objects

MATTI ILMARI NIEMI

I. INTRODUCTION

OBJECTIVITY IS A normative concept. It is used as a demand applying to the language of philosophy, science and humanities. Normally, sentences doomed to be subjective are not seen as acceptable: sentences can be 'polluted' by the subjective influence. Accordingly, objectivity entails rationality and meaningfulness.

At the general philosophical level, objectivity is closely related to the concept of truth. When the demand for truthfulness is set up, satisfaction of the demand for objectivity is a necessary but not a sufficient condition of truthfulness. The same holds true for the concept of acceptability or justifiability when the concept of truth is not employed.

Objectivity refers to the relation between a subject and the person speaking about it. With the help of the concept of objectivity, it is presumed that the subject is independent of the speaker. Is it possible to know the world without the influence of the person in the know? Nagel has enunciated the problem of objectivity in the following way: how to combine the perspective of a particular person in the world with an objective view of the same world, the person and his viewpoint included?[1] The problem is emphasised in the fields of social sciences and humanities where the subjects are artificial.

There are two different dimensions included in the dichotomy objective–subjective. There are, perhaps, even two different senses of this dichotomy. The first is a general philosophical issue and the second a specific one, relevant in the areas of ethics and legal studies.

---

[1] T Nagel, *The View from Nowhere* (New York and Oxford, Oxford University Press, 1986) 3.

The first dimension is cognitive. According to this dimension, objectivity is a distinctive mark of rational knowledge. Objectivity refers to the cognition of a subject directed to the world around the subject. Respectively, subjectivity means sentences manifesting the subject itself.

The second dimension is ethical. It refers to the problem of evaluation. Here, the crucial questions are whether it is possible to discuss values in a rational way and whether there are objective values. More specifically, can judgments on values bear knowledge, or are they merely expressions of the subject's attitudes, feelings or personal interests?

Both of these dimensions are important in the field of law and both of them have to be taken into consideration. In philosophy of law, these two dimensions are often entangled. No clear separation is made here either.

In this paper, I will study the concept of objectivity from the point of view and for the needs of conventional legal dogmatics. My aspiration is to introduce a workable conception of objectivity for it.[2] Because of these restrictions, the fundamental challenge of objectivity provided by critical legal studies is ignored here. No doubt, objectivity is a topic vulnerable to criticism.

II. SOME PRELIMINARY REMARKS

It is a tempting course of thinking to presume a certain structure of the world as the foundation for the demand of objectivity: objectivity is a relation between a statement and a certain defined object. Accordingly, objectivity is seen as mind-independent. This is, however, a strong philosophical commitment. It calls for realism and the correspondence theory of truth. They are often included in the positivistic thinking which bore great influence in legal philosophy during the first half of the twentieth century. These orientations had many different manifestations, including both the cognitive and ethical dimensions. Philosophical realism and correspondence theory are, nevertheless, highly problematic in the field of legal philosophy. Hence, I leave them aside.

---

[2] The question of objectivity of legal reasoning in legal dogmatics has to be separated from the question of objectivity of law and objectivity of reasoning within the law, for instance, the reasoning of a judge. Greenawalt has addressed the last two questions. See K Greenawalt, *Law and Objectivity* (New York and Oxford, Oxford University Press, 1992) 3, 11 and 193. MH Kramer is also interested in the objectivity of law, see MH Kramer, *Objectivity and the Rule of Law* (New York, Cambridge University Press, 2007) 3. In addition, the approach adopted here has to be separated from the question of objectivity of legal theory, which is at the centre of attention of many articles in this book. See J Hage, *Can Legal Theory Be Objective?* ch 2 in this volume. See also P Cserne, 'Objectivity and the Law's Assumptions about Human Behaviour' ch 9 in this volume. Cserne focuses on both law and legal theory. Stavropoulos' viewpoint can be seen as uniform with mine but he confines himself to legal concepts. See N Stavropoulos *Objectivity in Law* (Oxford, Clarendon Press, 1996) 7.

Nevertheless, the strong and traditional challenge provided by philosophical realism and correspondence theory cannot be ignored or passed quickly. Their influence on legal thinking has to be clarified and explained. This explanation constitutes the critical and, in this sense, the negative dimension of my paper.

On the other hand, it is fair to also demand a positive and constructive approach. For this purpose, I try to outline a different approach to and conception of objectivity. In accordance with the title of this paper, it is the conception of objectivity without any defined objects of knowledge. Objectivity is considered a quality of reasoning. It is a weak conception of objectivity. Its tenability will be founded on the commitments of conventional legal dogmatics and, basically, on the nature of law. A sound conception of objectivity is a clarification of the philosophical presumptions of legal knowledge for its part. In other words, the basic features of conventional and advanced legal argumentation stipulate its philosophical commitments, not the other way around.[3]

Why is the objectivity of legal dogmatics an important issue—or is it important? I consider it important and one of the cornerstones of legal dogmatics. Legal dogmatics is an important way to present knowledge of valid law. In order to perform this duty in an acceptable way, the demand of objectivity has to be imposed. In other words, the requirement of objectivity has to be met in the work of a legal scholar. In short, trustworthy legal reasoning is objective. Furthermore, the objectivity of legal reasoning can be seen as one of the objective values of contemporary Western societies.[4]

III. PHILOSOPHICAL BACKGROUND OF OBJECTIVISM AND SUBJECTIVISM

The problems of objectivity and objectivism are general philosophical issues. They are—naturally—conceptually related. Objectivism about a topic holds that judgments about it can be objective.

---

[3] Here, I agree with Stavropoulos that the adopted approach can be called a domain-sensitive way. On the other hand, I do not follow his lead in connecting legal issues with substantial semantics and social practices. As far as the later issue is concerned, Stavropoulos follows Hart. See Stavropoulos, *Objectivity in Law* (n 2) 6 and 53.

[4] According to Van Hoecke's critical viewpoint on this claim, objectivity provides good feeling in the corrupted and less-than-perfect world. See M Van Hoecke, *Objectivity in Law and Jurisprudence*, ch 1 in this volume, 4. This viewpoint is sceptical. Scepticism is a characteristic of the supporters of American Legal Pragmatism and the Critical Legal Scholars. They both deny determinate correct legal answers or predictable decisions in the frames of formal systems of law, that is, they dispute objectivity in this sense. It is not, however, guaranteed to result in certainty of the indeterminacy of law on the general level because of the uncertainty of correct answers in individual cases. See Kramer, *Objectivity and the Rule of Law*, (n 2) 19.

Objectivism is often contrasted with *projectivism*. According to projectivism, judgments about a topic are, as a matter of fact, merely objective-sounding expressions of attitudes or feelings. Our personal and internal attitudes or feelings are projected to appear as qualities of external objects.

These distinctions can be traced back to the philosophies of Locke and Hume. Locke adopted from Galileo Galilei the distinction between *primary* and *secondary qualities* and raised them to be the basic epistemic concepts of his philosophy of science.[5] There are two kinds of qualities according to Locke. Only some qualities are external, that is, real parts of the world. Many appearances are merely impressions of the mind. They are subjective experiences but not perceptions of facts.[6] This seems to be the root of the strong and influential positivistic dimension of Western philosophy.

Hume accepted Locke's point of departure. The source and origin of knowledge is either perceptions or emotions.[7] In the field of philosophy of science, this approach leads to nominalism and positivism: all knowledge and facts are founded on empirical perceptions. In the field of ethics, that is moral philosophy, this approach leads to ethical naturalism. According to Hume, moral distinctions are not the offspring of reasons, and judgments about goodness or badness cannot be derived from facts. The source of moral judgments lies in human feelings and passions.[8]

The Humean naturalism and emotivism is an important background of *ethical subjectivism,* which was a popular ethical view at the end of the nineteenth century and during the first half of the twentieth century.[9] Subjectivism, in turn, is an important ally of legal positivism.

Subjectivism is a version of projectivism and, hence, a way to deny objectivism. According to subjectivism, people are expressing their personal desires or feelings when they are making moral judgments.

IV. LEGAL POSITIVISM AND ETHICAL SUBJECTIVISM

The two most important characteristics of positivistic thinking are the *social thesis* and the *separability thesis*.[10] According to them, law is a matter of fact as decisions or as other social facts, and there is no necessary connection between law and morals. These theses are closely connected.

---

[5] B Russell, *The History of Western Philosophy and its Connection with Political and Social Circumstances from the Earliest Times to the Present Day* (London, George Allen & Unwin Ltd, 1982) 585.

[6] J Locke, *An Essay Concerning Human Understanding* (Oxford, 1894) book II, chs 1, 2 and 4, 175 and 178 available at www.markfoster.net/sociosphere/locke.pdf.

[7] D Hume, *A Treatise of Human Nature,* 2nd edn (Oxford, Clarendon Press, 1978) book I, 1, 7 and 25.

[8] Ibid book III, 458 and 468.

[9] For instance, the studies of E Westermarck, CL Stevenson and AJ Ayer.

[10] JL Coleman and B Leiter, 'Legal Positivism' in Dennis Patterson (ed), *A Companion to Philosophy of Law and Legal Theory* (Oxford, Blackwell Publishers, 1996) 241.

The social thesis is one of the cornerstones of the approaches of Kelsen and Hart. Kelsen saw legal rules as legal facts and as the content of the lawgiver's will.[11] For Hart, law appears as existing and valid rules identified by the rule of recognition. For him, the existence of a legal system is a social phenomenon.[12]

Both of these theses together entail the difference in quality between law and morals: descriptions of valid law (or expressions of valid law) differ radically from moral evaluations. The existence of legal rules is a social fact, but what is the quality or nature of morals?

My claim is that legal positivism, at least strong positivism that is so-called plain-fact or exclusive positivism, presumes ethical subjectivism. A true and consistent supporter of it has to see morals as a variety of different opinions, attitudes, feelings or personal interests, that is, subjective expressions of persons but not descriptions of a society.

This presupposition appears in the major texts of positivists. Relativity of moral values in these texts means, in fact, different and contrary personal moral evaluations or values or interests of different groups of persons but not values of societies, that is, shared values of the members of a society as the subjects of a legal system.[13]

In this respect, Morton's approach is illuminating. According to him, there is a qualitative difference between factual law as enacted norms and evaluative morals. The latter is a matter of personal attitudes and opinions or restricted group interests.[14] Accordingly, the plurality of values and dissension of morals is used as an argument against the moral foundation of law.

V. THE STRONG CONCEPTIONS OF OBJECTIVITY

With reference to the relation between law and morals defined by legal positivists (at least by strict or exclusive positivists), we are ready to define certain conceptions of objectivity. Here, I take advantage of the three concepts of objectivity introduced by Marmor.[15] I treat them as different conceptions, that is, interpretations of the concept of objectivity.

---

[11] H Kelsen, *Pure Theory of Law* (Berkeley, Los Angeles and London, University of California Press, 1970) 73 and 79.

[12] HLA Hart, *The Concept of Law*, 2nd edn (Oxford, Clarendon Press, 1994) 201.

[13] I interpret the texts of Kelsen and Hart as expressing the emotivistic or subjectivistic view on morals. See Kelsen, *Pure Theory of Law* (n 11) 63; Kelsen, 'Law, State and Justice in the Pure Theory of Law' (1947–48) *Yale Law Journal*, 377; Hart, *The Concept of Law* (n 12) 200; and Hart, 'Positivism and the Separation of Law and Morals' in HLA Hart (ed), *Essays in Jurisprudence and Philosophy* (Oxford, Clarendon Press, 1983) 82.

[14] P Morton, *An Institutional Theory of Law* (Oxford, Clarendon Press, 1998) 11, 194, 364 and 369.

[15] A Marmor, 'Three Concepts of Objectivity' in A Marmor (ed), *Law and Interpretation, Essays in Legal Philosophy* (Oxford, Clarendon Press, 1995). I have taken advantage of Marmor's distinctions, but on the other hand, I have not followed them in all respects. There

According to the traditional and simple conception, objectivity means congruence between a judgment and its perceivable object. A judgment is objective if, and only if, it describes its object as a part of the discernible world. If a judgment does not tell us about a discernible object, it tells us about the speaker. In this case, the judgment is subjective. This conception is the strongest and it can be called the *metaphysical* or *ontological* conception.

This conception presumes philosophical realism and the correspondence theory of truth. A judgment cannot be objective or true or false if there are no defined objects in the perceivable world. Otherwise, judgments are subjective.

In a sense, the approach of legal realists satisfies the demands of this conception. They are not, however, philosophical realists. They do not accept legal rules or concepts as the objects of statements. Instead, with the help of naturalistic replacement (reduction) they define other objects as the true objects of legal knowledge. These objects can be the acts of judges or attitudes or beliefs of citizens or judges. These objects are parts of the perceivable world and statements about them can be verified or falsified empirically in accordance with the principles of philosophical positivism.[16] Here, objectivity bears the strong mind-independence.[17]

According to this approach, existing evaluations can, on the one hand, be part of the object of knowledge but are, on the other hand, not part of legal knowledge. In other words, rational discourse on values at the level of science is not possible. There is no room for appealing to values or principles of justice. Even the room for legal interpretation is very narrow. For instance, appealing to the system of law, human rights or consequences of different interpretations seem to be excluded from legal dogmatics. These cannot be elements of knowledge, which means information of behaviour or beliefs. This approach is uniform with the one of Hume and has common features with the one of Kelsen.

At the general level, the metaphysical conception of objectivity is not acceptable: it is too strong and narrow. The demands of this conception cannot be satisfied, at least not in the area of social sciences or humanities. The same holds true in the areas of legal dogmatics.

There is also a weaker version of the previous conception. According to it, a statement is objective if it is a statement about a defined object. Otherwise, a statement is subjective. In this case, the defined object is

---

are significant deviations and differences. Compare with the six chief and few ancillary conceptions of objectivity introduced by Kramer in *Objectivity and the Rule of Law* (n 2) 2. Each of them can be included in the sphere of the strong conceptions of objectivity.

[16] See, eg F Cohen, 'Transcendental Nonsense and the Functional Approach' (1935) *Columbia Law Review* 821, 839 and 849 and A Ross, *Om ret og retfærdighed* (København, Nyt nordisk forlag Arnold Busk, 1953) 52, 56 and 58.

[17] For the distinction between strong and weak mind-independence, see Kramer (n 2) 4.

not necessarily a part of the perceivable world. On the other hand, it is presumed that the object is defined as a part of the reality in one sense or another.

In the field of law, Kelsen can be seen as a representative of this approach. He has adopted philosophical realism. For him, legal rules (basically, the legal ought in the form of imputation) are the defined and existing objects of the statements of legal dogmatics. These statements are true or false, and hence, they are value-free and objective descriptions of their objects. Moreover, Kelsen employs correspondence as the definition of truth. Accordingly, legal rules are social facts and there is a special branch of reality as the object area of legal dogmatics. On the other hand, the existence of legal norms differs from the perceivable reality. Here, existence means validity. The special kind of legal reality means the will of the lawgiver (in a non-psychological sense).[18] Existence of laws depends on the decisions of the lawgiver. With the help of these philosophical points of departure Kelsen defended legal dogmatics as an acceptable branch of science but, at the same time, as an independent branch. The criteria of acceptability were, however, provided by philosophical positivism.[19]

There seems to be no room for evaluations in the Kelsenian statements of legal dogmatics. For instance, interpretative sentences containing principles of justice are doomed to be subjective. Kelsen is a plain-fact or exclusive positivist.

The second conception of objectivity introduced by Marmor is *semantic objectivity*. According to this, a statement is objective if and only if it is a statement about an object. The crucial matter is the grammatical sense of a statement. In order to be objective, a statement has to give information about a defined object in a world other than in the speaker's mind. On the other hand, no ontology or truth is needed.

According to my interpretation, the correctness or acceptability of a statement can be justified by other means than truthfulness in the sense of correspondence as far as this conception is applied. In the field of legal dogmatics, the correctness of a statement can be based in its semantic meaning and the criteria of acceptability. Both correct meanings and the

---

[18] H Kelsen, *General Theory of Law and State* (New York, Russell & Russell, 1961) 30, 46 and 153, and *Pure Theory of Law* (n 11) 4, 72 and 76. I interpret the term 'norm' employed by Kelsen as a rule. El Karouni calls the Kelsenian conception of objectivity absolute and pure, see M El Karouni, *Legal Science Challenged by Cultural Paradigms*, ch 12 in this volume, 236.

[19] Humanities and social sciences were under a great pressure assessed by the prevailing positivistic philosophy during the first half of the twentieth century. Kelsen, like many other theorists, felt obligated to defend legal dogmatics as an acceptable branch of science. In addition, Kelsen found it necessary to transform legal dogmatics into a branch of science acceptable from the viewpoint of positivistic philosophy. On the other hand, supporters of legal realism advanced much further in this fallacious way.

criteria of acceptability can be traced back to the practices of people in the Wittgensteinian sense.

With the help of this interpretation of the semantic conception, it is possible to place the approach of Hart within the frames of this conception. In addition, and with the help of this conception, it is possible to answer the following question: how is it possible to define legal rules without ontological commitments and, at the same time, as a factual and contingent matter?

For Hart, the existence of legal rules or, rather, the existence of a certain legal system bears, on the one hand, social fact but, on the other hand, validity without any ontological commitments in relation to individual rules. The existence of rules is explained by the membership of a legal system. Validity for Hart is a certain way to understand language, which is basically a factual (and contingent) practice.[20] The criteria of validity, in turn, refer to certain rules of recognition adopted by a certain society in a certain time. These criteria are reduced in the same way to a certain established practice of people and a society.[21] Basically, the existence of the rules of recognition means the existence of a practice and, hence, Hart closes the gap between is and ought in the same way as Kelsen.[22] Here, objectivity bears the weak mind-independence.

Hart makes a clear distinction between the dynamic rules of law and static rules of morals. The latter are merely primary rules, rules of conduct and obligations, without official recognition and without the support of secondary rules (for instance, specific rules of recognition and change).[23] Moreover, Hart, like Kelsen, seems to adopt ethical subjectivism: people's allegiance to the system of law can be based on many different considerations.[24]

Even Hart's idea of the minimum content of natural law seems to emphasise this difference. There are certain characteristics which are necessary for any system of national law.[25] They are parts of the definition of the concept

---

[20] See, eg HLA Hart, 'The Ascription of Responsibility and Rights' in A Flew (ed), *Logic and Language*, first series (Oxford, Blackwell Publishers, 1960) 145; 'Definition and Theory in Jurisprudence' in *Essays in Jurisprudence and Philosophy* (Oxford, Oxford University Press, 1983) 23; and *The Concept of Law* (n 12) 94. The influence of the mature Wittgenstein on Hart is obvious here. That is why the phrase 'use in the language' ('*Gebraucht in der Sprache*') is important in this respect. An existing practice can be seen as the core of Wittgenstein's idea. See L Wittgenstein, *Philosophical Investigations* (Oxford, Blackwell Publishers, 1958) I, 43. At the level of legal issues, Hart interprets this approach as the thesis according to which a concept's meaning (content) is determined by its use (as a social practice). For the dynamic nature of positive law, see also Kelsen, *General Theory of Law and State* (n 18) 399.

[21] Hart, *The Concept of Law* (n 12) 101 and 109.

[22] Both Kelsen and Hart define a crucial crossing point which belong to the world of ought (*sollen*) and to the world of is (*sein*). Kelsen defines legal rules as existing facts with the content of ought. Hart defines the rule of recognition as a norm and, at the same time, an existing fact of a society. See Kelsen (n 11) 4.

[23] Hart, *The Concept of Law* (n 12) 170 and 175.

[24] Ibid 203.

[25] Ibid 199.

of law. On the other hand, when these minimum demands are satisfied, there seems to be no significant place for principles of justice or values in the frames of conventional legal interpretations or adjudication. Instead, there is much room for contingent legal rules, that is, rules with any kind of content within the borderlines shown by the criteria of the minimum content of natural law.

Hart shows himself to be a soft or inclusive positivist. According to a rule of recognition, moral principles or values can be incorporated into a legal system as criteria of validity.[26] There are, however, obvious problems involved.

A simple rule of recognition, like that of Kelsen, is clear and strong. With its help, it is easy to recognise the valid law. On the other hand, it is too strong: it is not realistic or acceptable to adopt such a narrow concept of law. It is not acknowledged in contemporary Western societies.

An extensive and complex rule of recognition is, in turn, powerless. It is not helpful any more. With its use, it is not possible to separate legal reasons from moral or other reasons. In other words, it no longer fulfills its function. In addition, a rule of recognition containing moral principles is not consistent with the social thesis or separability thesis.

When a system of valid law is seen as a social and factual phenomenon, it has to be separated from moral evaluations. They are different in quality. In addition, there is a clear separation between sentences expressing the existence of law and judgments about it. That is, separation between the questions of what the law is and what it should be.

Expressions referring to valid law are, in one sense or another, descriptions and for that reason it is presumed that it is easy to separate them from evaluative judgments. One consequence of this separation is the narrow conception of legal interpretation: it is only possible to elucidate the meaning of the given law by interpretation. If there are creative elements beyond these limits involved in legal interpretation, these elements do not clarify the meaning of the valid law. Instead, they are acts of discretion and lawgiving.[27] In the frames of legal dogmatics, these sentences cannot be objective statements describing the valid law but perhaps evaluations, other judgments about the law or proposals for a new law or a change of law. Furthermore, a scholar acting as a lawgiver cannot lean on principles of justice when the existence of objective values is denied.[28]

---

[26] Ibid 101 and 250.
[27] Kelsen (n 11) 355 and Hart, *The Concept of Law* (n 12) 252.
[28] Stavropoulos defines the strong conceptions as criterial models. They contain certain semantic assumptions appearing, for instance, as presumed extensions of legal concepts and interpretation. If a legal concept is a given matter, it cannot be an object of disagreement, that is, an object of different interpretations. In other words, there cannot be any genuine different interpretations of the content of the concept. This critic follows Dworkin. Stavropoulos (n 2) 2 and 5, and R Dworkin, *Law's Empire* (London, Fontana Press, 1986) 31 and 45. See also R Dworkin, *Justice in Robes* (Cambridge and London, Harvard University Press, 2006) 31 and 223.

I take it for granted that these conclusions are neither durable, nor acceptable. Conventional legal interpretation, both in legal dogmatics and adjudication, contains arguments, which means, for instance, appealing to general concepts, the system of law, principles of justice, goals of public policy and consequences of different alternative interpretations or applications. As parts of conventional legal reasoning, they cannot be doomed to be subjective. Instead, they are parts of knowledge of law.[29]

It is not an acceptable solution to separate two kinds of arguments, those describing the valid law and others justifying the particular choices in the frames of the previous ones. First, they are not different in quality. They are similar parts of legal argumentation and they have a similar effect. In addition, it is not possible to decide beforehand in an exhaustive way, what the effect and weight of different arguments are in different situations and cases.

Secondly, it is possible to make exceptional interpretations and deviations from the wordings of statutes or precedents (*contra legem*) and, at the same time, to regard statutes or precedents as the most important and primary sources of law.

The third conception introduced by Marmor is the *logical conception* of objectivity. According to that conception, a statement is objective if and only if it has a determinate truth value. This conception is not, however, helpful or interesting in this context. In addition, it leads us to the problems involved in the concept of truth and, hence, to another subject.

VI. A WEAK CONCEPTION OF OBJECTIVITY

In this context, the most interesting and, I think, the most useful conception of objectivity is introduced by Rawls. It is the *constructive conception* of objectivity.[30] It is much weaker than all three conceptions described above. I believe that the conception of objectivity has to be weak in order to be workable in legal dogmatics or in the field of law on the whole.

Accordingly, I will abandon the stronger conceptions described above, and I will apply Rawls' ideas in the following text.[31]

Rawls' conception focuses our attention on the criteria of objective reasoning, on arguments and conclusions and on their justification instead of entities or objects of knowledge. There is no need to presume any kind of object or descriptive nature of legal reasoning. Even the concept of truth

---

[29] For different kinds of legal arguments and the ways they are employed, see my article 'Form and Substance in Legal Reasoning: Two Conceptions' (2010) *Ratio Juris* 487.

[30] J Rawls, *Political Liberalism* (New York, Columbia University Press, 1993) 110 and 115.

[31] Compare with the critic of the strong objectivity of Van Hoecke, M Van Hoecke, *Objectivity in Law and Jurisprudence,* ch 1 in this volume, 7.

remains redundant. In other words, I adopt a conception of objectivity without objects.³²

In order to be objective, a sentence must be at the *general level* and *free from particular interests*. The additional requirements of objectivity at the general level are the following ones. A sentence must be constituted by common terms and common ways of reasoning; there must be an aspiration to well-justified conclusions; the criteria and priority of arguments are given beforehand; there is a clear difference from individualistic viewpoints; and the notion of objectivity and its criteria must be common to reasonable persons. In short, objectivity contains the ability to depart from the individual point of view and join the common and general discourse.³³

We can directly apply these general criteria of objectivity and they seem to be as familiar and common as the general presuppositions of legal interpretation. There seems to be much in common with the general rules of legal reasoning introduced by Alexy.³⁴ The function of these rules can be seen as an aspiration to warrant the objectivity of legal reasoning and interpretation.

It is worth noticing that this conception allows *different degrees of objectivity*. An adequate moral or legal notion of objectivity is not an either/or matter. Judgments can be more or less objective and more or less subjective; they can be more or less successful and more or less convincing and credible.

VII. OBJECTIVITY OF VALUES

There is an important question united with the problem of objectivity in the field of law, which cannot be passed: are there objective values?

At least in a minimalist sense, there have to be objective moral values in a society: as implications of valid legal rules adopted by the society. Here we can agree with Kelsen. A forbidden action is treated as a bad action.³⁵

---

³² In the same way, Nagel says in the field of ethics 'objectivity of moral reasoning does not depend on its having an external reference' and 'moral thought is concerned not with the description and explanation of what happens but with decisions and their justifications' (T Nagel, *The Last Word* (Oxford, Oxford University Press, 1997) 101 and 102). The difference between epistemological and ontological objectivity can be exploited here, as well. Epistemological objectivity does not entail ontological objectivity. See JR Searle, *The Construction of Social Reality* (New York, The Free Press, 1995) 63.

³³ 'We are to rely less and less on certain individual aspects of our point of view, and more and more on something else, less individual, which is also part of us.' (Nagel, *The View from Nowhere* (n 1) 67). Here, MH Kramer employs terms 'epistemic objectivity' and 'transindividual discernibility'. See Kramer (n 2) 46. His point of view is, nevertheless, different.

³⁴ See R Alexy, *A Theory of Legal Argumentation* (Oxford, Clarendon Press, 1989) 187. The idea of certain necessary and objective rules of rational argumentation can be also found in the philosophy of J Habermas. For these rules and critique on it, see B Wolthuis, *Objective Rules of Argumentation*, ch 6 in this volume, 115 and 117.

³⁵ Kelsen (n 11) 17. The existence of a rule is an objective matter, while its content as a prescription and as the will of the law-giver is a subjective matter. See also ibid 7.

The assumption of objective *values of a society* as the background for its valid law can be justified by the generality of law. Valid law as a whole concerns all members of society. Whether certain single rules apply to certain members depends, naturally, on their contents. According to Raz, when there are objective values, everyone has reasons to promote them.[36] When there are reasons to promote a certain value, there is an obligation to promote it. These obligations are general and objective. There is a clear difference to subjective values.[37] Subjective values appearing as personal desires and interests merely create personal reasons to promote them and can be in conflict with general obligations.

The problem of objectivity of values is a large and complicated issue and, as such, beyond the scope of this paper. There is, nevertheless, one obvious reason to give an affirmative answer to the question presented above. The wide range of legal reasons is adopted here. In other words, I have adopted a wide and open conception of law. For instance, appealing to the principles of justice has been mentioned as a type of acceptable and conventional legal reasoning.[38]

Do I appeal to my personal attitudes, feelings, personal interests or something similar when I appeal to the principles of justice in the role of a legal scholar? My unquestionable answer is no. Appealing to the principles of justice means appealing to the values of my society, and hence, I presume, the objective values of my society. It is another question whether my argumentation is well founded or credible in a particular case.

It is not possible to appeal to the principles of justice without a presumption of objective values. The same holds true for many other conventional legal arguments, for instance the consequences of alternative interpretations. It must be possible to compare the consequences, that is to evaluate them and the differences between them. Here again, the subject matter is often justice. For instance, in the field of civil law, a certain interpretation can lead to unfairly heavy burdens for a person or to unearned or unfounded benefits for another.

The adoption of the concept of objective values means the abandonment of projectivism, including ethical subjectivism and emotivism. In addition, it leads to suspicions about the credibility of legal positivism.

This conclusion raises a second question: is it necessary to adopt universal or other absolute values? My answer is negative. The way out is *ethical relativism*. It is possible to define objective values as values of a particular society at a particular time. Accordingly, there can be societies

---

[36] J Raz, *Practical Reasons and Norms* (Oxford, Oxford University Press, 1999) 29 and 34.
[37] If there are objective values, there must also be subjective values.
[38] Hence, law is not a house with certain walls separating the inside and the outside in an unambiguous way. See PC Westerman, *The Impossibility of an Outsider's Perspective*, ch 3 in this volume, 54.

having different values at the same time, and the values of a society can change.[39]

VIII. DIMENSIONS OF OBJECTIVITY

The aspiration of the general criteria of the weak conception of objectivity adopted above is to secure *ideal epistemic conditions* of reasoning.[40] With their help, correct reasoning and conclusions are possible. Hence, obeying the criteria promotes objectivity. In the field of law, ideal epistemic conditions refer to the advanced and conventional ways of legal reasoning. In addition, they provide us with usable criteria of criticism. As mentioned at the beginning of this article, objectivity is a normative concept.

The general criteria have to be specified at the level of legal reasoning.

Law is an interpersonal matter, referring to the relations between persons. Law regulates relations between persons. Accordingly, it is situated at the level of society. The objectivity adopted here appears as *inter-subjectivity*. It can be seen as a crucial dimension of objectivity.

In addition, law is a normative, artificial and conceptual matter and is dependent on the members of a society and on their conventions. It is constituted by the members of a society as a whole.[41] On the other hand, as a part of a society, law is a given in relation to individual members of the society.

One obvious dimension of legal objectivity is commitment to the *official sources of law*, statutes and precedents. Their existence can be explained in many ways, for instance as the will of the law-giver, adopted by Kelsen. Here, they are seen as the primary appearances of the *conventions* of a society and reflections of the other dimensions of the society.[42] Statutes and precedents are the visible, primary and objective ways a society expresses and imposes

---

[39] The change of values or moral principles of a society differs, naturally, from the change of statutes or legal praxis. By exploiting the Hartian concepts, no specific secondary rules of change are available. Instead, the change is slow and indefinite. On the other hand, no definite rules are needed. The final power and influence of values and principles depend on their general acceptability and applicability in the situation or case at hand. Of course, the static nature of morals does not mean that it is immutable.

[40] See JL Coleman and B Leiter, 'Determinacy, Objectivity, and Authority' in A Marmor (ed), *Law and Interpretation, Essays in Legal Philosophy* (Oxford, Clarendon Press, 1997) 263 and 272.

[41] The system of law is seen here as the traditional national system. It does not exclude the influence of international law and, especially, the significant role of European law.

[42] Conventions are not defined here merely as formal decisions tied to certain procedures at the surface level of a legal system, that is, in the narrow and positivistic sense. Instead, they are seen as reflections of the conventions at a deeper level and in the broad sense. They are expressions, applications and adjustments of the principles of justice and values in addition to other factors influencing the content of law. Hence, it is natural to use these principles and values as the premises of legal reasoning besides sections of statutes and precedents. Adjustment also refers to reconciliation and compromises between opposing interests.

its rules and, at the same time, expresses its values. As embodiments of these rules, they provide primary premises and a strong foundation for the objectivity of legal reasoning. As a matter of fact, they constitute the strongest foundation for objectivity. In short, passing or ignoring applicable sections of statutes or precedents is not acceptable in legal interpretation or adjudication. On the other hand, unconventional interpretations or applications as well as well justified *contra legem* interpretations or judgments are possible. The Kantian term objectivisation is applicable here.[43]

Affirmation of the strong position of statutes or precedents does not compel one to adopt exclusive positivism or, for that matter, any kind of positivism. Statutes and precedents are not enough, much more is needed. Sections of statutes and precedents are neither necessary nor sufficient reasons for the conclusions of legal dogmatics. As well as, and sometimes instead of them, many other kinds of arguments are used and needed. Many of them are substantive reasons and context-dependent and, therefore, it is not possible to enumerate all possible legal reasons beforehand in an exhaustive way. I suppose that *legal relevancy* is the only way to restrict the sphere of legal reasons. Hence, the concept of law adopted here is both wide and open.

As mentioned above, even the priority order of different legal reasons cannot be determined beforehand exhaustively. At most, it is possible to point out a prima facie order. The final weight and effect of different legal reasons varies in different situations and cases. Legal interpretations and applications are context-dependent.

Exceptional interpretations and deviations from applicable statutes or precedents are possible. Interpretation is always needed, even in easy cases. Accordingly, it is justified to consider sentences of statutes or precedents as *primary* reasons[44] rather than as exclusive reasons.

From the viewpoint of objectivity, relevant legal reasons or acceptable conclusions are not enough. They have to be used in a conventional and acceptable way. By the demands of *correct reasoning,* for their part, we try to warrant the objectivity of reasoning.

From the viewpoint of citizens, the objectivity of legal reasoning appears as *impartiality*. There are normative stands in this society to which a citizen appeals when he or she appeals to the law, independent of the stands or interests of certain persons or groups. Legal reasoning, as a response to this appeal, has to take place free from such disturbing factors. Most often this viewpoint is united with adjudication, the work of judges, but impartiality is a demand applying to legal scholars, as well. Through the concept of

---

[43] I Kant, *The Grounding for the Metaphysics of Morals* (Indianapolis and Cambridge, Hackett Publishing Company, 1981) 412ff.

[44] For sentences of statutes as the exclusive reasons, see J Raz, *The Authority of Law* (Oxford, Oxford University Press, 1979) 29 and 33.

impartiality we can introduce two new qualifications of legal objectivity: the *objective intentions* of interpreters or applicators and their *impartial positions*. In addition to judges, it is presumed that scholars are not disqualified.[45]

In this sense, the demands of law are *impersonal*. The call for objectivity in the most important sense is the ability to present warrants securing that the standpoint introduced is the standpoint of the society and an embodiment of its values, not a personal opinion or evaluation or another subjective or particular viewpoint.[46]

Even the use of relevant legal reasons and correct reasoning is not enough. I take it for granted that the *best possible conclusions* are the objects of legal scholars. Here we can see the aspiration to reach the most acceptable and objective standpoint of the law. It is a standpoint which is not personal but the most reasonable and acceptable one in a society to which the person presenting the reasoning belongs as a member. Here, I appeal to the notion of the best possible interpretation introduced by Dworkin.[47]

It is easy to notice that the dimensions of objectivity outlined above strongly resemble the demands regarding a disinterested and competent *judge*. It is not a surprise because, basically, their questions about the content of valid law are the same.

IX. CONCLUSIONS

Objective legal reasoning without objects is possible. It is not necessary to presume any defined objects as the pieces of reality and as the counterparts of the statements of legal dogmatics. Moreover, aspiration for objectivity is a necessary element of acceptable conventional legal reasoning. That is, objectivity is presumed in the texts of conventional legal dogmatics. It is a part of the sense of the concept of legal knowledge. On the other hand, the conception of objectivity has to be weak.

Both the demand and possibility of objectivity covers the whole range of different legal reasons including evaluative considerations. Moreover, all legal reasons as premises of interpretation or adjudication bear the same quality and similar effect. Legal statements and judgments are expressions, not descriptions of valid law. As expressions they always constitute

---

[45] Objectivity qua impartiality when the focus is on the objectivity of law, see Kramer (n 2) 53.

[46] Greenawalt uses the term 'interpersonal force', see Greenawalt, *Law and Objectivity* (n 2) 202.

[47] See Dworkin, *Law's Empire* (n 28) 338, 379 and 411. Even the notion of the one determined right answer to all legal questions introduced by Dworkin can be interpreted as the best possible answer. In other words, there is always the best justified answer. See R Dworkin, *Taking Rights Seriously* (Cambridge, Mass, Harvard University Press, 1978) 279ff and *Justice in Robes* (n 28) 41. Compare with the notion of 'community of interpreters' used by Van Hoecke (M Van Hoecke, 'Objectivity in Law and Jurisprudence', ch 1 in this volume, 8.

interpretation of law. Their plausibility is not founded on correspondence but on the justificatory effect of premises. Accordingly, it is possible to resign from the doctrine of legal positivism.

The approach adopted here is vulnerable to criticism. The wide concept of law implies a creative element involved in legal interpretation. The necessary judicial consideration implies creation to a certain extent.[48] Its conclusions are not determined beforehand by conclusive criteria. Accordingly, the crucial question is: is it possible to create law by the means of legal interpretation in an objective way? My answer is, without any doubt, affirmative. It is both possible and necessary. This kind of objectivity is the most important presupposition of the credibility of legal dogmatics. On the other hand and in the same way as in the case of adjudication, objectivity has to be secured with the help of more precise demands.

Law is an artificial and conceptual matter, that is, an outcome of human creation and a part of human culture. This is the fundamental reason for the nature of legal reasoning and interpretation as well as for the weakness of objectivity. Legal dogmatics has the same quality as the object it is expressing.

In the above, I have tried to describe the dimensions of objective reasoning. They are characteristics of legal reasoning of a high level. In short, objectivity means the demand of advanced legal reasoning.[49]

---

[48] The creative dimension does not mean discretion, free reasoning or issuing new rules in the sense adopted in legal positivism. Rather, it is the ability to reach the most objective and justified conclusion. The positivistic distinction between describing the law and creating a new law is not accepted or followed here.

[49] See Nagel who says: 'Objectivity is a method of understanding.' (Nagel (n 1) 4).

5
Legal Certainty as an Element of Objectivity in Law

JUHA RAITIO

I. INTRODUCTION

I WILL START by trying to do something impossible. I will try to define the principle of legal certainty. It has at least two dimensions, namely predictability and acceptability. The demand of legitimacy relates to the principle of legal certainty and to the interpretation process, which requires the courts to justify their decisions in a tried and tested way. So, the requirement of acceptability in judicial decision-making can be linked with legal certainty when considering the grounds of the judgment. Those grounds should be predictable and acceptable. This viewpoint is, in turn, closely related to some views of democracy because of the demand for openness, which makes external control of the decision-making activity possible. It is widely known that this dichotomy of legal certainty has many links to Nordic legal theory and especially to the Analytical School of Law. The question of an adequate justification of any court's judgments might be understood to be an aspect of legal certainty even on the basis of the case law of the European Court of Justice (ECJ).[1]

Additionally, there are cases on the grounds of which one might conclude that the democratic form of government can be held as a requirement of EU law.[2] So, democracy requires legal certainty, which in turn, presupposes a certain degree of respect for democratic values.[3] Legal decision-making ought to be loyal to the democratically elected legislature. On the other hand, when the law is vague or unclear, bases of interpretation other

---

[1] See Case 69/83 *Lux* [1984] ECR 2447, especially 2466–67.
[2] See H Rasmussen, *European Community Case Law, Summaries of Leading EC Court Cases* (Copenhagen, Handelshøjskolens Forlag, 1993) 83–84, Cases 93/78 *Matheus v Doego* [1978] ECR 2203, especially 2209–12, Case 138/79 *Roquette Frères* [1980] ECR 3333, especially 3360–61, para 33 in particular, and Case C-300/89 *Commission v Council* [1991] ECR I-2867, especially I-2900, para 20.
[3] See A Peczenik, *On Law and Reason* (Dordrecht, Kluwer Academic Publishers, 1989) 40.

than linguistic ones prevail. Aarnio has pointed out that one of the most important properties of a mature democracy is openness, which makes the external control of the decision-making possible. Courts do not fall completely outside democratic control, although they are independent of other power centres in society. The requirement of openness, in turn, leads one to conclude that decisions must be justified in such a way that considerations relating to moral or social values are revealed.[4] This kind of conception of democracy might be considered to be typical from the viewpoint of a Nordic nation-state, which does not necessarily mean that these ideas could not be applied *mutatis mutandis* in the framework of the European Union. In any case, the concepts of democracy, rule of law or legal certainty are definitely context bound and, therefore, one might pose the question of objectivity as regards the use of them. This is also the challenge for this short essay.

II. LEGAL REASONING, JUSTIFICATION AND VALUES

The issues concerning European values and human rights have recently become more and more important in EU law. This can be illustrated by referring to the Fundamental Charter of Human Rights, the Constitutional Treaty and recent case law of the ECJ.[5] Given the importance of the contemporary human rights discourse, it is relevant to ask whether there is a uniform moral system in Europe, if one tries to elaborate the criteria of acceptable and predictable judicial decisions in the EU. The theories of judicial argumentation and levels of justification in the judicial decision-making might illustrate the connection of how studies concerning the alleged common European value basis offer a valuable contribution to the studies of law. Ronald Dworkin's theory of law and justice, especially the rights thesis and the definition of legal principles, underlines the significance of political morality in judicial decision-making.[6] Dworkin's emphasis on morality

---

[4] See A Aarnio, *Reason and Authority, A Treatise on the Dynamic Paradigm of Legal Dogmatics* (Aldershot, Ashgate/Dartmouth, 1997) 193.

[5] See, eg on human rights and the free movement of persons Cases C-60/00 *Carpenter* [2002] ECR I-6279, C-413/99 *Baumbast and R* [2002] ECR I-709, C-109/01 *Akrich* [2003] ECR I-9607, and C-127/08 *Metock* [2008] ECR I-6241, or on human rights and free movement of goods or services Cases C-112/00 *Schmidberger* [2003] ECR I-5659 and C-36/02 *Omega Spielhallen* [2004] ECR I-9609.

[6] See R Dworkin, *Taking Rights Seriously*, With a New Appendix, *A Response to Critics* (Cambridge, Mass, Harvard University Press, 1978) 344. Dworkin does not maintain that there is no difference between moral and legal arguments in hard cases, so he does not represent 'traditional natural law theory'.

offers, at least to a certain extent, a theoretical basis for operating with the following levels of justification:[7]

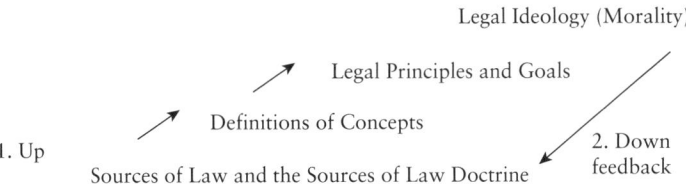

Figure 1: The Levels of Justification

The idea of the levels of justification is that the judicial decision should be justified at as low a level as possible. It would be a methodological mistake to move over to the next level of justification without the decisive resources of the lower level being exhausted. If a decision cannot be based on a clear source of law and if there is not any sound definition of concept to apply, one has to move to the next level of legal principles and goals. The principles may be more or less convergent or divergent and they may have a different dimension of weight. The weight given to a principle and the choice between divergent principles is in the last analysis a matter of morality, or legal/political ideology. When the court has reached the decision, it might become a source of law, a precedent. This is illustrated by the feedback in justification. The idea is actually an illustration of justification and how the judges heuristically proceed in the judicial decision-making. In the heuristic justification of the difficult cases the judge is bound to be influenced by local or national cultural or religious values, which in turn, require extra-legal studies concerning morality and values.

One could plausibly claim that it is not likely that the ECJ would normally rely on moral arguments in its judicial decision-making. It tends to refer to its previous case law and written sources of EU law in a precise and accurate way by relying on the literal meaning, although it is famous for its teleological interpretation.[8] However, there are certain circumstances in which the ECJ is even obliged to take into consideration questions of morality, that is moral values. This is evident as far as the free movement

---

[7] See, eg HT Klami, *Methodological Problems in European and Comparative Law* (Helsinki, Helsingin yliopiston yleisen oikeustieteen laitoksen julkaisuja 14, 1997) 11 and J Raitio, *The Principle of Legal Certainty in EC Law* (Dordrecht, Kluwer Academic Publishers, 2003) 301–302 and 376–79.

[8] See, eg S Sankari, *Legal Reasoning in Context, The Court of Justice on Articles 17 and 18 EC (20 and 21 TFEU) 2000–2008* (Helsinki, Juvenes Print, 2011) 282, in which she states: 'If simply semiotic criteria of interpretation did not provide an answer to the question of legal interpretation at hand, the Court of Justice applied systemic criteria of interpretation. It placed the norm in its norm-context and interpreted it in a way that best fit with preserving or developing the consistency and coherence of the normative framework of the field of law.'

of goods is concerned. For example, one could refer to Article 36 TFEU (ex Article 30 EC) and point out that the quantitative restrictions on imports or exports and measures having equivalent effect can be justified on grounds of public morality.[9]

Moral considerations may also sometimes come to the fore in the field of free movement of services. For example, in the *Grogan* case[10] the problem was that abortion clinics were prohibited in Ireland, but not in the UK. When a student organisation distributed free of charge information concerning abortion clinics in UK, the leaders of this organisation were prosecuted in a local court. In a Catholic country such as Ireland, it is not likely that people would adopt a more lenient stance towards abortion, so the ECJ wisely left it to the discretion of the local level to decide on the acceptability of abortion and did not emphasise the free movement of services in the context of the case. Certain extra-legal arguments of 'appropriateness' or 'public morality' can be linked to the cases concerning people's sexual behaviour in general. For example, the legal status of transsexual or homosexual employees might lead to a discussion, what are the limits of tolerance given the local culture and habits as premises.[11] This kind of discussion is not possible, if it is restricted to the first level of justification only.

In this context, one could point out that EU citizens might rely in particular on the fourth level of justification, the questions of morality, since they do not know what arguments can be employed at the lower levels of justification. While EU citizens or even politicians would, in the context of the Union decision-making, use colloquial expressions such as 'acceptability', 'reasonableness' or 'common sense' typical of the fourth level, the professionals would, in turn, emphasise third-level terms, such as the principles of efficiency, equality, subsidiarity and legality, and refer to the written sources of EU law or case law to justify and specify their views. It is obvious that the lower one proceeds in the levels of justification, the more one needs to know about EU law. At the fourth level of justification anyone is competent to argue in favour of or against a certain outcome to a certain moral problem. It is probably generally acknowledged, at least within the EU, that an act of 'ethnic cleansing' such as the one the Nazis organised during the Second World War is not 'acceptable'. The discussion concerning the acceptability of law leads to extra-legal argumentation, but nevertheless moral arguments should be taken into consideration in judicial decision-making, which is a requirement related to the legitimacy of the judgments in a democratic society.

---

[9] See on pornographic publications and public morality, Cases 34/79 *Henn and Darby* [1979] ECR 3795 and 121/85 *Conegate* [1986] ECR 1007.
[10] See Case C-159/90 *SPUC v Grogan* [1991] ECR I-4685.
[11] See, eg Cases C-13/94 *P v S and Cornwall County Council* [1996] ECR I-2165 or C-249/96 *Grant* [1998] ECR I-621.

Collins has described how the legal reasoning varies depending on the particular school of legal theory.[12] The legal positivists identify the ideal of the rule of law as one requiring strict observation of established legal rules.[13] From the positivist point of view, the legal reasoning ought to employ formal logical rationality,[14] which is the application of rules according to their established literal meaning. In such reasoning the emphasis is naturally on the first level of justification as described above. On the other hand, the 'idealists', or natural lawyers, conceive of the rule of law as a substantive principle, which embodies the liberal political settlement with its allocation of institutional responsibilities and a distribution of rights to individual citizens.[15] Consequently, the legal reasoning can be described as a type of substantive rationality[16] distinguishable in form and from other styles of practical reasoning by the duty not to upset the established order of power and wealth in a society. The upper levels of justification may then come to the fore. Collins seems to have ignored legal realism and concentrated only on the extremes, namely legal positivism and natural law theories.

But what about contemporary criticism against the levels of justification? I think the main critical arguments relate to the emphasis on literal interpretation, to the indeterminacy of language. For example, in Elina Paunio's recent dissertation on legal certainty and multilingualism in the EU, she advocates the idea that legal interpretation in general and in the EU law context in particular, should overemphasise neither the wording of legal texts nor linguistic arguments.[17] This seems to be a relatively common trend in Finland nowadays and one might wonder whether this would lead researchers to think that legal interpretation is so fuzzy and indeterminate that the following quotation from Lewis Carroll's *Through the Looking Glass* aptly describes it: '"When I use a word", Humpty Dumpty said in rather a scornful tone, "it means just what I choose it to mean—neither more nor less."'[18]

---

[12] See H Collins, 'Democracy and Adjudication' in N MacCormick and P Birks (eds), *The Legal Mind, Essays for Tony Honoré* (Oxford, Clarendon Press, 1986) 68–69.

[13] See J Raz, *The Authority of Law, Essays on Law and Morality* (Oxford, Clarendon Press, 1979) 217. The rule of law applies to judges primarily in their duty to apply the law.

[14] See HLA Hart, *The Concept of Law*, 2nd edn (Oxford, Clarendon Press, 1997) 155–84 or M Weber, 'Economy and Law' in G Roth and C Wittich (eds), *Economy and Society: An Outline of Interpretative Sociology* (New York, Bedminster Press, 1968) 656–57.

[15] See R Dworkin, 'Political Judges and the Rule of Law' in *Proceedings of the British Academy*, vol LXIV, 1978, (The British Academy, London, Oxford University Press, 1980) 259–87.

[16] See Weber, 'Economy and Law' (n 14) 656–57.

[17] See E Paunio, *Beyond Words, The European Court of Justice and Legal Certainty in Multilingual EU Law* (Helsinki, Unigrafia, 2011).

[18] L Carroll, *Through the Looking Glass and What Alice Found There* (London, The MacMillan Company, 1871). This citation can be found at the first page of Elina Paunio's dissertation (Paunio, *Beyond Words* (n 17) 1), which can be generalised as a study of indeterminacy of law in a multi-lingual EU. Suvi Sankari has also referred to Humpty Dumpty

Perhaps one should not overemphasise the recent discourse concerning indeterminacy of language in the field of EU law, since a well-balanced view on legal interpretation is presented by Suvi Sankari in her dissertation *Legal Reasoning in Context*.[19] One of the outcomes of her study is that she has not found a strong teleological undercurrent supporting the case law on EU-citizenship, although one would have expected otherwise. She has shown that the legal reasoning in the case law concerning EU citizenship has most often remained as close to applying semiotic (linguistic) criteria of interpretation as possible.[20]

For the sake of predictability one should begin with the linguistic interpretation. This, in turn, is connected to both rule of law and legal certainty. Then again, one may pose a question, whether the very reliance and reference on such obscure and multi-layered legal concepts shows that mere words do not suffice in legal interpretation. No, words do not suffice, but one should start from wording and after that enter the sphere of discourse, communication or 'behaviour', as Klami would probably have said. This way the considerations of norms, that is rules, principles and policies, lead us back to the sphere of language and linguistic interpretation.

III. PRINCIPLES AS NORMS AND DWORKIN'S BASIC LEGAL THEORY

Dworkin would argue that principles are legal arguments, which may only give direction to the outcome of the case in question, since they are often intertwined and suitable for 'weighing up and balancing'.[21] This, in

---

in her dissertation (Sankari, *Legal Reasoning in Context* (n 8) 3), which concerns case law on EU-citizenship in 2000–2008. Sankari has referred to Humpty Dumpty in the context of explaining the role of the European Court of Justice as follows: 'It enjoys interpretative autonomy over the law of the autonomous EU legal order which cannot be reduced to regular international law', which is not the same context than in Paunio's work. The indeterminacy of meaning and language has also been thoroughly analysed by Susanna Lindroos-Hovinheimo in her recent dissertation (S Lindroos-Hovinheimo, *Despairing Justice and the Ethics of Legal Interpretation*, (Helsinki, Unigrafia, 2011).

[19] See Sankari (n 8) 278, in which she concludes: 'In the light of the reasoning, the Court of Justice seems not to exhibit very much by way of activist tendencies, but at most silences eliminated by subsequent cases, and it most often employs systemic criteria of interpretation, never wholly abandoning the text of the law.' Sankari appears to be relatively legalistic and 'keeps her feet on the ground'. Sankari has relied on Bengoetxea's construction of the normal established criteria of interpretation (J Bengoetxea, *The Legal Reasoning of the European Court of Justice, Towards a European Jurisprudence* (Oxford and New York, Clarendon Press, 1993)) and the idea of silence speaking in addition to words (D Sarmiento, 'The Silent Lamb and the Deaf Wolfes: Constitutional Pluralism, Preliminary References and the Role of Silent Judgments in EU Law' in M Avbelj and J Komárek (eds), *Constitutional Pluralism in the European Union and Beyond* (Oxford, Hart Publishing, 2012).

[20] See Sankari (n 8) 281–82.
[21] See Dworkin, *Taking Rights Seriously* (n 6) 35.

turn, implies that principles do not necessarily have any specific scope of application, and therefore certain general considerations about the factual basis might be adequate. For example, the vague terms 'acceptability' and 'predictability' relate to questions of fact as general considerations. The situation is different where the rules are concerned. Then the scope of application is determined in a specific way. The rule either applies to the circumstances in question or it does not. The literal interpretation applies, especially when the observation of unambiguous fact premises are to be subsumed by clearly-formulated norm premises, whereas the anti-literal interpretation appears to be applicable in the context of vague clauses and general considerations of the facts at hand. Since the principle of legal certainty is an underlying principle of law, both the fact and norm premises are imprecise as well as the scope of application, in contrast to those of the principles of equal pay and the observance of discrimination based on sex.

According to Dworkin, the relevance of legal principles is not derived from their formal source of origin, but from a certain 'sense of appropriateness'[22] accorded to them, developed in time among the legal profession and the public at large, or their match with the soundest theory of political morality[23] in the legal community.[24] In this sense, a set of legal principles cannot be distinguished from moral or political principles. This is in coherence with his emphasis that rights are *ex ante*, so that individuals already have rights before the court or any other authority upholds them. In turn, it might be possible to link this to the modern way of thinking that certain individual rights are fundamental to the extent that they cannot be outweighed by any other legal norms.

Dworkin's idea of a basic legal theory is an essential element of his theory of law, because it justifies the legal decisions in the best possible way. The best possible justification will be achieved when the proposition is coherent with the basic legal theory, which includes the principles protecting the rights of individuals and the ones which give content to the demand of equality as well as policies related to collective interests. The crucial innovation is that legal systems are not based only on rules, but that principles and policies count in the judicial decision-making as well. The theory also gives an order of priority to the standards of the legal system by attributing weights to them. Such a theory should be the goal of every decision-maker, although in practice no one can ever reach it. However, Dworkin has, nevertheless, advocated the one-right-answer thesis. Dworkin's theory of

---

[22] Ibid 40.
[23] Ibid 66–68, 126.
[24] See R Siltala, *A Theory of Precedent, From Analytical Positivism to a Post-Analytical Philosophy of Law* (Oxford, Hart Publishing, 2000) 45.

law implies that there can not be only one right answer in every possible case, but in most cases there is such a solution.[25]

Dworkin describes an ideal judge, superhuman Hercules, who is able to create a basic legal theory, which brings the different elements of the legal order, including principles, into harmony with each other. No one can be like Hercules, but every judge should try to get as close to the competence and skills of Hercules as possible.[26] Hercules' theory of adjudication, or basic legal theory, identifies a particular conception of community morality as decisive in legal issues. Hercules must rely on his own judgment as to what the principles of morality are, not on the popular opinion of the community. This view encourages a judge to make his own judgments about institutional rights, which must be separated from goals in Dworkin's theory.[27]

As far as the judge's discretion is concerned, he is permitted to change an existing rule of law if there is a principle or a set of principles to justify the change. Dworkin pointed out, though, that not just any principle will do to justify a change, otherwise no rule would ever be safe. He implies the necessity of having some principles that count for more than others. The order of preference among principles could not depend on the judge's own preferences, because otherwise one could not hold any of the rules as binding. The limits of the judge's discretion according to Dworkin are also, for the most part, based on principles such as a set of principles that require the courts to pay a qualified deference to the acts of legislature. The discretion of judges is also limited by the doctrine of precedent, which according to Dworkin, is another 'set of principles reflecting the equities and efficiencies of consistency'.[28]

In the context of constitutional rights, Dworkin points out that many legal sentences or clauses referring to legal principles are vague. According to him, the clauses are vague only if one takes them to be incomplete or schematic attempts to lay down particular conceptions. If one takes them as appeals to moral concepts they could not be made more precise by being more detailed. Dworkin gives an example from everyday life to illustrate the difference between concepts and conceptions. If he tells his children not to treat others unfairly, he means that their behaviour is guided by the concept of fairness, not by any specific conception of fairness he has in mind at the time he gives this order. He would expect his children to apply his instructions to situations he had not thought about. On the other hand, his conception of fairness might turn out to be wrong at least in some respect.

---

[25] See Dworkin, *Taking Rights Seriously* (n 6) 279–90.

[26] Ibid 105–30, 358–59, and the comments in A Aarnio, *The Rational as Reasonable, A Treatise on Legal Justification*, (Dordrecht, D Reidel Publishing Company, 1987) 163–64 and J Pöyhönen, *Sopimusoikeuden järjestelmä ja sopimusten sovittelu* (Vammala, Suomalaisen lakimiesyhdistyksen julkaisuja, A:179, 1988) 26.

[27] See Dworkin (n 6) 126–30.

[28] Ibid 37.

In the latter case, he would simply say to his children that the instruction to treat others fairly covered the case. The conceptions of fairness may differ from each other, but the concept of fairness remains the same. When he appeals to fairness he poses a moral issue and when he lays down his conception of fairness he tries to answer it.[29]

The emphasis on moral weightings has led Dworkin to analyse how the courts should decide controversial constitutional issues. The programme of judicial activism holds that courts should accept the directions of the vague provisions referring to principles and that they should revise these principles from time to time in the light of what seems to the Court fresh moral insight. The policy of judicial activism presupposes a certain objectivity of moral principles and civil rights. Citizens have a moral right to equality against the state. In that sense they have rights *ex ante*.

Roughly speaking, the programme of judicial restraint in turn holds that courts should allow the decisions of other branches of government to stand, which according to Dworkin, can be based either on a theory of political scepticism or a theory of judicial deference. The scepticism entails the idea that citizens do not have moral rights against the state. They have only such legal rights as the constitution grants them or as established in the case law. The theory of judicial deference assumes that citizens have moral rights against the state beyond what the law expressly states, but it points out that the character and strength of these rights are debatable and it argues that political institutions instead of courts should decide which rights are to be recognised. The latter argument employs the demand of democracy in the sense that all unsettled issues, even moral ones, must be resolved only by institutions that are politically accountable to the citizens. The argument of democracy implies the idea that democratic institutions are, in fact, more likely to make sounder decisions than courts on the issues of rights and that their decisions are also fairer.[30] The distinction between soundness and fairness has no relevance in the sceptical theory of law, according to which there are no moral rights against the state.

IV. THE CONCEPT OF LEGAL CERTAINTY: ACCEPTABILITY AND PREDICTABILITY

The avoidance of arbitrariness has traditionally been regarded in the Finnish–Swedish concept of law as a basic norm for the judge.[31] Even the Scandinavian Reformer and author of the 'Judge's Rules', Olaus Petri,

---

[29] Ibid 134–36.
[30] Ibid 137–41.
[31] See Aarnio, *The Rational as Reasonable* (n 26) 4.

back in the sixteenth century had emphasised the idea that 'arbitrariness is not the law of the land'. In other words, the decision must be based on proven facts and valid legislation. Olaus Petri (1493–1552) was influenced particularly by the German Reformer Martin Luther (1483–1546) and by the Protestantism of that time. In his later work, Aarnio points out that the Judge's Rules manifest the Nordic ideal of legal reasoning and that this idea is nothing more than that of the Roman law tradition still followed at least in the Continental European countries.[32] However, this does not exclude the influence of the Lutheran Protestantism as far as the content of the Judge's Rules are concerned.

According to Aarnio, the expectation of legal certainty *sensu stricto*[33] means that every citizen has the right to expect legal protection.[34] Furthermore, the courts' obligation to give legal protection is such that the citizen's legal problem is dealt with in accordance with the law. The courts must also make a justified legal decision in the case at hand.[35] According to Peczenik, court's refusal to make a decision (*denegatio iustitiae*) is not morally acceptable, because people expect access to justice.[36] There might be exceptional reasons based, for example, on procedural law when the court decides not to give a judgment. Still, the courts have, in principle, a legal obligation to reach a decision irrespective of the difficulties relating to the decision-making. To sum up, Peczenik lists three conditions for legal decisions:

1. the decision is supported by a statute and/or another source of law;
2. in hard cases the decision is also supported by moral value statements; and
3. one can reconstruct legal decision-making as a logically correct process of reasoning.[37]

The problem of qualification and interpretation of a relevant norm characterises the judge's uncertainty in judicial decision-making as well as the epistemic challenge for scholars. In practice, the problems of qualification

---

[32] See Aarnio, *Reason and Authority* (n 4) 191 and compare with Peczenik, *On Law and Reason* (n 3) 35, in which he states: 'In the Roman republic, the *praetor* could thus order the judge to assume the fiction that the demands of *ius civile* were fulfilled in the case under adjudication. The *praetors*, acting in close contact with judicial practice, thus developed an entirely new legal system. A partly similar evolution took place in medieval England.'

[33] On the terms *sensu stricto*, *sensu largo* and *sensu largissimo*, see DN MacCormick and RS Summers (eds), *Interpreting Statutes, A Comparative Study* (Aldershot, Dartmouth, 1991) 12–13 and J Wróblewski, *The Judicial Application of Law* (Dordrecht, Kluwer Academic Publishers, 1992) 87–88.

[34] See Aarnio, *The Rational as Reasonable* (n 26) 3.

[35] See Aarnio, *Reason and Authority* (n 4) 189–90 and Peczenik, (n 3) 29–31.

[36] See Peczenik (n 3) 34. *Denegatio iustitiae* is forbidden by written or customary law in many countries. One can refer to the French *Code Civil*, which determines the criminal responsibility of a judge who refuses to decide the case at hand because the law is silent or unclear.

[37] See Peczenik (n 3) 29–31.

and interpretation are often intertwined. The qualification presupposes knowledge of the content of a relevant norm, which in turn may call for interpretation. And vice versa, interpretation may in some cases prove that a norm under scrutiny does not apply to the facts of the case at hand, which is a problem of qualification.[38] As far as the preliminary rulings of the ECJ are concerned, the qualification problem is not as significant as the problem of interpretation. As a rule, the referring national court or tribunal asks for a preliminary ruling on a certain specified EU norm, and the interpretation of that norm is the actual content of the ruling.

Uncertainty in judicial decision-making should not be evaded by merely referring to the authority of the court. This point of view has special significance in EU law. When the ECJ began to give preliminary rulings, it had relatively weak institutional authority among the courts in the Member States. However, preliminary rulings have gained in interpretative importance in courts other than the one that originally requested a ruling. This development is made possible not least because of the justification of the preliminary rulings offered by the ECJ. It is the thoroughness of the justification, which has, at least partly, created the basis for the confidence the national courts have in the ECJ. At the national level, the justification is also important from the point of view of an appeal, since more than one interpretation may be possible in a case and the appellant can receive sufficient information on the arguments relevant to the case.[39] In the context of preliminary rulings this latter point of view is especially significant when the referring court is a lower court in the national hierarchy.

The significance of legal certainty can be illustrated by employing the idea of judicial decision-making based on coin-flipping. Bix describes a case where an American judge decided the guilt or innocence of traffic violators by the flip of a coin when he could not decide the case on the basis of the testimony. Not surprisingly, this practice was not accepted by the state commission on judicial fitness. Intuitively judicial decision-making clearly cannot be based on such an irrational and random approach to a judicial problem. As Bix points out, to flip a coin is to provide no reasons for the choice offered.[40] Even though there might be uncertainty in establishing what has happened, that is, what are the fact premises of the case, the judgment ought to be based on a legal analysis of both facts and norms and on truth and law. Therefore, in the context of judicial decision-making one cannot argue that the outcome of the case is predictable, because by flipping a coin the probability of acquittal is 1:2.

---

[38] See Aarnio (n 4) 190.
[39] On the importance of thorough justification, see Aarnio, *The Rational as Reasonable* (n 26) 6–7.
[40] See B Bix, *Law, Language and Legal Determinacy* (Oxford and New York, Oxford University Press, 1995) 106.

According to Aarnio, the expectation of legal certainty *sensu largo* contains two substantial elements: the demands that arbitrariness must be avoided (formal legal certainty) and that the decision must be proper and thus acceptable (substantive legal certainty).[41] Formal legal certainty can be defended by stating that courts have to behave so that the citizens are able to plan their activities on a rational basis, which in turn is a necessary condition for the continuity of the society.[42] The need to eliminate randomness from the judicial decision-making requires in turn rational legal reasoning.[43] The minimum precondition for such reasoning is that the courts support their decisions with legal norms. This precondition is connected with the principle of legality, which has significance especially in criminal and penal law. On the other hand, the courts must use proper interpretation methods to adapt legal norms to moral or teleological arguments and to the facts of the case.[44] The expectation of legal certainty also requires that the decision, as an outcome of the rational legal reasoning, is reasonable. Thus the substantive aspect of legal certainty means that the judicial interpretation must be in accordance with the law and it has to meet certain minimum distinctive criteria of equity and justice.[45]

Formal and substantive legal certainty intertwine in judicial decision-making. Legal norms are not completely autonomous with respect to the moral or social norms of the society. Predictable decisions may not be acceptable according to the demands of justice and vice versa. Aarnio gives an example relating to the concept of equality. If the text of the law does not define the meaning of the principle of equality in the case at hand, one must take into consideration the non-legal norms dealing with equality in judicial interpretation.[46] This, in turn, may emphasise the need to apply the various patterns of interpretation and levels of justification in legal decision-making.

Peczenik has illustrated the importance of substantive legal certainty (*materiell rättssäkerhet*) by referring to the 'Hitler argument'.[47] According to this argument, the laws and decisions against the Jews were predictable, but they were not acceptable in the light of generally agreed moral norms. Therefore, the requirements of legal certainty were not fulfilled. The core of Peczenik's Hitler argument is shared by Aarnio, who has in turn referred to the Cambodia of Pol Pot as an example.[48] Although Peczenik's Hitler

---

[41] See Aarnio (n 26) 3 and Aarnio (n 4) 191 and Peczenik (n 3) 32.
[42] See Aarnio (n 26) 4.
[43] See Aarnio (n 4) 191.
[44] See Peczenik (n 3) 34.
[45] See Aarnio (n 4) 191–92.
[46] See Aarnio (n 26) 4.
[47] See A Peczenik, *Vad är rätt?, Om demokrati, rättssäkerhet, etik och juridisk argumentation* (Stockholm, Nordstedts Juridik AB, Fritzes Förlag AB, 1995) 97–98.
[48] See Aarnio (n 26) 38 or Aarnio (n 4) 191.

argument seems to be intuitively convincing, it reveals the weakness of defining substantive legal certainty with the help of practical examples based on politics.

There seems to be a tendency to criticise the Hitler argument, especially among the legal positivists, who would like to keep issues of law and morality separate. The Hitler argument leads one to wonder whether there are any universal criteria of acceptability in judicial decision-making. This question can be approached indirectly by studying the argumentation patterns, levels of justification and rational interpretation.[49] One might note the universal nature of human rights, though. The concept of 'acceptability' is related to the material content of the interpretation and not to the form of reasoning itself. The reasonable result of the interpretation must correspond to the knowledge and values of the legal community in question.[50] The scepticism as regards universal criteria of acceptability is in keeping with the opposition to the Dworkinian one-right-answer thesis.[51] The universal criteria of acceptability in legal decision-making would call for an objective value basis. One might question whether such universal values exist 'in the real world', to use an expression by Searle.[52] It would also be problematic to argue that a certain specific method of drafting the universal criteria of acceptability is the 'correct' one. This stance is not a novelty. For example, Aarnio has stated that 'due to the non-cognitive property of value judgments, acceptability is not universal'.[53]

To sum up, in Nordic jurisprudence both Aarnio and Peczenik have described the twofold conception of legal certainty.[54] The formal aspect of legal certainty refers to the requirement of eliminating randomness from the legal decision-making activity, which according to Aarnio intertwines with the concept of predictability. The substantive aspect of legal certainty requires in turn, that the solutions of the judicial decision-making must also be substantially right, which can be called the demand of acceptability.[55]

---

[49] On the various argumentation models from the comparative perspective see MacCormick and Summers, *Interpreting Statutes* (n 82) 9–27 and 461–551.
[50] On the concept of 'rational acceptability' as well as the terms 'L-rationality and D-rationality' see Aarnio (n 26) 158–229, especially 188–93.
[51] See Dworkin, *Taking Rights Seriously* (n 6) 279–90.
[52] See J Searle, *Mind, Language and Society, Doing Philosophy in the Real World* (London, Weidenfeld & Nicolson, 1999) 9–20. According to Searle, it is a 'default position' that there is a real world that exists independently of us, independently of our experiences, interests, thoughts or language.
[53] See Aarnio (n 26) 190–91.
[54] See Aarnio (n 26) 3–8, 44 or Aarnio (n 4) 189–93, Peczenik (n 3) 31–35 or Peczenik, *Vad är rätt?* (n 47) 89–100.
[55] See Aarnio (n 4) 191.

V. THE QUESTION OF ACCEPTABILITY IN LEGAL DECISION-MAKING AND NORDIC JURISPRUDENCE

In more recent Nordic jurisprudence, even more elaborate conceptions of legal certainty have been presented.[56] For example, Gustafsson has presented the idea of social acceptability and moral acceptability in the context of substantive legal certainty. My contribution, in turn, has been the threefold conception of legal certainty, namely the formal, factual and substantive legal certainty. The three elements of the conception of legal certainty may illustrate the Legal Positivism, Legal Realism and Natural Law theories, respectively. Factual legal certainty is a logical derivation of the Wróblewskian conception of factual validity.[57] Factual legal certainty can be perceived as the demand of efficiency and stability in law. Thus it intertwines with formal and substantive legal certainty.

For example, in the case of *desuetudo*, obsolete laws, although formally still valid, are considered no longer in force, because they have not been applied by the judiciary for a long time. If a court was to apply such an obsolete law unexpectedly, this would be against factual legal certainty. One could point out that the court's behaviour was unpredictable and thus against formal legal certainty. This idea is not tenable, however, because by definition formal legal certainty as a requirement of predictability is fulfilled, if the formally valid legal rules are applied in the judicial decision-making. On the other hand, one might also point out that legal certainty was breached because of the material reasons related to the conception of substantive legal certainty. This latter counter-argument to factual legal certainty is much more convincing because one might not consider the application of obsolete laws acceptable in the light of the social and moral norms of the society. Therefore, there might be plausible reasons to argue that the factual legal certainty is part of the broader conception of substantive legal certainty, which in turn resembles the idea of social and moral acceptability by Gustafsson. However, the idea of stability in the (factual) legal certainty is actually not new, since in the 1980s Bydlinski had already listed the following elements as a part of legal certainty: '*Rechtsklarheit, Sicherung der Rechtsdurchsetzung, Stabilität des Rechts, Zugänglichkeit des Rechts*'.[58]

In Denmark and Norway, there has been a tendency to advocate for substantive legal certainty, not only for formal legal certainty. In Sweden, Gustafsson presented the idea of social acceptability and moral acceptability.[59]

---

[56] See Raitio, *The Principle of Legal Certainty* (n 7) 347–87 and H Gustafsson, *Rättens polyvalens; En rättsvetenskaplig studie av sociala rättigheter och rättssäkerhet* (Lund, Studies in sociology of law no 14, 2002) 1ff.

[57] See Wróblewski, *The Judicial Application of Law* (n 33) 75–83. According to him, the validity of norms is based on systemic, factual and axiological validity.

[58] See F Bydlinski, *Juristische Methodenlehre und Rechtsbegriff* (Vienna, Springer Verlag, 1982) 325–29. Here *Stability des Rechts* refers to stability of legal system.

[59] See Gustafsson, *Rättens polyvalens*, 1ff.

In Finland, perhaps the most far-reaching attempt to emphasise the substantive legal certainty is presented by Paunio, specifically in the context of analysing the decisions of the multilingual ECJ. She seems to think that legal certainty consists of a more substantive element than that of predictability. According to her views, substantive legal certainty is related to substantive acceptability of legislation adjudication.[60] In many cases, legal certainty can be understood as a means for justifying a certain outcome or interpretative choice. Paunio claims that coherence in legal reasoning promotes legal certainty in its substantive form.[61] One might note that the underlying theoretical framework of Paunio's research is based on hermeneutical philosophy as well as on Habermas' work on discourse theory of law.

However, the problematic feature of substantive legal certainty is the obscure scope of application. In addition, the criteria for acceptability of judicial decision-making are not thoroughly described either. In this context one might ask the question of how formal the judicial decision-making should be. For example, in EU competition law the so-called *de minimis* rule cannot be defined in an exact way. It excludes the agreements of minor importance outside the scope of prohibition of Article 101(1) TFEU. Despite the case law concerning the *de minimis* rule, it still remains unspecific.[62] However, the obscurity of the *de minimis* rule is well founded. One cannot regulate certain economical structures with norms that are too exact. Yet, I would claim that the *de minimis* rule increases legal certainty, especially predictability, in competition law. Still, the *de minimis* rule is, in the first instance, hardly related to moral considerations. It is more or less connected to the practical economic analysis concerning the efficiency, continuity and stability of the market. So, even from this very practical standpoint there is room for factual and substantive legal certainty in addition to the formal one.

Inevitably, the substantive aspect of legal certainty is, at least partially, a subjective notion since there is scant evidence of a uniform value-basis in modern societies. Still, if the requirement of legal certainty is exhausted merely by reference to the predictability and legality of the judicial decision-making, this would make any legal decision acceptable irrespective of its content or consequences. In general, predictability can be related to the inner logic of judicial decision-making, to the subsumption of the fact and norm premises, whereas acceptability relates to the content of the decision. This in turn pinpoints to the importance of studying the objectivity in law.

---

[60] See Paunio (n 17) 7.
[61] Ibid 113.
[62] See, eg Cases 5/69 *Völk v Vervaecke* [1969] ECR 295, 22/71 *Bequelin* [1971] ECR 949 or C-234/89 *Delimitis* [1991] ECR I-935.

VI. WRÓBLEWSKI'S VALIDITY OF LAW REVISITED IN THE TERM 'FACTUAL LEGAL CERTAINTY'—BUT IS THERE REALLY ANY NEED FOR IT?

The question of acceptability and the Hitler argument can be linked to the issue of the validity of law.[63] Law is not valid unless it is acceptable. Wróblewski's three conceptions of validity—systemic validity, factual validity and axiological validity—are important for defining the concept of legal certainty. Aarnio makes similar distinctions in terms of systemic validity, the efficacy and acceptability of legal norms. Systemic validity can be defined with reference to a norm's formal source of origin, factual validity with reference to the operative 'law in action' and axiological validity with reference to a norm's acceptability in light of social and moral values. Siltala prefers the terms positivist, sociological and axiological (naturalist) validity, with reference to the basic postulates of Legal Positivism, Legal Realism and Natural Law Theory, respectively.[64] Aarnio concludes that the legal order established by Hitler's regime was valid in the systemic sense, but not in a material sense.[65] Thus the requirements of legal certainty were not fulfilled either.

In Wróblewski's theory, the systemic validity is the basic mode of legal validity for the statutory systems of law and that the notions of factual and axiological validity are applicable only exceptionally.[66] Siltala argues that the decisive priority accorded to the systemic validity conception is in line with the basic tenets of the positivist conception of law, as acknowledged by the representatives of Analytical Positivism, such as Aarnio or Wróblewski. The axiological validity conception overlaps with the notion of *proto-norms*, that is policies and principles in particular. Moreover, Siltala points out that the term 'validity' is misplaced in the context of legal principles and policies, since their impact on the outcome of the case at hand is based on a certain sense of appropriateness and institutional support only, reflecting the low level of legal formality.[67]

As described above, the point of departure is to approach the concept of legal certainty by employing the conception based on Aarnio's and Peczenik's definition. Legal certainty can be understood as consisting of the formal and substantive elements, or predictability and acceptability, respectively. In judicial decision-making, the formal aspect and substantive aspect

---

[63] See Aarnio (n 26) 33–38; Bengoetxea, *The Legal Reasoning of the European Court of Justice*, 56–57 or Wróblewski, *The Judicial Application of Law* (n 33) 75–83.

[64] See Siltala, *A Theory of Precedent* (n 24) 182. Siltala has adopted a term 'naturalist validity' instead of axiological validity.

[65] See Aarnio (n 26) 38.

[66] See Wróblewski (n 33) 76.

[67] See Siltala (n 24) 182–83.

are not necessarily equal in importance, which calls for a more elaborated view of legal certainty. The validity conceptions, that is systemic, factual and axiological, are not equally significant either.[68] The weighing of different validity concepts or aspects of legal certainty depends on the viewpoint of law in general. In Finland, for example, the legalistic and positivist attitude towards the law has been relatively significant especially in the first decades following independence in 1917 and the formal conception of legal certainty has prevailed in judicial practice at least during the twentieth century.[69]

If the Wróblewskian conceptions of validity[70] were employed in defining the conception of legal certainty, the factual validity of law might be perceived as the demand of efficiency or efficacy in law. The term 'operative law' refers to the law constituted by final judicial decisions. The most radical version of the concept of factual validity emphasises the idea that 'law in action' is the real law, as opposed to 'law in books': real law is law that is applied as 'law'.[71] Thus one would have three elements in legal certainty:

1. formal legal certainty, (predictability);
2. factual legal certainty; and
3. substantive legal certainty, (acceptability).[72]

Thus the factual legal certainty can be considered as a logical derivation of Wróblewski's threefold conception of validity. Since the administrative practice is easy to alter and not as public as legislation, one might argue

---

[68] Ibid 182, in which he describes how the prevalent Nordic legal source doctrine determines the different validity conceptions' mutual priority order in judicial decision-making: (1) statutory enactments, which satisfy the criteria of formal systemic validity, are qualified as strongly binding, mandatory reasons of law; (2) prior court decisions or precedents, which satisfy the criteria of factual validity, are qualified as weakly binding, persuasive reasons in law; and (3) general legal principles, moral principles, and consequentialist arguments, which satisfy the criteria of axiological validity, are permitted reasons in law, according to Aarnio's tripartite division of a judge's legitimate source material. Siltala refers to Aarnio (n 26) 93 in this respect.
[69] See Aarnio (n 4) 192.
[70] See Wróblewski (n 33) 75–83.
[71] Ibid 84 and comments in Pöyhönen, *Sopimusoikeuden järjestelmä* (n 26) 29–31. Wróblewski has also aptly pointed out that the operative law conception emphasises the role of the courts, because 'the court becomes the law-maker sometimes besides and sometimes against the legislator'. One might consider it to be a problem that within the operative law conception, one could hardly ask about the legality of judicial decisions.
[72] See K Tuori, 'Interests and the Legitimacy of Law', in A Aarnio, K Pietilä and J Uusitalo (eds), *Interests, Morality and the Law* (Tampere: Research Institute for Social Sciences, University of Tampere, 1996) 94–97. In addition to the formal (systemic) and factual validity Tuori has employed the concept of rationality instead of acceptability and he has referred to Habermas' conceptual framework of three aspects of practical reason, namely pragmatic, ethical and moral.

that it is not predictable and clear enough to be employed in support of the argument of factual legal certainty. To be more precise, factual legal certainty relates to the certain conduct of an administrative authority on which the protection of legitimate expectations can be based rather than the vague and general concept of administrative practice.[73]

The grounds of judgments gain special importance in circumstances where the ECJ tries to convince the national courts and authorities to adopt its rulings. Factual legal certainty does not put as much emphasis on moral evaluation as its substantive counterpart, and to this extent is a more appropriate term for approaching legal certainty in EU law—a legal system known for its 'economism', at least among the neofunctionalists. The substantive legal certainty and the questions of morality may come to the fore especially when the ECJ has to take into consideration issues of human rights in its decision-making.[74]

Regardless of how much I try to advocate the factual legal certainty, it does not seem to convince the academic audience. Can the reason for the 'polite silence' towards factual legal certainty be the obvious problem, which it reveals in a legal system? There should not be a situation in which law in books and law in action differ from one another. What about rule of law in such a scenario? But as I have tried to demonstrate, there might be such situations in the field of EU law. I still claim that Wróblewskian conception of factual validity or my factual legal certainty may sometimes come to the fore in the interpretation and application of law in contemporary legal systems.

Or might the reason for not applying factual legal certainty relate to the fact that it requires empirical research?[75] One should be able to answer the question, whether the expectations related to judicial protection are *in concreto* fulfilled. This question brings me back to the 1990s and I almost hear the late professor Klami lecturing in an enthusiastic voice: 'Law is interaction between norms and behaviour.' Legislation and the judicial application of law is considered to be behaviour but on the other hand, it sets forth norms, statutes or precedents, in order to regulate behaviour. It is obvious that my conception of factual legal certainty has been influenced by Wróblewski, Aarnio and Peczenik, but also by Klami and his finalistic theory of law.

---

[73] See Raitio, *The Principle of Legal Certainty* (n 7) 204–14 and 372–87.
[74] See Cases C-13/94 *P v S and Cornwall County Council* [1996] ECR I-2143 and C-249/96 *Grant* [1998] ECR I-621.
[75] See Paunio (n 17) 6.

VII. LEVELS OF JUSTIFICATION, VARIOUS ARGUMENTS, LEGAL NORMATIVITY AND THE ELEMENTS OF LEGAL CERTAINTY ARE INTERTWINED

My conception of legal certainty employs the theory of norms developed especially by Dworkin and Siltala, the types of arguments in judicial interpretation by the Bielefeld circle and the conception of legal certainty by Aarnio and Peczenik. I find these to be the basic elements of the objectivity in law and legal decision-making. It can be illustrated by using the following figure:

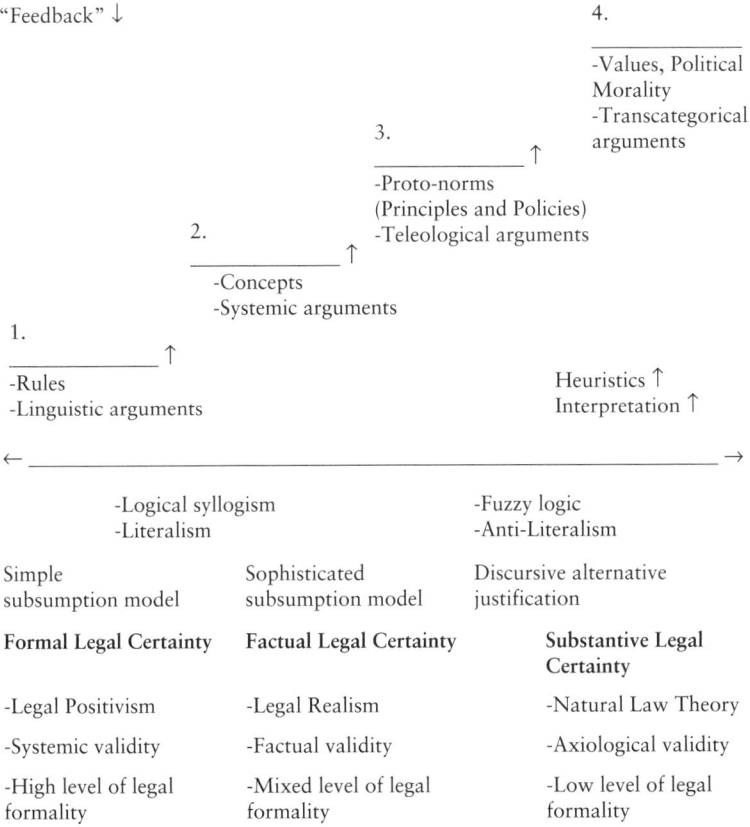

Figure 2: Threefold Conception of Legal Certainty (Rule of Law)

According to this framework, one must endeavour to justify a judicial decision at the lowest possible level. If a judicial decision cannot be justified by appeal to sources of law, one must move to argumentation using conceptual definitions and *proto-norms*, that is legal principles and policies. When determining the dimension of weight carried by different legal principles, it is important to consider and benefit from the respect and regard with which these principles are held at the highest justification level. One might argue that in practice normative contradictions concerning principles are not solved by moral arguments, but rather through practical reasoning by taking into account the practical consequences of decisions. In isolated cases this may lead to conflict situations between the safeguarding of human and fundamental rights and financially oriented objectives.[76] Irrespective of whether the decision-making is value- or objective based, deliberation that occurs at a certain level of legal ideology may be realised sometimes even as explicatory justification. On the other hand, transitions between justification levels also happen from the top down. A decision based on a *proto-norm* or conceptual definition argument may become a pattern-setting model and so become quoted as a source of law, in which case it is interpreted as a source to be studied in accordance with the source of law doctrine being applied by the court in question.

This also applies to the decision-making of the ECJ. For example, the linguistic arguments do not provide a sufficient basis for interpretation of Article 28 TFEU (ex Article 23 EC and ex Article 9 EEC) which prohibits the customs duties and all charges having equivalent effect between Member States. One should take into consideration the unity of the Union customs territory and the objectives of the Union as a whole. The ECJ has consistently held that the justification of the prohibition is based on the fact that any pecuniary charges imposed on goods by reason of the fact that they cross a frontier constitutes an obstacle to the free movement of goods.[77] However, in certain exceptional circumstances the prohibition may also apply to goods entering a region within the Member State. In the *Lancry* case, which concerned trade between continental France and its overseas departments, the ECJ held that:

> Since the very principle of a customs union covers all trade in goods, as provided for by Article 9 of the Treaty, it requires the free movement of goods generally, as opposed to inter-State trade alone, to be ensured within the union. Although Article 9 et seq makes express reference only to trade between Member States, that is because it was assumed that there were no charges exhibiting the features of a customs duty in existence within the Member States. Since the absence of such charges is an essential precondition for the attainment of a customs union covering all trade in goods, it follows that they are likewise prohibited by Article 9 et seq.[78]

---

[76] See, eg Cases 34/79 *Henn and Darby* [1979] ECR 3795, and 121/85 *Conegate* [1986] ECR 1007 related to public morality expressed in Art 36 TFEU (ex Art 30 EC) or cases related to sexuality such as Cases C-159/90 *SPUC v Grogan* [1991] ECR I-4685, C-13/94 *P v S and Cornwall County Council* [1996] ECR I-2143, C-249/96 *Grant* [1998] ECR I-621, C-117/01 *KB* [2004] ECR I-541 and C-423/04 *Richards* [2006] ECR I-3585.

[77] See Cases 2 and 3/69 *Brachfeld* [1969] ECR 211, especially 222, para 14.

[78] See Cases C-363/93, C-407/93, C-408/93, C-409/93, C-410/93 and C-411/93 *Lancry* [1994] ECR I-3957, especially I-3991, para 29.

The ECJ has confirmed this interpretation in its subsequent case law,[79] so one might rely on the *erga omnes* effect of this case law in the interpretation of Article 28 TFEU (ex Article 23 EC) and treat it as a source of EU law. Teleological arguments appear to be significant in the justification of this particular case law as well as in the context of case law related to Articles 30, 34 and 157 TFEU (ex Articles 25, 28 or 141 EC), in particular.[80]

Different justification levels can utilise different types of arguments. The objects of linguistic interpretation are the sentences defining the norms embodied in a source of law. The defining of concepts can create meanings that differ from those in everyday language, so the role of linguistic interpretation is especially emphasised at lower justification levels. Systemic interpretation, however, is emphasised especially at the conceptual definition level, because consistency of interpretation requires that the substantive meaning of concepts used in statute material being interpreted does not vary. Teleological and transcategorical interpretation of the law becomes important at the level of *proto-norms*. This proposed scheme is fuzzy and imprecise, especially with respect to transcategorical interpretation. It can be placed at the highest justification level, or equally well at all justification levels. Transcategorical arguments illustrate the possibility that several types of arguments can be valid simultaneously.

Within the Bielefeld group, justification has been examined from the perspective of the internal logic of a decision. Among the civil law countries, France is perhaps one example where a simple subsumption model is followed. This is reminiscent of predicate logic, which applies a statutory interpretation of the law in the spirit of strong legal positivism. In this model, the relevant norms are subsumed by facts and circumstances and a conclusion is reached, which forms the judgment. Often the judgment is pronounced in one long sentence expressed in rather formal language. Maybe a more typical model, for example, in Italy, Germany and Finland is a sophisticated subsumption model, where the final conclusion is deduced logically from premises, which are justified one by one by additional premises. In this way, the judgment, structurally speaking, consists of a chain of premises and deductions with each premise justified by several arguments. The sophisticated subsumption model represents a shift in justification away from an authoritative model towards a more dialectic model. Typical of the Anglo-American legal culture is the discursive alternative justification, which for its part is the result of juridical choices and statutory prioritisation. The judgment represents a conclusion based on an argument, which is, in a way,

---

[79] See Cases C-485/93 and C-486/93 *Simitzi* [1995] ECR I-2655, especially I-2676–I-2677, paras 21–22.
[80] See Cases 26/62 *Van Gend en Loos* [1963] ECR 1, 8/74 *Dassonville* [1974] ECR 837, the *Cassis de Dijon* case 120/78 *Rewe-Zentral* [1979] ECR 649 and 43/75 *Defrenne v Sabena* [1976] ECR 455.

victorious in a 'war of arguments'. The discursive alternative justification thus resembles the process of practical reasoning, where the judgment is not a logically deduced imperative from premises, but a proposition, which leads to a desirable conclusion from the perspective of the objectives of the legal system.[81] One might argue that all these patterns of argumentation can be discerned from the case law of the ECJ.[82]

As far as practical reasoning and teleological interpretation are concerned, one can refer, for example, to the *Van Gend en Loos* case in EU law.[83] A prerequisite for the realisation of a customs union was the prevention of new internal duties and charges being implemented within the EU, after the Treaty of Rome had come into effect in the Member States in 1958. A prohibition on new duties was clearly expressed in ex Article 12 EEC (now Article 30 TFEU, ex Article 25 EC), but its efficacy in practice required an individual right of action on the basis of Community law, from which developed the doctrine of direct effect of EU law. Practical reasoning is also often applied in situations where the decision-maker has to weigh the value of possible legal consequences and to choose a norm on that basis. I consider it exemplary that attention is being focused on the possible consequences of a judicial decision at the stage when that decision is being prepared, and so I find it difficult to consider the teleological method of interpretation problematic from the perspective of preservation of a fair legal system and the requirements of legal certainty.

VIII. CONCLUSIONS—OBJECTIVITY, COHERENCE AND LEGAL CULTURES?

Legal interpretation is context-bound. For example, the Wróblewskian view of the validity of norms is conditioned by the circumstances in Poland during the 1980s. If one claims that there is a clear difference between 'law in books' and 'law in action', one might ask the question of how democratic such a society is and how the rule of law is respected. This view on the validity of norms reflects the view on legal certainty. It shows how the legal cultures and legal theory may interact. The objectivity in legal decision-making

---

[81] See MacCormick and Summers, *Interpreting Statutes* (n 82) 492–94. In practical reasoning it is a question of an objective and the means essential to the achievement of that objective. There is no logical necessity between objective and means, instead the indispensability of certain means for the achievement of an objective is based on the inferrer's (eg the judiciary's) own beliefs on the matter. Such practical syllogism produces a technical norm, which contains the idea of what must be done to achieve an objective as a kind of practical necessity. The technical norm is not an imperative, simply a proposition stating the situation.

[82] See JJ Barceló, 'Precedent in European Community Law, in DN MacCormick and RS Summers (eds), *Interpreting Precedents, A Comparative Study* (Aldershot, Ashgate/Dartmouth, 1997) 411–15.

[83] See Case 26/62 *Van Gend en Loos* [1963] ECR 1.

and interpretation requires in my opinion more emphasis on literal interpretation than is common in some contemporary studies—even in the field of EU law.

I have used Paunio's work 'Beyond words' on translation problems and legal certainty in EU law as an example for this. I am a little hesitant as regards Paunio's emphasis on Soriano's originally modest notion of coherence,[84] which focuses on analysing legal reasoning of the ECJ instead of formulating the whole legal system as a coherent unit based on a limited number of principles. It ensures that value choices are expressed in the justification. I must admit that the modest notion of coherence is perfectly in line with her emphasis on substantive legal certainty and communicative rationality (discourse theory of law). However, her ideas lead me to additional questions. Will the emphasis on substantive legal certainty lead to increasing casuism, to context-bound discussions of fairness or to emphasising legal certainty too much from an individual's point of view instead of a more communitarian way emphasising stability and predictability? Will the emphasis on substantive legal certainty advocate a more Anglo-American way of justifying legal decisions than has been the Court's practise so far, the so called 'European way'?

My aim has been to challenge the ultra-teleological interpretation of law. The Court decisions should be context-bound, but this does not mean that the coherence of the legal system as a whole can be hampered. It is not enough to make sure that a decision contains coherent arguments from the beginning to the end. I call such a casuism 'the Casanova method', named after a famous playboy. Casanova was successful because he told his mistresses whatever they wanted to hear. He could trust that no-one really knew how the stories differed from one another depending on the casual wishes of his numerous partners. Courts do not have this possibility, because judgments are published and known. If the courts settle for casuism and neglect the systemic interpretation, the coherence of the legal system will be hampered. But, on the other hand, the 'Casanova method' seems to be very useful in letting the various legal cultural circumstances affect the outcome of the case.

Then again, one could argue that my criticism of the modest notion of coherence is too far-reaching and provocative. Therefore, I try to moderate and specify my point as follows. Soriano has emphasised the coherence of legal argumentation instead of coherence of legal rulings. A modest notion of coherence is meant as an indeterminate criterion of rightness, which is not able to provide an ultimate answer for every case. It provides 'a criterialess

---

[84] For a modest notion of coherence see LM Soriano, 'A Modest Notion of Coherence in Legal Reasoning. A Model for the European Court of Justice' (2003) 16 *Ratio Juris*, 296–323.

criterion of legal reasoning'.⁸⁵ He asks, whether the argumentation, which supports a certain ruling, cohere and how one can find coherence in connecting, or 'netting' reasons, which support the ruling. In his article, he has adopted as an example of the traditional approach to interpret EU law the following words originally written by Judge Edward:

> The judge's role cannot be confined to that of providing a technocratic literal interpretation of texts produced by others.(). As a system based on case law the judge must proceed from one case to another seeking, as points come up for decision, to make the legal system consistent, coherent, workable, and effective.⁸⁶

This quotation naturally underlines the significance that the rulings cohere, that is systemic interpretation, which is exactly my point as well. However, in my opinion Soriano has a point when he describes the logic of legal reasoning in the Court of Justice as follows:

> Indeed its decisions follow very much a logic-deductive pattern which excludes circularity: The focus is on the justification of the conclusion (the verdict), rather than on the justification of the premises themselves; it also focuses on deductive connections rather than plausible supportive structures. The lack of reciprocal justification of premises can be explained by the non-acceptance of circularity as a quality of legal reasoning.⁸⁷

If one wants to interpret Soriano's modest notion of coherence 'in a modest way', then it would merely mean that he underlines the 'netting of arguments' and advocates a better quality in the reasoning of the Court of Justice. This leads one to ask the question, whether Soriano has been misinterpreted, if the significance of the systemic arguments have not gained enough weight among the various arguments.

Finally, to sum up, all my considerations come back to the central idea that levels of justification, various legal arguments and legal normativity are intertwined, which is coherent with the basic tenets of the Analytical School of Law. And yes, there is some sort of objectivity in the general scheme of analytical approach to law, but the objectivity requires that one can make a distinction between the ontology of law, epistemology of law and the various interpretation models of law—not to forget the requirement of coherence in law, which relates to both rulings and legal reasoning. All of these elements should be taken into consideration when analysing the concept of legal certainty.

---

⁸⁵ Ibid 307.
⁸⁶ See D Edward, 'Judicial Activism: Myth or Reality?' in AIL Campbell and M Voyatzi (eds), *Legal Reasoning and Judicial Interpretation of European Law* (London, Treanton, 1996) 29–67, especially 66–67 and Soriano, 'A Modest Notion of Coherence' (n 84) 298.
⁸⁷ See Soriano ibid 318.

6
Objective Rules of Argumentation

BERTJAN WOLTHUIS

IT IS PROBABLY not uncommon to think of arguing with others as engaging in some sort of rule-governed activity, as playing some sort of game with rules that distinguish between what still counts as arguing and what no longer does. When you are arguing with someone, you are, for example, not allowed to threaten that person, or forbid him or her to ask questions or raise objections. Threatening someone or excluding someone from participating on an equal footing in the conversation, is clearly breaking the rules of the game. It means that you are not playing the game according to the rules, that you are not arguing at all, just as a field player who plays the ball with his hand is not playing football.

This elementary picture of arguing is called into question by recent controversies about the way populist politicians participate in parliamentary meetings. Particularly in some of Europe's northern countries, populist political parties have been able to win a considerable number of seats in representative bodies. What is interesting here is the deep disagreement among critics or commentators about the way these populists communicate in parliament. According to some critics, among them several members of parliament, populist members of parliament disregard the rules of argumentation, do not play the game by the rules. Other commentators, not necessarily supporters of populist policies, suggest that populists may be regarded as innovators of parliament, as players who change the rules of the game to some extent.[1]

This disagreement among critics raises critical questions about our elementary, unreflected picture of argumentation as a game. First of all, is arguing rightly considered as a game at all and, secondly, if so, what are its rules and, thirdly, what is the character of these rules? Are they objective? Can they be changed, adapted by the players to new circumstances? Or are

---

[1] In the Netherlands this difference of opinion (concerning the populist Geert Wilders) is displayed in eg M Peeperkorn, 'Stijl van Wilders krijgt navolging' (Wilders' style is followed) (2007) *de Volkskrant*, 10 March, Amsterdam. All translations from Dutch and German to English in this chapter are mine.

the ground rules of arguing fixed, just as the ground rule of football that you are not allowed to play the ball with your hand is fixed. If that rule is abandoned we should say that we no longer play football but some other game (handball, for instance). Questions such as these need to be addressed in order to properly analyse the controversies relating to populist politics.[2]

My position in this contribution to the volume is that arguing with others is a game, because it shares many of the key characteristics of a game (section II). I also claim, following Jürgen Habermas' train of thought, that the basic rules of arguing are fixed and objective (section III). However, these basic rules are *abstracted* from real practices of argumentation. Habermas reflects in his work on the general notion—what some philosophers would call 'the concept'—of argumentation. In order to get a clear view on controversies about real practices of argumentation, such as the controversy about populist parliamentary politics, we also need to research particular 'conceptions' of argumentation, specific games of argumentation and their rules (section IV). Here I find the example set by the studies of Michel Foucault very helpful. Foucault has shown in several publications that the rules of particular practices have become controversial at some point and have been adapted to new circumstances. However, my position is that these adaptations cannot come into conflict with the concept of argumentation (of which Habermas has provided an interpretation), if the participants still wish to play the game of argumentation (section V). The conclusion is that the basic rules of argumentation are objective in the sense that they are the rules of the game. They can be interpreted, modified and balanced against each other, in a multitude of contexts, but it is not possible to abandon these ground rules altogether and still play the game of argumentation (section VI). I illustrate my line of reasoning in these paragraphs with two cases of populism in the Dutch parliament. I introduce these cases below (section I).

I. POPULISM IN DUTCH PARLIAMENT

Geert Wilders is the leader of the Freedom Party (PVV) in the Netherlands. That party took 24 of the 150 seats in parliament after the 2010 election, which made it the third largest political party in the Netherlands. The Freedom Party is viewed by its adherents as anti-elitist and by its opponents as right-wing, populist, nationalist and Islamophobic. The party plays a key role in Dutch politics for it endorses the current minority cabinet of Liberal Democrats and Christian Democrats, especially the cabinet's social-economic programme. In return, the minority cabinet agrees to be strict on immigration.

---

[2] In this chapter these questions are answered. It paves the way for a thorough analysis of controversies concerning populist politics; such an analysis cannot be given here.

Since the rise of Geert Wilders in Dutch politics the population of the Netherlands has been split into two camps. On one side stand those who consider him and his partisans a threat to democracy, civility and the rule of law. On the other side are those who view the Freedom Party's leader as a sharp and effective debater, a true democrat (because he is anti-elitist) and a welcome breath of fresh air to parliamentary life. Here, I reflect on just one issue that divides the two camps: the way in which PVV representatives communicate in parliament. Their speeches in parliament have on occasion led to sharp controversy: some members claim that Wilders 'disregards every rule of discussion', that he 'does not play the game according to the rules'; while other commentators regard his lively and provocative parliamentary appearances as innovative and effective ways to engage in debate.[3]

In the rest of this contribution, I illustrate my line of reasoning with two cases. Both deal with issues of nationality and loyalty, issues central to rightwing populist politics. Some Dutch citizens (among them politicians) have more than one nationality because they or their ancestors have migrated to the Netherlands and have not given up their first nationality.[4]

On 15 February 2007, Sietse Fritsma, a member of parliament for the Freedom Party, submitted a motion in which he asked the government to prohibit Dutch citizens from having other nationalities and to exclude, in the meantime, citizens with multiple nationalities from the Dutch cabinet which was being formed at that time.[5] Although it is practice to support motions, so that they can be admitted and be voted on at a later stage, Fritsma's motion was severely attacked right away. The meeting was adjourned and in the interval Fritsma reluctantly agreed to delete the second part of the motion. Several members did not support Fristma's motion, because he questioned the integrity of two members of parliament with dual nationalities, who were about to enter the cabinet.

A few weeks later, on 8 March 2007, Geert Wilders asked Khadija Arib, a member of the Labour Party and a citizen of both Morocco and the Netherlands, to choose between her advisory work for a Moroccan board and her membership of Dutch parliament because by serving two countries, Wilders claimed, her loyalty to the Netherlands is not guaranteed.[6] During this meeting Wilders was strongly attacked and after the meeting the criticism referred to above, that he disregarded the rules of argumentation, was leveled against him.

---

[3] M Peeperkorn, 'Stijl van Wilders krijgt navolging' (n 1).
[4] Some countries do not allow their citizens to give up their nationality.
[5] *Handelingen II*, 15 February 2007, 44, 2571ff. The proceedings of the Dutch parliament are called 'Handelingen'. I refer to them by date, meeting number and page number, respectively. The proceedings have become available at www.overheid.nl (proceedings since 1995) and www.statengeneraaldigitaal.nl (1814–1995).
[6] *Handelingen II*, 8 March 2007, 46, 2746ff.

II. WHY ARGUING IS VIEWED AS A GAME-LIKE ACTIVITY

The critique that Wilders does not play according to the rules suggests that members of the Dutch parliament view argumentation as some sort of game-like activity with rules that differentiate between what does and does not count as arguing. Wilders evidently crossed the line, at least according to some critics. Let us take the criticism seriously and examine why the view of arguing as a game may be sound.

First, we need to address the question of what makes something a game. According to Ludwig Wittgenstein games differ enormously, there are possibly no characteristics that all games share. Still, we use the word 'game' to cover all these different activities. Wittgenstein claims that the activities we call 'games' share characteristics in the same way members of a family share resemblances. Members of a family share some resemblances, but there is not necessarily one feature they all share.[7]

The Dutch historian Johan Huizinga mentions a few resemblances that games share in this way. (1) Play is free. You cannot play and follow orders at the same time. Players act freely, they figure out new ways of playing. (2) A game is not part of normal, daily life. (3) It has a place and time of its own. It starts at a certain time and stops after a while. Players often take turns. (4) A game has a goal. The players have to accomplish something. A game is exciting because it is not certain that the players will succeed. (5) A game has rules. The player who disregards the rules is a killjoy, he destroys the game. The rules of the game are constitutive of the game, which means that when they are broken, the game is no longer played. The killjoy must not be confused with a cheat. The latter is a player who appears to play the game while the former may eventually start a new game, according to new rules.[8]

Argumentation is a game in this sense. (1) It is free. (2) It is not a part of, but instead some sort of reflection upon, daily life. (3) The speakers take turns. There is symmetry, as in other games. (4) The goal of argumentation is to reach agreement. (5) It has rules, too. When someone forces another to give up his position, for example by threatening, that person does not play the game of argumentation.

The position that arguing is *not* a game is, to my knowledge, not explicitly defended. Some may think that Jon Elster adopts this position, because he has researched arguing thoroughly, but never conceives it as a practice or game. The notion of a game in the sense explicated by Huizinga above, however, is

---

[7] L Wittgenstein, *Philosophical Investigations* (Oxford, Wiley-Blackwell, 2009), paras 66 and 67.

[8] J Huizinga, *Homo ludens* (Boston, Beacon Press, 1992) ch 1.

possibly not part of the vocabulary of Elster's methodological individualism.[9] Therefore, that Elster does not call it a game, does not imply that he would deny it to be a game-like activity. Moreover, Elster is particularly interested in argumentation from a cheater's point of view, a perspective that presupposes, indeed parasites on, an honest participant's view of arguing as a game. Elster's main contribution to argumentation theory is his explanation of why the cheat is also bound by the rules of the game.[10] The impartial justification with which the dishonest participant clothes his private interest must not fit it too neatly or else he will run the risk of exposure. Elster calls this the imperfection constraint. This constraint forces the hypocrite to find an impartial justification that serves not only his own interests, but also those of others. The second difficulty is that a cheat cannot simply select the justification that suits his interests best. 'Once a speaker has adopted an impartial argument because it corresponds to his interest or prejudice, he will be seen as opportunistic if he deviates from it when it ceases to serve his needs.'[11] Then he runs the risk of blowing his cover, in which case he is no longer capable of persuading others. Elster calls this the consistency constraint. So, although Elster does not call arguing a game, it is obvious that his deceiver's stance towards arguing *presupposes* just such a picture of argumentation. If arguers would not expect each other to be moved by the general interest, the deceiver could not deceive at all.[12] The expectations that those who are engaged in argumentation have with respect to each other's attitudes and actions, precisely entail that argumentation is a game with rules that determine what the players may and may not do if they wish to be considered to be engaged in argumentation.

III. JÜRGEN HABERMAS ON THE RULES OF ARGUMENTATION

The next issue relates to what kind of game argumentation is. What are the rules, what is its aim? We may, of course, not expect unanimity among theorists concerning this matter. A good point to start is perhaps Jürgen Habermas' influential notion of argumentation. Habermas takes up in his works the honest participant's point of view on argumentation right from the start. According to Habermas, arguing is a practice, in which the

---

[9] B Wolthuis, 'Jon Elster, Reason and Rationality' (2009) 38 *Netherlands Journal for Legal Philosophy and Jurisprudence* 263–65.
[10] Remember that the cheat does not want to be found out. He wants to further his own interests by appearing to be arguing sincerely.
[11] J Elster, 'Deliberation and Constitution Making' in J Elster (ed), *Deliberative Democracy* (Cambridge, Cambridge University Press, 1998) 104.
[12] J Habermas, 'Kommunikative Rationalität und grenzüberschreitende Politik. Eine Replik' in P Niesen and B Herborth (eds), *Anarchie der kommunikativen Freiheit. Jürgen Habermas und die Theorie der internationalen Politik* (Frankfurt am Main, Suhrkamp Verlag, 2007) 415, fn17.

participants reflect on, and attempt to repair, a dissensus. A dissensus is experienced as a problem when persons coordinate their actions by reaching agreement (*Verständigung*), that is, when they act communicatively. People engage in argumentation with each other when communicative action (*kommunikatives Handeln*), action in which coordination is based on agreement, breaks down simply because there is no agreement.

An argumentation is a reflexive type of communicative action.[13] This means that an argumentation is also a practice, just as communicative action is, in which free and equal persons aim to repair a dissensus without using force or deception. Only the force of the better argument is allowed. Communicative action and argumentation are manifestations of the values of freedom, equality and rationality. The dissensus can be repaired when the actors find a new basis for agreement as the result of an exchange of arguments. But that is only possible when some reasons are stronger than others.[14]

Are there criteria with which to determine whether a series of utterances qualifies as 'arguing' or 'discourse'? A solitary argument is not sufficient. An argumentation involves a contest about what are the better reasons.[15] A form of communication is viewed by Habermas as an argumentation when the participants attempt to reach a shared understanding by exchanging and testing reasons. This testing does not rule out competition. An agonic practice does not need to hinder the search for agreement, as long as the participants are prepared to accept the superior line of reasoning. Habermas speaks of a cooperative contest (*kooperativer Wettbewerb*).[16] A contest does frustrate a consensus, of course, when participants want to win at all costs.

In order to explain better what it is to engage in an argumentation, Habermas distinguishes four characteristics of argumentation: (a) inclusion (relevant contributors may not be excluded); (b) equality (all participants have an equal opportunity to contribute); (c) sincerity (all participants must mean what they say); and, finally, (d) freedom, or non-domination (the participants are not allowed to use force, except that of a better

---

[13] 'Eine Argumentation setzt verständigungsorientiertes Handeln auf reflexiver Ebene fort.' (J Habermas, 'Kommunikative Rationalität und grenzüberschreitende Politik. Eine Replik' in P Niesen and B Herborth (eds), *Anarchie der kommunikativen Freiheit. Jürgen Habermas und die Theorie der internationalen Politik* (Frankfurt am Main, Suhrkamp Verlag, 2007) 413).

[14] 'Der Übergang zur reflexiven Ebene des Diskurses kann die gestörte Verständigung nur dank der Überzeugungskraft besserer Argumente wiederherstellen.' (ibid).

[15] 'Einzelne "Argumente" bestimmen noch keinen Kommunikationsmodus im Sinne von "Argumentation" oder "rationalem Diskurs". Davon ist vielmehr nur im Falle eines Wettbewerbs um das "bessere Argument" die Rede.' (ibid).

[16] J Habermas, 'Eine genealogische Betrachtung zum kognitiven Gehalt der Moral' in J Habermas, *Die Einbeziehung des Anderen. Studien zur politischen Theorie* (Frankfurt am Main, Suhrkamp Verlag, 1996) 61.

argument).¹⁷ When people really try to reach an agreement by exchanging reasons, they cannot at the same time exclude or play down relevant contributions or participants (against (a) and (b)), deceive (against (c)), threat or force (against (d)) others. A genuine agreement means that previously dissenting parties are 'forced' by nothing but the same arguments and information to freely accept the same position.

The sharp criticism that was leveled against Fritsma and Wilders after their attacks on members of parliament with dual nationalities can perhaps be best explained by referring to characteristic (a) above. While Fritsma and Wilders did not exclude members with other nationalities from parliament, they made clear that they did not want them included in the Dutch cabinet (Fritsma) or in the Dutch parliament (Wilders), because of their possible lack of loyalty to the Netherlands. By stating this opinion in parliament, Fritsma and Wilders already question the presupposed equality between members of parliament.

Habermas refers to these four characteristics as presuppositions (*Voraussetzungen* or *Präsuppositionen*), indicating that participants *presuppose*, or *act under the assumption* that the others engaged in arguing accept each other as equals, say what they mean, do not use force and so on. So, what is presupposed is that the participants act according to these four standards or rules. This notion of a game with rules explains why Elster's hypocrite is bound by them, even if he only pretends to play the game. Another way to put it is that these are the rules of a game. 'These presuppositions are constitutive of the game of argumentation: the very moment we discover that somebody cheats and manipulates or excludes relevant persons or contributions, we realize that the game is over.'¹⁸ This is similar to a game such as football: engaging in a football match entails, for example, following the rule that you do not play the ball with your hand. When a player commits that foul, he no longer plays football. The referee stops the game and, after a penalty has been given, starts it again.¹⁹

The question is, of course, how to conceptualise the difference between these presuppositions and actual contributions to argumentation, in which these standards may not be fully met. The presuppositions idealise, Habermas

---

¹⁷ '(a) Niemand, der einen relevanten Beitrag machen könnte, darf von der Teilnahme ausgeschlossen werden; (b) allen wird die gleiche Chance gegeben, Beiträge zu leisten; (c) die Teilnehmer müssen meinen, was sie sagen; (d) die Kommunikation muß derart von äußeren und inneren Zwängen frei sein, daß die Ja/Nein-Stellungnahmen zu kritisierbaren Geltungsansprüchen allein durch die Überzeugungskraft besserer Gründe motiviert sind.' (ibid 62).
¹⁸ J Habermas, 'Concluding Comments on Empirical Approaches to Deliberative Politics' (2005) 40 *Acta Politica* 385.
¹⁹ See B Wolthuis, 'What we can learn from football about parliamentary argumentation' (2011) 9 *Commonwealth Youth and Development* 28–39.

admits. However, they are part of the practice.[20] Participants would not engage in practices without making these idealising presuppositions.

> Take the practice of general voting as an example. It depends on a voluntary participation of a large part of the citizens. Any democratic regime is finished without that. However, would citizens participate at all unless they *presupposed*, contrasting evidence notwithstanding, that one's vote does make a difference in the effective outcome? Would citizens bring to court any legal case unless they *presupposed*, contrary to beliefs of many lawyers and law professors, that outcomes more often than not qualify for the kind of fair administration of justice they expect? Would members of a parliamentary committee or a caucus engage again and again in discussions on normatively loaded issues (such as stem cell research) unless they *presupposed* that they can win over people by better arguments?[21]

So, these standards or rules of arguing are factual and counterfactual at the same time. They are counterfactual in the sense that in actual practice deliberations and participants fall short of these idealising presuppositions. The deliberations are not open to everyone, participants refuse to yield to better arguments, they act strategically and so on. On the other hand, Habermas stresses, participants cannot but presuppose that these standards are followed. Proof is that participants respond to deviations from these standards, as the criticism leveled against Fritsma and Wilders shows. Not all deviations lead to a withdrawal from the game. However, at some point participants will turn away from the practice. Where exactly this point lies can be researched empirically.[22]

One might wonder whether the rules or standards that are presupposed in the game of argumentation really apply to politicians contributing to, for instance, parliamentary proceedings or election debates. If we follow Habermas' line of reasoning that when we argue we cannot but make these presuppositions, it would seem that these do apply in these contexts, at least, as long as politicians really *argue*. That last point is sometimes difficult to assess as Habermas admits. In everyday scenes the communicative practices people are involved in often change quickly from arguing to bargaining and back. Observers will find it difficult to say *which* game is played *when*, because in everyday situations the attitudes of the players are decisive and they cannot be experienced directly by outsiders. In more formal situations,

---

[20] 'Solche impliziten Voraussetzungen [sind] *mit dem Vollzug* bestimmter Praktiken *unvermeidlich* verknüpft.' (J Habermas, *Ach, Europa. Kleine Politischen Schriften XI* (Frankfurt am Main, Suhrkamp Verlag, 2008) 150).

[21] J Habermas, 'Concluding Comments on Empirical Approaches to Deliberative Politics' (2005) 40 *Acta Politica* 385.

[22] 'Es ist eine empirisch Frage, ab wann eine wahrgenommene Differenz dieser Art nicht mehr als "normal" hingenommen wird, sondern eine Schwelle passiert, jenseits deren die Teilnehmer sich von einer etablierten Praxis entfremdet fühlen.' (Habermas, *Ach, Europa* (n 20) 151).

for example a parliamentary meeting or a court of law, the interpretation is much easier because the institutional arrangements decide which game is played, so to speak.[23] How is this possible? Well, in an informal setting, participants have to live up to the standards they presuppose all by themselves. In a formal context, institutions like the judge or the chairman and an agenda help to meet these standards.[24] Concerning Fritsma's motion the interference of the chairman, highly uncommon with respect to motions, is a clear example of a chairman who guards the quality of the discussion. 'I could not accept that Fritsma suggests that members have a double loyalty', Gerdi Verbeet, chairman of the *Tweede Kamer*, explained later.[25] So in a formal setting, the attitude of the speakers becomes almost irrelevant. Whether the participants act strategically or not, their contributions are heard and weighed, for example, irrespective of the speaker's intentions.[26] So, to conclude, the presuppositions apply whenever people argue and politicians will almost always participate in an argumentation because of the institutional context in which they speak.

The discussion so far indicates that arguing can be viewed as a game and that this game is played according to certain rules. When participants argue, they presuppose that these rules are followed or that these standards are met, at least to a sufficient degree. Political communication, as long as it is conducted in a parliamentary setting, is almost automatically structured as a discourse by that institutional context.

The question that concerns us now, brings us to the central discussion of this volume: are the rules of the game of argumentation objective? The answer is, of course, prepared in the discussion so far. What Habermas

---

[23] 'Formale Bedingungen fördern von Fall zu Fall eine relative Entkoppelung des Kommunikationsmodus von den Einstellungen der beteiligten Aktoren.' (J Habermas, 'Kommunikative Rationalität und grenzüberschreitende Politik. Eine Replik' in P Niesen and B Herborth (eds), *Anarchie der kommunikativen Freiheit. Jürgen Habermas und die Theorie der internationalen Politik* (Frankfurt am Main, Suhrkamp Verlag, 2007) 417).

[24] 'In den weichen Kontexten des Alltagshandelns wird den Aktoren, die sich auf Argumentationen einlassen, zugemutet, selber die erforderlichen Kommunikationsvoraussetzungen zu erfüllen. ... Diese Bürde wird den Aktoren abgenommen, wenn Diskurse als solche rechtlich institutionalisiert sind und institutionalisierte Verfahren die Vermutung begründen, dass alle potentiell Betroffenen hinreichend vertreten sind, dass die richtigen Themen behandelt sowie all relevante Beiträge zu Sprache gebracht und diskursiv verarbeitet, das heißt nach akzeptierten Begründungsmustern gefiltert und mit dem Ziel eines rational motivierten Einverständnisses selegiert werden.' (ibid 418).

[25] 'Beroering in Kamer over voorstel PVV om dubbele nationaliteit' (Disturbance in parliament about proposal PVV double nationality) *NRC Handelsblad* (15 February 2007).

[26] 'Exemplarisch ist der Gerichtsdiskurs, der gemäß formalen Feststellungs-, Beratungs- und Entscheidungsverfahren so klar institutionalisiert ist, dass die vorgetragenen Informationen und Gründe für eine gerechtfertigte Entscheidung des Richters ganz unabhängig davon "zählen", ob die Parteien ihre Beiträge in strategischer Absicht leisten oder nicht.' (J Habermas, 'Kommunikative Rationalität und grenzüberschreitende Politik. Eine Replik' in P Niesen and B Herborth (eds), *Anarchie der kommunikativen Freiheit. Jürgen Habermas und die Theorie der internationalen Politik* (Frankfurt am Main, Suhrkamp Verlag, 2007) 418).

emphasises throughout his work is that when you engage in the practice of argumentation, you cannot but presuppose these norms. This certainly implies that the rules of the game are objective. They do not depend on our preferences or opinions, but on the practice of argumentation as we have come to know it (since Socrates, in the Western tradition of thought). This practice is established, it is real. We can watch people argue. We can argue ourselves. The rules of this practice constitute an objective standard (*objektiver Maßstab*) against which our contributions can be measured.[27] To be sure, the rules of the game are not set in stone or inscribed in nature. They are agreed upon by human beings. The game is culture, not nature. However, in its basic aspects the game seems not *relative to* culture. The game can be found in all cultures and there does not seem to be an equivalent for it.[28]

IV. THE CONCEPT AND CONCEPTIONS OF ARGUMENTATION

Habermas' account of argumentation as a game with objective rules is convincing. It seems impossible to argue and, at the same time, disregard the basic rules of the game. Of course, the rules that Habermas has formulated may not be the final or best interpretation of the game's basic rules, but the idea that argumentation is characterised by ground rules concerning inclusion, equality, sincerity and non-domination, that you cannot depart from if you wish to argue seems right.

Some critics have pointed out that this notion of argumentation is too abstract to be relevant to particular practices of argumentation, such as parliamentary argumentation. Because Habermas focuses on what all argumentative practices share, he abstracts, according to James Tully, from the 'contingent presuppositions specific to *this* or *that* form of argumentation'.[29] Because of this focus on presuppositions that are common to *all* forms of rational argumentation, Habermas claims to have found norms and standards that cannot be questioned, 'because to do so would be to commit a performative contradiction'.[30] The critique is that this theoretical tactic

---

[27] 'Die Nachkonstruktion stillzweigend vorgenommener kontrafaktischer Voraussetzungen liefert einen objektiven Maßstab der Bewertung, der in den beobachteten Praktiken selbst wurzelt.' (Habermas(n 20) 151).

[28] 'Wir dürfen zwar davon ausgehen, daß die Beratungs- und Rechtfertigungspraxis, die wir Argumentation nennen, in allen Kulturen und Gesellschaften (wenn auch nicht notwendig in institutionalisierter Form, so doch als informelle Praxis) anzutreffen ist und daß es für diese Art der Problemlösung keine Äquivalente gibt.' (J Habermas, 'Eine genealogische Betrachtung zum kognitiven Gehalt der Moral' in J Habermas, *Die Einbeziehung des Anderen. Studien zur politischen Theorie* (Frankfurt am Main, Suhrkamp Verlag, 1996) 61).

[29] J Tully, 'To Think and Act Differently: Foucault's Four Reciprocal Objections to Habermas' Theory' in S Ashenden and D Owen (eds), *Foucault contra Habermas. Recasting the Dialogue between Genealogy and Critical Theory* (London, Sage Publications, 1999) 119.

[30] Ibid 111.

makes the approach less useful as a tool with which to appreciate real contests about argumentation, for example, about the way to participate in parliamentary meetings. When we leave the abstract realm of unquestionable objective presuppositions, and research the do's and don'ts of participating in a specific practice, in a specific time-frame, with all the rules and customs and habits that colour that practice, we will probably come across rules that *can* and *are* challenged and changed in the course of the game. 'One of the main reasons ... approaches [as that of Habermas] fail to understand the phenomenon they purport to study', writes Tully, 'is that they disregard one of its central characteristics, one which always exceeds the grasp of theory and explanation: the freedom of speaking and acting differently in the course of the game and so modifying the rules or even transforming the game itself.'[31]

This critique is serious and must be dealt with. However, I think that can be done without giving up the (Habermasian) picture of argumentation as sketched in section III. The point is that Tully and other critics, although they acknowledge that Habermas' work remains on an abstract level, assume too quickly that it is impossible to incorporate into the theory an account of institutionalised practices of argumentation. Habermas himself does not rule out this possibility. On the contrary, recently he has warned political scientists not to apply his general findings in a too direct way to specific practices of argumentation. In a discussion with political scientists he differentiates between two levels of research and acknowledges that there is a substantial task cut out for them.

> Research in constitutive presuppositions is part of conceptual analysis, a proper job for philosophers. However, such a philosophical analysis assumes more and more features of an empirical research, the more we depart from the level of generalized cognitive and linguistic practices and approach presuppositions of institutionalized and more or less conventional practices.[32]

It is clear that Habermas' work resides on the 'general' level. The job of political scientists is to reconstruct the rules of the particular games they try to analyse. This suggests that Habermas would take a critical stance towards approaches that copy/paste the presuppositions interpreted by Habermas on the level of 'generalized cognitive and linguistic practices' on particular instances of argumentation, for he sees 'research in constitutive presuppositions' on the level of institutions as an independent type of research.

An example of such a top-down approach to parliamentary meetings is the four country survey of parliamentary argumentation by Steiner et al. The researchers construct a 'Discourse Quality Index' to measure the

---

[31] J Tully, 'The agonic freedom of citizens' (1999) 28 *Economy and Society* 164.
[32] J Habermas, 'Concluding Comments on Empirical Approaches to Deliberative Politics' (2005) 40 *Acta Politica* 385.

discourse quality of speeches of members of parliament. That index is claimed to be based on Habermas' theory of argumentation or discourse.[33] The index is an operationalisation of the ideal of reaching a genuine consensus. The key element is that

> there should be a willingness on the part of all participants to yield to the force of the better argument, which means that the preferences of the participants should not be fixed, but open to change. ... This criterion is at the very core of the ideal of deliberative politics.[34]

The rather pessimistic conclusion Steiner et al draw is that argumentation in parliament almost never results in genuine agreement or 'constructive politics', as the researchers call it.

> [L]evels of constructive politics looked very similar across institutional settings, with positional politics being the norm. At least in legislative settings, it appears that it is very difficult to move actors away from positional politics in their speech acts and in the direction of consensus solutions.[35]

But is it also justified to draw the conclusion that members of parliament lack the willingness to yield to the better argument? I think not. The problem indeed is that the research is not built on an interpretation of the particular game of argumentation that is played in and outside parliament. Perhaps the participants were willing to yield to better arguments, but simply were not convinced by the other parties' speeches. Or the point of the argumentation game in parliament is possibly not to change the others' points of view at all, but just to test the rationality or consistency of the different positions. If that is the case the conclusion that few politicians changed position after the meeting, is no reason for pessimism but instead indicates that the positions were already well-informed, rational and consistent at the outset—perhaps because they were the result of a thorough argumentation process within political parties, behind closed doors and prior to the public parliamentary meeting in which they were defended.[36]

Authors, such as Tully, are correct in their criticism that because of the abstract nature of Habermas' theory changes in and controversies about the rules of the game of argumentation remain largely out of sight. But this does not mean that the picture of argumentation as a game in general with objective and unchangeable ground rules *provides no room* for controversy

---

[33] J Steiner, A Bächtiger, M Spörndli and MR Steenbergen, *Deliberative Politics in Action. Analysing Parliamentary Discourse* (Cambridge, Cambridge University Press, 2004) 53.
[34] Ibid 23.
[35] Ibid 136.
[36] For this interpretation of the game, see B Wolthuis, 'What we can learn from football about parliamentary argumentation' (2011) 9 *Commonwealth Youth and Development* 28–39. In Dutch: B Wolthuis, 'Het parlementair debat als spel' (2007) 36 *Netherlands Journal for Legal Philosophy and Jurisprudence*, 12–33 and B Wolthuis, 'Waarom parlementsleden met elkaar blijven debatteren terwijl dat ogenschijnlijk niets uithaalt' in J Tans et al (eds), *De grenzen van het goede leven. Rechtsgeleerde opstellen aangeboden aan Prof mr A Soeteman* (Nijmegen, Ars Aequi Libri, 2009) 191–98.

and change. Controversy may very well be part of particular practices of argumentation and also lead to change to some extent but not in a fundamental way because then the game would simply have evolved into an altogether different game.

The position I would like to propose takes seriously both Habermas' insights in the game-like character of argumentation and the critique leveled against him. It allows for change and controversy in the various *conceptions* of argumentation, but not in the *concept* of argumentation, that is what all conceptions have in common. Where Habermas has explained the concept of argumentation in general, political scientists interpret conceptions of argumentation, as these can be interpreted from specific argumentation games.[37]

V. DUTCH PARLIAMENTARY ARGUMENTATION: RULES AND TACTICS

Although the basic rules of argumentation are objective and fixed, the rules of specific games of argumentation may change in the course of time and within the limits set by these basic rules. I want to illustrate this picture of stability and change with some historical controversies about the game of argumentation in the Dutch parliament. The approach I adopt is inspired by the type of historical research that Michel Foucault called 'history of thought':[38]

> I would like to distinguish between the 'history of ideas' and the 'history of thought'. Most of the time a historian of ideas tries to determine when a specific concept appears, and this moment is often identified by the appearance of a new word. But what I am attempting to do as a historian of thought is something

---

[37] The relationship between concept and conceptions is familiar in philosophy. John Rawls adopts the distinction to explain how people disagree about justice and at the same time endorse some conception of justice, even if they prefer a different conception themselves. '[I]t seems natural to think of the concept of justice as distinct from the various conceptions of justice and as being specified by the role which these different sets of principles, these different conceptions, have in common. Those who hold different conceptions of justice can, then, still agree that institutions are just when no arbitrary distinctions are made between persons in the assigning of basic rights and duties and when the rules determine a proper balance between competing claims to the advantages of social life. Men can agree to this description of just institutions since the notions of an arbitrary distinction and of a proper balance, which are included in the concept of justice, are left open for each to interpret according to the principles of justice that he accepts.' (J Rawls, *A Theory of Justice*, rev edn (Cambridge Mass, The Belknap Press, 1999) 5.)

[38] Michel Foucault used this method in the historical studies he conducted shortly before his death. Particularly interesting for argumentation, is his history of free speech or '*parrhesia*' in ancient Greece. *Discourse and Truth: the Problematization of Parrhesia. 6 lectures given by Michel Foucault at the University of California at Berkeley, Oct-Nov. 1983*, edited by Joseph Pearson in 1985, foucault.info/documents/parrhesia/. Although Habermas and Foucault are often presented as rivals (in secondary literature; for example by Tully), I believe their insights can also fruitfully be combined, for example by locating Habermas' work mainly on the level of the concept of argumentation, while Foucault's methods inspire historical research of concrete argumentation practices. See this section and the previous one.

different. I am trying to analyze the way institutions, practices, habits, and behavior become a problem for people who behave in specific sorts of ways, who have certain types of habits, who engage in certain kinds of practices, and who put to work specific kinds of institutions. The history of ideas involves the analysis of a notion from its birth, through its development, and in the setting of other ideas which constitute its context. The history of thought is the analysis of the way an unproblematic field of experience, or a set of practices which were accepted without question, which were familiar and out of discussion, becomes a problem, raises discussion and debate, incites new reactions, and induces a crisis in the previously silent behavior, habits, practices, and institutions.[39]

I believe this approach to history serves our purpose well, because Foucault is interested in the history of a practice and in the way the participants, the players we might say, problematise their game. In Foucault's view these problematisations are not necessary or automatic, quite the contrary. He insists that the way in which the participants problematise their practice and innovate it as a result of that problematisation is in no way determined.

> [A] given problematization is not an effect or consequence of a historical context or situation, but is an answer given by definite individuals (although you may find this same answer given in a series of texts, and at a certain point the answer may become so general that it also becomes anonymous). ... A problematization is always a kind of creation; but a creation in the sense that, given a certain situation, you cannot infer that this kind of problematization will follow. Given a certain problematization, you can only understand why this kind of answer appears as a reply to some concrete and specific aspect of the world.[40]

The basic rules of argumentation as Habermas views them are in two respects far removed from what Foucault calls 'problematisations'. The basic rules are *basic* to begin with. They leave a lot of questions unanswered. A specific game of argumentation needs specific rules of order that a chairman can apply in order to guard the order of the discussion. Take, for example, the ground rule that says that no-one who can make a relevant contribution may be excluded. Of course, in a parliament, only those elected may participate. But given that, do we view all 'members' at all times as persons who can make a relevant contribution? What if they contribute in a harmful way, for example, when they insult another member? Every parliament needs to draw up rules to settle these issues. I discuss this below, under (1).

Secondly, the basic rules are far removed from the problematisations of the players because they are *rules*. A game cannot be completely understood just by looking at its rules. The reason is that the rules of a game never instruct the players *how to play*. The rules tell them what is *not* allowed. You may not play the ball with your hand. You may not harm a player. You

---

[39] Foucault, *Discourse and Truth* (ibid) ch II.
[40] Ibid ch VI.

may not threaten the person you argue with. How you actually score a goal or convince the other party, is up to you or your team or party. That is what Huizinga means when he says that play is free. To think of a way to play a game is precisely its purpose. However, in order to play the game well, to actually score a goal or to succeed in testing the opponent's position, players may agree to follow a specific mode or way of playing. A way or mode of playing the game can be called a 'tactic'. In parliamentary argumentation a certain tactic can be considered the best way to argue. Often, these tactics are not laid down in the rules of order. Tactics can lead to changes in the rules of order, for certain tactics may be regarded as a problem by some players. See below, under (2), about tactics.

(1) Let us first discuss some problematisations concerning the rules of order. The rules of order I focus on here are related to the first two rules Habermas distinguished: (a) the rule that no-one who can make a relevant contribution may be excluded; and (b) the rule that all participants must be given an equal opportunity to contribute.

(a) The topic of exclusion became an issue in Dutch parliamentary history when members of parliament started to problematise what may and may not be said in parliamentary meetings, after the First World War, when communist and socialist political parties entered parliament. They made that a problem because these political parties jeopardised the parliamentary system itself. Although these parties came to accept the parliamentary system in the decades after World War II, their original plan was to overthrow parliamentary democracy and install a communist or socialist regime. They entered the parliamentary arena with some reluctance, because they knew that entrance implied acceptance, at least to some extent. They attended parliamentary meetings, but acted sometimes in a provocative, sometimes subversive manner. I want to highlight two interventions.

At the end of the First World War the socialists ended the regime of the German Emperor Wilhelm II and founded a republic. Dutch socialists hoped for a revolution in Holland too. On 5 November 1918, the leader of the socialist party, Troelstra, exclaimed in parliament: 'Realise that when the time has come that you cannot remain in power, other forces will take your place. Then the working class, the new power, will ask you to step aside and give her the place she deserves.'[41] A few days later Troelstra preached in favour of revolution ('the working class in the Netherlands now takes command') at a party meeting.[42] In parliament, he was less outspoken and said that 'the working class can *claim* to take power' and that 'it is our

---

[41] *Handelingen II*, 5 November 1918, 15, 259.
[42] PJ Oud, *Het jongste verleden. Parlementaire geschiedenis van Nederland 1918–1940, Deel I* (Van Gorcum, Assen, 1948) 227.

job to seize this moment to elevate the working class'.[43] The chairman did not intervene. The revolution never happened.

The chairman did intervene, however, when on 23 October 1930, the communist Wijnkoop said that 'the communists will use all means, including illegal means, to put a stop to this war [Wijnkoop referred to the rise of Hitler in Germany. He expected him to start a war] and end it'.[44] Apparently, what made the difference was that the communist referred to violence, while the socialist always stressed a peaceful surrender of power.

Parliament prepared itself for future threats to the parliamentary system when it decided, on 14 February 1934, with 67 against four votes, to add the rule that it is prohibited to approve of or encourage illegal actions (the 1849 Rules of Order already prohibit insults and speaking out of order). Extreme left-wing parties protested against the rule. They feared being 'muffled' by this 'undemocratic' measure that prevented 'unrestrained discussion'. The proponents of the rule explained that it is necessary 'to prevent members from using parliamentary rights to ruin parliamentary democracy'.[45]

According to the new rule, members of parliament who insult, interrupt or endorse illegal action when parliament is in session, run the risk of exclusion: 'He who makes insulting remarks, disturbs the order or encourages illegal actions, is reprimanded by the chairman.' The chairman is entitled to deny that speaker the floor, if he continues to insult, etc and can even exclude him from the assembly for a day or more. The fear was that in the future certain members would want 'to destroy parliament. What has happened abroad, can serve as a warning'. Critical members noticed that the chairman is entitled to exclude members for more than a year. 'This is politically dubious', these members said, 'because in a time of excitement, a majority could strengthen its position by excluding a minority for a long time.' The proponents thought this danger was not likely, because 'it conflicts with the nature of the Dutch people'.[46]

Seventy-three years later Fritsma motioned the Dutch government to prohibit citizens from having multiple nationalities, but also, 'in the meantime', as he phrased it, to exclude persons with dual nationality from government. Although members of parliament criticised Fritsma for questioning the integrity/loyalty of those with dual nationalities, they also pointed out that Fritsma requested government 'not to execute the law'.[47] Fritsma explicitly asked government to put aside existing law that allows Dutch citizens to have multiple nationalities. Did Fritsma 'encourage illegal actions'? Possibly so. Fritsma withdrew the second part of his motion.

---

[43] *Handelingen II*, 12 November 1918, 19, 347.
[44] *Handelingen II*, 23 October 1930, 10, 227.
[45] *Handelingen II*, 14 February 1934, 35, 1216–32.
[46] *Handelingen II*, 14 February 1934, 35, 1216–32.
[47] *Handelingen II*, 15 February 2007, 44, 2575.

(b) The topic of equality is fundamental to rules of order. Rules of order are meant to ensure that all members are given a fair opportunity to have their say. The practice in Dutch parliament was, and in essence still is, that you have to get the floor from the chairman before you can speak. It is prohibited to interrupt a member who has the floor. The 1849 Rules of Order state in Article 34: it is not permitted to interrupt a speaker, unless he needs to be reminded to follow the Rules of Order. During a meeting in 1855, Van Hoëvell interrupted Minister Van Hall who claimed that Van Hoëvell always voted in favour of his budget proposals. Because Van Hall responded, the stenographer had to report the interruption in order to make the proceedings intelligible.

> 'No, always against!', Van Hoëvell interrupted.
>
> Van Hall: 'Then I am pleased to find him here so consistent with himself.'
>
> Van Hoëvell: 'Always, not just here!'
>
> Van Hall: 'Then I beg your pardon; for then my argument collapses.'
>
> Van Hoëvell: 'If you please.'[48]

This is recognised as the first interruption in Dutch parliamentary history.[49] Five years later, Van Hoëvell interrupted the same minister again. This time Van Hall explained in his speech why he agreed to accept a new term as minister, after a time away from politics.

> Van Hall: 'I resigned in 1856. ... I led a life in seclusion and did not interfere with politics, until I noticed the rise of a new cabinet, in which many of my old friends took part. I regarded it as my duty to support this party.'
>
> Van Hoëvell: 'Heaven forbid such support!'
>
> Van Hall: 'Mister Chairman, I do not know how Mister Van Hoëvell, who appears to take the floor, thinks about this, but I regard it as my duty!'
>
> The chairman adjourned the meeting for half an hour, after which Van Hall complained that he was being 'attacked'. 'At my age one does not pick a fight.'[50]

A day later Van Hoëvell referred in his speech to the interruption.

> Yesterday there was an incident that I want to discuss shortly. I heaved a sigh that came out rather harsh and that will appear in the proceedings. I have no issue with that: if necessary my darkest secrets, if they concern politics, may be admitted in the proceedings.[51]

---

[48] *Handelingen II*, 20 November 1855, 123. (Meeting numbers were not used in those days.)
[49] J Turpijn, *Mannen van gezag. De uitvinding van de Tweede Kamer 1848–1888* (Amsterdam, Wereldbibliotheek, 2008) 75.
[50] *Handelingen II*, 26 November 1860, 28, 290.1 and 290.4.
[51] *Handelingen II*, 27 November 1860, 29, 300.

Both the reaction of Van Hall and Van Hoëvell's qualification of the interruption as an incident indicate that interruptions were rare. That changed only slowly in the following years. More and more interruptions were made, but interruptions were still considered to be interferences of the order of the day. As discussed above, repeated interruptions were even considered a reason for excluding a member from a meeting. However, interruptions were also often allowed by the chairman because these spontaneous interventions could lift the level of the discussion, if they were done in good faith. So the problem became how to maintain order and guarantee equality, on the one hand, while at the same time, fostering spontaneous discussion. The solution that was discovered in practice was explicated in 1966, when parliament amended the rule: 'The chairman can allow interruptions.'[52] The reason parliament amended the rule at that particular point in time was prompted by the newly-held hope that parliament would develop into an arena of serious and lively discussion. This hope is illustrated by the 1966 proposal to forbid members of parliament to read their written speeches out loud. Although the proposal was rejected, both proponents and critics underscored its main goal, which is to improve discussion. 'We need to respond more to each other's speeches, make the discussion livelier.' 'It is important to show that we try to convince each other.'[53]

The criticism most often levelled against Wilders is that he evades discussion, that he avoids the questions raised by his opponents when they interrupt his speeches. Wilders also acted similarly in the meeting about Arib. When a member of parliament confronted him, for example, with research that concluded Arib's advisory work poses no problem for her membership of the Dutch parliament, Wilders simply replied: 'There is a problem. For me,'[54] without providing any reasons. His critics view his reluctance or refusal to answer these interruptions as a *withdrawal* from the game of argumentation. 'He disregards every rule of argumentation.' 'He does not play according to the rules.'[55] The history of the Dutch parliament reveals an interesting development here. Interruptions were prohibited at first and allowed later by the chairman. But today, members who refuse to respond to such interruptions are considered to be a killjoy. Whether the populist abandons the game by refusing to answer, or introduces a new tactic within the limits of the game, future analysis must tell.

(2) More on tactics now. The 1848 Constitution conferred important powers to parliament. In the decades following 1848, parliament matured and developed. One of the things that parliament had to figure out was how to conduct its business; how to organise the meetings, how to discuss

---

[52] *Kamerstukken II*, 1964–65, 8042, no 2, 11.
[53] *Handelingen II*, 29 June 1966, 56, 2160 and 2166.
[54] *Handelingen II*, 8 March 2007, 46, 2749.
[55] See n 1.

matters. Some politicians feared the disorder and the revolution they witnessed in February 1848 in France and later in Germany and other countries. This fear produced very strict rules of order. The rules did, for example, not explicitly allow motions in which parliament could give its opinion on urgent matters. The Rules of Order included two rules about motions. Rule 27 explained that

> the order can be broken, when a member asks the floor to ... propose a motion .... Rule 32 said that 'a motion of order to propose to adjourn the meeting, must be seconded by four members, other than the mover, before the chairman can bring it before the assembly'.[56]

These rules had already become a problem in May 1849, when the government wanted to learn parliament's position on a certain deal it was about to make with the Dutch Trade Association. On 21 May 1849, member De Man found a solution to this problem. He proposed adding parliament's opinion concerning this topic to the motion to adjourn.

> I thought about it and wondered whether there is a way to make parliament declare its position regarding the matter. ... At first, I thought to propose a motion of order, but we already are in the order of the day. ... I then got the idea to use the right, under article 32 of the Rules of Order, to propose to adjourn the meeting, and on that occasion, in that decision, to include the declaration. ... On these grounds, I propose the following motion: 'The assembly, judging that the proposed arrangements with the Dutch Trade Association cannot be made without cooperation of the legislative power, adjourns the meeting.'[57]

Several members warned that the motion of De Man was in conflict with both the Rules of Order and the Constitution. These members feared that accepting De Man's innovation could lead to rash decisions, 'the consequences of which were regretted elsewhere'.[58] Others feared an omnipotent parliament or a parliament attaining more and more power, like the (constituent) assemblies in Frankfurt and Paris. But in the end, a majority of 40 against 19 votes decided the motion of De Man should be allowed. It has become practice since then to support motions, as a sign of comradeship among political rivals, because each motion deserves to be treated properly. That Fritsma's motion concerning double nationalities was not seconded, was highly unusual.

A second aspect of how to argue with each other concerned the tone of the discussion. At the start, parliament saw itself as a congregation of gentlemen, who discussed matters of common interest in a dignified manner. However, when conservative members of parliament were increasingly

---

[56] JG Pippel, *Het reglement van orde van de Tweede Kamer der Staten-Generaal. Zijne geschiedenis en toepassing* ("s-Gravenhage, Staatsdrukkerij, 1950) 130–31.
[57] *Handelingen II*, 21 May 1849, 513.
[58] Ibid.

crowded out by their liberal opponents, discussions slowly became less gentle. Historical research interprets this change of approach as a conflict between an aristocratic style and a style that is much more progressive, liberal and egalitarian.[59] The conflict is illustrated by the clash in 1854 between the Minister of War, a Baron with a long military career, Forstner van Dambenoy, a true aristocrat, and the young Van Zuylen van Nijevelt, who also belonged to the nobility but had joined the liberal party. Forstner used to appear in parliament in his full military uniform. He always said as little as possible. He did not accept the authority of parliament wholeheartedly. He just honoured the King, as he used to say. In 1854, the rumour went that the King was not allowed to command his troops, which was his constitutional prerogative. Van Zuylen took the opportunity to criticise Forstner's attitude to parliament. 'I hear government say "to honour the King", but what does that mean, when the King's most uncontroversial prerogative is curtailed?' Forstner played dumb and requested an explanation of Van Zuylen, 'if he is an honest man', for Forstner interpreted Van Zuylens remark as an accusation of treason and perjury. Van Zuylen told Forstner not to exaggerate and that he had to accept the freedom of discussion in parliament. Forstner did not accept this and insisted that Van Zuylen would state his case, exclaiming: 'I demand an explanation from him as a man of honour!' and drawing the rapier that was part of his military outfit. The chairman immediately adjourned the meeting, after which Van Zuylen referred to the rumour.[60] That Forstner took out his rapier continued to dominate parliamentary affairs in the days after the incident. The writer of the 1848 Constitution and the leader of the liberal party, Thorbecke, seised the occasion to articulate a new, liberal rule of sharp, not overly polite or restrained, argumentation.

> I always thought that the rules of parliamentary courtesy are not different from the rules a gentleman abides by. However, parliamentary language has its own peculiarity, because we have to judge freely and examine stringently. In that language words sometimes have a different meaning than they would have in society. I give an example. I can be forced to say: I lost my faith in that Minister. That would be an insult in ordinary life. But here it does not concern the Minister as an individual or a person, it concerns his governance.[61]

At the conclusion of his speech, Thorbecke urged the Ministers not to take things personally, or parliament cannot do its job properly. In the years that followed, parliament succeeded in developing and maintaining 'its own

---

[59] Turpijn, *Mannen van gezag* (n 49) ch II.
[60] *Handelingen II*, 25 November 1854, 135 and 136. See also Turpijn (n 49) 71–72.
[61] *Handelingen II*, 27 November 1854, 144.

peculiar language'. The aristocratic tactic, which meant that parliament could not discuss matters freely, was abandoned for good.[62]

Is the direct and confronting language used, for example, by Wilders in the debate about Arib, one might wonder, not a perfect example of unrestrained parliamentary language, such as the nineteenth-century liberals dreamt of? While others may see some room for discussion here, it seems decisive that Wilders did not criticise what Arib did. He just questioned her loyalty, solely on the basis of her dual nationality.

VI. CONCLUSION

The controversies and changes referred to in the last section illustrate that the basic rules of argumentation, as interpreted by Habermas, are far removed from a specific game of argumentation, such as the game that is played in the Dutch parliament. Nevertheless, at the same time, they provide the limits within which this game is played.

(1)(a) To the rule that no-one may be excluded, Dutch Parliament added the exception that those who sympathise with violence may be excluded. Does this constitute a departure from the basic rule? I believe it does not. It is a specification that intends to protect free parliamentary speech from those who want to end parliamentary politics *violently*. Recall that it is not prohibited to argue for a peaceful regime change, as the case of Troelstra shows.

(1)(b) The basic rule that everyone must have equal opportunity to participate in argumentation is mirrored in the Dutch parliamentary rule that only those may speak who have been given the floor by the chairman. However, this rule frustrated free, improvised discussion, and so it was amended in the end. Interruptions may be allowed by the chairman. The new rule aims to improve the level of discussion but, on the other hand, does not eliminate equality. The chairman can still see to it that discussions are conducted under fair conditions.

(2) The rules of a game secure the freedom to develop a variety of ways to play the game. The innovation of De Man, who cleverly introduced in the Dutch parliament the 'non-procedural' motion, is a good example. Or what about the creation of a 'peculiar parliamentary language', as Thorbecke called it, by liberal politicians in the nineteenth century, in order to overcome the lack of freedom of discussion that resulted from a too civil tone? Parliament needed a sharp vocabulary to be able to bite. Both instances illustrate the creativity that Foucault saw as the key element in the history of thought.

---

[62] Turpijn (n 49) ch II.

These changes of the rules and tactics do not challenge the basic rules of argumentation themselves. If such basic rules are abandoned in the history of the game, the historian simply ought to admit that people have started to play an altogether different game. The rules and tactics of specific argumentation games can, of course, become the object of controversy and may, in the end, change within the limits set by the basic rules.

These basic rules are objective in the sense that they reflect wide and deep agreement about how discussions are to be conducted, as explained in section III. It is not possible to disregard these basic rules altogether if participants wish to argue with one another. The objectivity of these rules, however, does not mean that specific practices of argumentation cannot change. These practices are shaped by specific rules and tactics that can be challenged, and are sometimes changed, in the history of these practices, within the limits set by the presuppositions of argumentation, of which Habermas has provided an interpretation.

I hope a thorough analysis of controversies as those between deliberative and populist politicians about argumentation in parliament can benefit from such a picture of argumentation. One of the questions that such an analysis should answer is whether twenty-first-century populists aim to change the character of the game or wish to abandon it altogether.

7

Easy Cases and Objective Interpretation

NIKO SOININEN

I. INTRODUCTION

Objectivity is often theorized as a relationship between an assertion and some state of affairs in virtue of which the assertion is "objectively true". The nub of the argument is that assertions or beliefs are true in virtue of the way things are (ie facts). Facts make assertions and beliefs true, and objectively so, for facts are not mere matters of mind: they are a function of the way things are.[1]

IN OBJECTIVISM, THE idea is roughly that rules are like rails and the application of a rule is strictly connected to those rails. The interpretation of rules then proceeds in a predetermined direction without any chance of deviating from the predetermined path. Researchers defending objectivity in law argue that there is some sort of objective standard for evaluating the correctness of legal interpretation and this standard is independent of the rule itself. By using this standard, we can see whether or not a rule has been followed.[2] Wittgenstein objected to the idea of 'rules on rails' because even if we use some objective standard for interpretation, the standard itself must first be interpreted and that can be done in multiple ways. There is no one right interpretation of the standard, which ought to guide our interpretation of the law.[3] Objectivism then seems to fail catastrophically.[4]

---

[1] D Patterson, 'Normativity and Objectivity in Law' (2001) 43(1) *William and Mary Law Review* 326.
[2] See, eg MS Moore, 'A Natural Law Theory of Interpretation' (1985) 58 *Southern Californian Law Review* 294. For a summary of objectivism in law, see Patterson, 'Normativity and Objectivity in Law' (n 1) 330–34.
[3] L Wittgenstein, *Philosophical Investigations*, 2nd edn (trans GEM Anscombe) (Oxford, Basil Blackwell Ltd, 1958) para 218. See for the interpretation of Wittgenstein on this issue Patterson (n 1) 333–34.
[4] Patterson (n 1) 334.

In modern jurisprudence, the Wittgensteinian critique against objectivity and one right answer has been adopted and developed, for example by Hage, Leenes and Lodder who have argued that there are no easy cases because in any case the facts and/or the interpretation of the law can be questioned. Furthermore, legal conclusions do not (ever) follow purely formal logic. Thus, there cannot be one right answer to a case, not even to an easy case, because by arguing a different view on the legal norms or facts the case can be turned into a hard one.[5]

In this article, I oppose this view by stating that there are some easy cases in which formal logic is the only used form of inference and that it can be used as the soul justification of the case. Furthermore, I argue that the interpretation of the law adopted in an easy case is the only possible one and that this application is objective because there is not and cannot be any alternatives for the interpretation of the law in easy cases. In other words, I argue that objective legal interpretation is possible in easy cases and that there is also undeniable justification for that interpretation. There is still space for an objectivistic view towards law but this view has to be narrowed down from earlier conceptions and to a certain extent redefined.

My conception of objectivity in law then rests heavily on the lack of choice in interpretation. The lack of choice in interpretation on the other hand rests on the differentiation made between easy, in-between and hard cases by which I intend to develop and specify the traditional categorisation between easy and hard cases.[6] I argue that the analytical differentiation between easy and hard cases is not fine enough and has to be supplemented by adding a third category of in-between cases in order for the relevant differences between cases to be illuminated.

I must highlight that in any other case than an easy case, one right answer does not exist. Legal inference cannot follow purely formal logic and there is no objective legal solution to in-between or hard cases.[7] With regard to in-between and hard cases I agree with the arguments put forward by Wittgenstein and Hage, Leenes and Lodder above.[8] It is in easy cases where our views differ.

I start constructing my argument by dividing judicial cases theoretically into three categories (easy, in-between and hard). This categorisation allows us to see the paramount differences between different cases in both

---

[5] JC Hage, R Leenes and AR Lodder, 'Hard Cases: A Procedural Approach' (1994) 2 *Artificial Intelligence and Law* 113–18.

[6] The distinction between easy and hard cases stems from HLA Hart, *The Concept of Law* (Oxford, Oxford University Press, 1961) and R Dworkin, *Taking Rights Seriously* (Cambridge, Mass, Harvard University Press, 1978).

[7] Already HLA Hart, 'Positivism and the Separation of Law and Morals' (1958) 71(4) *Harvard Law Review* 607–08 stated that in hard cases where the interpretation of a legal concept falls within the penumbra, deductive logic or deductive reasoning are not sufficient. Hart on the other hand stated that although these hard cases do not follow formal logic, this does not mean that there is not some other kind of logic involved in legal inference in harder cases.

[8] Hage, Leenes and Lodder, 'Hard Cases' (n 5) 113–18.

interpretation and argumentation. As a result of this differentiation, I argue that the conception of objectivity in law should be based on easy cases. I further illustrate the categorisation between cases and the idea of objectivity in easy cases by analysing three cases from Finnish administrative law, more specifically from water law.

II. NEW GROUNDS FOR OBJECTIVE INTERPRETATION AND JUSTIFICATION

A. Easy, In-between and Hard Cases

Huhn views easy cases as being those where a clear rule[9] can be adopted in order to solve a legal problem and the validity of the rule is not questioned. On the contrary, Hage, Leenes and Lodder argue that cases categorised as easy by Huhn are not necessarily easy cases in reality because hard conceptual problems can occur even though a clear rule can be adopted and the validity of the rule is not questioned.[10]

In my view, both observations are correct. However, Hage, Leenes and Lodder do not take into account that an easy legal problem can, at first, be a hard one, but becomes part of established case law following multiple interpretations and precedents. At first, all cases can be hard cases. It is by iterative interpretation and constant application of the law that some legal problems become easier to solve. It is no surprise then that the concept of a routine or easy case is often affiliated with the frequency of similar cases on the legal authority's desk.[11] In these circumstances, some hard legal problems become easy ones over time because other similar cases have already been solved.[12] Behind the use of analogy is the norm 'every similar case should be treated similarly if there is no legitimate reason to deviate from

---

[9] By a clear rule I am referring to Hart's famous distinction between core and penumbra of legal concepts, see Hart, 'Positivism and the Separation of Law and Morals' (n 7) 607–08.

[10] W Huhn, 'The Use and Limits of Deductive Logic in Legal Reasoning' (2002) 42 *Santa Clara Law Review* 848; Hage, Leenes and Lodder (n 5) 113–18.

[11] Also Aulis Aarnio has stated that routine cases are cases, which occur frequently and are structurally clear; A Aarnio, *Laintulkinnan teoria. Yleisen oikeustieteen oppikirja* (Juva, Werner Söderström Oy, 1989) 158. This means that a legal authority applying the law has a clear picture of the details of the normative and factual premises of the case. Using terminology developed by Kaarle Makkonen, a mirror image-like relationship exists between the rule and a certain fact; K Makkonen, *Oikeudellisen ratkaisutoiminnan ongelmia. Rakenneanalyyttinen tutkimus* (Helsinki, Vammalan Kirjapaino Oy, 1981) 102–05.

[12] I am aware that my reference to empirical facts contains a hidden ideology, which can be traced to legal realists. In my view, the ontology of law can be traced both to the empirically observable real world of legal practices (*sein*) as well as to the world of legal norms (*sollen*) and these two are inseparable in legal thinking. For such ontology of law, see, eg R Siltala, *Oikeustieteen tieteenteoria* (Vammala, Vammalan Kirjapaino Oy, 2003) 53.

the case law'.[13] In easy cases, all the cases are similar in all legally relevant respects. If the premises differ, a case is not necessarily easy because there is no established case law. In a situation like this it may be likely that the case is easy but this remains to be seen in relation to future cases.

The (legalistic) reader might argue that there are some easy cases, which are easy from the first application, and that there is no need to define easy cases as being cases that have been solved at least once before. Even though we could theoretically say that the premises of a theoretical case cannot be disputed and there is no conflict of interpretations or interests involved, we can only know this for certain after the case (or similar cases) has been solved.[14] In order for a theory of easy cases to take into account the process nature of law as suggested by Hage, Leenes and Lodder, there has to be established case law before a case can be categorised as easy.

It is now established that we need case law to able to say how different facts and interpretations of the law will play out in the real world. However, this does not suffice for the definition of an easy case. How can we evaluate if the interpretations made in the case law are legally justified of not?

To answer the above question we have to add criteria to the definition of an easy case. Perhaps the most important characteristic of an easy case is that there can be no multiple interpretations of the law (normative premise) because a certain legal system can only function if the normative premise is constructed in a certain way. I will further illustrate this argument later on in section III B but for the time being suffice it to say here that if a certain interpretation would not be made in a certain case where the semantic formulation of a rule is clear, the rule could not be applied to any case and it could not fulfill the aims it was enacted for. In addition, in an easy case all the interpretative arguments support only one interpretation. In easy cases there is no conflict between the sources of law or different interpretative arguments.

---

[13] S Shapiro, *Legality* (Cambridge, Belknap Press of Harvard University Press, 2011) 15 has used the term 'truism' to describe certain generally accepted ideas about law.

[14] As Hage, Leenes and Lodder (n 5) 114 state: 'It is the decision making process that determines whether a case is hard; hardness is not solely a logical property of the combination of case and the law.' In my view this statement can be broadened: if the hardness of a case has been decided on in earlier cases (processes) and if the premises are the same in the case at hand, the present case too will be easy and solved like the previous similar case. RE Susskind, *Expert Systems in Law, A Jurisprudential Inquiry* (Oxford, Clarendon Press, 1987) has distinguished between two senses in which a case can be clear. First, a case can be clear retrospectively, which means that a judicial body has already solved the case and it was not contentious. Secondly, a case can be potentially clear if the case, when brought before a judicial body, would undoubtedly be clear. According to Susskind, only retrospectively clear cases are clear in the most demanding sense of the word. My conception of an easy case might be described by the term 'analogously clear', which is an application of Susskind's retrospectively clear case. In analogously clear cases similar cases have already been solved with similar premises and unless the normative or factual premises have changed, the present case shall also be solved similarly to those earlier cases.

When defining the hardness of the case, it is not sufficient to discus only the interpretation of the law. Also the facts have to be taken into consideration because as Hage, Leenes and Lodder stated, arguing a different view on the facts the case can be turned into a hard one. Would not the argument lose its justification if there was no conflict about the facts? What if all the parties agreed on the facts?

In an easy case only one interpretation of the law can be justified. All the interpretative arguments point to the same interpretation and a certain interpretation is vital for the functioning of a certain part of the legal system. This is why there is no discretion in the formulation of the normative premise. The same argument can be made for the factual premise: if all the parties agree on the facts in a certain case and all the evidence points in the same direction, also the factual premise seems to leave no discretion what so ever. In easy cases, legal inference follows formal logic and because the premises do not allow multiple interpretations, there is only one right answer to an easy case.

Siltala has stated that the concept of one right solution to a legal problem requires an interpretational reference point to which the 'right solution' is compared.[15] In my conceptualisation of easy cases, such an interpretational reference point is formed in an earlier case similar to the present case. For Dworkin this kind of interpretational reference point is the concept of law as integrity.[16] My view is that unless a legal problem has been solved at least once before, it is not certain that the problem is easy, rather it is only likely that it will be easy. This follows from the process nature of law: the hardness of a case is always defined in a process.[17]

As a conclusion from the above discussion, a case is easy only when (1) similar cases have been solved earlier; (2) the premises in these cases are similar in all legally relevant respects; (3) all similar cases are solved in a similar manner; (4) there can be only one legally relevant interpretation of the law and the facts; (5) there are no legally relevant conflict of interpretations of facts or the norm(s) and as a result (6) the use of legal discretion is

---

[15] Siltala, *Oikeustieteen tieteenteoria* (n 12) 92–93. Siltala's view conforms with the view of Wittgenstein in *Philosophical Investigations* (n 3) para 218.

[16] See R Dworkin, *Law's Empire* (Oxford, Hart Publishing, 1998) 176 and 225–75.

[17] According to Hage, Leenes and Lodder (n 5) 114 it is the judicial process which defines the interpretation of the law and the facts. However, the differences between, for example, civil and administrative process have to be taken into account. Naturally normative and factual premises are decided in a process every time the law is applied regardless of the field of law; but in a civil process strategic choices can have a paramount impact on the legal decision. On the other hand, in the Finnish administrative law the legal authority or administrative body has a legal obligation to know the content of the law and to apply it even though the parties have not made any claims about the applicable provision of the law (or facts). Also the legal authority has to make sure that the decision is based on sufficient knowledge of the facts of the case. This is so regardless of whether the parties have pleaded to the relevant facts or not.

not possible.[18] Easy cases are technical legal decisions, not legal conflicts, which are usually present in legal decision-making.[19] In an easy case the judicial or administrative body only confirms a certain legal act.

On the contrary, in-between cases are cases requiring the use of legal discretion.[20] In other words, the legal norms or the facts allow multiple interpretations. However, in in-between cases the different interpretations can be reconciled in some rational way, for example, by using meta-principles of *lex specialis*, *lex superior* or *lex posterior*. In-between cases are not entirely clear (as easy cases). On the other hand, they do not require delving deeper into the legal system or extensive weighing and balancing between different interpretations of the law (as hard cases). In hard cases, there is a gap in the legal system or the margin for discretion is very wide leaving multiple choices of interpretation that are equal in weight.[21]

In in-between and hard cases legal norms can be interpreted in multiple conflicting ways. There is sufficient justification for the interpretation to go either way and there is a conflict of interests involved in the process. However, here is the main difference between in-between and hard cases. In in-between cases, although multiple interpretations can be defended, there is a greater probability that the case is decided in a certain way and one interpretation of the law and the facts can rationally be placed above others. In in-between cases there is no one right answer but there is one probable answer after all the pros and cons of different interpretations have been taken into consideration. In a hard case, there may be equal grounds for a legal decision to go either way. In hard cases there is no sense in even speaking about probabilities.

In a way, I am intending by the above categorisation (easy/in-between/hard) to develop and to modify the traditional differentiation made between easy and hard cases. By this, I mean that I am adding the new category of in-between, which takes the place traditionally reserved for easy cases. By an easy case I mean something far easier than has traditionally been the case.

---

[18] By relevant conflict of interpretation I mean a situation where the premises can legitimately be questioned in a judicial process. Conflict in the interpretation of the law has been taken as one of the main arguments against objectivity in law: 'It is the breakdown of consensus at this level that fuels claims for lack of objectivity in law.' Patterson (n 1) 358.

[19] In contrast, A Marmor, 'No Easy Cases?' in D Patterson (ed), *Wittgenstein and Law* (Aldershot, Ashgate Publishing, 2004) 328 has argued that there is nothing 'mechanical' or 'automatic' in easy cases.

[20] In terms used in TF Gordon, 'An Abductive Theory of Legal Issues' (1991) 35 *International Journal of Man-Machine Studies* 209–44 in in-between and hard cases legal knowledge allows incompatible answers.

[21] This category is for the especially hard cases in which a legal decision has to be made without explicit and clear normative support or the normative support is very open to interpretation and possibly self-conflicting. See an example of such a case in the Finnish administrative law concerning the construction of a large water reservoir: Case KHO 2002:86 of the Supreme Administrative Court.

It has to be stated that in easy cases I am mostly thinking of administrative permits or simple judicial application procedures. In-between and hard cases, on the other hand, mostly deal with situations where two legally legitimate interpretations of the law can be placed against each other. Taking an example from Hage, Leenes and Lodder, a pro and contra method of weighing different arguments in a case may be fairly simple in an in-between case although there are at least two interpretations of the law available to the case and the facts of the case may be contested. In such a case, one interpretation of the normative and factual premises can be deemed as the best interpretation after the comparison between pros and cons of every interpretation has been made.

The differentiation between easy, in-between and hard cases can be further illustrated using Hart's famous categorisation of the core and penumbra of a legal concept. The idea is that every legal concept has easier core instances where the interpretational problems are more easily solved.[22] If the interpretation of a certain legal concept in a given case is situated in the core meaning of the word, the case is easy. If the interpretation is situated in the penumbra, this results in interpretational choices, which cannot be justified using purely deductive logic. When the interpretation is situated in the penumbra of the concept, the case is an in-between or hard one.

But how can we know whether the concept is situated in the core or the penumbra? Fuller has criticised Hart's categorisation and stated that legal rules do not pose in themselves the ability to be placed at the core or the penumbra of a legal concept. We have to know the purpose of the legal norm in question in order to be able to place events of the real world at the core or the penumbra.[23]

In my view, there is no harm in taking Fuller's critique as a part of Hart's categorisation. For this article, it would mean that there is a core and penumbra in every legal concept but the boundaries between them have to be drawn by using arguments other than semantic ones. I see no harm in identifying the boundaries between the core and the penumbra using all the legitimate interpretative methods available in law as long as the differentiation can be made.

One important feature in categorising cases is that the context of interpretation defines the case as easy, in-between or hard.[24] Although hermeneutics and the concept of the hermeneutical circle have been mostly adopted by the researchers defending subjectivism against objectivism, the concept can

---

[22] Hart (n 6) 607–08.
[23] LL Fuller, 'Positivism and Fidelity to Law: A Reply to Professor Hart' (1958) 71 (4) *Harvard Law Review* 662–64.
[24] See also J Raitio, 'Legal Certainty as an Element of Objectivity in Law' in this volume (ch 5) 86 and 106.

be useful here in explaining the nature of easy cases. Tontti has defined the hermeneutical circle in the following way:

> The relationship between the whole and its parts in interpretation is necessarily and always circular. It is thus possible to interpret a particular part of an object of understanding only in context ... The whole, however, is not given, it is constructed through the process of interpreting the parts.[25]

First, it is important to notice that interpretation is always a prerequisite for understanding.[26] This is why I have referred to interpretation of the normative and factual premise. I use the concept of interpretation in the way hermeneutics does: understanding always follows interpretation. Secondly, it is necessary to notice that interpretation always takes place in a context, and it is that context which defines cases as easy, in-between or hard. There are no easy, in-between or hard cases per se, regardless of the context.[27] For this article, it suffices to say that the context contains all the legal knowledge in a given legal system. For an individual case this means that the context is formed by the nature of the legal system (civil law, common law) and legal norms in the system.

Evaluation of evidence can also be an important factor in evaluating the hardness of a case. However, I have paid no attention to it because in easy cases the evidence is always 'perfect' as the case is not based on a conflict. All the parties in the process accept and usually present the evidence themselves. For example, in an affirmation of divorce both parties have agreed to get divorced and a judicial body only confirms this agreement. A similar situation can be found from the civil process where the judicial body is confined to the agreement reached by the parties. It has no choice but to confirm the agreement (if one is presented).

B. Objectivity in Easy Cases

Patterson has eloquently formulated the subjectivist critique towards objectivism in stating that from a subjectivist point of view there is a problem in the differentiation between mechanical (easy) and non-mechanical (in-between and hard) cases:

> The dilemma comes down to this: For a theory to generate answers, it must be mechanical, yet no mechanical theory can render an adequate account of our experience of legitimate moral choice. We cannot even escape the dilemma

---

[25] J Tontti, *Right and Prejudice. Prolegomena to a Hermeneutical Philosophy of Law* (Aldershot, Ashgate Publishing, 2004) 28.

[26] Michael Inwood, *A Heidegger Dictionary* (Oxford, Blackwell Publishers, 1999) 106 states that: 'Our everyday life is pervaded by interpretation, both of ourselves and other entities. Everyday "circumspect" interpretation is prior to the systematic interpretation, and prior to the explanations of the natural sciences.'

[27] Or as Hage, Leenes and Lodder (n 5) 114 state 'hardness is not solely a logical property of the combination of case and the law'. The case does not bear any mark by which we could recognise the case automatically as being easy, in-between or hard regardless of the context.

by trying to make some of our choices (the 'core') mechanical and some (the 'periphery') open-ended: No mechanical choices appear to be unequivocally valid.[28]

Subjectivists seem to suggest that there is always a choice in legal interpretation.[29] I do not agree with this view for all cases. Easy cases are purely mechanical and there is no choice involved. On the other hand, they form the objective grounds for any legal system[30] and in some fields of law are prerequisites for harder cases. The idea of an easy case functioning as a prerequisite for the application of law in a certain field of law is developed more fully in section III B. However, there are easy cases, which are not prerequisites for some other application of law but are mechanical in the sense that no choice is available in legal interpretation. These are cases where there is no conflict involved, for example, cases where an individual seeks an affirmation for a legal act from a judiciary or administrative body. Such a legal act can be confirmation of a divorce,[31] undisputed real estate acquisition or some form of notification.[32]

In an easy case, there is one right solution to a legal problem at hand and it is the one adopted before the present case in a similar case in which normative and factual premises were clear and where there was no conflict of interests or interpretations involved. Dworkin has also adopted the concept of one right solution to a legal problem, which follows from his theoretical principle of legal integrity.[33] Also Aarnio accepts Dworkin's view from the standpoint of legal authority because every legal process requires a final answer. In contrast, Aarnio criticises Dworkin's view of one right solution from a theoretical standpoint because Dworkin does not differentiate between a 'final' and 'right' answer. According to Aarnio there can be one final solution to a legal problem but no one right solution.[34] In my conceptualisation of easy cases I define one right solution as the one final and the one right solution to an easy legal problem.

---

[28] Patterson (n 1) 335.
[29] This argument has also been presented by Hage, Leenes and Lodder (n 5) 113–18.
[30] Here, by a legal system, I mean a system, eg inside an Act, such as the Finnish Water Act, not the legal system as a whole.
[31] In a situation where both parties are applying for the divorce in mutual agreement.
[32] These notifications might be lighter versions of a permit procedure, see, eg s 65 of the Finnish Environmental Protection Act (86/2000).
[33] Dworkin, *Law's Empire* (n 16). For the interpretation of Dworkin's legal integrity as an occurrence of the doctrine of one right solution, see Siltala (n 12) 94.
[34] Aarnio (n 11) 271. This was also the argument used by Hage, Leenes and Lodder (n 5) 116. In contrast, Aarnio (n 11) 158 argues that easy routine cases are mechanical and no discretion whatsoever is involved in a legal decision between different legal interpretations. In my view Aarnio is arguing that no one right answer exists in all the cases, especially hard cases but in easy cases there can be one right solution to a legal problem. In contrast, Marmor (n 19) 328 criticises this view by stating: 'Nor is there any intended implication here that application of the law in easy cases is in some way "mechanical" or "automatic", as is sometimes suggested'.

Why is it then that easy cases can be solved objectively? As stated above, in easy cases deductive logic is used in inference and the premises are given.[35] In this way, the only possible legal solution to an easy case is the conclusion of a syllogism. The end result of the logical operation is identical in all the similar easy cases because the premises are formed from similar easy cases. This is what I mean by there being only one right solution to an easy case: it is the one adopted earlier in a case where the question of the case's easiness was first touched upon. The objectivity of legal argumentation follows directly from the use of deductive logic and the presence of one right answer: a judicial body does not have any choice in the interpretation of the law nor in the interpretation of the factual premises and thus has no choice in its decision in easy cases.

Objectivity then stems from the lack of options in judicial decision-making. If there is no choice to decide differently, then the conclusion is objective and by referring to the given premises, the argumentation of the court is also objective. One might also say that there is no room (at all) for subjectivity, which in this case is the same thing as objectivity.[36] The concept of objectivity in law can be redeemed from Wittgenstein's critique: if there are no possibilities to interpret the law differently the need for an objective standard itself disappears.

Objectivity and subjective choice can be placed on a scale, where the subjectivity of an interpretation increases with the hardness of the case. In an easy case, the case can be solved objectively by using formal logic on a given set of normative and factual premises and as a result there can only be one right answer to the case. In in-between and hard cases this is not so and the subjective elements gain more and more ground on objectivity as one moves towards harder cases. The harder the case, the more subjective choice is involved in the decision making process.

As Patterson has shown, objectivity is related to the context in which it is applied. Objectivity might be discussed, for example, in physics, economics and law. In doing so, they use different concepts (language) to describe the

---

[35] Strictly speaking they are not given but constituted in each case individually. However, my point here is that although the factual and normative premises are constituted anew in every case they are also a given because the premises are the same in the current case as they were in earlier similar cases. In this way the premises are a given in an easy case although they have to be taken up in the process at hand. Here we see one major difference between civil and administrative law (at least in Finland). In a civil procedure, a party has to introduce a judicial body to the arguments it wishes the judicial body to decide upon, but in an administrative process a judicial body has a formally binding obligation to find and formulate the relevant information needed to interpret the law. In this way the process and different winning strategies are highlighted in civil law, eg in Hage, Leenes and Lodder (n 5) 118, but not in administrative law (at least in Finland).

[36] Objectivity in law is something other than objectivity in eg natural sciences, see M Van Hoecke 'Objectivity in Law and Jurisprudence' (ch 1 in this volume) 7. See, on the different meanings of objectivity, M Niemi 'Objective Legal Reasoning—Objectivity Without Objects' (ch 4 in this volume) 73–79.

world. Objectivity is relative to a certain domain, to a certain language and to a certain context.[37] My conception of an easy case being objective speaks of easy cases in the language of law and in the context of law. As they are cases in which there is no option in interpretation, the lack of subjective choice creates objectivity in the context of law. Easy cases are objective in law's domain and in law's normative terms. The vocabulary of law is embedded in us through legal education and it defines the way a lawyer sees the world.[38] In this world, there can only be one right answer to an easy case and it is objective in the domain of law because it lacks the possibility of a subjective choice.

C. Three Levels of Justification

Legal arguments have been categorised at least from the 1800s beginning with the works of von Savigny. Since then, many reclassifications have been made and the content has widened somewhat, but the core of the categorisations has remained.[39] Here, I am not concentrating on the categorisation or identification of different argument types but on the way they should be employed in relation to the difficulty of the case at hand.

Demands for legal argumentation are not identical in all cases. They vary with the hardness of the case. My view is that the demand for argumentation has three levels, which have a reference point in the above categorisation of cases.[40] On the first level (easy cases), it suffices that the legal authority gives all relevant legal facts and makes a reference to the wording of the

---

[37] Patterson (n 1) 363.

[38] As Wittgenstein (n 3) para 198 states, it is the training that defines how we react to a legal problem: 'Then can whatever I do be brought into accord with the rule?—Let me ask this: what has the expression of a rule—say a sign-post—got to do with my actions? What sort of connexion is there here?—Well, perhaps this one: I have been trained to react to this sign in a particular way, and now I do so react to it.'

[39] FC von Savigny, *System des Heutigen Römischen Rechts* (Veit & Co, Berlin, 1840) has categorised legal arguments as text, precedent and legal science. In temporary legal theory W Huhn, 'The Use and Limits of Deductive Logic in Legal Reasoning' (n 10) 845 and *The Five Types of Legal Argument*, 2nd edn (Durham, Carolina Academic Press, 2008) has categorised legal arguments into text, intent, precedent, tradition and policy. P Bobbit, *Constitutional Interpretation* (Oxford, Blackwell Publishing, 1991) 12–13, on the other hand, speaks of modalities, which are historical, textual, structural, doctrinal, ethical and prudential arguments. RS Summers and ND MacCormick, 'Interpretation and Justification' in RS Summers and ND MacCormick (eds), *Interpreting Statutes* (Aldershot, Ashgate Publishing, 1991) 512–16 speak of linguistic, systemic, teleological, evaluative and trans-categorical arguments.

[40] My categorisation of argumentation resembles closely categorisation made by Huhn, *The Use and Limits of Deductive Logic* (n 10) 862: 'A system of pure logic works only in easy cases..... Hard cases are solved by complex balancing intra-modal and intermodal arguments, in which the court evaluates not only the strength of individual arguments, but also the relative weights of the values that support our legal system.' According to Huhn, at 828–29 'the very definition of a hard case is that it is one that cannot be resolved deductively'.

statute.⁴¹ In easy cases, there is no strict necessity for further argumentation or justification because the conclusion of a legal inference can be deduced⁴² from the premises and the premises are given.⁴³ In easy cases, formal logic in a form of a syllogism can be used as a heuristic tool for reaching a conclusion and also as the sole justification for the legal interpretation.⁴⁴

Easy cases follow de facto deductive logic and a legal conclusion can be reached using logical syllogism. In my conceptualisation of easy cases no external justification is required because the normative (major) premise is clear and justified by the wording of the statute. The factual (minor) premise is agreed upon (by the parties) and the present case is similar in all relevant respects to the previous cases. Internal justification is not needed because deductive reasoning is the only form of inference, which can maintain the truth-value of the premises. Deductive reasoning is in itself the justification in easy cases in the internal sense of justification. In easy cases, a decision can be externally justified simply by referring to the wording of the statute and to the factual premises at hand.

Also MacCormick states that in some routine cases legal inference is deductive by nature.⁴⁵ In my view, MacCormick means by this that legal inference is in some cases de facto deductive by nature, not merely argued

---

⁴¹ Summers and MacCormick (n 39) 526 see 'single-type arguments' as permissible in routine cases where the single argument of the wording of the statute suffices to justify a legal decision. See also K Malin, 'Hallinto-oikeuksien kaavapäätösten perustelut' (2008) 2 *Oikeus* 200, where Malin states that the argumentation in easy cases in the context of city planning in Finland does not have to be extensive. Malin studied the argumentation of the Finnish Administrative Courts, which have the same argumentative demand that concerns water permit judgments. In contrast, K Nuotio, 'Oikeuslähteet, "supernormistot" ja ratkaisujen perustelu' in J Tala and K Wikström (eds), *Oikeus—kulttuuria ja teoriaa* Juhlakirja Hannu Tolonen(Turun yliopisto, Vammalan kirjapaino, 2005) 133 states that it is not (ever) enough for a legal authority to refer only to semantic arguments; that is to say to the wording of the statute.

⁴² In the context of Finnish water law, some instalments of ducts and cables can serve as examples of an easy case. In contrast, Nuotio (n 41) 133 and R Siltala, *Oikeudellisen ajattelun perusteet* (Turku, Painosalama Oy, 2010) 247 do not accept the conception of legal inference as deductive by nature in any case. R Alexy, *A Theory of Legal Argumentation. The Theory of Rational Discourse as Theory of Legal Justification* (Oxford, Clarendon Press, 1989) 1 states on the subject that: 'In *many* cases the singular normative statement which expresses a judgment resolving a legal dispute in not logical conclusion.' (emphasis added). In my view Alexy's formulation leaves room for deductive reasoning in some (easy) cases.

⁴³ Hage, Leenes and Lodder (n 5) 118 state that: 'Any legal argument that leads to a particular legal conclusion must be based on premises but there are no premises which can be taken for granted. One always needs a procedure to establish the premises from which a legal argument can start. Most often such a procedure will have an expected outcome … but this need not to be the case.' This process that Hage, Leenes and Lodder are talking about has already taken place in an earlier similar process and although the factual premises have to be evaluated anew in every legal process, the end result in easy cases is that they are the same as in the earlier similar case(s).

⁴⁴ Also Huhn, (n 10) 817 states that in easy cases where there is no ambiguity in rules and where the validity of the norm is not contested, legal conclusion follows deductively from the legal norm.

⁴⁵ N MacCormick, *Legal Reasoning and Legal Theory* (Oxford, Oxford University Press, 1978) 19. Also Huhn, (n 10) 828–29 states that deductive logic is used in easy cases.

or justified in the form of a logical syllogism. This is to say that the context of discovery is deductive by nature in some cases. In contrast, for example, Siltala states that legal inference advances from norm and fact premises to an interpretative clause and is not deductive by nature because the inference does not maintain the truth-value of the premises although legal inference can afterwards be presented in a deductive form.[46] In other words, Siltala differentiates between deductive logic as the de facto used form of legal inference (context of discovery) and deductive reasoning (context of justification).

It should be noted though that MacCormick does not suggest that legal inference is always deductive by nature but that it can be in some (easy) cases. This being the case, the justification and argumentation of legal inference cannot be based purely on formal logic because it does not cover all instances of legal inference. On the other hand, this conclusion does not mean that deduction is never de facto used when reaching a decision in legal inference or cannot be used in easy cases as justification of a certain interpretation.

In in-between cases (the second level of justification) a legal norm leaves a margin for discretion after the interpretation has been performed. The use of this margin must be justified by referring to valid law and using other than semantic arguments.[47] In in-between and hard cases semantic arguments do not suffice because the wording of the legal norm can be interpreted in multiple conflicting ways. This is why there has to be some justification in addition to the semantic arguments: the legal conclusion

---

[46] Siltala, *Oikeudellisen ajattelun perusteet* (n 42) 247. The observation that legal argumentation is also something other than deductive reasoning has, on the other hand, been significant in bringing forth logical-deductive facade reasoning into discussion. Deductive logic has been accused of hiding non-judicial grounds for legal decision-making, see eg LD Eriksson, 'Om olika argumentationsmodeller' (1979) *Tidskrift Utgiven av Juridiska Föreningen i Finland* 50, and on the other hand of the justification of concise legal reasoning J Virolainen and P Martikainen, *Pro & Contra—Tuomion perustelemisen keskeisiä kysymyksiä* (Helsinki, Talentum Oy, 2003) 47–48. This critique towards deductive reasoning has also been criticised from the point of view that deductive reasoning cannot be attached to facade reasoning or concise legal reasoning as such but is only one tool in the toolbox of judicial decision making which complements other tools without being good or bad in itself (S Sajama, 'Argumentaatio oikeudellisessa tutkimuksessa' in T Miettinen (ed), *Oikeustieteellinen opinnäytetyö*, 2nd edn (Joensuu, Joensuun yliopisto, 2004) 42–43. From the administrative judicial point of view see P Vihervuori, 'Totuudesta hallintolainkäytössä' in R Nuolimaa, P Vihervuori and H Klemettinen, *Juhlakirja Pekka Hallberg 1944–12/6–2004* (Helsinki, Gummerus, 2004) 496. Vihervuori has stated, that administrative decisions do not usually follow formal logic. This has been particularly so when discussing interest comparison in the water permit judgments in Finland, at 508.

[47] In this category cases cannot be justified solely on 'We find that ...' -type of argumentation because the inference is not by nature deductive. In in-between cases a source of law could be interpreted otherwise but because no one right solution to a certain legal problem can be deduced from the legal system, justification which goes beyond formal semantic argumentation is needed. In such cases multiple legal arguments have to be used for justification. See also MacCormick and Summers (n 39) 526–27.

does not follow directly from the premises but requires a normative choice between interpretations.

In hard cases (third level of justification) it is mandatory to use all the interpretative methods in order to justify a certain interpretation of the law.[48] Multiple interpretative methods can be used to defend and to oppose a certain interpretation of the law. If we are to pick one interpretation over another in a hard case, the argumentation has to be extensive and take into consideration the arguments for and against a certain interpretation. Only after careful and visible weighing between different interpretations can a legal decision in a hard case be justified.[49]

The applications of all the different methods of interpretation follow from the fact that no one right solution to any case other than an easy case (levels 2 and 3 of justification) exists. It is necessary for a legal authority to also give internal justification for a legal decision because in in-between and hard cases, the legal inference does not follow formal logic and is not by nature deductive reasoning, which could justify itself (in the internal sense of justification).

By using Tuori's concept of the levels of law,[50] in easy cases a legal interpretation can be justified simply by referring to the surface level of the law. For example, a reference to the wording of the statute justifies a certain interpretation, which is predetermined in easy cases. When moving on to harder cases, the legal demand for argumentation increases. In hard cases, the use of interpretative choices has to be justified using not just the

---

[48] Huhn, *The Five Types of Legal Argument* (n 10) 85–91. A similar approach to legal argumentation has been used by Alexy, *A Theory of Legal Argumentation* (n 42) 246; MacCormick and Summers (n 39) 526–27; S Laakso, *Oikeudellisesta sääntelystä ja päätöksenteosta: erityisesti julkisoikeuden alalla* (Helsinki, Valtion Painatuskeskus, 1990) 180.

[49] Following the terminology used by J Hage ('Can Legal Theory Be Objective?' (ch 2 in this volume) 26–31) a legalistic approach towards law is used in easy cases without any opportunity to take reasonability arguments into consideration. When moving on to in-between and hard cases a legalistic approach is not sufficient and has to be complemented with interpretive, activist and deviant logical approaches towards law.

[50] K Tuori, *Critical Legal Positivism* (Aldershot, Ashgate Publishing, 2002) 214. In Tuori's theory of law, the legal system is divided into three levels: on the surface level there are all the textually formulated formally binding norms (statutes, law making documents etc). On the second level reside general doctrines of law and some legal principles; and on the deep level the paramount ideas and ideologies inherent in the western legal system such as human rights, the principle of rule of law etc. These levels of law have different conceptions of time: the surface level can change very rapidly, whereas the change slows down when moving on to the deeper levels of law. The different levels of law also have several interrelationships. For instance, the deeper levels of law constitute the surroundings (the context) in which we develop and apply norms of the surface level and the level of legal culture has an interpretational effect on the surface level. The deeper levels of law also restrict certain legal activities on the surface level. Tuori claims that his theory is a critical legal positivistic theory of law because the legal surface can have a slow gradual effect on the deeper levels of the law. By this process all the levels of law come into the realm of discretionary acts. In contrast, R Siltala, 'Fragmentteja, osa III: Mistä puhumme, kun puhumme oikeudesta?' (2000) 4 *Oikeus* 481–82 has criticised Tuori's claim of the theory of legal levels being a positivistic theory of law.

surface level of the law but also the level of legal culture (that is, eg general doctrines of law) and the deep level of law (that is, constitutional principles, human rights argumentation etc).[51]

III. ANALYSIS OF THREE CASES IN FINNISH WATER LAW

A. Legal Norms Guiding Finnish Water Permit Judgments

In this main section, I analyse three cases from Finnish water law. Most readers might not be familiar with the contents of the Finnish Water Act (587/2011) regulating the issue, so I will start by outlining the legal norms regulating the cases in the light of which the three cases will be evaluated.[52] All three cases consider whether a water permit can be allowed in a specific situation. A water permit has to be applied for when an undertaking causes structural alterations to water bodies, causing physical change to the water area and violating private or public interests listed in the Water Act. A water permit is also needed if an undertaking restricts a waterway, which is used for transport, timber floating or the passage of fish.

The permit judgment is usually based on a comparison of interests or weighing and balancing of interests stated in Chapter 3, Section 4 of the Finnish Water Act. All relevant economic interests such as agriculture, forestry, water traffic, hydroelectric power, damage or benefit to properties, fishing, floating of wood, water supply and sewerage, as well as non-economic interests such as human health, living conditions, effects on the environment, townscape, land use planning, cultural heritage or landscape, shall be included in the weighing of interests (Chapter 3, Sections 2, 6 and 7 of the Finnish Water Act). When the positive effects for different interests clearly outweigh the harm caused by the undertaking, the permit shall be allowed. The positive and negative effects shall be measured in economic terms if this is possible and if not, the comparison shall be conducted from a general point of view (Chapter 3, Section 4 of the Finnish Water Act).[53]

---

[51] MI Niemi, 'Lainopillisen argumentoinnin kaksi tasoa. Kolme tutkielmaa laista ja oikeudesta, osa 3/3' (1998) 5 *Lakimies* 757–58, has divided legal justification into formal justification, which relies on the pedigree and hierarchical status of the norm and into contentual justification, which relies on contentual reasoning by way of referring to teleological, systemic or evaluative arguments. Using Niemi's concept of formal and contentual justification, the easy cases can be justified solely using formal justification and as we move towards harder cases, the demand for contentual reasoning increases.

[52] Naturally this legal doctrinal introduction is very crude and short but makes it possible for the reader not familiar with the Finnish water law to understand and to evaluate the conclusions made in the case analyses discussed below.

[53] Performing the comparison from a 'general point of view' is a very tricky task as there is no uniform criteria upon which the comparison or weighing of interests could be based. This lack of criteria for weighing of interests is also one of the main reasons why most water permit judgments are in-between or hard cases.

B. Easy Case: There Can be Only one Right Answer

Installation of a water duct can be categorised as an easy case in my categorisation.[54] It is typical for these cases that no relevant harm is caused by these undertakings. This means that when interest comparison is performed, harm is 0 and the benefit is the economic value of the undertaking, which the Finnish Water Act clearly states as one of the interests to be taken into account (in this case the value of sewage). As was stated above in section II, in easy cases the legal inference and justification follow formal logic in a form of a syllogism:

Major (normative) premise:	If the benefits of an undertaking clearly outweigh the harm caused, the permit shall be allowed.
Minor (factual) premise:	Benefits of an undertaking clearly outweigh the harms caused (the undertaking causes no harm at all).
Conclusion:	The permit shall be allowed.

The legal question here is: what does Section 4 in Chapter 3 of the Finnish Water Act mean by stating that benefits of an undertaking have to clearly outweigh the harm caused? The reader might ask: is this not a classic example of a hard case which cannot be solved using purely semantic arguments and to which no one right answer can exist? My answer is yes and no. It is yes in the sense that the two examples below (in sections III C and III D) of an in-between and hard case are confronted with the same provision of the Water Act and thus the interpretational problem is in principle the same in all the cases regardless of the hardness of the case. It is no in the sense that a certain interpretation has to take place in this easy case in order for the Water Act to function at all and in the sense that the facts of the case differ greatly from in-between and hard cases. Although the interpretational problem is the same regardless of the hardness of the case, the application of the law has to be different when comparing easy cases to in-between or hard cases.

So how can it be that the same provision of the law can be interpreted objectively in certain cases and not objectively in others? Why does the interpretation of the Water Act differ between easier and harder cases? The answer to this question has to do with the prerequisites of the interpretation of the Water Act. By this I mean that if a certain interpretation is not adopted in easy cases it undermines the application of the provision in harder cases. If the easy case at hand is not solved in one particular way,

---

[54] No reference to any particular case is made here because these cases are very frequent and there are no legal problems involved concerning interest comparison.

all the other undertakings (harder cases) have to be dismissed. Any other interpretation in an easy case would lead to a situation where water permits could not be allowed in any case and this would result in the Water Act being completely useless. In order for the Water Act to function at all, water permits in easy cases always have to be granted (if there is no harm and there is some benefit). This is a prerequisite in applying the provision of the Water Act.

I shall explain why this is so. The interpretation of the legal and factual premise is clear in this case. First, the undertaking causes no harm whatsoever (from the viewpoint of the Water Act). This means that there is no reference value for harm in this case and so any amount of benefit has to be interpreted as clearly outweighing the harm caused because the relative difference between harm and benefit is infinity. If a permit judgment would not be allowed in an easy case like this, all the other permits would have to be rejected. Consequently, the whole water permit system would be pointless because in any case other than an easy case the difference between benefits and harm is less than infinity, in other words it is finite.

If we do not allow the permit in a case where benefits outweigh the harms by infinity, we cannot allow permits in any case. As a result of this, the Water Act would ban all water-related undertakings without exceptions. As this is not and cannot be the case, there is only one right solution to the case regardless of the interpretative method (text, precedent, intent and so on) used. These easy cases are purely mechanical processes, which do not require any use of discretion because of the lack of choice in interpretation.

C. In-between Case: Minor Ambiguities in Interpretation

In an in-between case the situation changes considerably when compared to easy cases. Here we have no one right answer although we might have more and less probable answers. An example of an in-between case is that of a bilateral high voltage electric cable, which would be installed on the ocean floor.[55] The benefits to different interests listed in the Water Act total in excess of €100 million. The damage of the undertaking would consist of minor blurring of the water, harmful effects to recreational uses of the water area and minor harm to fish and other sea creatures. These damages would last for two weeks and after which there would be no further harm. There would also be a risk of (greater) harm to other environmental interests, mostly to endangered species and the aquatic environments should anything go wrong. So the legal question here is: how does the economic

---

[55] Case ESAVI 206/2010/4 of the Regional Administrative Agency.

benefit of €100 million compare to the minor harm caused by the digging of the seabed and to the risk to endangered species?

The hardest legal question here is how to compare benefits and damages when they are incommensurable. Should we put different interests on the same scale so that they could be compared? Or should we only look at the normative support for each interest in order to define which interest weighs more heavily? The makings of a hard case stack up quickly. Why is it then that this is not a hard case but an in-between case? The answer is quite straightforward. In this case, the benefits are very high and the harm consists of only minor harm caused to recreational uses of the sea and of minor harm to the aquatic environment. This harm lasts only for two weeks and after that the aquatic environment will return to its original state. Demanding certain precautionary measures from the applicant can lessen the risk to endangered species. There is also a strong possibility that this risk might not materialise. However, some consideration and value in the comparison has to be given to the mere risk of harm.

When the case seems this easy, why is it not an easy case? The answer is simple: because there is no one right answer to the problem. This case does not follow deductive logic because the undertaking causes harm to certain interests and there is interpretative choice to value the harm because it cannot be measured purely in monetary terms. The decision can be presented in a logical syllogism but multiple conflicting syllogisms can be made on the premises of the case by disputing the normative and/or factual premise(s) at hand. It is by persuasive legal argumentation that a case is decided, not by logic. This is not to say that it is not probable that a permit will be granted and that a case is decided in a certain way. In in-between cases there is the probability that a case will be solved in a certain manner but there is no certainty. As a result of this, multiple plausible interpretations of the law can be made and, hence, there can be no objectivity in in-between cases. There is only subjectivity, which has to be backed by convincing legal arguments.

D. Hard Case: Major Ambiguities in Interpretation

In a hard case there are major ambiguities in the interpretation of the law and/or the facts. In my example of a hard case we have an undertaking, which will result in a large international port for cargo.[56] This port would be located near the Natura-2000 site and would cause significant harm to the environment in the area. As a result of the undertaking, the port area would be totally transformed from its natural state and all the environmental

---

[56] Case KHO 2002:64 of the Supreme Administrative Court.

values in the area would be permanently lost. The benefits of the undertaking, however, come to hundreds of millions of euros.

The legal question here is the same as in the in-between case: how can economic interests be weighed against environmental or any other non-economic interest? Although the case resembles the in-between case, the difference is that now the harm caused by the undertaking is much more substantial. As a result of this, the use of legal discretion becomes increasingly difficult. Theoretically, the same observations can be made here that were made in the in-between case. There is no one right answer to the problem and the decision of the case cannot be purely based on formal logic. As a result of this, there is no objective view to the case because normative choices are present. The right answer is conjured in a process as Hage, Leenes and Lodder state.[57] Rationally, the decision could go either way.

IV. CONCLUSIONS

In section II, I argued that legal cases can be categorised as easy, in-between and hard and that this categorisation describes more accurately different legal cases than the old distinction between easy and hard cases. Easy cases can be described as mechanical routine cases where there is an established application of the law and no conflict of interpretations of the law or the facts is involved in the process. Easy cases are usually cases in which the judicial or administrative body only confirms a certain state of affairs, for example, affirmation of a divorce which was agreed upon by both parties. In addition, in easy cases there is a well established case law backing a certain interpretation of the law.

In-between cases are cases in which conflicting interpretations of the law or the facts can be presented but they can usually be solved relatively easily. In hard cases, the justifiable interpretations of the law increase because there is a gap in the legal system or different conflicting interpretations of the law can be equally justified. In in-between cases there might be a high probability that a case is decided in a certain way but in hard cases such probabilities do not exist.

In-between and hard cases differ from easy cases in many ways. First, there is no one right answer to an in-between or a hard case because the interpretation of the premises can always be rationally and legitimately criticised and the use of different interpretative methods leads to different outcomes in the application of the law. As a result of this, there cannot be an objective interpretation or solution to in-between and hard cases. However, in in-between cases a particular interpretation of the law is not

---

[57] Hage, Leenes and Lodder (n 5) 114.

certain it is only probable. Even probabilities have to be dismissed in hard cases because the legal solution could go either way. As one moves towards harder cases, normativity claims space from objectivity.

Also legal argumentation has to adapt to the paramount differences in interpretation between different cases. In in-between or hard cases legal argumentation cannot be based purely on semantics. It is the semantics that the argument is about. As one moves towards harder cases the use of different types of legal arguments is required. In the hardest cases, all the interpretative methods available have to be used in order to legally justify a certain decision.[58]

In easy cases there is only one right interpretation[59] of the law and the interpretation is objective because there is no space for subjective choices. Legal inference follows formal logic and the premises are given. By given premises I mean that there is only one possible interpretation of the law. The factual premises have been agreed upon (by the parties) involved so there is no conflict involved. In addition, a case's easiness has been confirmed in earlier case law.

Interpretation in easy cases is as close to objectivity as it is possible to get in law.[60] As the difficulty of the case increases, the interpretative methods and argumentation must also transform. In an easy case textual interpretation is enough and purely referring to the wording of the legal norm can function as the justification of a legal decision. No further justification is required because the conclusion necessarily follows from the premises using deductive logic and the premises are given (and not contested).

As was noted in section III in the case of the Water Act, easy cases have to be decided in a certain way in order for the permit system to function at all. Taken in a broader context, this is not always the case. Easy cases can most commonly be described as mechanical routine cases, when no conflict is involved. A judicial or administrative body merely affirms some state of affairs in its decision. By an easy case, I mean something far easier than has previously been the case.

---

[58] Huhn (n 10) 85–91. A similar approach to legal argumentation has been used by Alexy (n 42) 246; MacCormick and Summers (n 39) 526–27; and Laakso (n 48) 180.

[59] One can question the use of the word 'interpretation' here altogether because in easy cases there is only one right answer which is almost self-evident. I use interpretation here in the sense that any provision of the law has to be interpreted before it can be said that there is only one option to choose from, see, eg (n 37) 106. I do not use the word interpretation in the sense that there would be any options, freedom or vagueness in the application of the law.

[60] In other words, some compromises have to be made when naming legal interpretation or argumentation 'objective'. See also Niemi, 'Objective Legal Reasoning—Objectivity Without Objects' (ch 4 in this volume) 78–79.

IV. Human Behaviour and its Objective Foundation

8

Can Inalienable Rights Provide an Objective Foundation for Law and Morality?

MAIJA AALTO-HEINILÄ

I. INTRODUCTION

IN MODERN MULTI-CULTURAL Western societies, tolerance of different cultures and value-systems is an important moral and political ideal. Yet this tolerance has its limits: most of us do not want to accept full-blown ethical relativism, that is, a way of thinking according to which there are no universal, objective moral values and, according to which, what is right and wrong depends entirely on each culture's or individual's own preferences. We think, when faced with violent and brutal cultural practices which harm innocent people, that there are some things people should not do to one another, no matter what culture and society they belong to. And that every legal system, no matter what idiosyncrasies it may otherwise contain, must respect some fundamental prohibitions. In other words, most people believe that there is an objective foundation for morality and law: a firm ground that sets limits to policies of tolerance.

But what does this firm ground consist of? Most people nowadays would answer: in universal human rights. As Jonathan Gorman observes, there is 'a widespread respect for rights as if they were absolute standards of morality ... If anything does, respect for human rights expresses what others might see as the moral fundamentalism of Western civilization'.[1]

Belief in human rights as the foundation of morality and law is not only a popular belief, but also a view endorsed by many eminent philosophers. Philosophers who base their ethics and political theory on universal, objective human rights include for example, John Locke (whose belief in the natural rights of 'life, health, liberty and possessions' is echoed in the

---

[1] J Gorman, *Rights and Reason* (Montreal and Kingston, McGill-Queen's University Press, 2003) 2.

US Declaration of Independence);[2] Robert Nozick (who begins his book *Anarchy, State and Utopia* by declaring that: 'Individuals have rights, and there are things no person or group may do to them (without violating their rights)'),[3] and Ronald Dworkin, who characterises individuals' rights as 'trumps' which outweigh considerations of general utility in political decision-making.[4]

The idea that certain basic human rights provide the objective foundation for law and morality is perhaps most emphatically expressed in the claim that those rights are *inalienable*. Inalienable rights are understood to be rights that do not depend on social conventions for their existence, but belong to everybody naturally or inherently. These are the firmest and strongest type of rights there can be and thus serve well as a basis for our legal and moral systems. Inalienable rights are mentioned, for example, in the Universal Declaration of Human Rights (1948), which opens by stating that 'recognition of the inherent dignity and of the equal and inalienable rights of all members of the human family is the foundation of freedom, justice and peace in the world', and in the US Declaration of Independence (1776), according to which 'all men are created equal, [and] they are endowed by their Creator with certain unalienable Rights, that among these are Life, Liberty, and the pursuit of Happiness'.

In this paper, I want to clarify the concept of rights, and especially that of inalienable rights, in order to see whether they can take up the role that is commonly ascribed to them (as an objective ground for law and morality). Most of the paper will be devoted to the exposition of the so-called will theory of rights. This theory links rights with the possibility of expressing one's own choice or will, which means, if we accept the theory, that there are no inalienable rights: any right can, in principle, be alienated. I try to bring out the advantages of the will theory and, in particular, to show that it need not lead to any morally drastic conclusions. Thus, granting that the will theory is a plausible account of the nature of rights, we should perhaps look for the objective foundation of law and morality elsewhere than in (inalienable) rights.

II. THE IDEA OF INALIENABLE RIGHTS

Let us first clarify what we mean by inalienable rights. According to *Collins Cobuild English Dictionary* (1987), 'inalienable' means 'not able to be transferred to another; not alienable (the inalienable rights of citizen)'.

---

[2] J Locke, *Two Treatises of Government and A Letter Concerning Toleration*, I Shapiro (ed) (first published 1690, New Haven, CT, Yale University Press, 2003) Book ii, ch 2, para 6.
[3] R Nozick, *Anarchy, State and Utopia* (New York, Basic Books, 1974) ix.
[4] R Dworkin, *Taking Rights Seriously* (Cambridge, Mass, Harvard University Press, 1978) xi.

In the *Stanford Encyclopedia of Philosophy*, James Nickel gives the following definition: 'To say that a right is inalienable means that its holder cannot lose it temporarily or permanently by bad conduct or by voluntarily giving it up.'[5] Marvin Schiller captures the essence of inalienable rights by saying simply that they 'are logically and morally impossible to alienate'.[6] It is hard to think of a more secure foundation for law and morality than rights that are of this kind. But what, more precisely, would it mean to have such a right?

If there are some things that it is logically impossible to alienate, then it seems those things cannot be *external* to the owner. Thus, to be in possession of an inalienable right would be to be in possession of something that belongs to the right-holder's essence, her inner being or nature. It is logically impossible to alienate something which belongs to the essence of a thing without turning that thing to another, different thing. For example, if personhood or the freedom of will were thought to be the essential characteristics of human beings, then those features cannot be alienated from humans without turning them into non-humans. For example, Hegel seems to understand inalienable rights in this way:

> I may relinquish property, since it is mine only by virtue of my having put my will into it. I may let a thing go unowned by me or pass it over to the will and possession of another; but this is possible only so far as the object is in its nature something external....
>
> Some goods, or rather substantial phases of life are inalienable, and the right to them does not perish through lapse of time. Those comprise my inner personality and the universal essence of my consciousness of myself, and are personality in general, freedom of the will in the broadest sense, social life and religion ...
>
> The right to nothing that is inalienable can be forfeited through lapse of time.[7]

Ernst Cassirer, while explaining the ideals of the political morality of the seventeenth century, writes that:

> There is, at least, one right that cannot be ceded or abandoned: the right to personality ... There is no *pactum subjectionis*, no act of submission by which man can give up the state of free agent and enslave himself. For by such an act of renunciation he would give up that very character which constitutes his nature and essence: he would lose his humanity.[8]

If this is the standard way of understanding inalienable rights, then, to be more precise, the 'logical inalienability' is in fact connected to the essential *things* or features which constitute our humanity, and not to entities

---

[5] plato.stanford.edu.entries.rights-human.
[6] M Schiller, 'Are There Any Inalienable Rights?' (1969) 79 *Ethics* 4, 309, 314.
[7] GWH Hegel, *Philosophy of Right* (trans SW Dyde Kitchener) (first published 1821, Ontario, Batoche Books, 2001) s 65-6.
[8] E Cassirer, *The Myth of the State* (New Haven, CT, Yale University Press, 1963) 175.

called *rights*.⁹ The role of the right is to protect these essential features (for although it is logically impossible to remove the essence of humanity from someone so that she still remains human, it is, of course, not physically impossible to destroy humans).

Thus, 'right' in 'inalienable rights' seems to refer to an (unwaivable) *duty* to protect and maintain the essential features of humanity in oneself and others, or to a *prohibition* to attack or destroy these features. This, as far as I can see, is what is meant by saying that it is not only logically, but also 'morally impossible' to alienate inalienable rights (*cf* Schiller's definition above): we cannot release ourselves or anyone else from these fundamental duties. The duty to protect the inalienable, essential features of humans can have various grounds. A Lockean philosopher would appeal to the idea that since we are all created by God, we do not have the moral authority to destroy anybody's life, health or property; a Kantian would say that human *dignity* enforces certain absolute moral requirements upon us; an Aristotelian virtue theorist would claim that there are some things that are so important for human well-being that it is inconceivable that anyone would ever want to forgo them. Thus, it is not only conceptually incoherent to try to renounce one's right to, for example, personhood, but also *bad* to try to do so. The renunciation would be an offence against God, or a degrading of human dignity, or would severely damage human well-being and happiness (which no human voluntarily wants).

We can summarise the results of this brief analysis in the following way: in 'inalienable rights':

1. *inalienable* refers to features of humanity, which it is logically impossible to alienate (in the sense that if those features are alienated, one ceases to be human); and
2. *right* refers to a non-waivable moral duty to preserve the essential features of humanity in oneself and others.

Let us grant that there are some properties in humans, which are essential to them (although what those properties are may be far from clear). What I want to question is the understanding of the term 'right' which emerges out of this analysis. Can we have rights, which leave us no options—which

---

⁹ Joel Feinberg draws our attention to two possible ways of understanding inalienable rights: the *thing* to which one has a right may be inalienable, or the *right* to that thing may be inalienable. See J Feinberg, 'Voluntary Euthanasia and the Inalienable Right to Life' (1977) 7 *Philosophy and Public Affairs* 2, 93, 114–17. But it seems that even in the latter case, the 'inalienability' of the right means in fact that humans possess certain abilities or characteristics (eg freedom of choice) that they cannot give up, rather than that entities called 'rights' are firmly attached to them. If, for example, an inalienable right to property is understood so that one can give away one's *property* if one wants to, but not one's *right* to property, this means just that one always has the *option* of acquiring property (whether one uses that option or not). So what is inalienable is the capacity to choose whether or not to own things, and not a mysterious right-entity.

force only one way of acting upon us (in this case, preservation of the essence of humanity)? Or could we express the thought behind appeals to inalienable rights in some other way—without using the concept of a right at all? Could we, for example, talk simply of our fundamental *duty* to respect humanity (in ourselves and others), or of the equal and non-forfeitable *entitlement* or *desert* of everyone to be treated as a human being? Let us next look at a description of rights, which restricts the application of the term only to those cases when the right-holder can voluntarily give up or alienate her right, and at the merits of that description.

III. HLA HART'S WILL THEORY OF RIGHTS

The theory in question is the so-called *will* or *choice* theory of rights. The most famous (although not the purest) representative of this theory is HLA Hart. We shall first look at how Hart explains the nature of *moral* rights, and then at his theory of legal rights. To clarify briefly this distinction, moral rights exist prior to or independently of their recognition by the legal order. Morally conscientious people should recognise and perform the duties that correlate with moral rights, but those duties need not be legally binding. So moral rights are powerful, but not necessarily legally enforceable, claims against other people. If such claims are also recognised by the state, so that they can be legally enforced, then they are legal rights as well. The assumption behind the rhetoric of inalienable rights is clearly that these are moral rights (which all governments should also legally respect).

A classical analysis of moral rights can be found in HLA Hart's article 'Are there any natural rights?'[10] The starting-point for Hart's analysis is that all human beings (or more precisely, all adults with normal cognitive capacities) are *free* and that freedom is something that we *value highly*.[11] Moral rights are the products of this fundamental human freedom. Moral rights (and corresponding moral obligations or duties) arise when we choose to *use* our freedom to create special relations with other people. For example, I can voluntarily promise to babysit my friend's children while she runs some errands. By making this promise my friend acquires a moral *right* (to the thing that I promised to do) and I am consequently under a moral *duty* to carry out what I promised. What is essential here, according to Hart, is that my friend can, if she wants to, release me from my duty or alternatively

---

[10] HLA Hart, 'Are There Any Natural Rights?' in J Waldron (ed), *Theories of Rights* (Oxford, Oxford University Press, 1984) 77–90. Hart's article appeared originally in *The Philosophical Review* (vol LXIV, no 2 April 1955).

[11] Hart, 'Are There Any Natural Rights' ibid 75, 88. Hart calls this freedom our only natural *right*; but in my view his analysis does not depend on whether the natural freedom of human beings is a right or not. What is crucial is simply that we *are* free. If this is a right, then it is a different type of right from all ordinary rights. I shall briefly return to this issue later.

insist that the promise will be held. She has a morally legitimate reason to *restrict* my freedom in a certain way (if I babysit her children, I will not be able to do many other things), but she also has the power or authority to release me from my moral duty. To have a moral right means, according to Hart's analysis, to be such a 'small-scale sovereign' in some matter. If the parties in the right–duty relationship are called Y and X, then:

> Y is ... morally in a position to determine by his choice how X shall act and in this way to limit X's freedom of choice; and it is this fact ... that makes it appropriate to say that he has a right.[12]

Not only promises but all voluntary transactions when a person consents or authorises another 'to interfere in matters which but for his consent or authorisation he would be free to determine for himself' create moral rights, that is, legitimate excuses to interfere with some person's freedom.[13]

Hart supports this analysis of moral rights by appealing to the way we ordinarily use the word 'right'. There are two typical contexts: (a) where we explain to others why we intrude someone's sphere of personal freedom ('I have a right to open her letters because she gave me her permission'); and (b) where we resist or object to some interference with our freedom ('You have no right to forbid me from saying what I think').[14] These examples reveal that rights are needed as justifications to interfere with other's freedom and privacy, and that we value freedom so highly that we *demand* justifications if someone attempts such interference.

Two important points need to be made. First of all, Hart's analysis is purely *formal* and does not specify to what kinds of things we can acquire moral rights. For example, in the case of rights arising out of promises, 'the right and obligation arise not because the promised action has itself any particular moral quality, but just because of the voluntary transaction between the parties'.[15] In other words, what is essential to the formation of moral rights and duties are the specific voluntary transactions between specific, determined persons, and not the *content* of those transactions.[16] This seems to leave us with the possibility that people can acquire moral rights to clearly immoral things. No matter what cruelties one person is asked to perform upon another, she would have a moral right to perform those actions if the other person consented to it.

---

[12] Ibid 82.
[13] Ibid 85.
[14] Ibid 84.
[15] Ibid 84.
[16] According to Hart, 'it is important for the whole logic of rights that ... the person who has a right (to whom the performance is *owed* or *due*) is discovered by examining the transaction or antecedent situation or relations of the parties out of which the "duty" arises'. Hart (n 10) 84.

However, the second important point is that Hart claims nowhere that rights exhaust the whole realm of morality. That is, he does not claim that as long as the right–duty relations are created in the right way (through the free choices of individuals), everything is morally in order. Rights form only a *part* of morality; in addition to them, there are other (and often much stronger) moral considerations that need to be taken into account in morally problematic situations. We shall return to this point at the end of the paper.

IV. THE WILL THEORY AND LEGAL RIGHTS

Does the will theory also explain the nature of legal rights? The theory captures at least those rights that exist under civil law. According to Hart, civil law gives a special status or place for individuals:

> The idea is that of one individual given by the law exclusive control, more or less extensive, over another person's duty so that in the area of conduct covered by that duty the individual who has the right is a small-scale sovereign to whom the duty is owed.[17]

Hart distinguishes three different levels at which the individual can exercise this control over another person's duty: (1) the right-holder can extinguish the other person's duty or leave it in existence; (2) after breach (or threatened breach) of the duty, the right-holder may sue or not sue for compensation; and (3) the right-holder may or may not extinguish the obligation to pay compensation to which the breach gives rise.[18]

In criminal law individuals are not given this kind of control: 'a person protected only by the criminal law has no power to release anyone from its duties'.[19] But the will theorist must then conclude that people have no rights under the criminal law. In fact, we do not have a right against murder or against serious assaults, since we have no legal authority to release anyone from the duty not to kill or assault us. This consequence of the will theory—that is the denial that criminal law gives us rights against such actions as murder—has been much criticised,[20] but Hart seems to think that

---

[17] HLA Hart, 'Legal Rights', in HLA Hart, *Essays on Bentham* (Oxford, Oxford University Press, 1982) 162, 183. The article appeared originally in *Oxford Essays in Jurisprudence*, 2nd series (Oxford, Clarendon Press, 1973).
[18] Hart, 'Legal Rights' ibid 184.
[19] Ibid 184.
[20] See, eg N MacCormick, 'Rights in Legislation' in PMS Hacker and J Raz (eds), *Law, Morality and Society. Essays in Honour of HLA Hart* (Oxford, Clarendon Press, 1977) 196–97, and M Kramer, 'Rights Without Trimmings' in M Kramer, N Simmonds and H Steiner, *A Debate Over Rights* (Oxford, Oxford University Press, 1998) 71.

it is rather one of the advantages of the will theory that it keeps civil law and criminal law apart:

> The crucial distinction ... is the special manner in which the civil law as distinct from the criminal law provides for individuals: it recognizes or gives them a place or a *locus standi* in relation to the law quite different from that given by the criminal law.[21]

Civil law recognises and attempts to protect the rights that arise through voluntary transactions between autonomous individuals. Criminal law, however, can be seen to be about our fundamental *duties*, to talk about rights in this context would be superfluous or redundant according to Hart.[22]

Hart did, however, admit that there are some legal rights, which the will theory of rights cannot account for. These are *immunity* rights that protect citizens from the whims of the legislator. 'Immunity' is a term that derives from Wesley Hohfeld. Hohfeld famously analysed legal rights into four different types of 'jural relations': rights proper (or claim-rights), privileges (or liberties), powers[23] and immunities. To define these very briefly:

> A right is one's affirmative claim against another, and a privilege is one's freedom from the right or claim of another. Similarly, a power is one's affirmative 'control' over a given legal relation as against another; whereas an immunity is one's freedom from the legal power or 'control' of another as regards some legal relation.[24]

At first, Hart thought that the will or choice theory of rights explains neatly what the 'unifying element' is in all these four different types of rights distinguished by Hohfeld. Thus, Hart writes in his early article 'Definition and Theory in Jurisprudence' that

> in all four cases the law specifically recognizes the *choice* of an individual either negatively by not impeding or obstructing it (liberty and immunity) or affirmatively by giving legal effect to it (claim and power) ... Of course, when we say in any of these four senses that a person has a right we are not referring to any *actual* choice that he has made, but either the relevant rules of law are such that *if* he chooses certain consequences follow, or there are no rules to impede his choice *if* he makes it. If there are legal rights which cannot be waived these would need special treatment.[25]

---

[21] Hart, (n 17) 183.
[22] '[N]othing seems to be gained in significance or clarity by translating eg the statement that men are under a legal duty not to murder, assault or steal from others into the statement that individuals have a right not to be murdered, assaulted or stolen from.' Hart (n 17) 182.
[23] About the concept 'power', see J Hage's article in this volume (ch 2).
[24] W Hohfeld, 'Some Fundamental Legal Conceptions as Applied in Judicial Reasoning' (1913, November) *Yale Law Journal* 16, 55.
[25] HLA Hart, 'Definition and Theory in Jurisprudence' in HLA Hart, *Essays in Jurisprudence and Philosophy* (Oxford, Clarendon Press, 1983) 35–36. The article appeared originally in *The Law Quarterly Review* (vol 70, January 1954).

As the last sentence reveals, Hart recognised very early that unwaivable legal rights cause a problem for the will theory. Later, he solved this problem by admitting that a theory of rights which is 'centered on the notion of a legally respected choice, cannot be taken as exhausting the notion of a legal right'.[26] The will theory of rights, according to Hart's later view, is an account of the rights of citizen against citizen—that is rights under the 'ordinary law'.[27] But Hart talks also of 'fundamental rights', which are the rights of citizen against legislature and which limit the legislature's powers to make or unmake the ordinary law. According to (the later) Hart, the choice theory is 'not sufficient to provide an analysis of such constitutionally guaranteed individual rights. These require for their analysis the notion of an immunity.'[28] The function or purpose of immunities is to protect 'basic or fundamental human needs';[29] and in so far as such immunities are unwaivable by an ordinary citizen, they lie outside the reach of the will theory.

V. MODERN DEFENDERS OF THE WILL THEORY

So Hart, in the end, does not think that his analysis of rights explains the nature of all legal rights. Hart's followers and modern defenders of the will theory think that Hart need not have made that concession; they think that the will theory can easily account for Hohfeldian immunity-rights also. For example, Nigel Simmonds thinks that Hart should have adhered to his early suggestion according to which an immunity 'recognizes the right-holder's choice not *positively* by giving effect to it, but *negatively* by ensuring that one's legal position is not affected by anyone else's choices'.[30] In general, any right (not only a Hohfeldian immunity) which is rendered unwaivable can be accommodated within the will theory. As Simmonds sees it, even nonwaivable or inalienable legal rights give the right-holder certain important options which she would lack without the right—namely, the option of suing or not suing those who violate the right. So even though the option of completely extinguishing the right does not exist for the right-holder, there are other ways in which the right-holder can exercise control and express her own will.[31]

It is debatable whether this account of unwaivable legal rights is consistent with the will theory—does not the right-holder lose a significant portion of her freedom and autonomy if the option of not alienating the right does

---

[26] Hart (n 17) 189.
[27] Ibid 190.
[28] Ibid 191.
[29] Ibid 193.
[30] N Simmonds, 'Rights at the Cutting Edge' in M Kramer, N Simmonds and H Steiner, *A Debate Over Rights* (Oxford, Oxford University Press, 1998) 228.
[31] See Simmonds, 'Rights at the Cutting Edge' ibid 229.

not exist for her? However, as regards moral rights, Simmonds is more consistent. Moral rights are always alienable by the right-holder. Thus, if a person consents, for example, to a serious beating, she has no moral right to complain afterwards, 'for we cannot reasonably complain of something to which we have consented'.[32] So even though initially everyone has a moral duty not to beat me, I have the freedom to release someone from that duty, that is I can waive or alienate my moral right not to be beaten. (Of course, my consent may not be enough to release anyone from their *legal* duties not to beat others.)

Another way to include unwaivable Hohfeldian immunities (or any unwaivable legal rights) within the will theory is to hold, as Steiner does, that they are unwaivable or inalienable only from the viewpoint of ordinary citizens. However, 'ordinary citizens' inabilities to waive these immunities do not imply that they are unwaivable. Hart is looking in the wrong place—at the wrong persons—in seeking, and failing to find, powers of waiver with respect to immunities against legislative enactments.'[33]

Hart should be looking at those officials who are legally empowered to determine the meaning of constitutional immunities, and who have the power to choose whether to uphold or nullify legislators' enactments.[34] The actual right-holder is in fact the official who has such discretionary power. The same applies to criminal law: although ordinary citizens cannot release anyone from their legal duty not to kill anyone, there are state officials who have the power to grant even licenses to kill. If we want to talk about rights in criminal law, then the real right-holders are those who have the authority to release ordinary citizens from their criminal-law duties.[35]

This sounds strange to many people because we are accustomed to thinking that rights always benefit the person who has them: so that if the right against murder is beneficial to *me,* then it is *my* right (and not some state officials' right). But this test for identifying right-holders leads to many problems. For example, if two people make a contract and create a right–duty relationship then the performance of the duty (correlative to the right) might benefit numerous other people who are not parties to the contract. Still we do not want to grant rights (enforceable claims) to all the possible beneficiaries of some duty—we cannot even know beforehand all of them. (In contract law, third parties do not always count as right-holders—they cannot sue for compensation—no matter how much they lose if the contract is breached.) And it is also quite conceivable and not uncommon that the actual right-holder does not benefit at all from her right. Instead of

---

[32] Ibid 232.
[33] H Steiner, 'Are There *Still* Any Natural Rights?' in M Kramer, C Grant, B Colburn and A Hatzistavrou (eds), *The Legacy of HLA Hart* (Oxford, Oxford University Press, 2008) 249.
[34] Steiner, 'Are There *Still* Any Natural Rights' ibid 249–50.
[35] Ibid 248–49.

identifying the right-holder by asking 'Who benefits?', it is much simpler, according to Steiner, to ask 'Who chooses?'—or, more precisely, 'Who is vested with the powers both to waive, and alternatively to demand and if necessary enforce compliance with [a recognised legal] duty?'[36] If we use this formal test (which does not look at who benefits from the performance of the duty), then we can see that unwaivable legal rights are unwaivable only from the perspective of the person who is most directly *affected* by the use (or violation) of the right. But they are not unwaivable in an absolute sense—that is they are not inalienable. So according to Steiner, with respect to unwaivable immunities or criminal law rights, ordinary citizens are in the position of third-party beneficiaries (who benefit from someone else's exercise of the right), rather than in the position of genuine right-holders.

VI. ADVANTAGES OF THE WILL THEORY

As we saw earlier, the will theory of rights provides a simple criterion for recognising right-bearers: when a person is in a position to release someone else from a morally or legally enforceable duty, that person has a right against the other person (or persons). To have a right means to have such discretionary power, that is the possibility to choose whether or not to demand the performance of someone else's duty. One advantage of the will theory is just this clarity and simplicity: it gives a clear criterion with which rights can be demarcated from other types of moral or legal claims.

The rival of the will theory, the so-called interest (or benefit) theory of rights, identifies rights on the basis of interests, which are so important that they generate duties for other people (to protect those interests). Then this person whose interest is protected has a right.[37] But the interest theorists do not usually say much about *whose* interests and *what* interests are so important that they generate rights. Defining rights in terms of important interests may mean that all adults or all humans or all living beings or all living and even some inanimate beings have rights (if they have protection-demanding interests). The interest theorists regard this as an advantage of their theory—that is that it can, in principle, cover a larger group of right-holders than the will theory—but the other side of the coin is that the sphere of right-holders might expand so much that the concept of a right suffers serious inflation. It loses its distinctive role and force in our moral discourse if nearly any entity can have rights.

---

[36] Ibid 246.
[37] The interest theory is advanced eg by J Raz (see J Raz, 'On the Nature of Rights' (1984) XCIII *Mind*, 194–214, MacCormick, 'Rights in Legislation' (n 20) and Kramer, 'Rights Without Trimmings' (n 20).

Besides, one may note that if the interest theorist allowed rights for beings who are incapable of making choices and using the rights, those rights would be useless for their holders (unless there was someone who could use and defend the rights on their behalf). It would be a very strange kind of right with which the right-holder could not do anything; as Hart puts it, 'it is hard to think of rights except as capable of *exercise*'.[38] So even the rights of, for example, animals, require someone who exercises those rights. Is not the right then in fact that person's right who can use it?

Moreover, the will theory's demand that rights can also be exercised 'negatively'—that is the right-holder always has the option of not using or even completely alienating her right—is not difficult to understand. If there were rights which were not 'discretionary' but 'mandatory' (to use Feinberg's terminology),[39] or which granted only a 'single' but not a 'paired' liberty or power (to use Leif Wenar's terminology),[40] they would look more like duties than rights. For example, if a policeman has a licence to break into someone's house while catching a murderer, but also *has* to break into the house if it is the only way to catch the criminal, then it would be more accurate to call this licence the policeman's duty rather than a right. Similarly, a judge has the power to issue legally binding judgments, but the judge also *has* to issue them: she has no choice. If we call this power a right, it is again inseparable from a duty. But when a right leaves one the option of not using it—when one *must not* always demand from others what the right entitles one to demand—then the right is clearly distinguished from a duty. Thus, one of the advantages of the will theory is that it keeps rights (which involve the possibility to do otherwise) apart from duties (which do not involve the possibility to do otherwise).

It is true that many of those (putative) rights, which involve no possibility to do otherwise are beneficial to the right-holder, therefore they do not *feel* like duties, but rather like privileges. For example, although the right to education is a mandatory right—it cannot be waived by school-children or their parents and is, therefore, as much a duty as a right—we usually regard it as our privilege and point out how good, advantageous, beneficial and so on it is if someone questions the usefulness of compulsory education. Therefore we do not hesitate calling it our basic right.

But this opens the door for paternalism. When those duties which are beneficial to the person under the duty are declared to be this person's rights, the underlying thought seems to be that people do not necessarily know themselves what is in their best interests—what best promotes their well-being. By declaring certain things (which typically promote human

---

[38] Hart (n 17) 184.
[39] Feinberg, 'Voluntary Euthanasia' (n 9) 105.
[40] L Wenar, 'The Nature of Rights' (2005) 33 *Philosophy and Public Affairs* 3, 223, 226.

well-being) everyone's inalienable rights, people are denied the opportunity of choosing themselves the things that are most important for their well-being (or the opportunity of preferring something else than their own well-being in their lives). It is of course understandable to deny children for example, the opportunity to choose whether or not to attend school. But if, say, unemployed adults are forced to educate themselves for a new profession, this often raises angry reactions, especially if the duty is expressed in terms of the rights of the unemployed. As Feinberg puts it: 'The concept of a mandatory right ... would seem to be a paternalistic notion, reasonably enough applied to children, but offensively demeaning when imposed on presumably autonomous adults.'[41]

The point here is not to deny that certain interests are so important that they demand protection, perhaps even against a person's own will. The point is just that when we are talking about the kind of protection of interests which leaves no choice for the person protected, then it would be clearer to talk about everyone's (including the person whose interest is protected) *duty* not to destroy or interfere with the interest in question. There may be rational and convincing arguments for this kind of duty and the word 'duty' does not always have to bear negative connotations (we accept happily many of our duties). But in so far as such duties cannot be waived by ordinary citizens, there is something misleading in calling them their 'rights'.

To sum up, the will theory of rights captures many of our intuitions about rights, and is clearer and simpler than rival theories about rights (which connect rights with interests, benefits or well-being). The consequence of the theory is that the group of right-holders is not as large as most people are accustomed to thinking, for example, small children and animals cannot have rights according to the will theory. The other significant consequence, as has become clear, is that there are no inalienable rights. It belongs to the concept of a right that it can be transferred, waived, even completely abandoned, if the right-holder so chooses. This requires that right-holders are free: they have the freedom to choose even a life without any rights. But since freedom is something that belongs to the essence of right-holders (is an inalienable aspect of them), then freedom is not something that belongs to the realm of rights. It underlies all the various rights; it is the precondition for acquiring and using or waiving and alienating different rights. So contrary to Hart, I would not call freedom our only natural (inalienable) right, but the transcendental condition of all rights.

---

[41] Feinberg (n 9) 106.

VII. A RIGHT TO DO WRONG?

The acceptance of the will theory of rights and the consequent denial of inalienable rights seems to leave us with a morally unpleasant situation. If we admit that there are no inalienable rights (in the strong sense suggested by declarations of human rights), do we then have to accept the possibility that people can have moral rights to beat, mutilate, kill and even eat each other if the victim voluntarily consents to such a treatment?[42] And, more generally, do we have to conclude that there is no objective foundation for law and morality, that we cannot, in advance, put any constraints on individuals' free choices (except the merely formal constraint that everyone's choices must be mutually compatible)?

A will theorist does have to admit that it is theoretically possible for two people, if they both act fully voluntarily and are well-informed about all the relevant facts, to form a right–duty relationship the content of which is clearly morally very dubious. But the will theorist can add that it is quite another thing to verify *in practice* when there has been genuine, well-informed and uncoerced consent to some immoral proposal. As Onora O'Neill points out, even the formal procedures used in the legal context to signify consent, such as signatures or formal oaths, are defeasible: they do not constitute genuine consent if there is, for example, ignorance, misrepresentation or pressure.[43] And of course, when there are no established formal procedures, it is all the more unclear what constitutes real agreement. The lack of clarity is mainly due to the fact that people have differing abilities to assess the meaning and implications of some proposal. For example, if a doctor asks the patient's permission to perform some complex medical operation upon the patient, it is hard to ascertain whether the patient's consent is genuine. People who are not experts cannot easily understand complex medical procedures. But, as O'Neill points out, if the doctor gives a simplified account of the operation, then the patient does not consent to what is actually done to her.[44]

This is a difficulty that besets all cases of consent (and not only those where the other party clearly has less knowledge about the relevant facts). We may always have only a partial understanding of what others want from us (and in this sense our abilities to consent may always be impaired). This is because consent is an intentional concept, that is it is always *about*

---

[42] In 2000, a German computer technician, Armin Meiwes, searched through the internet for a voluntary victim for slaughter. He found a victim who consented to his proposal with the following words: 'I offer myself to you and will let you dine from my live body.' The slaughter was effected and Meiwes was eventually convicted of murder and sentenced to life in prison. About this case, see V Bergelson, 'The Right to Be Hurt: Testing the Boundaries of Consent' (2007) *George Washington Law Review* 165–235.

[43] O O'Neill, 'Between Consenting Adults' (1985) 14 *Philosophy and Public Affairs* 252, 254.

[44] Ibid 256.

something, and that 'something' can be given different descriptions, it can be understood differently by different people. Thus:

> When we consent to another's proposal we consent, even when 'fully' informed, only to some specific formulation of what the other has it in mind to do. We may remain ignorant of further, perhaps equally pertinent accounts of what is proposed, including some to which we would not consent.[45]

For example (to use a case from the Finnish Supreme Court), when a doctor proposes to do a 'standard investigation' on a woman who suspects she has breast cancer, part of the meaning of the 'standard investigation' for the doctor may be oral examination of the breasts. This is not at all what the patient agrees to when she gives her permission to the procedure.[46]

Due to these difficulties in determining when there really has been fully informed, well considered and uncoerced consent or agreement, it is a wise policy not to accept consent as a legally valid excuse when the proposal is clearly harmful for the consenting person. We can always presume that 'no one in his right mind, fully informed, would sell himself to permanent poverty or slavery or sell his discretionary right to life'.[47] But, as Feinberg continues, that presumption is 'quite consistent with the acknowledgment that even the natural right to life is alienable *in principle*, though not in fact'.[48] So, although we may never know whether a person who gives up one of her basic human rights does so fully voluntarily, this is not inconsistent with claiming that there are no truly inalienable rights.

VIII. A NEW FOUNDATION?

Appealing to the practical difficulties in determining when there has been a fully voluntary alienation of some right is perhaps not felt to be enough: many people would also want to block the *theoretical* possibility of letting people voluntarily harm each other (or themselves). And the natural way to block this possibility is to declare that some rights cannot be alienated (and thus to adopt a different theory of rights than the will theory).

However, the will theorist need not be committed to thinking that that there is *nothing* morally wrong in cases where well-informed voluntary adults form right–duty relations which seriously harm someone. As was already pointed out earlier, the view of the will theory of rights is that there is *more* to morality than rights. As Steiner points out, it is only if rights are seen as *peremptory*—if they are seen as 'trumps' in relation to other

---

[45] Ibid 256.
[46] www.finlex.fi/fi/oikeus/kko/kko/2011/20110001.
[47] Feinberg (n 9) 123.
[48] Ibid 123.

moral values—that the will theory of rights appears objectionable.[49] But, as he continues, 'rights do not, and arguably cannot, exhaust the moral universe'.[50] Let's suppose that I own a boat, and have a legal and moral right against others' using it without my permission. If someone is drowning and the only (or quickest) way to rescue her is to take my boat, it is within my rights to refuse to loan the boat to the rescuers, but 'so much for the worse for my rights', the rescuers have a more powerful moral *duty* to take my boat and effect the rescue.[51]

Thus, if we abandon inalienable rights as providing the objective foundation for law and morality, this need not mean that there are no such foundations. The objective moral foundation could be found, for example, in some basic moral duties or prohibitions and these duties could be constructed from certain uncontested, self-evident facts about humans and the human condition in the world. An example would be Hart's attempt to derive the basic rules of morality and law from the 'minimum content of natural law'. According to Hart, there are some 'universally recognized principles of conduct' which are based on 'elementary truths concerning human beings, their natural environment, and aims'.[52] The aim of human beings, generally speaking, is simply to live. When we combine this uncontestable starting-point with equally uncontestable truths about human vulnerability, approximate equality, limited altruism, limited resources, and limited understanding and strength of will, we shall arrive at basic requirements of law and morality.[53] These requirements are usually formulated in negative form as prohibitions ('Thou shalt not kill') rather than in positive form as rights or entitlements.

Onora O'Neill starts similarly from a few basic facts about all humans and, using the Kantian principle of universalisation, arrives at our fundamental moral duties. In other words, O'Neill's strategy is to identify and reject 'any principle of action that *cannot* guide the action of all members of a plurality of approximately equal rational beings'.[54] If such principles are found, then 'their rejection will be obligatory for rational beings'.[55] For example, if I was about to deceive someone with my words and then applied the Kantian method of universalisation to the principle of my action, I could figure out that 'a principle of deceit *cannot* guide all communication among a plurality of rational beings, since its adoption is incompatible with

---

[49] H Steiner, 'Working Rights' in M Kramer, N Simmonds and H Steiner, *A Debate Over Rights* (Oxford, Oxford University Press, 1998), 257.
[50] Ibid 259.
[51] Ibid 259.
[52] HLA Hart, *The Concept of Law* (Oxford University Press, 1961) 193.
[53] Ibid 192–97. About Hart's minimum content of natural law, see also Peter Cserne's article, 'Objectivity and the Law's Assumptions about Human Behaviour', ch 9 in this volume.
[54] O O'Neill, 'Children's Rights and Children's Lives' (1988) 98 *Ethics* 445, 456.
[55] Ibid.

maintaining conditions of trust, so with the possibility of communication that deceit itself requires'.[56]

Because the principle of deceit, when universalised, leads to the impossibility of deceit (since as a universal principle it would make all communication impossible), we may conclude that 'nondeceit (at least) is an obligatory fundamental principle of action among a plurality of rational beings who communicate'.[57]

This is not to say that there are no problems involved in these two strategies. However, my aim here is not to argue extensively in favour of duty-based ethics, but only to suggest that rights need not be taken to be fundamental in moral (or legal) argumentation. When rights are placed in the fundament of our moral system, then rights typically mean unwaivable or inalienable rights. But we have seen that the idea of inalienable rights is conceptually contestable: there are many advantages for reserving the term 'right' only to those claims or entitlements which it is, in principle (if not always in practice), possible to waive or alienate.

Furthermore, the idea behind inalienable rights can in fact be expressed without appeals to 'rights' at all. For the underlying thought seems to be that there are some things that we *cannot* do to any human being, we cannot destroy their freedom of will, their personality, or any other feature which makes them human. I do not see any gain in clarity or persuasive force if we express this moral demand in terms of individual's inalienable rights rather than simply *forbidding* certain actions. And the fundamental prohibitions could be constructed from what can be called 'objective' facts about humans. 'Objective' here need not mean that humans possess an immutable essence or necessary nature (as those appealing to inalienable rights typically hold), but only that there are some minimally contestable facts about us as we are now in this world. As things are, we are, for example, vulnerable, relatively rational, communicative and dependent on each other, therefore we need (and *can* have) some basic rules which regulate our conduct. So, denying that there are such things as inalienable rights need not have any morally drastic consequences, nor need it mean that there can be no objective foundations for morality and law.

---

[56] Ibid 456.
[57] Ibid 456.

9

Objectivity and the Law's Assumptions about Human Behaviour

PÉTER CSERNE

I. INTRODUCTION

A. The Law's Assumptions and their 'Objectivity'

MOST GENERALLY, THE law's assumptions refer to theoretical and empirical presuppositions behind legal concepts, rules and doctrines about factual and normative features of the world. It seems obvious that the law makes or is based on such assumptions, especially about human behaviour. Although the law sets *normative* expectations in the sense that the violation of a norm does not invalidate it,[1] it would be hard to imagine a legal system that could work without, in some ways, taking into account some facts about its subjects whose behaviour it purports to regulate or for whom it claims to provide reasons for action.[2] Legal rules typically assume that to some extent people act out of self-interest and/or they respond rationally to 'carrots and sticks', in the sense of seeking the former and avoiding the latter. For instance, there seems to be an implicit assumption behind the rules on intellectual property in the US Constitution that granting temporary monopoly to authors and inventors

---

[1] Cf N Luhmann, *A Sociological Theory of Law* (London, Routledge & Kegan Paul, 1985) 31–48, on cognitive and normative expectations and the 'handling of disappointments' (*Enttäuschungsabwicklung*).
[2] Modern laws also make assumptions about 'legal' persons, ie non-human entities. These are, as we know them now, ultimately acting through human beings. Technological developments, however, raise the question whether the law could or should assign rights and duties to non-humans, such as animals or robots, without recurrence to human agents' responsibility for them. See G Teubner 'Rights of Non-humans? Electronic Agents and Animals as New Actors in Politics and Law' (2006) 33 *Journal of Law and Society* 497–521.

over the result of their creative activities gives them an incentive to innovate and engage in socially beneficial activities.[3]

Sometimes the law makes its assumptions explicit. This is the case when a written constitution explicitly discusses certain features of human nature as a basis for human rights or when the official legislative motives for certain consumer protection rules refer to consumers' (lack of) capacity to take well-considered economic decisions. Most assumptions, however, are implicit: it is for either courts or legal theorists to reconstruct them from rules and doctrines of the law.[4]

How is this issue related to the objectivity of law and legal theory? In case of explicit assumptions, 'objectivity' roughly refers to the question whether the law's assumptions are 'true' or 'adequate'. Criticisms of particular laws often go along these lines, arguing that 'false assumptions in the law violate law's objectivity'. Prima facie, it seems desirable that when the law takes into account empirical facts about its subjects, this happens not only in an impartial and transparent manner but also in a substantively correct way. In this sense, the objectivity of the law's assumptions is mainly a problem of legislation or more broadly, legal policy or regulatory design.

Implicit assumptions raise an additional question concerning the 'objectivity' of rival reconstructions of these assumptions. As far as the analysis of laws with implicit assumptions is concerned, there are different ways to discern or reconstruct them. Here, objectivity concerns the method courts or theorists follow in explicating the assumptions behind legal rules and doctrines. This is a problem of legal reasoning in case of courts, and jurisprudential methodology in case of legal theorists.

Intuitively, then, the law's assumptions about human behaviour are related to objectivity in several ways. Without going into details here, it should be noted that in philosophy, one usually distinguishes three 'dimensions', 'types' or 'kinds' of objectivity: ontological (metaphysical), epistemic and semantic.

---

[3] US Constitution Art I s 8 para 8: 'The Congress shall have Power ... [t]o promote the Progress of Science and useful Arts, by securing for limited Times to Authors and Inventors the exclusive Right to their respective Writings and Discoveries.' To be sure, the official justification of intellectual property is not simply and not everywhere related to such incentive effects. Traditionally, in continental Europe the explicit emphasis has been on neither the incentive effects of intellectual property rights nor the social benefits from the progress of science and useful arts but on the moral rights of authors and inventors. This justification, in turn, rests on assumptions about authors and inventors as possible holders of moral rights.

[4] For instance, such a reconstruction takes place when a constitutional court elucidates the concept of human dignity as a basis for human rights, or when a legal scholar analyses the 'social model' behind classical civil codes, as in F Wieacker *Das Sozialmodell der klassischen Privatrechtsgesetzbücher und die Entwicklung in der modernen Gesellschaft* (Karlsruhe, Müller, 1953).

The extensive literature on objectivity in law and in legal theory[5] usually relies on these distinctions as an analytical framework.[6]

At first sight, the theoretical status of the law's assumptions refers to the semantic dimension of objectivity, that is, the 'truth-aptitude' of legal statements.[7] Law is said to be objective in this sense when it excludes certain kinds of utterances, among them 'statements characterized by pre-suppositional failures'.[8] Note, however, that truth-aptitude does not refer to the idea that the law should be based on assumptions which correspond to facts of the world, let alone to human nature. According to Kramer, a domain of statements is objective in this semantic sense if (among others) it does not include (too many) statements that suffer from 'radical reference failures', such as the statement 'The present king of France is bald'.[9] Thus, the theoretical status of the law's assumptions seems rather related to the ontological and epistemic dimensions of objectivity, in particular to what Kramer calls 'cognitive reliability'.[10] While he argues that cognitive reliability is not a self-standing conception of objectivity but 'subsumable under previous conceptions',[11] irrespective of the proper locus of the problem in his conceptual framework, the objectivity of the law's assumptions about human behaviour raises jurisprudential issues that seem worth examining. Do laws rely on 'true' or 'adequate' assumptions? Should they? How do these assumptions relate to empirical facts, discovered by behavioural and social sciences? What is the role of legal theory with regard to these assumptions?

B. Reconstruction and Confrontation

While legal constructs and doctrinal theories are often well-articulated and on the surface have a clear technical meaning, they also half-knowingly reflect philosophical ideas of earlier ages ('the metaphysics of the Stone Age'[12]) or express common sense beliefs and evaluations (of 'the man on the

---

[5] See, eg K Greenawalt, *Law and Objectivity* (New York, Oxford University Press, 1995); N Stavropoulos, *Objectivity in Law* (Oxford, Clarendon Press, 1996); B Leiter (ed), *Objectivity in Law and Morals* (Cambridge, Cambridge University Press, 2001); MH Kramer, *Objectivity and the Rule of Law* (Cambridge, Cambridge University Press, 2007).
[6] B Leiter, 'Law and Objectivity' in B Leiter, *Naturalizing Jurisprudence. Essays on American Legal Realism and Naturalism in Legal Philosophy* (Oxford, Oxford University Press, 2007) 258–75; Kramer, *Objectivity* (n 5) 1–100.
[7] Kramer, (n 5), 68–82.
[8] Ibid 69–70.
[9] Ibid 69–70.
[10] Ibid 99.
[11] Ibid 99.
[12] HLA Hart and T Honoré, *Causation in the Law*, 2nd edn (Oxford, Oxford University Press, 1985) 2.

Clapham omnibus'[13]). Such obscure, naïve and often implicit theories seem satisfactory for everyday operations of the law but at closer look, especially in the eyes of an analytical philosopher or an empirical scientist, this 'legal world view' turns out to be strange and deeply problematic.

When we talk about the law's assumptions about human behaviour or even a legal 'model of human nature', the epistemic and methodological character of these assumptions is rather unclear; at any rate, it appears to be quite different from those in behavioural and social sciences. The core task of this chapter is to analyse this difference and to see what happens when the assumptions and doctrinal constructs of the law get confronted with insights, experiments and models of social and behavioural sciences.

The general idea that legal policy and legal scholarship should rely on empirical research is, of course, hardly a new one: legal realism, socio-legal studies, 'law in context' all professed and expressed an interest in empirically informed legal research and reforms. Arguably a new phase began in the last two decades, when under the label 'behavioural law and economics'[14] and 'neuro-law'[15] both legal policy and legal scholarship have increasingly referred to psychological research and neuroscience in justifying or criticising new regulatory ideas such as 'smart regulation',[16] 'libertarian paternalism'[17] or 'nudging'.[18]

While empirical results from psychological and neuro-scientific research become more and more prevalent in public policy debates, including both practical and academic legal discussions on regulatory reforms, much less attention is paid to the implications of this development on legal doctrine and legal theory. How and to what extent is this increasing awareness and enrichment of legal policy expected to change the doctrinal scaffolding of complex legal systems? How does this incorporation of empirical insights challenge and change the assumptions embedded in fundamental legal concepts and doctrines?

---

[13] See en.wikipedia.org/wiki/The_man_on_the_Clapham_omnibus.

[14] See, eg CR Sunstein (ed), *Behavioral Law and Economics* (Cambridge, Cambridge University Press, 2000).

[15] See, eg B Garland (ed), *Neuroscience and the Law. Brain, Mind, and the Scales of Justice* (New York, Dana Press, 2004); S Schleim, TM Spranger and H Walter (eds), *Von der Neuroethik zum Neurorecht?* (Göttingen, Vandenhoeck & Ruprecht, 2009); MS Pardo and D Patterson, 'Philosophical Foundations of Law and Neuroscience' (2010) *University of Illinois Law Review* 1211–50.

[16] See, eg N Gunningham and D Sinclair 'Designing Smart Regulation' in N Gunningham and P Grabovsky (eds), *Smart Regulation: Designing Environmental Policy* (Oxford, Oxford University Press, 1998).

[17] CR Sunstein and RH Thaler, 'Libertarian Paternalism in Not an Oxymoron' (2003) 70 *University of Chicago Law Review* 1159–202.

[18] R Thaler and CR Sunstein, *Nudge: Improving Decisions about Health, Wealth, and Happiness* (New Haven, Yale University Press, 2008).

Analytically, such an inquiry requires two steps: reconstruction and confrontation. First, one has to identify and rationally reconstruct the assumptions about human behaviour behind both larger legal domains and specific legal doctrines. Whether one wants to criticise law's implicit presuppositions or not, making them explicit and discussing their 'objectivity' is an important theoretical task in its own right. The reconstruction pursued in this chapter reveals, in general terms, that legal epistemology is rather complex: the law's assumptions derive from a mixture of common sense beliefs and moral intuitions, moral principles, obsolete and current scientific theories and philosophical ideas, as well as scientifically informed deliberate design.

The second step is confrontation of the law's assumptions with new technological developments or research insights. The question to be raised is whether it is possible, necessary or desirable to revise legal rules and theories in light of these new developments.

Both reconstruction and confrontation can occur at three levels: legal practice (legal proceedings, especially adjudication); legal policy or design (deliberate changes of legal rules, institutions, and structures); and legal theory or philosophy. These levels or contexts raise partly different concerns.[19] In section II, I approach this problem through the lenses of legal theory. Taking Herbert Hart's views on legal epistemology as a starting point, I suggest a heuristic typology of the various cases when the assumptions behind legal rules or doctrines become problematic and discuss the kinds of responses this can generate at the level of legal scholarship. Section III focuses on legal design: assuming a broadly instrumental view of law, I discuss a few general ideas on how policymakers should confront the law's assumptions with the results of empirical research in designing legal regulations. I argue that the epistemic and methodological differences between the law's assumptions and empirical sciences provide a key to a better understanding of both the objectivity of law and the role of legal design.

C. Domain-specificity and System-specificity in the Law's Assumptions

Briefly and metaphorically, the theoretical reconstruction of legal epistemology is concerned with 'how the law thinks'.[20] One can, of course speak about 'the law' and its assumptions at different levels of abstraction. These

---

[19] I discussed certain aspects of the confrontation problem at the level of legal practice elsewhere. See P Cserne 'Consequence-Based Arguments in Legal Reasoning: a Jurisprudential Preface to Law and Economics' in K Mathis (ed), *Efficiency, Sustainability, and Justice to Future Generations*, Law and Philosophy Library 98 (Berlin, Springer, 2011) 31–54.

[20] *Cf* G Teubner, 'How the Law Thinks. Toward a Constructivist Epistemology of Law' (1989) 23 *Law and Society Review* 727–57.

assumptions are sometimes considered as common to entire legal cultures ('modern Western law'), families ('Continental laws') or legal systems ('French law') but often they attach to specific doctrinal constructs ('strict liability') and 'theories' ('contractual capacity'). For a theoretical reconstruction of the law's assumptions, the first step is to draw finer distinctions within the broad category of 'the law'. The two most important divisions concern legal domains (or areas) and legal systems (or cultures). In other words, the law's assumptions are, at least potentially, both domain-specific and system-specific.

Domain-specificity means that similar doctrinal constructs that figure in distinct legal areas rely on different assumptions. For instance, the legal criteria for 'consent' in a commercial transaction, in case of marriage or in the context of rape do not necessarily coincide. As another example, criminal law and private law sometimes adopt different 'theories' of causation, capacity or intention. These differences are related to other features of these legal domains. Thus, commercial law, family law and criminal law make different assumptions about and set different criteria for voluntary human action. Domain-specificity surely has a lot to do with accidents of institutional history but it is, at least in part, related to normative and functional differences between legal domains that are prone to substantive theoretical discussion. Regarding the theoretical significance of domain-specificity an obvious question to ask is whether these legal domains, for example, commercial transactions, marriage or (non)consensual sexual relations, presuppose or can be coherently mapped on distinct domains or aspects of human practice.[21]

Not only do criminal and private law have different 'theories' of capacity or causation, but each legal system potentially has idiosyncratic 'theories'.[22] An example of this system-specificity is when Belgian tort law's 'theory' of causation differs from the Finnish one, if not in terms of outcome, at least in doctrinal construction. Comparative legal scholarship, especially in its 'culturalist' vein, deals with these idiosyncrasies by contrasting similarities and overlaps in legal outcomes with deep-rooted differences in legal cultures or *mentalités*, often arguing that differences in doctrinal constructions result in insurmountable barriers to their functional analysis, let alone transplantation or harmonisation. System-specificity obviously raises many questions for comparative legal scholarship. For instance, can it be meaningfully said that the Belgian theory of causation is better, more appropriate and so on than the

---

[21] Although I cannot go into details here, my hypothesis is that at least in complex modern legal systems various domains of the law assume or reflect different 'models of man' in the sense that they rely on specific presuppositions about preferences, motivations and behaviour of legal subjects which correspond, to some extent, to different aspects of human practice.

[22] Arguably, even the distinctions between legal domains themselves are system-specific, at least in the sense of their historical development.

Finnish? Is there an objective measure? Can such differences between legal systems be related to rival philosophical theories of causation, consent or intention or to rival 'styles' of philosophising in different legal cultures? For instance, is it meaningful to relate the differences between the French and the English concept of contract to 'Cartesian' and 'Humean' philosophy, respectively, as hallmarks of radically different national cultures?[23] Or are these differences the result of historical accidents without deeper theoretical meaning? Can we infer from system-specificity to the incommensurability of legal cultures?[24] In general, both domain-specificity and system-specificity indicate that behind the generalisation 'the law' there are important differences and subdivisions that have to be taken into account in any in-depth discussion on the epistemic and methodological character of doctrinal legal constructs.

II. 'HOW THE LAW THINKS': RECONSTRUCTING LEGAL EPISTEMOLOGY

A. Theoretical Perspectives on the Epistemology of Law

The epistemology of law and the implicit theories behind particular legal constructs can be analysed from numerous perspectives.

Generally, legal anthropology is relevant here inasmuch as it is concerned with the *Weltanschauung* reflected in concepts and doctrines of various legal cultures. Although not legal anthropologists in the disciplinary sense, French legal scholars Legendre and Supiot, use a similar methodology for uncovering basic ideological commitments behind (modern) Western law. Combining historical inquiry with a more critical stance, they uncover what they call the 'dogmatic nature' of the law.[25]

Donald Kelley's equally erudite but less critical historical inquiry suggests that for several centuries Western jurisprudence (re)presented itself as the 'true science of society', as the centre of scientific inquiry on human nature

---

[23] *Cf* C Valcke, 'Convergence and Divergence of the English, French, and German Concept of Contract' (2008) 1 *European Review of Private Law* 29–62.

[24] These questions indicate that a comparative analysis of system-specific assumptions of the law provide a fertile area for theoretical discussion. Under some interpretation of legal objectivity, it may indeed be a matter of concern that systemic differences are based on historical accidents and arbitrary assumptions. Certainly, system-specificity can be seen as problematic for the objectivity of law when the latter is associated with uniformity or universality of the law but also (although not in the same way) when theoretical legal discourse aspires for trans-cultural validity. *cf* the contributions of Jaap Hage and Jaakko Husa in this volume (chs 2 and 10).

[25] P Legendre, *L'amour du censeur. Essai sur l'ordre dogmatique* (Paris, Editions du Seuil, 1974); A Supiot, *Homo juridicus. On the Anthropological Function of the Law* (London, Verso, 2007).

and social interaction.[26] He reconstructs the historical development of legal scholarship as the primary sphere of human practice aiming at understanding and shaping of the social world in a 'human measure' by also making this humanistic view normatively appealing. Kelley also discusses how this view was continuously challenged and almost completely washed away by the rise of modern social sciences.[27] The rise and fall of law as 'the oldest social science' was reconstructed in a somewhat different narrative by Tim Murphy[28] who argued that the 'epistemic shift [away from law] was a consequence of the rise of statistics'.[29]

Different versions of systems theory and social constructivism aim at both theoretical reconstruction and philosophical justification of the autonomy of legal epistemology with respect to scientific rationality and political interests, mainly in terms of self-referentiality.[30] Based on the theoretical background and methodology of Anglo-American legal philosophy, Jeremy Waldron defends the conceptual schemes and doctrinal constructions of modern legal systems against 'realist' attacks by referring to the coherence of legal systems and the role of this 'systematicity' in pluralist societies.[31]

B. Herbert Hart on Legal Epistemology: Philosophy as 'Rational and Critical Foundation' of the Law[32]

In the following sections, I take HLA Hart's views on legal epistemology as a starting point for analysing the theoretical status of the law's assumptions about human behaviour. I will discuss what Hart said or would have said about legal epistemology and the way he confronted legal doctrines with

---

[26] D Kelley, *The Human Measure. Social Thought in the Western Legal Tradition* (Cambridge, Harvard University Press, 1990).

[27] Ibid ch 14: 'From Civil Science to the Human Sciences'. The sections in this chapter are tellingly entitled: 'Law Transcended by Philosophy', 'Law Subverted by Economics', 'Law Surpassed by Anthropology', and 'Law Overpowered by Sociology'. The concluding chapter contrasts 'Social Scientism' with 'The Human Measure'.

[28] WT Murphy, *The Oldest Social Science? Configurations of Law and Modernity* (Oxford, Oxford University Press, 1997).

[29] G Samuel, 'Interdisciplinarity and the Authority Paradigm: Should Law Be Taken Seriously by Scientists and Social Scientists?' (2009) 36 *Journal of Law and Society* 431, 445.

[30] Luhmann, *A Sociological Theory of Law* (n 1); R Wiethölter, 'Social Science Models in Economic Law' in T Daintith and G Teubner (eds), *Contract and Organization: Legal Analysis in the Light of Economic and Social Theory* (Berlin, Walter de Gruyter, 1986) 52–67; Teubner, 'How the Law Thinks' (n 20).

[31] J Waldron, 'Transcendental Nonsense and System in the Law' (2000) 100 *Columbia Law Review* 16. See also D Nelken, 'Can Law Learn from Social Science?' (2001) 35 *Israel Law Review* 205–24.

[32] This section is based on P Cserne 'Between "Metaphysics of the Stone Age" and the "Brave New World": HLA Hart on the Law's Assumptions about Human Nature' in MA Jovanovic and B Spaic (eds) *Jurisprudence and Political Philosophy in the 21st Century: Reassessing Legacies* (Frankfurt, Peter Lang, 2012) 71–87.

ordinary views, empirical research, and philosophical arguments. In the analysis, I mainly rely on Hart's so-called specific jurisprudence, especially *Causation in the Law*, co-authored with Tony Honoré, and the collection of essays in *Punishment and Responsibility*.[33] While Hart's approach is mainly analytical, he also sees that a thorough analysis of the law's assumptions has to provide a 'rational and critical foundation' for the law, which also requires going beyond conceptual analytical and positivist description. This combination of reconstruction and 'therapeutic'[34] arguments shows that Hart did not confine himself to conceptual and descriptive analysis. To borrow a term from his essay on Bentham, he was open to the 'demystifying' role of legal philosophy.[35] In various ways and instances his 'expository' reconstruction of legal doctrine combines with his critical or 'censorial' jurisprudence.[36]

At least in the first edition of *Causation*, Hart and Honoré 'drew on the philosophical currents of the fifties. At that time the analysis of ordinary language was regarded by many as the key to the clarification of conceptual difficulties'.[37] They argue that 'the language of ordinary people and of lawyers both revealed and obscured the truth about causal concepts'.[38] They also explain why conceptual analysis involves going beyond description:

> [I]f ordinary language and legal discourse contain clues to the existence of these various notions and to the analogies and dysfunctions between them, they also have a pathological aspect. For though in everyday life we make a distinction between conditions and causes, and, with the help of the distinction, explain puzzling events, control our environment, and assign praise or blame, we are often unable to explain the principles on which we do so. Hence lawyers in particular, when called upon to give an account of the causal principles they apply, often resort to obscure metaphors of 'causal potency', the 'exhaustion' of causes, and the 'breaking of causal chains'. Here, our aim was therapeutic. We tried to translate the bewildering metaphors into factual terms and to dissipate the sense of mystification they engender.[39]

---

[33] Hart and Honoré, *Causation in the Law* (n 12); HLA Hart, *Punishment and Responsibility. Essays in the Philosophy of Law* (Oxford, Oxford University Press, 1968).
[34] Hart and Honoré (n 12) xxxiv.
[35] HLA Hart 'Bentham and the Demystification of the Law' (1973) 36 *Modern Law Review* 2–17.
[36] Focusing on Hart's special jurisprudence also allows seeing parallels between Hart's and Fuller's views on the law's assumptions about personhood, thus throwing a different light on their theoretical debate on the concept of law and the methodology of jurisprudence.
[37] Hart and Honoré (n 12) xxxiii. Note here that they mention *conceptual* difficulties, not normative or empirical ones. Although the law's assumptions about human behaviour are not only a conceptual but a substantive matter, their view is that these two cannot be separated. Indeed, their analysis of legal theories of causation is based on the assumption that one should not be concerned with the duality of 'words and things'. *Cf* HLA Hart, 'Analytical Jurisprudence in Mid-Twentieth Century. Reply to Professor Bodenheimer' (1957) 105 *University of Pennsylvania Law Review* 953, 967.
[38] Hart and Honoré (n 12) xxxi.
[39] Ibid xxxiii–iv.

This version of ordinary language philosophy takes up a critical task with regard to doctrinal constructs although not necessarily in light of moral values. This raises the question about the relation of description and therapy. Looking at legal doctrines, how much of the embedded ordinary views (common sense, folk psychology) on the one hand, and which aspects of the professional jargon and metaphors on the other, can or should be retained? What and how should be 'translated into factual terms'? Is it indeed the case that doctrinal theories or their assumptions can be translated into 'factual terms'?

Below, I will suggest a more comprehensive answer to these questions but if we continue reading the preface, Hart and Honoré indirectly hint at a possible answer. They mention changes in philosophical background theories between the two editions of *Causation*, in particular the rise of 'a wider conception of philosophy, more receptive to general theory'.[40] In its immediate context this statement suggests that in the early 1980s in Anglo-American legal philosophy it was accepted, maybe even 'fashionable' not to merely analyse linguistic practices of ordinary people or legal officials but to be critical towards their use of legal doctrinal categories. This is, of course, nothing to a serious discussion of the proper relation between description and evaluation. What it probably indicates is that in the authors' view there is no general or absolute standard for the proper relation: there are different viable philosophical approaches and standards change in time. Juxtaposing the 'factual' with 'metaphorical' is certainly one way for theorists to justify, at least rhetorically, a certain combination of description and demystification in their analysis. If we look at Hart's other writings, for example on the principles of punishment and criminal law doctrines,[41] the legal enforcement of conventional sexual morality[42] or the legal regulation of abortion,[43] we observe that their 'therapeutic' and critical tenor varies, depending, among others, on the audience, the context, and the weight of the doctrinal construct on Hart's own critical moral scale.

In fact, even in the case of *Causation*, the link between legal doctrinal constructs, ordinary people's view and the task of legal theory is not only an epistemic matter but related to moral issues. Discussing the role of causation in the attribution of responsibility, Hart and Honoré argue that causal connection is neither necessary nor sufficient in every case but it is often

---

[40] Ibid xxxiv.
[41] Hart, *Punishment and Responsibility* (n 33).
[42] HLA Hart, 'Immorality and Treason' (1958) 59 *The Listener* 162; 'The Use and Abuse of Criminal Law' (1961) 4 *Oxford Lawyer* 712; 'Social Solidarity and the Enforcement of Morality' in HLA Hart, *Essays in Jurisprudence and Philosophy* (Oxford, Oxford University Press, 1983) 248; HLA Hart, *Law, Legislation, and Liberty*, 2nd edn (Oxford, Oxford University Press, 1989).
[43] HLA Hart 'Abortion Law Reform: The English Experience' (1972) 8 *Melbourne University Law Review* 388.

necessary and sometimes sufficient. Those cases when it is both necessary and sufficient 'form a paradigm against which the variations can be easily understood. That we are responsible for the harm we cause is a principle that makes an immediate appeal to *common moral sensibility*.'[44] The reference to 'common moral sensibility' indicates that the theoretical question about the 'central', 'focal' or 'paradigmatic' case of a legal concept (here responsibility) is linked to moral issues. To be sure, 'common moral sensibility' as mentioned here can be understood from a detached perspective, referring to conventional social morality.

Later in the preface, discussing alternative theories of tort law, they argue that

> the law of tort cannot be accounted for solely as an instrument for maximizing future wealth or utility or some other socially desirable end. Backward-looking aims, such as redress of wrongs, play at least some part in it and will continue to do so in any society in which regard continues to be paid to *the moral sensibility of ordinary people*. For one of *our most widely shared intuitions* concerns the redress of wrong we do and that we ought in a proper sense to pay compensation for it.[45]

In this quote there is, once more, no clear indication that the 'moral sensibility of ordinary people' would be necessarily endorsed by the authors' critical morality. Still, it conveys the idea that not only conceptual but also moral arguments are relevant in the choice between alternative theories of tort law.[46]

Hart thought that common sense moral views are relevant for lawyers in general and for legal design in particular.[47] However, he clearly opposed the

---

[44] Hart and Honoré (n 12) xxxv.
[45] Ibid lxxv.
[46] Hart explains this point more generally, elsewhere: 'There is of course much justice in the claim that in order to understand certain features of legal institutions or legal rules, the aims and purposes they are designed to fulfil must be understood. Thus, a tax cannot be distinguished from a fine except by reference to the purpose for which it is imposed; but to recognize this is not to abandon an analytical study of the law for an evaluative one. The identification of something as an instrument for certain purposes leaves open the question whether it is good or bad, although such identification may indicate the standards by reference to which this question is to be answered.' HLA Hart 'Problems of Philosophy of Law' in Hart, *Essays in Jurisprudence and Philosophy* (n 41) 111.
[47] 'These notions [of causation and responsibility] have very deep roots in all our thinking and in common ideas of when it is just or fair to punish or exact compensation. Hence even lawyers who most wish the law cut loose from traditional ways of talking about causation concede that at certain points popular conceptions of justice demand attention to them' Hart and Honoré (n 12) 1. At a later point in the preface, Hart and Honoré give a rather vague hint as to why tort law should not run against common moral sensibilities and intuitions. Although here they use another term, 'moral principles', they note that 'there are obvious reasons why the law should not here conflict with moral principles' (ibid lxxviii). A plausible interpretation of this is that social acceptance and effectiveness of the law requires avoiding conflicts with moral principles. Under this interpretation, 'should' indicates a hypothetical imperative for a rational legislator to avoid conflicts between legal rules and widely held moral views.

view that law should be a 'mouthpiece of the moral sentiments of society'.[48] He argued that legal philosophical analysis should play a role in 'demystification' and 'enlightenment'. In the 'therapeutic' aspect, critical deliberation about ends and scientific knowledge about means (facts) should play a key role but it is unlikely to shock commonly held moral intuitions.[49]

Coming back to the relation of ordinary man's views and the law's assumptions, Hart and Honoré argue that in case of causation, there is not much difference between the two: the latter is based on and refines the former.[50]

What is then the task of legal theorists who, following Hart's hermeneutic or interpretative method,[51] want to understand a certain legal concept and the relations between ordinary usage and legal usage? The answer seems to be encapsulated in the methodological credo of *Causation*: 'to put a *rational and critical foundation* under the case law as it stands'.[52]

---

[48] Hart, *Punishment and Responsibility* (n 33) 170. At another point (ibid 131), he suggests that law should not simply give effect to but rather 'control resentment, however natural, in the interests of some deliberate forward-looking policy, much as we control our natural fears in the interest of forward-looking prudential aims'.

[49] '[F]or the community to think that there is something sacrosanct about its scale of moral evaluations may, as Mill long ago told us, stultify its advance. For these evaluations may plainly rest on inadequate understanding or appreciation of facts. Should we, for example, wish common estimates of the moral seriousness of bad driving on the roads to be taken as the prime determinant of punishments? Or should we hope that the law might, here and elsewhere, not passively reflect uninstructed opinion but actively help to shape moral sentiments to rational common ends?' ibid 171.

[50] '[C]ourts have continually claimed that it is the ordinary man's conception of cause that is used by the law and enters into various forms of legal responsibility. Though in legal contexts that conception has to be refined and modified in various ways, the clarification of the structure of ordinary causal statements was and is an indispensable first step towards understanding the use of causal notions in the law.' Hart and Honoré, (n 12) xxxiv. See also ibid 1: 'the assertion often made by the courts, especially in England, that it is the plain man's notions of causation (and not the philosopher's or the scientist's) with which the law is concerned, seems to us to be true'. This is not always the case. Hart notes elsewhere that 'the judgment of the reasonable man very often is a mere projected shadow, cast by the judge's own moral views or those of his own social class.' Hart, *Punishment and Responsibility* (n 33) 171.

[51] See Hart, *Essays* (n 42) 13–14, ND MacCormick *H.L.A. Hart*, 2nd edn, Jurists: Profiles in Legal Theory (Stanford, Stanford University Press, 2007) 46–55. The similarity between Hart's approach in *Causation* and *Punishment and Responsibility* and what later became Dworkin's own 'interpretive' approach was already noted by Dworkin in his review of *Punishment and Responsibility*, *cf* NLacey 'Analytical Jurisprudence versus Descriptive Sociology Revisited' (2006) 84 *Texas Law Review* 962.

[52] Hart and Honoré (n 12) xxxv. They also note (ibid) that courts are not always aware of applying the common sense causal criteria. Does it matter whether courts do this 'consciously' or 'unconsciously'? What would 'unconsciously' mean? It can either mean that courts are not aware that they adopt the ordinary man's views on causation, or that while courts consciously adopt the ordinary man's views, they are not concerned whether what they do is also philosophically sound. The former would mean that judges behave in this respect like ordinary people and legal doctrine is continuous with ordinary language. The second interpretation indicates that judges are less (self-)reflective about their practice than legal philosophers. In some cases this is also relatively unproblematic but, as mentioned by Hart in another context (see n 50), judges might enforce their own views or that of their social class which they believe to be widely held in society.

Hart and Honoré's theoretical strategy was to put a philosophical structure behind 'causation talk'[53] by distinguishing the central or paradigmatic case of legal causation from subsidiary uses of causal terms. They also suggested corrections to the practice by eliminating what they consider as 'obscuring metaphors'. Legal doctrine, case law, ordinary views and philosophical arguments add up to a theory which then should feed back to the practice of law itself, by providing 'a rational and critical foundation'.

In case of causation, the authors' critical morality largely supports doctrinal views, case law and ordinary people's views. As they argue, 'the limits to responsibility set by common sense causal principles are *appropriate* to the law'.[54] 'Appropriateness' is left undefined here but it does not seem too far-fetched to relate it to the Aristotelian notion of practical reasonableness. In sum, for the authors ordinary notions of causation more or less make sense and the relevant segment of the law is more or less doing what it should. In this respect, causation is a particular 'fortunate case'.

Although Hart always discusses the interrelations of epistemic and moral common sense with empirical facts and critical morality in specific contexts, his essays on criminal law supplement the picture gained from analysing the case of causation.[55] Inspired by these further remarks, for heuristic purposes one can roughly define 'fortunate cases' such as causation and contrast them with a typology of various 'unfortunate cases'.

In a (relatively) 'fortunate case' the ordinary views are reflected in legal doctrines and, in their main lines both are also philosophically (epistemologically, metaphysically, and normatively) sound. The most fortunate but most unlikely case is when, in addition to these, there is general agreement among theorists and competent participants of the practice that this congruence holds. This last condition is unlikely to hold in modern societies characterised by moral pluralism.[56]

In contrast to this, there are unfortunate cases of various kinds. The first occurs when the ordinary views are 'unenlightened', for example, they are restrictive of individual freedom to an unnecessary extent and the law caters these views.[57] Hart clearly indicates that his moral standpoint differs

---

[53] Lacey 'Analytical Jurisprudence versus Descriptive Sociology Revisited' (n 51) 966.
[54] Hart and Honoré (n 12) lxxix–lxxx.
[55] See Hart, *Punishment and Responsibility* (n 33) 2 ('orthodox, or common sense principles (untouched by modern psychological doubts)'); 3 (to assess whether the institution of criminal punishment 'has been eroded by, or needs to be adapted to, new beliefs about the human mind'); 32 ('scientists and plain men differ as to the relevance of some excusing conditions'); 97 (the remnants of 'the metaphysics of the Stone Age'); 170–72 (populist references to common moral sentiments); 179 (the ideology of science); 190 (dispute between doctors and lawyers).
[56] Ibid 171.
[57] These unfortunate cases are discussed in terms of Hart's critical morality. This does not imply that I subscribe to all of his substantive views. As examples of unenlightened views, he discusses the criminal protection of conventional sexual morality and the use of criminal law for pure retribution. See his works cited in n 42.

from the majority view as reflected in conventional morality and sanctioned by criminal law. His goal as legal theorist was to support legal reform by generating and participating in public moral debate. In short, this kind of unfortunate cases requires 'enlightenment'.

A second type of unfortunate case occurs when the ordinary people's views are diffuse, uninformed or based on false or unproven factual (empirical) assumptions. This lack of clarity is generally reflected in legal doctrine.[58] In this case, the therapy provided (or, rather, encouraged) by the legal theorist should be 'expertise' about facts.[59] As we will see below, this is the main channel of 'importing' empirical research into the law.

In a third type of 'unfortunate cases' Hart criticised legal doctrines or constructs for being expressed in metaphorical terms or based on obsolete or obscure philosophical arguments, in brief representing 'the metaphysics of the Stone Age'.[60] What is needed here is 'demystification'.

To be sure, 'fortunateness' is a matter of degree and unfortunate cases can be mixed. Two further types of unfortunateness will be discussed in the next sections. The point of this typology is to suggest that when legal theorists provide 'rational and critical foundations' for legal doctrinal constructs, the hermeneutic method of understanding is combined with enlightenment, expertise, and demystification. In Hart's specific case, this shows how he combined the 'progressive idealist' with 'a hard-headed empiricist'.[61]

C. Law as a Distinctive Form of Social Control

Criticisms of *Causation* showed that others did not see legal doctrines on causation as much of a 'fortunate case' as the authors. Hart and Honoré's theoretical enterprise indeed has a polemic aspect. Their main target is 'causal minimalism' which they see as a legal theory aiming at the wrong kind of 'demystification' or rather oversimplification. Causal minimalists hold that most problems that courts discuss in terms of causes, 'are rather issues of legal policy in disguise, better answered by asking whether, all things considered, the defendant should be held liable for the harm which

---

[58] An example is Hart's reference to the 'stock of knowledge' of medical science that would be needed, instead of relying on 'a judge or jury's speculation' about the effect of 'lesser mental abnormalities' on *mens rea*. Hart, *Punishment and Responsibility* (n 33) 262.

[59] An example of the relevance of expertise is the death penalty, see Hart, *Punishment and Responsibility* (n 33) 88. See also Hart, 'Analytical Jurisprudence in Mid-twentieth Century' (n 37) 973.

[60] Hart and Honoré (n 12) 2. An example in point is his analysis of the legal conception of 'intent' in English criminal law, see Hart, *Punishment and Responsibility* (n 33) 97–104, 142–45.

[61] J Gardner, '[Book review of] A Life of HLA Hart: The Nightmare and the Noble Dream' (2005) 121 *Law Quarterly Review* 329, 330.

ensued'.⁶² Hart and Honoré argue that to reduce causality to a matter of legal policy is a theoretical mistake that leads to less, rather than more conceptual clarity.⁶³ The reason why they reject causal minimalism is resistance to sceptical temptations to reduce causal issues to policy issues *tout court*. They argued that legal theorists should not blur distinctions and categories in ordinary use of language that can also be interpreted in a philosophically sound manner.

This methodological principle could be called Hart's 'Aristotelian perspective'⁶⁴ in legal philosophy: to describe the views of participants of the practice without blurring relevant distinctions in legal language. In a certain sense, over-simplification is a fourth type of unfortunate case when legal theorists do not take ordinary people's views and legal doctrine seriously.

The polemic against causal minimalists takes Hart and Honoré into discussing their deeper reasons for the rejection of causal minimalism and other versions of scepticism towards causation and legal responsibility and their views on the nature of responsibility and personhood. After causal minimalists who are sceptical about the legal vocabulary of causation they respond to 'causal maximalists' who want to eliminate the requirement of fault from responsibility; then to sceptics who question the justifiability of the entire institution of legal responsibility; finally to those real or imaginary discussants who doubt that the law is preferable to psychological manipulation.

One sceptical question to answer is whether it serves any social or ethical end to make people responsible for the harm they cause in this legal sense. As a response, it is not sufficient to refer to 'common moral sensibilities' and to the 'obvious reasons why the law should not here conflict with moral principles'.⁶⁵ For the sceptic asks further:

> Why should a legal system bent on minimizing the harm arising from human conduct by its regulation of that conduct pay attention to our ordinary concepts of action? Why should it attend to the way in which we identify separate actions, and so the limits of action?⁶⁶

---

⁶² Hart and Honoré (n 12) xxxiv–xxxv.

⁶³ 'In the interests of clarity ... causal issues should be kept separate from issues of legal policy' and the different policy goals themselves 'should be carefully distinguished from one another' (ibid xxxv–xxxvi). They do not deny that to determine the basis of legal responsibility and the role of causation in this is a matter of legal policy: 'The impact of legal policy is that the law, correctly interpreted, defines the conduct which must be shown to be causally relevant to the harm, and, by allocating the burden of proof, determines the result when convincing evidence is likely to be unobtainable.' (ibid xlii).

⁶⁴ *Cf* Gardner, Book review (n 61) 331.

⁶⁵ Hart and Honoré (n 12) xxviii.

⁶⁶ Ibid lxxix.

This question touches upon the very problem this chapter is concerned with: the epistemological and methodological character of doctrinal constructs, in this case, legal responsibility. Should they reflect ordinary people's views and common sense psychology? Do we need the construct at all?

Hart and Honoré give an answer that might be surprising at first: 'the answer to the sceptic must be thought mainly in the *virtues of the distinctive form which the legal control of conduct takes*'.[67] This argument, as it were, is a reference to the *nature of things*. The legal way of controlling human conduct seems to have, if not an essence, at least a distinctive form.[68]

Hart uses nature-of-things arguments at other points as well, most famously when he discusses the 'core of good sense in the doctrine of natural law' theories.[69] In his 'minimal content of natural law' argument, the 'necessary' content of the law is required not by logic but the human predicament, that is, empirical facts about general features of human life. These features are necessary 'in our world', as we know it. Similarly, in our world, we individuate actions and think of human persons as responsible for their doings, at least in central cases.[70]

Hart's idea of the 'minimal content of natural law' is different from Fuller's 'inner morality of law', both substantively and methodologically but shows close parallels with Fuller's remarks on 'the view of man implicit in legal morality'.[71] Fuller claims:

> To embark on the enterprise of subjecting human conduct to the governance of rules involves of necessity a commitment to the view of man that is, or can become, a responsible agent, capable of understanding and following rules, and answerable for his defaults.[72]

---

[67] Ibid (emphasis added).

[68] This argument is reminiscent of Fuller's analysis in *The Morality of Law* where he explicitly stated that the inner morality of law is an expression of the *nature* of the institutions of legislation and adjudication, in an Aristotelian teleological sense, namely governance of human conduct by general rules. The eight requirements of law's inner morality follow from the nature of the law in the sense of its distinctive form. See LL Fuller, *The Morality of Law*, 2nd edn (New Haven, Yale University Press, 1969).

[69] HLA Hart, *The Concept of Law*, 2nd edn (Oxford, Clarendon Press, 1994) 199. *Cf* Hart, *Essays* (n 42), 113: 'Arguments along these lines may be viewed as a modest empirical counterpart to the more ambitious teleological doctrine of natural law'.

[70] We could indeed imagine that instead of being moderately selfish, people were angels; or that instead of moderate scarcity, they would enjoy abundance in all resources necessary for human needs (or at least for peaceful survival); or that instead of being vulnerable to physical violence, humans 'were clad perhaps like giant crabs with an impenetrable carapace' that made one person's injuring another more difficult, see Hart, *Essays* (n 42) 80. Similarly, a world with the institution of legal responsibility is not logically necessary either: we could imagine a different world without it.

[71] Fuller, *The Morality of Law* (n 68) 162–67.

[72] Ibid 162. He adds that 'the whole body of the law is permeated by two recurring standards of decision: fault and intent'. (ibid 167).

Hart makes it clear that the features of human nature he refers to are so basic that they could even be called 'natural' necessity. The logical possibility of their change is not a real prospect for any visible future: it rather belongs to 'science fiction'.[73] Of course, a number of scientific and technological achievements that in Hart's lifetime seemed to belong to 'science fiction' turned out to be real and became part of human practice.

This raises questions about how much the law's assumptions are related to what is technologically possible. Indeed, towards the end of the preface, Hart and Honoré make an anti-utopian reference:

> It is thinkable that legal control of conduct might take the form of Brave New World conditioning, so that people were never tempted to disobey the law, or of preventive or incapacitating measures, so that people were unable to disobey. In contrast with such forms of control the law of crime and tort, quite apart from sanctions, makes its primary appeal to individuals as intelligent beings who are assumed to have the capacity to control their conduct, and invites them to do so. It defers coercion and punitive measures until it is shown that this primary appeal has broken down, viz. until a crime has been committed or some harm has been done. The latter is the price to be paid for a form of control that invites the subject's obedience and so, by preserving the possibility of disobeying, maximizes freedom within the framework of coercive sanctions.[74]

While this passage confirms Hart's commitment to the value of individual freedom,[75] the reference to the Brave New World shows yet another parallel with *The Morality of Law*. After Rex I's disastrous experience (or experimentation) with guiding human behaviour through legal rules, Rex II turned from law and legal experts to different mechanisms of governance. Fuller cryptically hints here at an alternative world without rules, that is, without law:

> The first act of his successor, Rex II, was to announce that he was taking the powers of government away from the lawyers and placing them in the hands of psychiatrists and experts in public relations. This way, he explained, people could be more happy without rules.[76]

---

[73] Hart, *Essays* (n 42) 80.
[74] Hart and Honoré (n 12) lxxix.
[75] Hart, *Punishment and Responsibility* (n 33) 23: 'Criminal punishment as an attempt to secure desired behaviour differs from the manipulative techniques of the Brave New World (conditioning, propaganda, etc) or the simple incapacitation of those with anti-social tendencies, by taking a risk. It defers action till harm has been done; its primary operation consists simply in announcing certain standards of behaviour and attaching penalties for deviation, making it less eligible, and then leaving individuals to choose.'
[76] Fuller (n 68) 38.

D. Law, Personhood and Naturalism

At the very end of the preface, Hart and Honoré sketch an alternative response to the sceptic:

> [T]he idea that individuals are primarily responsible for the harm which their actions are sufficient to produce without the intervention of others or of extraordinary natural events is important, not merely to law and morality, but to the preservation of something else of great moment in human life. This is the individual's sense of himself as a separate person whose character is manifested in such actions. Individuals come to understand themselves as distinct persons, to whatever extent they do, and to acquire a sense of self-respect largely by reflection on those changes in the world about them which their actions are sufficient to bring about without the intervention of others and which are therefore attributable to them separately. This sense of *respect for ourselves and others as distinct persons* would be much weakened, if not dissolved, if we could not think of ourselves as separate authors of the changes we make in the world.[77]

In a different context, Hart made a similar argument:

> Human society is a society of persons; and persons do not view themselves or each other merely as so many bodies moving in ways which are sometimes harmful and have to be prevented or altered. Instead persons interpret each other's movements as manifestations of intentions and choices, and these subjective factors are often more important to their social relations than the movements by which they are manifested or their effects. ... This is how human nature in human society actually is and as yet we have no power to alter it. The bearing of this fundamental fact on the law is this. If ... it is important for the law to reflect common judgments of morality, it is surely even more important that it should in general reflect in its judgments on human conduct distinctions which not only underlie morality, but pervade the whole of our social life. This it would fail to do if it treated men merely as alterable, predictable, curable, or manipulable things.[78]

In sum, the law is seen here as being based on the common sense idea of personal responsibility, which assumes that there are persons who consider themselves and each other as authors of their doings and care about each other's intentions and faults in their interactions. Hart also claims that these 'fundamental facts' about human personhood and society should be taken into account in the law. But what kind of 'should' exactly is this? Where does the law end? How much cure, manipulation, conditioning and propaganda are allowed?

In one sense, this question concerns a conceptual problem and the criteria that would disqualify these techniques of 'governance' or social control from the semantic field of law. But the question can also be understood as asking for a point where the frequency of legislative or administrative uses

---

[77] Hart and Honoré (n 12) lxxx–lxxxi (emphasis added).
[78] Hart, *Punishment and Responsibility* (n 33) 182–83.

of these practices would turn a legal system into non-law in a substantive sense, even if the rules that authorise these governance techniques are formally valid. There are other normative practices or governance mechanisms distinct from the central case of law. In some cases, these can achieve certain ends better than the law. Just as sometimes sending people to a psychiatrist or hiring experts in public relations is the reasonable course of action, in some cases fault-based liability is too costly for society and instead technical specifications or physical barriers are more reasonable to use in order to shape the action space of individuals within which they can decide on their conduct.

The few longer quotes above elaborated the idea that the law is (or should be) closely linked to 'our world', that is, the phenomenological world, including not only 'our moral intuitions' but deep-rooted factual beliefs. Now, here seems to lurk a fifth type of unfortunate case, probably the most difficult one. If epistemic and moral common sense, legal doctrine and powerful moral arguments are on one side, empirical science and naturalised epistemology on the other, is it obvious that the legal theorist should side with the former?

This unfortunate case is different from the second one where factual mistakes and false beliefs about issues of 'local importance' can be corrected by expertise. This case is about a potential conflict between generally held fundamental ideas about human nature on the one hand and a 'naturalistic' world view on the other. From a 'naturalistic' perspective, the phenomenological world view according to which people are responsible agents, capable of following rules, and conceive of themselves as authors of their doings, is an illusion.[79] This allows for the possibility that what science says about how things 'really are' on the one hand, and what the law says or assumes about our phenomenological world on the other, become fundamentally distinct, at least on certain points.

Can the law uphold its assumptions about personhood and responsibility, embedded in fundamental legal doctrines even if, to borrow Kelsen's phrase, they cannot stand firm 'before the tribunal of science'?[80] It seems that the answer to this question depends, among other things, on the epistemic character of these assumptions. To the extent that they are normative themselves, then their counterfactual character is both explained and vindicated. This suggests an epistemic position where legal theory does not 'take sides' between the 'naturalistic' and 'phenomenological' perspectives but simply 'observes' the discontinuity between these two and draws conclusions from

---

[79] J Greene and J Cohen 'For the Law, Neuroscience Changes Nothing and Everything' (2004) 359 *Philosophical Transactions of the Royal Society Series B*, 1775–85.
[80] H Kelsen 'The Natural-Law Doctrine before the Tribunal of Science' (1949) 2 *Western Political Quarterly* 481–513.

this discontinuity for legal design and legal practice. This position could probably be called a 'constructivist' epistemology of law.[81]

This 'constructivist' perspective can be developed in an instrumental direction as well. Hart argued convincingly that law is an artefact, a social phenomenon formed by the group whose law it is,[82] in short, a means.[83] From such an instrumental perspective, law's assumptions about human nature can, and in some sense should be, counter-factual and the 'objectivity' of these assumptions will not be a primary concern. In the next section I discuss briefly the consequences of this perspective for legal design and the 'import' of empirical research into the law.

III. THE LAW'S ASSUMPTIONS, EMPIRICAL RESEARCH, AND LEGAL DESIGN

The general question to be discussed in this section is that if law is seen from this instrumental perspective, that is, in light of certain moral values and prudential goals that the legal system should (allow its subjects to) realise, how should legal design take empirical research on human behaviour into account. In other words, what is the role of normative ideas and ideals and scientific knowledge in law within this instrumental perspective? What happens if legal doctrines and the implicit assumptions behind them are confronted with empirical research on human behaviour?

For instance, if we want to reform laws on the learning-disabled and their legal capacity, a lot of value-laden questions about autonomy arise. But if we want to have a sound theory of legal capacity, we also need some criterion or set of criteria to choose: should it be the best available theory? The one best accepted by the public? By experts? The one easiest to administer? The one that fits most easily in the doctrinal system of law? We come to see that we need criteria to choose between imperfectly compatible or partly incomparable theories. It seems that in legal design all 'unfortunate cases' discussed above resurface in some form. In fact, in a 'fortunate case' there does not seem to be scope for legal reform.

To the extent that the law is subject to deliberate change its assumptions can also be changed. If we want to change or criticise a law or, more generally, the law (or 'modern', 'bourgeois' etc law), a possible line of argument is to show or suggest that it is based on questionable, out-dated or simply wrong theories and assumptions. Indeed, a typical reason for legal reforms is that the legislator's perceptions or ideas about the world change and from this

---

[81] *Cf* Teubner (n 20).
[82] *Cf* MacCormick, *HLA Hart* (n 51) 49–50.
[83] L Green, 'Law as a Means' in P Cane (ed), *The Hart-Fuller Debate in the Twenty-First Century* (Oxford, Hart Publishing, 2010) 169–88.

flows a supposed need for legal change in light of changed circumstances or new facts. Intuitively, one also expects domain-specific differences in how closely these assumptions follow technological changes and how quickly they respond to development in empirical research.

The argument that the legal world view should be challenged in light of empirical data is based on the view of law as a specific social technology.[84] In this instrumental (or regulatory or pragmatic) view, the reason why legal policy should be informed by empirical research on human behaviour is straightforward: rational (legal) policy design requires reliable predictions about the incentive effects of legal rules. It is important to see, however, that even if we assume an instrumental perspective, it does not follow that legal scholarship unavoidably becomes a simple instrument of translating scientific insights into legal rules and doctrines. Empirical research can tell 'how' certain regulatory goals are most effectively achieved but it cannot tell what the goals should be. For instance, empirical research can tell what is impossible to achieve through law. In this sense, empirical research points at the limits of instrumental use of the law for promoting policy goals. It can also assist in designing reasonable proxies.[85] An example for more or less reasonable proxies is the 'compartmentalisation' of contract law. In a number of jurisdictions contract law is becoming (the first time, or again) compartmentalised into business-to-business, business-to-consumer, and consumer-to-consumer regimes. This is often justified by the different cognitive and motivational characteristics and risk attitudes of consumers and professional businesses.

The instrumental view of law raises two general questions. First, to what extent is it *possible* to design legal regulation based on empirical research? Second, to the extent this is possible, is it always *desirable* to do so?

As for the first question, as we know more and more about how people behave, including how they respond to regulation, it seems increasingly relevant whether the implicit model of human behaviour behind the law is compatible with these insights. What makes the issue more complex is that at present these empirical findings cannot be formulated in such a general manner that could be meaningfully contrasted with the law's assumptions. Not only is the implicit legal model fragmented but the findings of empirical sciences also tend to be particularised. They proved at most 'regional'

---

[84] H Albert, 'Law as an Instrument of Rational Practice' in T Daintith and G Teubner (eds), *Contract and Organization: Legal Analysis in the Light of Economic and Social Theory* (Berlin, Walter de Gruyter, 1986) 25–51; H Albert, *Rechtswissenschaft als Realwissenschaft: Das Recht als soziale Tatsache und die Aufgabe der Jurisprudenz* (Baden-Baden, Nomos, 1993).

[85] Proxies, in general, raise questions about rule-based decision-making. See F Schauer, *Playing by the Rules. A Philosophical Examination of Rule-Based Decision-Making in Law and in Life* (Oxford, Clarendon Press, 1991).

empirical theories with a relatively low level of abstraction. Any instrumental approach should also have a rather narrow focus.

Another problem is theoretical indeterminacy. Simply put, as theories are always revisable, policymakers and experts do not and cannot know before deciding on policy questions what the right theory is. There are various pragmatic ways out of this: relying on the overlapping consensus among scientists; using a rule of thumb to pick one theory; or simply conducting more empirical (case, event) studies without an underlying theory.

Finally, there are also more practical or secondary considerations that limit the usefulness of empirical research in legal design. These are related to the institutional constraints in both legislation and administration (regulatory impact assessment) and adjudication (consequence-based judicial reasoning): time constraints in political and legal procedures, limited expertise, and capture of public offices by private interests. These limits probably would not matter in an ideal world without transaction costs but still need to be taken into account in a second-best world.

As to the second question, is it desirable that legal rules are based on 'objective' or 'true' assumptions about human behaviour, to the extent possible? Intuitively, the answer seems negative. For instance, in the context of consumer law, it can be argued that regulation should not 'map' and thereby stabilise behavioural shortcomings and cognitive biases of consumers. Rather, consumer law should 'overshoot' with its assumptions about the consumers' capacity for rational choice in order to let them learn from their mistakes and thereby develop. Such dynamic considerations seem to suggest overestimating consumers' autonomy compared to how they actually behave. At closer look, however, it turns out that even in this instance a rational policymaker would need first to 'get the facts right', before deciding whether there are reasons to under or overestimate with its assumptions about the rationality and the motivational attitudes of individuals.

IV. CONCLUSIONS

This chapter analysed the epistemic and methodological character of the law's assumptions from two aspects. First, I discussed in what sense these assumptions can or should be objective. Inspired by Herbert Hart's views on legal epistemology in *Causation in the Law* and *Punishment and Responsibility*, I argued that the presuppositions behind the law in general and behind specific legal doctrines show domain-specific and system-specific combinations of ordinary people's views, common sense moral intuitions, philosophical theories of earlier ages and scientific knowledge. If the Hartian idea of the task of the legal philosopher, that is, to provide 'rational and critical foundation' for legal doctrines is taken seriously then this does not only include an epistemic ideal of objectivity to be attained through conceptual clarification. It also involves the legal theorist into enlightenment about empirical facts, demystification of metaphysical obscurities and substantive moral argumentation in terms of human nature and practical reasonableness.

The second aspect of the analysis concerned how the growing body of empirical knowledge on human decision-making and judgement can be integrated into legal policy and legal doctrines. I showed the main reasons for and challenges to including insights from behavioural and social sciences in legal regulatory design by pointing at the limits set by institutional, systemic and normative features of the law to this inclusion.

V. (Legal) Cultures

10

Kaleidoscopic Cultural Views and Legal Theory—Dethroning the Objectivity?

JAAKKO HUSA

> first call of a theory of law is that it should fit the facts[1]
>
> Oliver Wendell Holmes
>
> demand to admit only those theories which will follow from facts leaves us without any theory[2]
>
> Paul Feyerabend

I. INTRODUCTION

IT SEEMS POSSIBLE to claim that every scientific discipline or scholarly defined area of knowledge has a certain kind of mental base upon which it is based. Scholars are supposed to use *rational* thinking and arguments in their line of work. But, it has been argued that scientific rationalism or the general Western appeal to reason is actually empty.[3] This argument may stretch too far but undoubtedly one may hold that the very idea of science is closely connected to the idea of *objective research*, which leads to genuine knowledge. And yet, there is no single commonly agreed definition of knowledge and there are numerous theories to explain what knowledge actually is.[4]

When it comes to Western academic legal theory it seems there is an underlying (rational) assumption, which appears to be that of *universality*

---

[1] OW Holmes, *The Common Law* (Boston, Little Brown and Co, 1881) 211.
[2] P Feyerabend, *Against Method*, 3rd edn (London, Verson, 1996) 50.
[3] See P Feyerabend, *Farewell to Reason* (London, Verso, 1987) in which it is argued that science is one tradition among many and there is no genuine 'objectivity' free of cultures.
[4] See for more detailed discussion, eg K Lehrer, *Theory of Knowledge* (London, Routledge, 1990).

as opposed to relativism. Take any 'grand legal theory' such as HLA Hart's or Hans Kelsen's and it soon becomes quite clear that these theories seek to state something universal/general about the nature of law, rather than merely deal with the specific characteristics of a given legal system. Jaap Hage formulates this basic idea, on the basis of Hart's theory, by saying that according to this thinking: 'it is possible to say something sensible about the law in general, and not only about concrete legal systems'.[5]

The very concept of *iurisprudentia* (or 'legal theory' or 'legal philosophy') contains unspecified interest in things like the concept of law, the structure of legal system and the content of general legal concepts (for example, obligation, contract and so on). Thus, legal theory has been built upon meta-ideas of objectivity, which may assume strong views as Kelsen's *Reine Rechtslehre* or a modest view like Hage in his contribution to this book. Whereas Kelsen's idea was unhesitant about the very urge to purge all subjective elements from legal science, Hage's objectivity is different for it advocates objectivity (or 'truth') 'by convention' only.[6] However, Hage's thesis concerning modest objectivity differs clearly from the classical ambitions of legal theory of the twentieth century that is the grand theories of law crafted in the twentieth century are constructed on an idea of objectivity, thus, claiming universality at least implicitly.

A. Objectivity of Legal Theory and Primary Epistemology

Openly or clandestinely alleged objectivity of legal theory leans on *Anschauungen,* which assumes that legal theorist can be free of personal feelings or prejudices concerning theoretical analysis of law. This kind of strong objectivity inherently holds that legal theory (in substantive sense) should and can be unbiased and is supposedly based only on rational arguments or undisputed facts.[7] But, when one reads any of the grand legal theories it soon becomes clear that theoreticians are in fact not completely free from implicit prejudices or at least, certain covert culturally conditioned views about law are tenaciously present. Dworkin's ideas about law carry certain American conceptions (how legal cases ought to be decided); Kelsen held certain German (in cultural sense) ideas about law's nature (formal deductions from the valid rules); whereas Ross had many impulses from Nordic legal thinking (Scandinavian legal realism underlining social

---

[5] Hage ch 2 in this volume.

[6] Hage reminds also that as conventions they are not really 'true' or 'false'. See also M Van Hoecke, *Law as Communication* (Oxford, Hart Publishing, 2002) 200–201 (speaking of 'objective' truth within a *certain* community only).

[7] This, too, has been challenged by relativist Feyerabend who argued that there is cultural dependency between theory and the culture which the theory in question is part of; see Feyerabend, *Farewell to Reason* (n 3) 83–89.

utility); and Alexy's theory has been built largely on the praxis of German *Bundesverfassungsgericht* and so on.

Put differently, it seems very difficult to be truly free of the subconscious effect of one's own legal culture or at least those legal cultures best known to the theoretician: some shreds of prejudices and bias seems to be so resilient that they cannot be eradicated from the way one does legal theory. So, the effect of one's 'primary epistemology of law' does seem to survive even the eviction-efforts of the most dedicated legal theoreticians: cultural immersion in one's own law is rooted too deep to be ignored.

Primary epistemology of law refers to inbuilt and subconscious epistemic foundation of law and everything that is deemed legal. This kind of understanding is normally based on one mother-system, which is one's own law. The effects of this kind primary epistemology concern the manner one regards as a proper theorising about law. With this, we are dealing with an implicit mono-epistemology, which makes legal theoreticians regard their own system as 'normal' and other systems as 'not-normal' or, at least, something which is 'less-normal'.[8] Importantly, this is subconscious in nature; it has not to do with things like legal colonisation or other politically motivated ways to theorise about law.[9] As a result, a lack of genuine objectivity must be read in this chapter as unconscious injection of one's own primary epistemology into legal theory which is, notwithstanding, sought to be constructed honestly and to be as general and objective as possible.[10]

This paper challenges the possibility of universally neutral legal theory (in the strong sense) and it is done in the light of legal-cultural differences known from comparative study of law. The sketched argument here is not targeted toward any legal theory in a substantial sense but rather toward the meta-theoretical manner in which legal theories are normally constructed, that is on the foundation of the idea of generality and, thus, a more profound idea of objectivity. It will be argued that global legal pluralism should have distinct effect on *how to do* legal theory. This is done through the help of metaphorical device of kaleidoscope.[11]

---

[8] See for more details, J Husa, 'Turning the Curriculum Upside Down: Comparative Law as an Educational Tool for Constructing Pluralistic Legal Mind' (2009) 10 *German Law Journal* 913–28 (available at www.germanlawjournal.com/index.php?pageID=11&artID=1129).

[9] See for more detailed discussion, D Kennedy, 'The Methods and Politics of Comparative Law' in P Legrand and R Munday (eds), *Comparative Legal Studies* (Cambridge, Cambridge University Press, 2003) 345–434.

[10] Reasons for this cultural-specivity are not difficult to conceive: one's own law is *also* a theoretical perspective which contains concepts and categories used by legislators, jurists and legal scholars as well, *cf* P Westerman, 'Open or Autonomous? The Debate on Legal Methodology as a Reflection of the Debate on Law' in M Van Hoecke (ed), *Methodologies of Legal Research* (Oxford, Hart Publishing, 2011) 87–110, 90.

[11] This is very much the same approach as adopted by Pauline Westerman in this book when she uses the house metaphor (among other entertaining metaphors) (ch 3 in this volume).

II. KALEIDOSCOPE OF LAW AND LEGAL CULTURES

In comparative study of law it has almost always been understood that there are both differences and similarities between legal systems or, more broadly, between legal cultures. This view underlines the fact that even the black-letter standardisation or harmonisation is not going to bring about genuine harmonisation concerning intrinsic internal meanings of law.[12] In other words, even when legal systems are quite similar on paper there may be great differences in the day-to-day legal realities as has been the case with the Civil Code in Switzerland and its practically copied counterpart in Turkey.[13] Or, one can transplant literally a legal norm or legal institution from one system to another but the actual outcomes may still be completely different because of the surrounding legal cultures.[14]

It is quite likely that none of this comes as a true surprise for a legal theoretician and yet it is less acknowledged by them than it is by legal comparatists and sociologists. Altogether, it would seem futile to argue that the crafters of grand legal theories would have been ignorant of differences.[15] Yet, it seems that the plurality-lesson learned from the comparative study of law has had an insufficient effect on the manner in which legal theories have been constructed. These continue to claim their genuinely general or truly objective nature.[16] One possible way to analyse and understand how these legal-cultural differences could be taken into account is by relying on the metaphor of kaleidoscope.

A. Kaleidoscopic View of Law?

The idea of looking at the law and at different theoretical ways to conceive it as a kaleidoscope is a little used legal theoretical metaphor, but it is not completely unknown either.[17] But, what does it mean when one speaks of a

---

[12] On this argument, see, eg R Cotterrell, 'Is It so Bad to be Different? in E Örücü and D Nelken (eds), *Comparative Law—A Handbook* (Oxford, Hart Publishing, 2007) 133–54, 138–42.

[13] See for more details, eg YM Atamer, 'Rezeption und Weiterentwicklung des schweizerischen Zivilgesetzbuches in der Türkei' (2008) 72 *Rabels Zeitschrift für ausländisches und internationales Privatrecht*, 723–54.

[14] A well-known example is that of the '*Treu und Glauben*' clause in English common law, see G Teubner, 'Legal Irritants: Good Faith in British Law or How Unifying Law Ends Up in New Differences' (1998) 61 *Modern Law Review* 11–32.

[15] See, eg H Kelsen, *Reine Rechtslehre*, 2nd edn, 1960, reprint (Vienna, Verlag Franz Deuticke, 1967) 259–60 (discussing the nature of common law as a form of *Gewohnheitsrecht*).

[16] In other words, Western legal theories have been (knowingly) concentrating mainly on domestic law of modern nation states. cf Van Hoecke, *Law as Communication* (n 6) 1–2.

[17] This author is aware of only one example: H Tolonen, 'Oikeus ja sen tulkinnat' (Law and Its Interpretations) in Juha Häyhä (ed), *Minun metodini* (My Method), (Helsinki, WSLT, 1997) 279–97.

kaleidoscope of law in metaphoric sense? To answer this question one must first know what kaleidoscope actually is.

In a technical sense, a kaleidoscope is a device with a circle of mirrors containing loose, coloured objects and bits of glass, through which one looks. In practice, when looking into one end, light enters the other end and creates a colourful pattern due to the reflections of the mirrors. The word 'kaleidoscope' itself comes from a combination of ancient Greek words. The first word is καλός which normally means beautiful or good. The second word is είδος which means form or thing. And the third word is a verb σκοπέω which means to look around or to observe. Putting these three words together gives 'a tool for observation of good things/forms' (καλειδοσκόπιο). But, when using the concept of a kaleidoscope in a metaphorical sense, its normal usage is different. I may allude to things like a series of changing phases or events, or to the expression of a kaleidoscope of illusions. Now, in the context of this text we may speak of *a kaleidoscope of law*. Law, in this context, means law in a broad general sense, not law in relation to any specific legal system or other defined bodies of rules, domestic, international or supranational.

The core idea of this metaphor is to conceive that there is no single 'right' view of law, that is there is nothing in the law/legal sphere which would exclude cultural variety. Concurrently, we have different forms of laws such as indigenous laws, religious laws, professional laws, Western laws, African laws and so on. So, to use the idea of a kaleidoscope means to embrace the global legal pluralism instead of trying to conceive law from one culturally fixed angle.[18] However, it is important to stress that this metaphoric device does not imply surrendering to full relativism: kaleidoscope creates different images of law but it is still limiting other ways of grasping law even while it allows a certain number of variations.

When it comes to this metaphor and the accompanying arguments, they are not unheard of, they have taken other kinds of forms in the work of others. For example, Werner Menski has tried to mould legal theory for the purposes of plurality-focused understanding of law, thus, challenging Western legal theories which claim universal validity even while representing only a small portion of global humanity.[19] Also William Twining's work has struggled to inject comparative law learning experience into Western legal theory and, thus, challenging some of the very basic Western

---

[18] The present situation is described by Esin Örücü: 'today, "law", spans the range of positive law and then moves to non-state law, rules, custom and tradition', in 'Developing Comparative Law' in E Örücü and D Nelken (eds), *Comparative Law—A Handbook* (Oxford, Hart Publishing, 2007) 43–65, 60.
[19] See W Menski, *Comparative Law in a Global Context: The Legal Systems of Asia and Africa* (Cambridge, Cambridge University Press, 2006).

assumptions about law in general.[20] In general, both of them underline the importance of placing law in its own cultural context which produces a great challenge to the idea of universal and objective legal theory by adopting broad theoretical conception of law. However, these approaches do not necessarily lead to relativism; rather they seem to embrace law as a truly universal phenomenon which takes different culture-specific manifestations.[21] Consequently, despite commonalities, there is also going to be diversity.[22]

B. Legal Cultures—Challenge to Universalism

Recently, comparative study of law has increasingly used the concept of legal culture. To generalise: today the stress has moved from legal system to 'legal culture'. The use of this concept is widespread especially among comparatists.[23] However, there is no clear-cut definition of what it actually means and, in fact, it seems that not all comparatists use it in any specifically coherent manner.[24] Even so, in general we may characterise legal culture as a kind of 'extra-plus' of narrowly understood law. It brings forth the context of written rules, precedents and legal doctrines. The basic tenor while using this concept seems to be that when studying legal systems comparatively one needs much more than formal legal rules and institutions. The quintessential idea is that there is more to law than only legal rules or legal institutions and that these things should be taken into account. Of relevance are, for instance, underlying values, shared beliefs, common ways of thinking and interests of lawyers, lawmakers as well as private citizens.[25] In short, legal culture requires placing law in a societal and historical context and,

---

[20] See W Twining, *General Jurisprudence: Understanding Law from a Global Perspective* (Cambridge, Cambridge University Press, 2009).

[21] *Cf* Menski, *Comparative Law* (n 19) 499.

[22] This point here concerns the nature and content of legal cultures and it should be kept separate from the debate concerning the question about whether similarities or differences should be studied.

[23] HP Glenn even says grudgingly that: 'Everyone talks about culture these days, though no-one knows what it really is', HP Glenn, 'Comparing' in E Örücü and D Nelken (eds), *Comparative Law—A Handbook*, (Oxford, Hart Publishing, 2007) 91–1080, 97.

[24] See for more detailed discussion, D Nelken, 'Using the Concept of Legal Culture' (2004) 29 *Australian Journal of Legal Philosophy* 1–28 ('But the concept of legal culture is certainly not a simple one. Not only is it used in a variety of ways, some authors have even suggested that it is so misleading that it should be abandoned', 2). See also Van Hoecke (n 6) 57–58.

[25] *Cf* R Cotterrell, 'Comparative Law and Legal Culture', in M Reimann and R Zimmermann (eds), *Oxford Handbook of Comparative Law* (Oxford, Oxford University Press, 2006) 709–37, 710–11.

thus, abandoning the narrow point of view of classical jurist: laws are conceived in various epistemic contexts acknowledging the plurality of law.[26]

When considering studies in which the notion of legal culture is applied, these typically set out to explore empirical variation in the manner law is conceived and constructed and to map the existence of different *concepts* of law. A crucial auxiliary idea is to celebrate cultural differences and to reject the idea of similarity between different legal systems/cultures. Importantly, if one looks at grand legal theories something sticks out: the mainstream legal theory seems surprisingly unable to recognise pluralism and differences between legal cultures. Grand legal theories seek unity and, thus, seem insensitive to recognise the reality of global law. Or as Roger Cotterrell puts it: 'Traditionally mainstream legal theory has set out to demonstrate unity or system in legal doctrine and legal thought, and to portray legal regimes as relatively comprehensive, unified, and integrated normative structures.'[27] This tendency is very distinct in theories of Hart and Kelsen.

But, today's comparative study of law wishes to celebrate and to openly recognise legal-cultural differences, which is the opposite aim to that of demonstrating unity in law. Moreover, there seems to be a clear contradiction here: legal theory wishes to establish *the* concept of law and to seek unity or even to establish universal truths about the nature of law, whereas legal culture-oriented study of law seeks to demonstrate and underline the plurality of the concepts of law and the multiplicity of contexts of law.[28] And yet, this contradiction is all but clear.

But, what does this mean when theorising about law? Roughly we may say that legal theory is theory of law's origin, use, and study.[29] Or in other words, legal theory deals with the ontology, epistemology and methodology of law. Is this really so different from comparative study of law? Not necessarily, because comparative law means the study of differences and similarities between the laws of different systems/cultures. Furthermore, it is crucial to grasp that the underlying question is, nevertheless, the same: both of these

---

[26] This means that law and legal systems are 'embedded in larger framework of social structure and culture that constitute and reveal the place of law in society', D Nelken, 'Legal Culture' in J Smits (ed), *Elgar Encyclopedia of Comparative Law* (Cheltenham/Northampton, Edward Elgar, 2006) 372–81, 375.

[27] Cotterrell, 'Comparative Law' (n 25) 727.

[28] However, if one looks at how legal theory (jurisprudentia) has been constructed in England, the Nordic countries and Germany from the 19th century, one thing becomes clear: theories were crafted for national doctrinal or practical purposes. See, eg chapters by M Lobban ('Theory and Practice in the Development of the Nineteenth Century Common Law', 131–56), M Lyles ('Tradition, Conviction or Necessity?' 159–77), and J Schröder ('Das Verhältnis von Rechtswissenschaft ...', 313–37) in C Peterson (ed), *Rechtswissenschaft als juristische Doktrin* (Stockholm, The Olin Foundation for Legal History, 2011).

[29] It should be noted that this way to define legal theory (or 'general legal science') is derived from Aulis Aarnio, see, eg A Aarnio's *Philosophical Perspectives in Jurisprudence* (Helsinki, Acta Philosophica Fennica, 1983).

disciplines need to give some kind of answer to the question *what is law*.[30] Comparative law and legal theory both need some kind of definition of what it is that they are interested in.[31] This definition may be explicit or implicit. Typically, comparatists do this implicitly whereas most of the legal theoreticians do it explicitly (that is/are being rational about law) because it is part of what they are supposed to do.

What is the problem here? If comparatists of today are able to take into account the inherent pluralism, then why it is that legal theory does not seem to survive that obstacle with such ease? In order to give at least some tentative answer to this question, we need to look at why the unity and conceptual coherence of legal theories meet problems when encountering legal pluralism.

III. THREE ARCHETYPES OF HOW TO DO LEGAL THEORY—AND WHY THEY STUMBLE

From the point of view of mainstream Western legal theory it is possible to generalise and separate three basic theoretical approaches to law. These archetypes of legal theory include three kinds of ingredients which are: (1) values (religion, ethics, morality); (2) state-centred rules (legislation, precedents); and (3) empirical reality (socio-legal approaches).[32] From this theoretical triangle, three ways to define law seem to emerge: three different cultural (legal theory) images of law which are presented here briefly.[33]

Natural image of law. In a broad sense, we may describe natural law theories as such theoretical constructions that consist a body of normative rules which are considered as derived from non-positive (non man-made) source. Sources of these rules lie in, for example, nature, reason or religion. Moreover, these rules are regarded as normative as to their character so that they are at least ethically binding in all human societies. Clearly the idea of universalism and, thus, underlying objectivity (that is lacking partiality) are quintessential parts of natural law theories. Now, without going deeper into details we may argue that ancient (whether it be Greek or Roman) so-called rational and even more modern branches of natural law thinking consider it important that there are meaningful connections between, say, cosmic order of the world, morality or religion and legal sphere. The three

---

[30] Or, as Van Hoecke says: 'A definition of law is in fact nothing else than the core of a theory of law' *Law as Communication* (n 6) 6.

[31] See for more detailed discussion J Husa, 'Überlegungen zu einer Theorie der Rechtsvergleichung als Rechtsphilosophie' (2009) 40 *Rechtstheorie* 473–92.

[32] *Cf* Menski (n 19) Part I (constructing his own 'legal theory of pluralism' by combining all three elements of this theoretical triangle).

[33] Yet, these are, of course, not separate from others: one can very likely find all of those elements from virtually any legal system.

first mentioned are the ultimate sources of non-positive law from which one may derive natural law that is moral principles which are rules.

Typically, these kinds of rules are conceived as timeless, sometimes of divine origin, existing 'naturally'. Whereas ancient and religious natural law theories are either dead or regarded largely as not supported. In fact, what we have today are different versions of the so-called rational natural law theories. A good example of how the very concept of 'natural law' is to be understood in a 'rational' sense comes from Thomas Hobbes who said that this kind of law is 'a precept, or generall Rule, found out by Reason'.[34] But, if we take into account the pluralism of law and give epistemic weight to it, then it is empirically clear that the 'natural image of law' is actually a culture-specific reflection and they cannot claim (truly) universal validity or objectivity: they can be fully legitimate and justified in one or even many communities but not necessarily in all.[35] The problem with these is always the same: no religion, no certain form of rationality or morality can ever be truly universal. This is not difficult to grasp: compare some of the basic ideas of Islamic law and Western law (for example, gender equality) or the Western idea of human rights and Chinese conception of the actual scope and nature of human rights. It is very hard to reconcile legal pluralism and normative natural law theory.

Positivistic image of law. As with natural law theories, positivism is also difficult to define in a precise manner that is positivistic images of law are all somehow different from each other even while they also contain some important common ingredients and features. To simplify a great deal, the very basic idea of positivism is an idea which is in direct opposition to the natural law ideas. Namely, that it is not only possible but also valuable to construct a morally neutral descriptive/conceptual theory of law. So, for Kelsen, his *Pure Theory of Law* was general theory of positive law, not a theory of any specific legal system or interpretation of national or international legal norms.[36] However, Kelsen clearly failed to uphold the strict objectivity (or purity) of his system because he constructed *Grundnorm* which he assumed to be existing.[37] But this kind of norm is actually of an empirical nature, which has its true foundation in a certain community of humans which is willing to obey the first constitution. In other words, even

---

[34] T Hobbes, *Leviathan*, (first published 1651, Oxford, Clarendon Press, 1909) Pt 1, Ch XIV (at 99).
[35] Alf Ross presented this critique sharply by asking: 'Cannot my intuition be just as good as yours?' A Ross, *On Law and Justice* (Berkeley/Los Angeles, University of California Press, 1959) 261.
[36] 'Die Reine Rechtslehre ist eine Theorie des positiven Rechts; des positiven Rechts schlechthin, nicht einer speziellen Rechtsordnung. Sie ist allgemeine Rechtslehre, nicht Interpretation besonderer nationaler oder internationaler Rechtsnormen', Kelsen, *Reine Rechtslehre* (n 15) 1.
[37] Ibid 203–209.

this theory has roots in certain legal culture which may or may not choose to respect its *Grundnorm*.

The fundamental idea is to underline the role of man (no matter whether the role is intended or unintentional) in the making of law and legal system. But it would appear that modern developed versions of legal positivism are clearly embedded in certain legal cultures. For example, for Hart, the ultimate criterion of validity in a legal system was not like for Kelsen presupposed *Grundnorm* but rather a social rule which existed because it was actually *practiced* that is, it was effective. According to Hart:

> those rules of behaviour which are valid according to the system's ultimate criteria of validity must be generally obeyed, and ... its rules of recognition specifying the criteria of legal validity and its rules of change and adjudication must be effectively accepted as common public standards of official behaviour by its officials.[38]

Now, Hart seems to think that basically law is distinct from areas such as political system or morality, something which stands on its own. And, in this specific sense legal theory about law is not a theory fitted to one system/culture only, but it has a more general objective. However, the pluralistic argument stemming from various legal cultures seems to undermine the very idea of generality and objectivity. If one requires, like Hart, that (a) rules are generally obeyed, and (b) rules are effectively accepted, then it becomes clear that these requirements are of empirical nature. And, as empirical requirements they are necessarily embedded in certain non-universal context.

Another question raised by Hart concerns the fact that pluralism of today means the existence of several competing and overlapping legal rules within one system. There can be no general abeyance or effectiveness because there is not one commonly accepted rule of recognition but many. This is the reason why John Austin's idea requiring laws to be the commands by the sovereign is in trouble. There is no one sovereign: in a system one may have a national legislator, European Union, the Court of European Union, national supreme courts, European Convention on Human Rights and the European Court of Human Rights.[39] Crucially this is not only the case with Austin: even TE Holland's modified version of Austin's theory continued along the universalistic and seemingly objective path. Typically for the analytical tradition, Holland assumed common elements existed

---

[38] HLA Hart, *The Concept of Law*, 2nd edn by P Bulloch and J Raz (Oxford, Clarendon Press, 1994) 116.

[39] Basically, Austin held that law is the command of the 'sovereign', see J Austin, *The Province of Jurisprudence Determined* HLA Hart (ed) (first published 1861, London, Weidenfeld & Nicholson, 1954) Lecture VI.

everywhere and sought general methods, ideas, and purposes which would have been *common* to every system of law.[40]

So, these grand legal theories are, in fact, meant to work in such systems where there are mainly domestic rules without true competition between rules. Clearly this state of affairs must be deemed as profoundly problematic in 2010s.

Socio-legal image of law. These images are also theories about law which may be labelled as realistic or sociological branches of jurisprudence. Roughly, these kinds of approaches to law have meant demystification of doctrinal and judicial rhetoric within and about law. Now, we can at least separate two kinds of theoretically ambitious views ('grand theories') of law which may be described as realistic/sociological jurisprudence: American and Scandinavian. These views have in common that they directly oppose such formalistic views of law upheld by Kelsen in his *Pure Theory of Law*.[41]

Again, I have to generalise a great deal by saying that American version of realism had at least three typical features which were (1) recognition of the difference between law in action and law in books; (2) the attempt to explain the actual behaviour of courts; and (3) legal instrumentalism (so-called 'social engineering' view to law). These views were presented influentially, first, by theorists such as Roscoe Pound.[42] In practice, the key function of legal science was understood to make scientifically exact predictions concerning the future behaviour of courts. In other words, these predictions were meant to take place within a certain system (in this case American common law). This, in turn, means that American realism was contextually bound to its surrounding legal culture: no-one concerned themselves with general predictions of courts belonging to other jurisdictions.[43] All the same, this was not actually a problem for American legal realism because it understood the limits of legal theory. As Oliver Wendell Holmes said:

> The condition of our thinking about the universe is that it is capable of being thought about rationally, or, in other words, that every part of it is effect and cause in the same sense in which those parts are with which we are most familiar.

---

[40] See Lobban, 'Theory and Practice' (n 28) 141–42.

[41] Obviously one could also class under the heading 'legal realism' other kinds of approaches too such as the Critical Legal Studies movement (basically saying that law covers the clashes between interest groups and ideologies) or various post-modernistic ideas (rejecting the 'grand narratives' and underling the irrational and unconscious nature of human action). However, these have been omitted here. See RM Unger, *The Critical Legal Studies Movement* (Cambridge, Mass, Harvard University Press, 1983) and C Douzinas, *Postmodern Jurisprudence: The Law of Texts in the Texts of Law* (New York, Routledge, 1991).

[42] See the seminal article R Pound, 'Law in Books and Law in Action' (1910) 44 *American Law Review* 12–36.

[43] It is no surprise, then, that today Pound's legacy is understood specifically in the context of American legal culture, not in a universal manner. See KJ Bybee, 'Law in Action' (2006) 59 *Political Research Quarterly* 415–16.

> So in the broadest sense it is true that the law is a logical development, like everything else. The danger of which I speak is not the admission that the principles governing other phenomena also govern the law, but the notion that a given system, ours, for instance, can be worked out like mathematics from some general axioms of conduct.[44]

First, Holmes clearly renounced the use of logic while talking about law. He saw the nature of law as something that cannot be truly grasped with a logical approach. Secondly, Holmes was aware that when he spoke of law he spoke of 'that of a given system, ours' which shows that legal realism was not meant to be general legal theory but rather something which was meant to have a meaningful purpose and function within American law. And yet, when one reads national legal literature of different countries one can see that the theoretical legacy of this branch of legal realism is dealt with as if it was general or not bound to its own legal culture; take any decent book about legal theory (like this one) and you are sure to see citations (including in this article).

In Scandinavia, legal realism was more theoretical and it has a pronounced philosophical background which was roughly based on the work of Axel Hägerström. But, in fact, the actual legal theoretical content of Scandinavian realism was crafted by such theorists as Karl Olivecrona. He was a legal realist who stressed the empirical base of law which was to him, ultimately, the use of power (as it was for Kelsen). Olivecrona underlined the importance of a monopoly of force as the quintessential basis of all law.[45] However, as Alf Ross's thinking shows, Scandinavian realism too was aware of its legal-cultural boundaries. Ross wanted to avoid the problem of how to define law, and one of his ways to try to avoid this classical task of legal theory was to underline that:

> The problem of definition would only arise if we were to class these various systems together under the heading of 'law' or 'legal system ... it is not necessary to know anything about what this system of norms has in common with other systems of norms which could be classified together under the heading 'law' or 'legal system'.[46]

So, it would seem that Ross's legal realism could also have been able to avoid the objectivity problem by concentrating only on a certain system of rules. However, this is not the case because Ross's theoretical main ambition was to define the meaning of the concept of 'valid law' and this was to him something that was 'based on the fact that the norms are effectively complied with because they are felt to be socially binding'.[47] Now, in a

---

[44] O Wendell Holmes, 'The Path of Law', originally an address delivered in 1897, (1997) 110 *Harvard Law Review* 991–1009, 998–99.
[45] See K Olivecrona, *Law as Fact* (London, Oxford University Press, 1939).
[46] Ross, *On Law and Justice* (n 35) 30.
[47] Ibid 29.

pluralistic system one cannot assume this kind of social abidingness. For instance, rules of indigenous people may be felt as socially binding by those who are members of that people but not by others. The problem is, once again, the idea of the purity of legal system which does not fully recognise that there are overlapping systems and various bodies of valid norms which can be applied. There is no clear-cut theoretical answer to the question who's 'feeling of social abidingness of norms' is the right one.

On more general terms, we can see that natural law theories as well as different analytical attempts to craft general legal theory are all in difficulties with legal pluralism which seems to undermine the possibility of objectivity in a strong sense. But, the problem may exist, even more obscurely, in the very fabric of modern Western legal science in general. Rudolph von Jhering's words still linger with us after 150 years: true legal science should not be degraded into national study of law only.[48] And here lies the problem: the urge to universalise and stretch rigorous conceptual and semi-logical analysis *beyond* cultural borders may mean unawareness of concealed differences.

IV. KALEIDOSCOPIC VIEW TO LEGAL THEORY?

It seems that basic ways of doing legal theory and some of the important fundamental ideas behind grand legal theories are not very well equipped for confronting the new legal pluralistic world. They seem rather ill equipped while facing pluralistic phenomena, such as the optional civil code, European human rights or transnational law. Some of these problems were addressed in the previous chapter. However, it is not the task of this chapter to carve a new legal theory or a new way to understand what the legal-cultural epistemological limits are when it comes to *doing* legal theory. Instead, I can try to offer a series of hints to throw some light on the heuristic benefits of the kaleidoscopic view of law and, thus, on the way we understand what it means to *do* legal theory. So, some tentative key-ideas can be formulated.

Should one try to comprehend legal cultures as changing images of a kaleidoscope as an explicit epistemic base on which legal theories are being constructed, then one would probably have to underline a certain amount of relativity, which would not mean that everything goes. Rather it would mean accepting the value of legal-cultural factors for legal theory. In a more philosophical vein, one would also need to accept that there is no 'God's eye'

---

[48] von Jhering, *Geist des römischen Rechts auf den verschiedenen Stufen seiner Entwicklung*, Band I (Leipzig, Breitkopf & Härtel, 1852) 14–15 ('Die Rechtswissenschaft ist zur Landesjurisprudenz degradiert, die wissenschaftlichen Gränzen fallen in der Jurisprudenz mit den politischen zusammen. Eine demüthigende, unwürdige Form für eine Wissenschaft').

view of law. This implies accepting Hilary Putnam's epistemic idea according to which, man cannot have a 'God's eye' view of reality for man is always limited to his own conceptual schemes.[49] In a similar manner, legal theory cannot have God's eye view of law. Moreover, even most rigorous analytical study of legal concepts is not genuinely universal or void of the effects of law's legal cultural context: even legal theoreticians have their epistemic home-bases.

Legal theory's kaleidoscopic view of law would also mean to *refuse relying on* conceptual similarities. In short, English 'law', German '*Recht*', Finnish '*oikeus*' and Arabic '*shari'a*' have conceptual similarities which are based on textual interpretation. However, literal translations of legal-culturally loaded concepts are almost invariably misleading.[50] Moreover, by accepting a kaleidoscopic view we would have to acknowledge that law is always law-in-context or that the world of law juridiversity is the order of today.[51] Juridiversity means acceptance of the cultural diversity in law and also protecting different legal forms so that the richness of legal species could be protected against unnecessary uniformisation of law. But does this not leave us on a very theory-barren landscape indeed? Perhaps the situation is not sliding unavoidably to a dead end. As Mark Van Hoecke points out there may be reasons to be optimistic that some inter-subjective consensus among scholarly community may be reached on many jurisprudential matters: legal cultures do not exist in isolation from each other.[52] This possibility for optimism is also clearly the intellectual fuel for H Patrick Glenn's famous view on the sustainable diversity on law in terms of legal traditions.[53]

So, the suggested kaleidoscopic view would help the legal theorist to place himself in a witting relation with the kinds of laws he is studying by grasping that each time he is actually gazing into the viewfinder of a kaleidoscope he is seeing varying images of law/legal which are constantly changing (or that he remains within certain image-view only). Yet, because of the personal legal-cultural embedding or theoretical background of a

---

[49] See for a larger discussion of Putnam's view his *Reason, Truth, and History* (Cambridge, Cambridge University Press, 1981) in which he explains his internal and realist conception of truth.

[50] See for a more detailed discussion J Husa, 'Understanding Legal Languages—Linguistics Concerns of the Comparative Lawyer' in J Baaij (ed), *The Role of Legal Translation in Legal Harmonisation* (The Hague, Kluwer Law International, 2012) 161–81.

[51] Obviously this concept is derived from the biological concept of *biodiversity* which normally refers to the degree of variation of different life forms within a given ecosystem or even in relation to an entire planet. This concept entails the existence of a wide range of genotypes, species, or biotopes, in a given area or during a specific period of time; it 'embraces the whole of the incredible variety of life found on earth', see AP Gautam, 'Biodiversity' in *Encyclopedia of Environment and Society* (Sage Publications, 2007) available at www.sage-ereference.com/view/environment/n79.xml.

[52] See Van Hoecke's contribution to this volume (ch 1).

[53] See HP Glenn, *Legal Traditions of the World*, 4th edn (Oxford, Oxford University Press, 2010).

theoretician, the object, that is, the law, actually remains the same: the legal theorist seeks to point the kaleidoscope (where the light comes, a limited number of shapes and colours of particles of different object images) toward that which interests him and is a part of his understanding. And in this sense, the kaleidoscope would also entail a certain amount of similarity. For instance, if one was interested in the doctrine of precedent one could conclude from the comparison of the Islamic law's '*illah*' with that of the common law's '*ratio decidendi*' that we are dealing with basically different reflections/view images of the same type of thing. This is because both of these doctrines are meant to allow flexibility and adaptability but also maintain constancy and stability/predictability in legal systems as it is maintained and developed by the courts.[54]

On the down side, the kaleidoscopic view is perhaps a merely hopelessly heuristic idea which underlines the importance of not assuming conceptual or theoretical similarity without taking into account the effects of legal culture. In other words, it is a metaphoric remainder of the importance of looking beyond the text and beyond one's own legal-cultural epistemic matrix. Yet, as such a remainder, it would make visible that legal theorists are conceiving images of law that are shifting on each turn of the kaleidoscope.[55] In short, the point is to be aware of changes taking place even while the conceptual framework stays still.

V. IS THERE A LESSON FOR LEGAL THEORY?

The classical ambition still present in any modern Western grand legal theory has been at the root of constructing a general, universal and/or objective definition of law (seemingly) out of any particular context. Whereas socio-legal theories may actually gain a certain objectivism if they stay within a certain legal culture, natural law and positivistic theories are more problematic because they claim to be general theories about law. Recent discussion within comparative law and growing legal pluralism have, nevertheless, brought to light the inability of grand legal theories (such as Hart's and Kelsen's) to genuinely take into account the plurality of law. It is certainly beyond the scope of this chapter to try to solve these great theoretical problems. However, the

---

[54] See for more detailed analysis UF Moghul, 'Certainty in Ratiocination: How to Ascertain the Illah (Effective Cause) in the Islamic Legal System and How to Determine the Ratio Decidendi in the Anglo-American Common Law' (1999) 4 *Journal of Islamic Law* 125–200.

[55] No originality can be claimed here: in the 1800s Sir Henry Maine had already posed this (comparative and historical) point against the theory of Austin. Maine argued that Austin's conceptions made no sense in ancient or primitive communities. However, Maine's contextuality-based critique did not really change the way legal theory was considered; legal theory remained largely analytical in England throughout the 1800s and 1900s. See Lobban (n 28) 137–43.

concept of the kaleidoscope might be one useful way to picture a heuristic metaphor, which would take into account the plurality while constructing legal theories. Now, I will not finish with any truly conclusive statement here but rather with a sketch of the kaleidoscopic view of legal theory tentatively claiming that it might be a heuristic tool for a better self-understanding of the legal theories meta-epistemic boundaries: we do not possess 'God's Eye View' of law.

Finally, a kaleidoscope of law *could* be an instrument for viewing differing theoretical reflections of law where each reflection has a specific legal-cultural shape (for example, precedent law, statutory law, customary law, mixed-shapes). In terms of kaleidoscopic views, this would entail viewing a first object image (for example, legal rule) surrounded by a second object image (for example, doctrine on sources of law) all encompassed by a tertiary image (for example, structure of legal system) and so on. This would require conceiving that legal-theoretical ideas have set shapes (for example, formalism or realism) which allows the overall *shape* of the image (law as view finder) to remain constant regardless of changing *content* (coloured objects and bits of glass that is, rules, cases, institutions, doctrines) of the images. To put it another way: analytical analysis of legal concepts is not the same as looking into the microscope and gazing at an object which remains unchanged. Even analytical attempts mean looking through the kaleidoscope of law.

In conclusion, we may ask, what does the above said mean for legal theory? Two points are of importance here: (a) the kaleidoscopic view is not the same as surrendering to relativism; and (b) the kaleidoscopic view of legal theory is not itself a legal theory. Yet, this view underlines the importance of not locking any theory with its primary epistemology: it is only by understanding different viewpoints of law that we can also obtain a better understanding of legal theory itself. And, as Hage points out, this may mean that objective legal theory is possible 'at least to some extent'.[56] The kaleidoscope metaphor's lesson seems to be the call of the lack of theoretical pretentiousness.

---

[56] See Hage ch 2 in this volume.

11

Translators and Legal Comparatists as Objective Mediators between Cultures?

CAROLINE LASKE

IN WESTERN EUROPEAN culture, there is a deep-level and intrinsic link between language and law, as law cannot be imagined without the use of language and, in particular, the use of written language. If we want to study how this particular link informs legal theory in general, and comparative law in particular, we need to ask three preliminary questions: what is language, what is law, and what is the nature of the point at which they cross. The present paper will explore the possibility of using linguistic disciplines as cognitive models for comparative law and of adopting some of the linguistic and translation studies methodologies to suggest a more 'objective' basis for research in comparative law, which will in turn also influence legal theory. The complex issues surrounding the activity of legal translation are outside the scope of this paper, though they may get touched upon in the discussion.

I. LANGUAGE

The term 'language' has two meanings: the general concept of language, on the one hand, and a specific linguistic system, on the other. It is not within the scope of this paper to discuss in detail all the definitions and theories that have been developed in relation to language as a concept. Three main theories will be mentioned briefly, but only the one relating to language as an act of communication will be discussed in detail.

A. Mental Faculty

Language as a mental faculty refers to the notion that human capacity for language is universal and altogether innate and a unique development of the human brain. Chomsky's theory of Universal Grammar is a prominent exponent of this school of thought.

B. System of Symbols

Language as a system of symbols is a structuralist view, which sees language as a closed system in which elements are held in balance and according to specific (grammatical) rules. First introduced by de Saussure,[1] it is a conception of language as a socially shared and real system of signs, each of which consists of the arbitrary conjunction of an abstract concept (*signifié*/signified) and an acoustic image (*signifiant*/signifier).[2] Hence, 'meaning' is not given in advance but is created with the formation of the sign itself and it is not rooted in some universal logic but is the result of entirely arbitrary decisions on the part of each linguistic community. Consequently, if two communities construct different meanings, there is no objective basis for deciding which one is better or right.

C. Act of Communication

Language as an act of communication is a pragmatic view which stresses the function, notably the social function, of the use of language when people interact with each other. This approach has been adopted mainly in the context of socio-linguistics and linguistic anthropology.

In the context of examining the use of language in relation to law and to comparative law more particularly, the view which emphasises usage, communicative function and the social context of language seems the most appropriate to adopt. The theory of language to be discussed here is generally known as systemic functional linguistics, or systemic functional grammar or just systemic linguistics and was first developed by Michael Halliday.[3] It offers an account of language as it is used in actual social situations and is, in this sense, always concerned with the meaning, communicative functionality and rhetorical purposes of language. At the heart of systemic linguistics is the understanding of the communicative properties of written and spoken texts of all types (why a text means what it does and why it is valued as it is), as well as the understanding of the relation between language, on the one hand, and culture, community, social grouping and ideology, on the other.[4]

---

[1] F de Saussure, *Cours de linguistique générale* (first published 1916, Paris, Payot & Rivages, 2005).
[2] Developed in particular in his third course of lectures (1910–11).
[3] The standard reference work for systemic theory is M Halliday, *An Introduction to Functional Grammar* (London, Edward Arnold, 1985/1994).
[4] Ibid xxix.

For functional linguists, language appears to have developed and is being used for three main purposes, which Halliday has called metafunctions:

(i) *Ideational metafunction*, encodes meanings of experience which realise field of discourse ('experiental meanings'). It refers to the use of language to represent experience and construct a view of reality with the various categories language offers to talk about real-world happenings. There are three main constituents: processes (typically expressed as verbs identifying happenings and state of affairs); participants (typically expressed as nouns identifying entities); and circumstances (typically expressed as adverbs or prepositional phrases acting to provide some context to the first two elements).

(ii) *Interpersonal metafunction*, encodes meanings of attitudes and relationships which realise tenor of discourse ('interpersonal meanings'). It refers to the use of language to represent interaction between speakers, the way they construct and fill social roles, adopt and/or express attitudes/points of views, form relationships and alliances and so on. A speaker can adopt four basic interpersonal positions (which can be complicated, qualified and extended): it can be declarative (offering information), interrogative (demanding information), imperative (commands in relation to action or response rather than information) and offer (willingness to supply action and response).

(iii) *Textual metafunction*, encodes meanings of text development which realise mode of discourse ('textual meanings'). It refers to the use of language to organise the experiential and interpersonal meanings into a coherent, connected and unified entity. The most prominent textual function in this context is what has been termed the 'theme', which indicates the angle or the point of departure adopted by the speaker.

These meanings are encoded in what linguists call 'text' which is a piece of language in use that can be of any length and in either written or spoken form. It is 'language that is functional'.[5] A text, in this sense, is a coherent collection of meanings appropriate to its context. The way the text's meanings are combined together gives the text its texture and the text's structure rests on the mandatory structural elements used in the combination of these meanings.

The way these meanings are encoded depends on two surrounding contexts, illustrated in Figure 1 below. The 'context of culture' refers to the general outer cultural environment in which a text occurs. It includes elements such as conventions of address, politeness, discourse and so on, which shape meanings within a particular culture. The context of culture has been described 'as the sum of all the meanings it is possible to mean in that particular culture'.[6]

---

[5] M Halliday and R Hasan, *Language, Context and Texts: Aspects of Language in a Social Semiotic Perspective* (Geelong, Deaking University Press, 1985).
[6] D Butt, R Fahey, S Feez, S Spinks, C Yallop, *Using Functional Grammar: An Explorer's Guide* (Sydney, Macquarie University, 2000) 3.

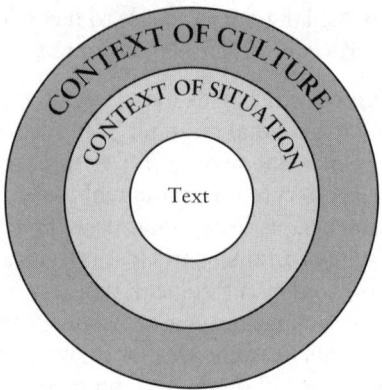

Figure 1: Text in context

Within that general context of culture, there is an inner context, which functional linguists have named the 'context of situation' and which refers, as the term indicates, to the specific situation in which a text occurs and in which meanings are formed. It includes 'the things going on in the world outside the text that make the text what it is'.[7] Linguists have identified three basic parameters of the situational differences within context of situation, namely field, tenor and mode. Field relates to experimental meanings, tenor to interpersonal meanings and mode to textual meanings, as described above in relation to the metafunctions of language (also illustrated in Figure 2 below).

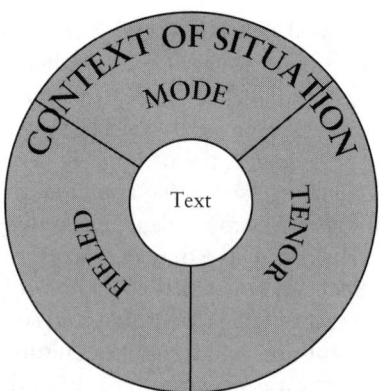

Figure 2: Parameters of context of situation[8]

[7] Ibid 4.
[8] Ibid 4.

To give an example, if you go into a corner shop in an English country village to buy some groceries, you will probably take a number of items off the shelf on which the exact price is marked and will proceed to the counter to pay and maybe chat with the shopkeeper and other customers about the weather. The text (spoken in this case) that accompanies this scene is likely to be very different if you go to a corner shop to do the grocery shopping in, let us say, Marrakech or Cairo or maybe even in Chinatown in London. The context of culture in the English village is that prices are clearly labelled and you are expected to pay at the counter what is written on the price ticket. Whereas in Marrakech or Cairo there are likely to be no price labels and the shopping is accompanied by barter and trading. And you would probably not talk about the weather with the shopkeeper but rather inquire about his health and family. Furthermore, the field, tenor and mode, as the parameters of the specific context of situation of the two texts will inform us how meanings are constructed in the two situations, such as, for example, the way you will address the shopkeeper or other customers, how you are going to introduce what you want to say and so on.

The analysis of language using methods that have been developed by linguistic disciplines such as functional grammar, allows us to show how meanings are encoded, including the consideration of the extra linguistic levels of context of culture and of situation.

II. LAW

It is not within the scope of this article to discuss the numerous theories on the definitions of law. For the purpose of this paper, law is to be understood not merely as a set of rules assembled in a coherent system that governs civil society, but in terms of a concept of legal culture which embeds the understanding of how law in a particular system is created, practised and interpreted in an understanding of the socio-political, cultural and historical context of the system in question.[9]

Culture is a rather vague concept,[10] which has been defined in the literature in relation to similarly vague notions, such as 'states of mind and ideas'.[11] In some of Friedman's descriptions general (national) culture appears in terms of a residual category of a general environment of beliefs,

---

[9] M Van Hoecke and M Warrington, 'Legal Cultures, Legal Paradigms and Legal Doctrine: Towards a New Model for Comparative Law' (first published 1998) reprinted in M Del Mar, W Twining and M Giudice (eds), *Legal Theory and the Legal Academy*, The Library of Essays in Contemporary Legal Theory, vol III (Farnham, Ashgate, 2010) 291–332.

[10] R Cotterrell, 'The Concept of Legal Culture' in D Nelken (ed), *Comparing Legal Cultures* (Aldershot, Dartmouth, 1997) 13. See also Jaakko Husa, in ch 10 in this volume.

[11] LM Friedman, 'The Concept of Legal Culture: A Reply' in D Nelken (ed), *Comparing Legal Cultures*, ibid 35.

ideas, and practices, 'a kind of aggregate, hard to compare with other aggregates'.[12] It is similarly difficult to identify the constitutive elements of the concept of legal culture. Van Hoecke describes the fabric of legal culture to lie in the combination and mutual interaction of a number of elements, such as 'world view', 'ideology' or 'habit'. 'Law thus starts from *general* values, worldviews and so on. In a second stage, however, law and practices *create* some *legal* values, worldviews, traditions and habits, in other words: a legal culture'.[13] Hence, 'legal culture is as much the product of the system as it is its generator'.[14] In other words, it appears difficult to define and delimit the elements that constitute legal culture beyond the use of a priori notions, often abstract or intuitive. Both in comparative law[15] and in legal sociology,[16] the concept of culture is used in this vague way apparently without much research in relation to proving the assumptions made about the notion of culture. Friedman concedes legal culture not to be 'one of these happy concepts … that we can measure with some degree of precision'.[17] And yet, a little later he admits that the states of mind for which legal culture is a generic term could, in principle, be 'discoverable empirically, but this is no easy task'.[18] Indeed, it is no easy task, but that should not preclude any attempts to find some empirical basis for the concept of legal culture, even if only on a partial basis. Placing the search for what constitutes legal culture on a more objective footing, will allow for greater understanding of this vast concept and will inform research in legal theory and, in particular, in areas such as comparative law and legal sociology.

Language is a reliable indicator of a great number of underlying cultural elements that a text (written or spoken) may contain. The linguistic disciplines and translation studies are good guides for gaining deep-level and multi-layered understanding of the phenomena that surround us and which have been expressed using language. Contrastive linguistics, corpus linguistics, systemic functional grammar, socio-linguistics, discourse analysis and translations studies, just to name a few, have all developed methodologies

---

[12] LM Friedman, *The Legal System: A Social Science Perspective* (New York, Russell Sage Foundation, 1975) 209.
[13] M Van Hoecke, *Law as Communication* (Oxford, Hart Publishing, 2002) 57.
[14] E Blankenburg, 'Civil Litigation Rates as Indicators for Legal Cultures' in D Nelken (ed), *Comparing Legal Cultures* (Dartmouth, Aldershot, 1997) 65.
[15] P Legrand, *Fragments on law-as-culture* (Deventer, WEJ Tjeenk Willink, 1999). P Legrand, 'The Same and the Different' in P Legrand and R Munday (eds), *Comparative Legal Studies: Traditions and Transitions* (Cambridge, Cambridge University Press, 2003). T Wilhelmsson, E Paunio and A Pohjolainen (eds), *Private Law and the Many Cultures of Europe* (The Hague, Kluwer Law International, 2007).
[16] LM Friedman, *The Legal System* (n 12) 15–16; also in D Nelken, *Comparing Legal Cultures* (Dartmouth, Aldershot, 1997): see Cotterrell, 'The Concept of Legal Culture' (n 10) 13 and Friedman, 'The Concept of Legal Culture: A Reply' (n 11) 33.
[17] Friedman, *The Concept of Legal Culture* (n 11) 33.
[18] Ibid 35.

that allow for analysis to move away from intuition and onto an altogether more objective and even empirical basis. So far, the objects of such studies have more often been literary, political or religious rather than legal texts.

III. LANGUAGE AND LAW: MEETING POINT

If we consider law as 'legal culture' relating the legal system to the culture of the society it governs and language beyond a narrow semantic meaning referring also to socio-cultural, political and historical contents, we discover there to be a parallel between language and law also on a conceptual level. To the extent that in our Western societies law cannot do without the use of language, that is the initial meeting point between the two concepts. There is, however, also an ongoing dynamic interaction between these two internally coherent systems in the sense that law creates language and language creates law. 'Language ... creates reality, a different legal language produces another kind of 'legal reality'.[19]

Law is institutionalised discourse, first and foremost within individual societies, but also in interaction with other (neighbouring) legal traditions. Legal systems, like languages, have always influenced each other across frontiers whether these were geographical, geo-political or cultural, whether in time or space. Hence, both legislation and languages are identifiable with a particular state/region/people/culture and are also the results of international/intercultural interaction and thus contain some borrowed, imported, transplanted elements and are always based on previous bodies of texts and discourses.[20] Interesting in this context is, for example, the position of Latin as the former lingua franca of law and its impact on the English, French and German legal languages, because legal terminology was frequently the result of the use of loanwords from Latin, the language of the *ius commune*.[21] Another important historical example is the use of French as a language of law in some English common law courts, which used neither Latin nor English, but Law French, which by the time of its disappearance in the early eighteenth century had degenerated into a hybrid of bastardised French, Latin and English.[22]

---

[19] Van Hoecke and Warrington (n 9) 535.
[20] J Lambert, 'The Status and Position of Legal Translation: A Chapter in the Discursive Construction of Societies' in F Olsen, A Lorz and D Stein (eds), *Languages and Law: Key Perspectives* (New York, Palgrave Macmillan, 2009) 76–95.
[21] There have been few studies on this. For an early example, see J Kabatek, *Bolognesische Renaissance und der Ausbau romanischer Sprachen. Juristische Diskurstraditionen und Sprachentwicklung in Südfrankreich und Spanien im 12. und 13. Jahrhundert* (Tübingen, Niemeyer, 2005).
[22] J Baker, *Manual of Law French* (Letchworth, Avebury, 1979); K Kerber, *Sprachwandel im Englischen Recht. Vom Law French zum Englischen* (Münster, LIT Verlag, 1997).

IV. TRANSLATION STUDIES AND COMPARATIVE LAW: ANOTHER MEETING POINT

Having established an intrinsic link between law and language, we can now consider a similar link between comparative law and linguistic disciplines, such as translation studies and to some extent contrastive linguistics. In their respective fields of activities, comparatists and (legal) translators are bound to consider each other's disciplines. Comparative lawyers are regularly confronted with the difficulties of translating legal terminology, concepts and legal discourse. As contrastive linguists and translators, they develop *tertium comparationis* to make independent comparisons possible. Legal translators in their quest to find equivalents in the target language need to engage in comparative law (or legal history), especially when there is no equivalent in the target legal language and system. In other words, the undertaking of comparison as such is a part of the core work in these disciplines.[23] Furthermore, law can be seen in terms of translation to the extent that legislation and legal discourse are the result of prior legal-discursive traditions.[24] Historically, law has always been intertwined with translation, as practically no area covered by a particular law system has ever been monolingual.

There are other similarities between the disciplines of translation studies and comparative law. Both have a descriptive and normative branch (what is the best translation/what is the best law); both draw more or less on other disciplines due to an acute awareness that context is important; both mediate between cultures and try to grapple with the 'foreign' and the 'unfamiliar'; and both have suffered from the common culture syndrome of Herder and Savigny and the obsession of the incompatible difference. There is even some shared vocabulary, terms such as 'transplants' or 'inside/outside view' can be found in the academic writings of both disciplines.

Translation can be seen as a language contact point, while comparative law establishes contact points between different systems of law. Starting from the underlying assumption that all texts are acts of communication, we can use as a cognitive model for comparative law the way a translator, as a mediator between cultures, approaches a text for translation. In the words of Robinson 'a useful way of thinking about translation and language is that translators don't translate *words;* they translate *what people do with words*'.[25] It is a hermeneutical approach, but linguistic and translation studies have developed methodologies and tools that enable the contents of the different language levels to be exposed on an objective (linguistic and discourse analysis) and even empirical basis (using corpus

---

[23] J Husa, 'Understanding Legal Languages—Linguistics Concerns of the Comparative Lawyer' in J Baaij, *The Role of Legal Translation in Legal Harmonization* (The Hague, Kluwer Law International, 2012).
[24] J Lambert, *The Status and Position of Legal Translation* (n 20).
[25] D Robinson, *Becoming a Translator* (London, Routledge, 2003) 142.

linguistics techniques). Similarly, in comparative law, we need to look beyond mere juxtapositions of two sets of positive rules and take on board social, economic, historical … aspects, what people *do with them*, to use Robinson's words by analogy.

V. COMPARATIVE LAW METHODOLOGIES

Comparative law has often been considered the poor cousin in the 'family' of law and legal theory. It is an area of law that is said to lack coherent theoretical basis and some have even argued that comparative law is not strictly law, but 'has by common consent the somewhat unusual characteristic that it does not exist'.[26] As the term suggests, we are dealing with a scholarly undertaking that involves law as its subject and comparison as its process. And immediately we are confronted with the question about what it is we are comparing and why, which in turn poses a number of epistemological and methodological issues that have been discussed extensively throughout the literature. Comparative law certainly appears as a kind of umbrella concept encompassing different kinds of activities that are being undertaken for diverse motives and goals.[27] To that extent, methodological pluralism is part and parcel of comparative law. It would be unrealistic to believe that one particular methodology can cover the entire spectrum of comparisons of a multi-layered concept, such as law, governing multidimensional and complex civil society.

If, for the purpose of comparative law, we regard law not merely as a textual, positive and authoritative phenomenon, but place it within its social realities, we need to embrace interdisciplinarity and also consider some of the social science methodologies.[28] 'An enquiry into methodology must … look at reasoning methods, schemes of intelligibility, paradigms and approaches that have been fashioned to promote an understanding of the object under consideration.'[29] The complexities of human society cannot be *reduced* to a single equation, an abstract scheme to which inductive and deductive reasoning can be applied, but can be *represented* in terms of schemes of intelligibility,[30] which will thus reveal social reality only in parts

---

[26] O Kahn-Freund, 'Comparative Law as an Academic Subject' (1966) 82 *Law Quarterly Review* 40.
[27] M Van Hoecke, *Deep Level Comparative Law*, EUI Working Papers, Law No 2002/13.
[28] G Samuel, 'Taking Methods Seriously' (Part One) and (Part Two) (2007) 2 *Journal of Comparative Law* 94 and 210.
[29] Ibid 219.
[30] Berthelot has identified six schemes of intelligibility: causal, functional, structural, hermeneutical, actional, dialectical; see JM Berthelot, *L'intelligence du social* (Paris, Presses Universitaires de France, 1990) 43–85, JM Berthelot, 'Programmes, paradigms, disciplines: pluralité et unité des sciences sociales' in JM Berthelot (ed), *Epistémologie des sciences sociales* (Paris, Presses Universitaires de France, 2001) 484.

and according to the scheme or combination of schemes used. This type of model falls short of the mathematical ones used in the natural sciences. It does not provide a 'scientific model, but a number of schemes that underpin the *art* of interpretation'.[31] This should, however, not preclude any efforts to ground the research in objectively and empirically ascertainable parameters, even if these can only provide a partial representation of social reality and the law it governs.

Functionalism has been the word in the mouths of a great many comparative lawyers and this for many decades now, whether to express their appraisal,[32] rejection[33] or redefinition[34] of the method. In terms of intelligibility, functionalism provides a representation of social reality that is based on the function of laws to be compared and, hence, enables the establishment of seemingly neutral facts for *tertium comparationis*. And yet, in the exercise of establishing facts, a number of other schemes of intelligibility may come into play, such as, for example, the hermeneutical scheme when facts have been subject to some prior selection, representation and interpretation, in which case the *tertium comparationis* is less of a neutral common denominator.

The issues surrounding the selection and presentation of facts for comparison is at the heart of some of the fiercest criticism of functionalism. Legrand contends that functional comparatists should not confuse resemblance with representation, indeed he believes representation to be *re*-presentation. 'The very fact of cognitive selection displays the contingent character of the product of that selection.' And 'it is impossible for the comparatist-as-observer ever to demonstrate sameness non-ethnocentrically because any understanding on his part assumes integration into his already-understood world, a world he cannot actually reflect himself out of'.[35] But what Legrand fails to recognise is that neither linguistic communities, nor legal systems, nor civil societies/communities live in isolation from each other. There has always been cross-fertilisation, whether geographical, geo-political or cultural, whether in time or space and these 'commonalities' need to be recognised as much as the differences Legrand advocates. Comparative law can only make sense if both these elements have been taken

---

[31] Samuel, 'Taking Methods Seriously' (n 28) 109.
[32] One prominent example: K Zweigert and H Kötz, *Einführung in die Rechtsvergleichung* (Tübingen, Mohr Siebeck, 1996).
[33] Two prominent examples: G Frankenberg, 'Critical Comparisons: Re-Thinking Comparative Law' (1985) 26 *Harvard International Law Journal* 411–55. P Legrand, 'The Same and the Different' in P Legrand and R Munday, *Comparative Legal Studies: Traditions and Transitions* (Cambridge, Cambridge University Press, 2003) 240–311.
[34] Two prominent examples: J Husa, 'Farewell to Functionalism or Methodological Tolerance?' (2003) 67 *RabelZ* 419–77. R Michaels, 'The Functional Method of Comparative Law' in M Reimann and R Zimmermann, *The Oxford Handbook of Comparative Law* (Oxford, Oxford University Press, 2006) 339–82.
[35] P Legrand, 'The Same and the Different' in P Legrand and R Munday, *Comparative Legal Studies: Traditions and Transitions* (Cambridge, Cambridge University Press, 2003) 254–55.

on board and grounded in some objective rather than vague parameters, and the baby has not been thrown out with the bath water in favour of one view over the other.

VI. LINGUISTIC AND TRANSLATION STUDIES METHODOLOGIES

While legal functionalists defend the common ground argument (the raison d'être of all legal systems is to solve same/similar problems) and difference theorists argue for the uniqueness of each legal system, neither side of the argument have come up with very convincing objective frameworks to sustain their theories.

In view of an intrinsic link between law and language in Western societies, this is precisely the point where some common ground may be established among the systems, namely that one of their basic constitutive features is the use of language. And if we can adopt as working hypothesis that the essence of language are communicative acts, then we can point to this as a further element in our common ground landscape. In other words, comparative lawyers can reasonably assume that texts[36] in law have used language and that their basic function is communication.

The comparatist now wants to establish the deep-level meanings and contents of the texts in order to get a better understanding of the extent to which they can be compared. For this purpose a text corpus will have to be collected and constructed. That is the very point when the comparatist will be plagued by the same question as so many before her: what texts should be selected? Is the selection not inevitably a biased *re*-presentation to use Legrand's term? The answer is indeed yes, and it is bound to constitute some partial revealing of the social reality, as discussed above. But attempts can be made to reduce to a minimum the elements of bias (dependent on the (financial) means one can dispose of). The selecting team should be multi-disciplinary and multi-lingual, especially if more than one language is involved. The corpus should be large and accessible electronically and according to the technical norms required by standard corpus linguistic research.[37] And legal comparatists could take a leaf out of the book of linguists and translators to the extent that the latter are less likely to be bound by an epistemological approach of *authority*, but by one of *inquiry*.[38]

---

[36] This paper adopts Halliday and Hasan's definition of 'text' as a piece of language in use, independent of its length and which can either be spoken or written, see Halliday and Hasan, *Language, Context and Texts* (n 5).
[37] Corpus linguistic research is also preoccupied with the representation issue, see D Biber, 'Representativeness in Corpus Design' in *Literary and Linguistic Computing* (1993) 8 (4) 243–57 (staff.um.edu.mt/albert.gatt/teaching/dl/biber93.pdf).
[38] Samuel (n 28) 94.

'In order to compare legal systems we have to know what it is that causes a number of legally relevant elements to form a "legal system"'[39] and by using the corpus to analyse the text both synchronically and diachronically, the terminology, the linguistic-discursive and translational elements of the language used in the laws to be compared, we can retrieve meanings on the different content levels and thus gain a deep-level understanding of the laws in question, including their development throughout time and space. It is beyond the scope of this paper to enumerate and discuss the vast array of possible analytical techniques. Instead, specific attention will be paid to two particular, though related aspects: the mediating role that translation plays and has played between different legal cultures, and the phenomenon of translational features in legal texts.

A. The Mediating Role of Translation

The epistemology of authority prominent in the study of law has a number of negative side effects on comparative work, which is much deplored by Samuel.[40] It leads to what he calls 'intellectual conservatism' not only in the sense of the difficulties to go beyond the textual authority of one system in relation to another, but also in the sense of the notion that national law is based on self-sufficient textual authority specific to one particular society. Legislation and legal discourse are always the results of prior legal-discursive traditions, which have, at some stage, made use of translation.[41] In this way, legal texts have to some extent integrated intercultural features and interlinguistic/translational components as constitutive elements, and translation, as a major source of discourse shifts, has had a mediating role between the different legal cultures. To understand this mediating role of translation in the field of legal culture would enable a much better knowledge of the development of legislation and legal discourse.[42]

The questions that need to be examined relate to whether the translation strategies are to any extent determined by the importance of the cultures involved, whether texts are indeed more often translated from dominant to peripheral cultures rather than the other way around and whether translators tend to be more attentive to the norms of the target culture if

---

[39] Van Hoecke and Warrington (n 9) at 497.
[40] Samuel (n 28) 235–37.
[41] This has been particularly intensified throughout the last half century with the emergence of several forms of multilingual economic, political and military integration on the European and on the global level (EU, UNO, WTO, NATO etc).
[42] The mediating role of translations is well-known in the field of culture and literature (S Bassnett, *Post-colonial Translation: Theory and Practice* (London, Routledge, 1998)) but has not been studied extensively in the field of legal culture.

that culture is a dominant one.[43] Of similar interest is to study the extent to which translation influences the discourse of the receiving culture, as it has been argued that specific discourse and sentence structures typical of the source language are adopted by the target language, even outside the framework of translation.[44] Methodological models such as terminological configurations and traditions, parallel or divergent priorities in discourse, their paradigmatic meaning from the perspective of dominant/peripheral tendencies will allow us to understand the reception, use and development of legal concepts and texts in national as well as in international (for example, EU) legal systems.

B. Translational Features

Related to the notion that intercultural features and interlinguistic/translational components are constitutive elements of legislation and legal discourse, is the idea that translations systematically present specific features, which make them identifiable as translations. This has been discussed particularly in the field of corpus-based translation studies, though not in relation to any specific corpus of legal texts.

The literature has identified three main translational features in translated discourse:

(i) *explicitation*, which is the tendency of translated text to be more explicit than non-translated text,[45] that is, the tendency to express meanings left implicit both in source texts and in similar original texts of the target culture;
(ii) *normalisation*, which is the tendency of translated text to conform to linguistic norms of the non-translated target discourse, sometimes even in an exaggerated way (for example, overuse of idiomatic expressions[46]);
(iii) *simplification*, which is the tendency for translated text to be usually syntactically and lexically poorer than source text.[47]

---

[43] L Venuti, *The Translator's Invisibility* (London, Routledge, 1985). M Rudvin, 'Translation and Myth: Norwegian Children's Literature in English' (1994) *Perspectives: Studies in Translatology* 199–211.

[44] V Becher, J House and S Kranich, 'Convergence and divergence of communication norms through language contact in translation' in K Braunmüller and J House, *Convergence and Divergence in Language Contact Situations* (Amsterdam, John Benjamins Publishing Company, 2009).

[45] S Blum-Kulka, 'Shifts of Cohesion and Coherence in Translation' in J House and S Blum-Kulka (eds), *Interlingual and Intercultural Communication* (Tübingen, Günter Narr, 1986) 17–35.

[46] G Toury, *In Search of a Theory of Translation* (Tel Aviv, The Porter Institute for Poetics and Semiotics, 1980).

[47] R Vanderauwera, *Dutch Novels translated into English: The Transformation of a 'Minority' Literature* (Amsterdam, Rodopi, 1985).

Given the special nature of legal discourse and, in particular, of legislation, the analysis of translational features in legal translated texts may add to a better understanding of the development of such texts. In view of the fact that legal concepts can differ from one legal culture to another, explicitation is likely to play an important role in translated legal discourse. It has been argued that in legislation adequacy in translation has priority over acceptability.[48] Adequacy refers to the intertextual equivalence between the source text and the target text, whereas acceptability refers to the intralingual relationship between target texts and other kinds of text in one language. In multi-lingual legislative environments such as the EU, for example, equally authentic legislation in different languages is expected to produce the same legal effects. It may be hypothesised that translational features, which could diminish adequacy are expected to be absent, whereas ones that could favour adequacy are likely to be present. As far as normalisation is concerned, no research has as yet studied this issue. Finally, simplification is less likely to be found in translated legal texts than in other fields, due to the extreme importance of accuracy in legal translation.

Corpus-based research on legislation and legal discourse to examine the presence of translational features would enable the identification of areas of legal discrepancy due to the translation process itself rather than to lexical or grammatical mismatch between versions. Combined with a comparative law approach such research would allow for some deep-level understanding of how legal concepts and cultures have developed and will, therefore, inform us on what elements of law are culturally determined and how, and what elements are less connected to culture. These in turn are essential elements for legal comparative work.

VII. CONCLUSIONS

This paper has explored some of the possibilities of using linguistic disciplines as cognitive models for comparative law and of adopting some of the linguistic and translation studies methodologies to suggest a more 'objective' and even empirical basis for research in comparative law. The working hypothesis has been that there is a deep-level and intrinsic link between language and law, as law (in Western culture) cannot be conceptualised and practiced without the use of language. To the extent that language is a reliable indicator of a great number of underlying notions that a text (written or spoken) may contain, the linguistic disciplines and translation studies are good guides for gaining deep-level and multi-layered understanding

---

[48] S Sarcevic, *New Approach to Legal Translation* (The Hague, Kluwer Law International, 1997).

of the phenomena that surround us and which have been expressed using language. Legislation and legal discourse are no exceptions to this.

Linguistic and translation studies have developed methodologies and tools that enable contents on the different language levels to be exposed on an objective (linguistic and discourse analysis) and even empirical basis (using corpus linguistics techniques). The analysis of language using methods that have been developed by linguistic disciplines such as functional grammar, allows us to show how meanings are encoded, including the consideration of the extralinguistic levels of context of culture and of situation.

Similarly, in comparative law, we need to look beyond mere juxtapositions of two sets of positive rules and take on board socio-political, economic, historical aspects, in other words the legal culture. Comparatists may establish *tertium comparationis* among the systems to be compared on the basis that a constitutive feature is the use of language and that the essence of language are communicative acts. Studying the language of legislation and legal discourse as a carrier of culture will provide some evidence on what constitutes and determines elements of legal culture. More specifically, examining the influence of prior legal-discursive traditions and translational features will allow for some deep-level understanding of how legal concepts and cultures have developed and will, therefore, inform us on what elements of law are culturally determined and how, and what elements are less connected to culture. These sorts of findings will help the legal comparatist to steer her little boat through the troubled water of vague and a priori notions and paradigms.

12

Legal Science Challenged by Cultural Paradigms: 'Subjective Objectivity' in Legal Scholarship

MUSTAPHA EL KAROUNI[*]

I. INTRODUCTION

THE RELATIONSHIP BETWEEN law and legal culture is a subject of growing interest and an increasingly large volume of literature (*Law as culture*). The object of this contribution is to illustrate that not only law, but also legal science, are linked to a cultural dimension.[1] It remains largely unchallenged that law, in the drafting stage, is the outcome of political and axiological choices. Its application (adjudication), study and teaching (legal science–legal scholarship) are expected to meet the criterion of 'objectivity', a condition for its legitimacy.[2]

According to our hypothesis, the influence of culture, which all-in-all constitutes a form of 'collective subjectivity' corresponding to a given group, means that this highly sought objectivity regularly takes a form that we will call subjective ('subjective objectivity').

To back up these hypotheses, we must establish how and to what degree of intensity culture affects law and the science of law. This influence is not exercised trivially and explicitly, but implicitly and often unconsciously via paradigms.

To get a clear idea of the phenomenon, we need to develop the concept of a *cultural paradigm*. The starting point for this concept is the idea of a paradigm as developed by Thomas Kuhn—in a way it is an extension and generalisation of that concept. This cultural paradigm approach makes

---

[*] I would like to thank Mark Van Hoecke for his helpful comments and reading. My thanks also go to Jaakko Husa, who invited me to the conference for which this paper was written, and to Jacques Perilleux for re-reading my article. Any errors are mine alone.

[1] We envisage 'legal science' in the broadest sense, either that of the old expression 'jurisprudence' used on the continent or the term 'jurisprudence' as currently used in the British and American legal literature. It includes the doctrine, philosophy of law and legal theory.

[2] For a description of the developments in the meanings of objectivity in law and some concrete examples, see M Van Hoecke, 'Objectivity in Law and Jurisprudence' ch 1 in this volume.

it possible to consider the cultural dimension at a higher level of abstraction and generalisation than can be reached with a traditional approach in terms of (legal) culture against which harsh objections have occasionally been made.

The debate between Cotterrell[3] and Friedman[4] on this issue is very revealing, illustrating two trends: Friedman makes (legal) culture a central theme in his work, whereas Cotterrell objects to this approach. His first criticism, based on the polysemic nature of the idea of culture, is hardly convincing, since polysemic concepts are the rule and concepts on a single aspect are an exception. What matters in an analysis is an explicit description of the content and meaning, and their constant and consistent use.

The problem lies not so much in the definition of (legal) culture as in another related question. In our opinion, the scale of observation of the cultural dimension is more fundamental.

We attempt to draw the conclusions that this approach implies for legal theory. Each issue discussed in this paper should be analysed in depth, but within the scope of this paper we must limit ourselves to the exploratory stage and to the description of the issues to be developed subsequently.

II. LEGAL THEORY AND CULTURAL PARADIGMS

A. The Fundamental Question of the Scale of Observation

There are various levels of culture. The culture of a society can be distinguished within the borders of a nation state, such as the French culture. This dimension (scale) of culture is regularly found in the concept of legal culture, and quite logically so. In fact, despite globalisation, law is a phenomenon of nation states. However, it is also possible to distinguish ethno-linguistic culture[5] and cultures based on religious elements, such as Catholic or Protestant culture.[6] Similarly, regional cultures can be pinpointed within the same nation state.[7] These distinctions are sharper when adding a criterion of social

---

[3] *Cf* R Cotterrell, *The Concept of Legal Cultures* in David Nelken (ed), *Comparing Legal Cultures* (Aldershot, Dartmouth, 1997) 13–31.

[4] *Cf* L Friedman, *The Concept of Legal Cultures: A Reply* in *Comparing Legal Cultures* ibid 33–39.

[5] Such as in Belgium, that includes both a Latin French-speaking culture and a Flemish Germanic culture.

[6] Max Weber developed his famous theory on the relation between Protestantism and the spirit of capitalism on this basis. *cf* M Weber, *The Protestant Ethic and the Spirit of Capitalism* (Mineola, New York, Dover Publications, 2003). We can also say that this religious substrate was also what led to the historical constitution of Belgium which was created by grouping Catholic French speakers and Dutch speakers who obtained their independence from the largely Protestant Dutch.

[7] In the American context, for example, significant differences can be noticed between the culture in the southern states (considered to be more conservative) and those on the East Coast or the West Coast (considered to be more progressive). Those differences will be still greater when comparing, eg the culture of southern farmers and the bourgeoisie from New York.

identity. From another standpoint, we can also distinguish minority cultures within a society.[8] All these criteria can be combined to give many variants of cultural identity.

What is at stake is fundamentally a question of scale. Depending on the scale chosen, the benchmarks and reality observed are transformed, so the question of rationality changes. This observation can be applied by analogy to a geographical scale: depending on the scale chosen, reality is perceived differently. Some elements appear and others disappear.[9]

For better comprehension, it is important to adopt an approach that is both general and broad. In other words, the level with the largest angle of vision and the highest degree of generality must be adopted. Consequently, a broad definition of culture should be used—one that can be widened and can integrate the various levels of analysis and expression of culture. This is the macro-cultural scale of large cultural sectors, where the identity that characterises the *mesocultural* or *microcultural scale* is (partially) formed. This is the dimension that requires a systemic, overall vision of the legal phenomenon. Under the influence of Cartesian philosophy and positivism, this analytical approach has been given priority in analysing law. From the standpoint of a legal theory that attempts to be global and systemic, these two approaches are more complementary than contradictory. They constitute two stages in an approach to scientific knowledge. Blaise Pascal had already perceived the problem when he wrote: 'I consider that it is impossible to know the parts without knowing the whole, but not to know the whole without knowing the parts.'[10]

In the European and American context, modernity is the system of legitimate representation that dominates and serves as the basis of Western culture. This new anthropological perception of man appeared during the Renaissance, to be passed on by the thinking of the Enlightenment and take concrete form all over the West as nation states on politico-legal level in the post French- and American-revolution societies. Modernity is the context for establishing legitimacy/illegitimacy of all cultures on the level of nation states and regions. It accordingly functions as the meta-culture of legitimisation. Before the Reformation and the Renaissance, Christianity fulfilled this role of meta-culture. This approach extends well beyond society, the continent and civilisation. It aims to reach the anthropological matrix which imparts meaning to the entire mental universe. Expressed more simply, the easiest way to understand a phenomenon is to go to its source.

---

[8] This can be the case for a community of immigrants and their descendants or for native populations such as the American Indians. These communities maintain a system of representation of the world and law that can be partially different from that of the global society. To this must be added acculturation phenomena that complicate the understanding of the cultural dimension, which appears to be relatively variable at this scale.
[9] *Cf* D Desjeux, *Les sciences sociales* (Paris, PUF, 2004) 5.
[10] B Pascal, 'Pensées' in *Oeuvres Complètes* (Paris, Seuil, 1963) 527.

We feel that a distinction must be made between two interpretations of modernity. The first is the one that was adopted through the French Revolution on the European continent and beyond, that we will refer to as *exclusive modernity*. It is exclusive in that it considers itself to be self-sufficient and that its relation to the past and to tradition is that of a breach or, in other words, opposition. It could also be called pure, or orthodox modernity, acting as a model whose ambition is to fully achieve the revolutionary anthropological project of the Enlightenment. In this sense, Anthony Carty calls the model produced by the French revolution the '*most complete modern project*'.[11] This is generally the concept of modernity that is used as an ideal–typical reference both from a common sense standpoint and in academic writings. Max Weber, who made the study of modernity and its specificity the centre of his work, illustrates this trend. Conversely, modernity in the American culture can be called *inclusive modernity*. In other words, this is a concept of modernity in a reform/continuity with the past. It is inclusive in that it contains dimensions that are not exclusively modern (for example, pre-modern notions). These characteristics are found quite clearly in the Common Law systems. This distinction, which can be considered as the foundation of the two (legal) cultures, is not sufficiently taken into account.[12]

Because of its very nature, modernity, as it has developed since the *Renaissance* as a civilisation project, must be envisaged as an ideal type and not as an existing empirical variable. The cultures that developed from it or that were modelled in the context of this metaculture, like the French or German cultures, could be the object of a more empirical approach. From this standpoint, the distinction between the ideal–typical and the empirical points of view is a corollary to the question of scale, and not of culture as such. This distinction between culture considered as an ideal example and culture understood empirically is not contradictory. These are two different levels of understanding and explanation.[13] These considerations have brought me to choose an approach in terms of paradigms and, more specifically, one special type of paradigm: the [macro] cultural paradigm.

---

[11] A Carty, *Post-Modern Law: Enlightenment, Revolution and the Death of Man* (Edinburgh, Edinburgh University Press, 1980) VIII.

[12] On this distinction, see M El Karouni, 'Les systèmes juridiques français et américain en perspective: essai de contribution à une nouvelle grille d'analyse' in D Ginocchi, D Guinard, S-M Maffesoli and S Roche (eds), *Les modèles juridiques français et américain: influences croisées* (Paris, L'Harmattan, 2008) 9–30.

[13] Cotterrell argues that: 'At least in modern complex societies, it is best to treat legal culture not as a description of empirical variability but as an ideal-type category to be used heuristically'; see D Nelken, 'An Introduction' in Nelken, *Comparing Legal Cultures* (n 3) 2–3.

B. Scientific Paradigms and Cultural Paradigms

(i) Paradigms in Scientific Activity: Kuhn and the Idealistic Theory of Knowledge

According to Thomas Kuhn, scientific activity takes place within a paradigmatic framework. A paradigm is a set of beliefs, recognised values and techniques, which are common to the members of a given scientific group.[14] Researchers of a discipline work in the context of a paradigm, which provides them with a conceptual context and a context of reference, constituting what Kuhn calls '*normal science*'. On occasion, this paradigm can no longer respond to a series of questions, which therefore appear as insoluble enigmas. This situation calls for a new paradigm able to resolve these anomalies. This change of paradigm constitutes a scientific revolution. According to Kuhn, this is the scheme that leads to progress in scientific research.

Knowledge of reality is thus not possible in a direct way. It is acquired via 'paradigms', which in a sense are lenses through which one sees the world. Kuhn further insists that the passage from one paradigm to another does not take place on a strictly objective basis. He goes on to explain that the change, which takes place in the individual at the time of a change of paradigm is similar to religious conversion. Kuhn bases his demonstration on numerous examples drawn from the history of sciences. These examples are often taken from physics, which is regarded as the model of modern science.

Kuhn stresses the importance of extra-scientific factors (values, metaphysics, social anchorage) in scientific research since, in his opinion, a paradigm draws on a vision of the world, as well as on basic principles and values. This analysis has fundamental consequences for our conception of scientific activity. In fact, in view of the subjective dimension found in scientific activity, this conception should be the object of scientific study in itself, with the central objective of looking into what brings about consent of the academic community in the context of scientific controversy. Here too, there is a need to find a meta point of view pertaining to science itself. One of the central dimensions of Kuhn's analysis is what he calls '*metaphysical paradigms*' or '*the metaphysical part of paradigms*'. By this, he refers to collectively adhering to certain beliefs.[15] Metaphysics is one of the facets of culture seen in a broad sense as we do. Metaphysics contributes to a system of representation of man by orienting his values and his relationship to reality. This precision (or hesitation) of Kuhn concerning the metaphysical (internal) dimension of paradigms, or the existence of metaphysical paradigms, brings us back to the key role that the axiological/cultural dimension plays in scientific activity.

---

[14] T Kuhn, *The Structure of Scientific Revolution*, 3rd edn (Chicago, University of Chicago Press, 1996) 175.
[15] Ibid 184.

(ii) Cultural Paradigms

Thomas Kuhn developed his approach by working solely in the field of 'pure' sciences, but without excluding the possibility of its wider applicability.[16] Kuhn's approach has since been used broadly in human and social sciences.

In fact, it seems evident a fortiori that if extra-scientific determinants contribute to the development of the exact sciences, whose results tend towards *certainty*, they contribute even more to the development of human and social sciences (including legal science) that tend towards *probable* results. Similarly, if paradigms structure 'soft' sciences, one can conclude that a fortiori, this holds for cultural and social representations.

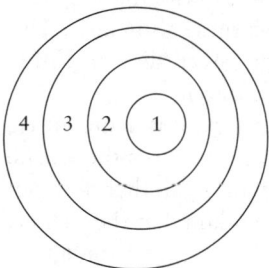

1. Exact sciences
2. Soft sciences (legal sciences/internal legal culture)
3. Cultural and social representations (external legal culture)
4. (Macro) cultural paradigms

This is the way we use the notion of a cultural paradigm. It is a structure of thought, which determines and is determined by a culture, a *vision of the world*. This type of paradigm is by extension a macro paradigm, which determines mesoparadigms and microparadigms (paradigms of legal science).[17]

C. Legal Theory and Cultural Paradigms: What are the Implications?

According to the hypothesis put forward, the paradigms of the science of law are the expression of wider (macro) paradigms. In the context of Western law, it is the (macro) paradigm of modernity, which builds the *cognitive* and *legitimising* framework of the jurists' theories and practices of law.

What are the epistemological consequences of this proposal on the legal systems and the science of law, which ideally fulfils a triple function of describing, understanding and explaining the legal phenomenon?[18] How does that translate into internal debates on legal theory?

---

[16] Ibid 208–09.

[17] In a way this concept of 'cultural paradigm' can be related to what Edgar Morin calls the 'major paradigms', see E Morin, *La méthode* (Paris, Seuil, 1991) 216–18.

[18] The function of prescription could be added in the context of jusnaturalism or if legal literature is considered to be part of legal science.

Subjective Objectivity in Law   235

This cultural dimension tends not to appear as such in internal discussions on legal theory. Legal thought (as well as scientific thought and common sense) is generally structured in a much more binary way and its dynamic is that of an opposition of these two competing poles of thought. This competition between concepts and paradigms takes the form of reasoned discussions on the respective methods of a rational point of view pertaining to the theories at hand. These discussions reach their full content only in a broader world, whose presuppositions are not all explicit. Systemic triangulation would show this conceptual dynamic as follows (Figure 2). In fact, discussions in legal science that take the form of these 'objective' discussions based on an exchange of rational arguments are to be suppressed the expression of preconceptions that are determined at a meta level. Cultural paradigms trace the outline of the cognitive frame within which the legal theorist does his analyses of the legal phenomenon.[19]

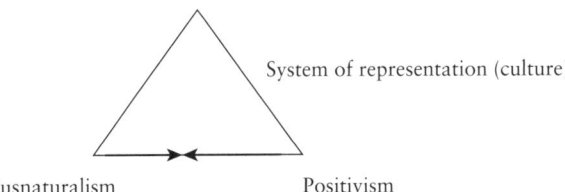

This approach has fundamental consequences for legal science. According to Mark Van Hoecke, the 'general theory of law is usually understood to be a positive science of law, aiming to be objective and non-normative, which studies problems common to all (or the majority of) legal systems from an external point of view, by using a pluri- or an inter-disciplinary method'.[20]

Legal theory that attempts to be objective must eliminate any source of subjectivity from its methods and assumptions. However, the (cultural) paradigm constitutes an a priori factor which comprises a form of subjectivity and consequently constitutes an epistemological obstacle to scientific knowledge. Indeed, culture prescribes whereas science describes.

---

[19] Cf Jaakko Husa's 'kaleidoscopic view on law'. Husa writes 'legal theory cannot have a God's Eye view of law. Moreover, even the most rigorous analytical study of legal concepts is not genuinely universal or void of the effects of law's legal cultural context: even legal theoreticians have their epistemic home bases.' 'Kaleidoscopic Cultural Views and Legal Theory—Dethroning the Objectivity?', ch 10 in this volume.

[20] M Van Hoecke, verbo 'Théorie générale du droit' in A-J Arnaud (ed), Dictionnaire encyclopédique de théorie et de sociologie du droit, 2nd edn (Paris, LGDJ, 1993). Compare the slightly different wording the same author used in 1999 in verbo 'Jurisprudence' in CB Gray (ed), The Philosophy of Law. An Encyclopedia (New York, Garland Publishing, 1999) vol 1, 459.

The notion of a paradigm has made headway in legal science and is the object of extensive literature.[21] As has been suggested earlier, the notion of a paradigm can be regarded as on a par with the concept of Bachelard's epistemological obstacle. Both cases involve a category or a representation, which is fundamental to a theory, and which either conditions the development of research or hinders its development.[22]

(i) Paradigm and Rationality: 'Objective Objectivity' versus 'Subjective Objectivity'

This form of subjectivity, at the level of paradigms, is not the trivial one as in common understanding, as it takes the form of rationality of a given thought structure within a specific paradigm. These considerations lead to a change in perspective in the way we think of objectivity. The ambition of traditional Cartesian modern science is an absolute objectivity, '*objective objectivity*', pure objectivity that supposes the absence of any subjective element. In this sense, Kelsen designed his pure theory of law, following Kant, who developed his *Critique of Pure Reason*.[23] Kelsen had the ambition of developing a theory of law centred exclusively on law, without any external elements. To reach this objectivity, the subject must fade away. Under Popper's theory, for example, it is imperative to identify the outline of this subjectivity to be certain that it does not interfere with what he calls *world* 3, which is the world of the mind's objective constructions.[24]

'Objectivity' in the classical sense [objective objectivity] is the quality of that which is valid in all times and places. It is universal. It is based on the clear separation of factual judgment and value judgment, of knowledge and belief.

If one accepts that science integrates paradigms a priori, then this pure objectivity must be reconsidered and be placed in its paradigm-related context. The ideal of pure objectivity therefore takes the form of '*subjective objectivity*'. In fact, this objectivity will be expressed in a frame of thought, a paradigm whose acceptance will depend on a complex series of elements and finally be based on a *belief* in the preferable nature of this paradigm as compared to the competing paradigm. This can be observed particularly in social sciences, where probability is at stake, when compared to the exact sciences, where certainty is aimed at.

---

[21] F Ost and M Van de Kerchove, 'De la bipolarité des erreurs ou de quelques paradigmes de la science du droit' in *Archives de philosophie du droit*, vol 33 (Paris, Receuil Sirey, 1989) and see quoted references at 181.
[22] Ibid.
[23] I Kant, *Critique of Pure Reason* (London, Penguin, 2008).
[24] P Nadeau, *verbo* 'Objectivité' in D Lecourt (ed), *Dictionnaire d'histoire et philosophie des sciences* (Paris, PUF, 2006) 818.

In the context of this 'subjective objectivity', the goal sought by the academic is indeed 'objectivity' first and foremost, but that objectivity will be determined in the end by the pre-established cognitive framework or, in other words, the paradigm. Therefore, this subjectivity is not the traditional subjectivity of an individual—something that is much easier to spot—but that of a community. This community can consist of a few hundred or a few thousand researchers in a particular field in the case of paradigms in Kuhn's sense. It can also be hundreds of millions of individuals in the case of (macro) cultural paradigms.

Let's take the example of two legal scholars who are asked to analyse the same Supreme Court decision. The former refers to a positivist paradigm, while the second favours an American realistic approach. They will no doubt explain the grounds for the decision differently. They have both considered the same object, but have seen different things.

The two forms of objectivity (pure and relative) must be contrasted with different forms of subjectivity. In fact, the goal of the project of modernity is to consider man's future in the perspective of progress by using a vision of the world that claims to be objective—pre-modern subjectivity being the basis, in this conception, of irrationality and obscurantism.

Subjectivity can also be split, as we have done earlier for objectivity. The most blatant subjectivity, 'subjective subjectivity' is a form of pure, absolute subjectivity, the counterpart to 'objective objectivity'. This 'subjective subjectivity' is wholly determined by sentiments, values and beliefs. It corresponds to a universe, where the vision of the world is wholly based on what is sacred, natural and supernatural. 'Subjective subjectivity' as a means to relate to truth/reality has little chance of lasting in the long term and in groups that are not fairly small. Indeed, life in society or in a community supposes at least some objectifying, if only for reasons of communication.

The second form of subjectivity in our classification is 'objective subjectivity', where beliefs, values and feelings have been made coherent by means of rationalisation. This is the case, for example, of theology in monotheistic religions. The purpose of objectifying is to make a belief shared by the faithful accessible universally, *in the same way*, in all times and places. The purpose of this effort to objectify is to ensure that the same religion is understood and observed *in the same way* by the members of the religion (internal function). Its purpose is also to present a set of proposals considered to have the value of transcendental truth *in the same way* to those who do not accept the proposals presented as a transcendental truth (external function).

In other words, the purpose of theology is to present a corpus of beliefs and representations of the religion in a systematic way so that they are universally accessible. The 'objective subjectivity' tends to raise beliefs to the level of representations that are, or could be, shared universally. This is not limited to theology, but can also concern political doctrine, for example. It is a process of objectifying a belief.

This is the type of knowledge that prevails in principle in traditional contexts. For example, in Europe before the modern era, monks essentially had a monopoly over knowledge and its transmission.

Objectifying consequently serves a belief (or is in any case important for a belief or at least is deployed within the limits of a belief). In the context of 'subjective objectivity', subjectivity is, on the contrary, subordinate, at least in principle, to objectivity.

Objectivity and subjectivity are generally thought of as opposites, and mutually exclusive. Our approach attempts to more realistically describe the real complexity of these categories, both in scientific practice and in their common meanings.[25]

From the ideal–typical standpoint, we consequently have four concepts and four viewpoints in relation to truth/reality. The fifth is the meta viewpoint that transcends the others. If these points are placed on a tradition–modernity axis that structures the dominant macroparadigm, we can visualise a possible modelisation of these relations to objectivity. On adopting a modern (exclusivist) point of view, the three other points of views (from 1 to 3) become illegitimate. In addition, they are perceived in an evolutionist perspective as former stages of the evolution of knowledge. We have seen, however, that a powerful trend in philosophy of knowledge, notably illustrated by Kuhn, questioned this vision which had become generally accepted. The meta point of view considers the other viewpoints as structures in relation to a vision of the world and not necessarily as logical

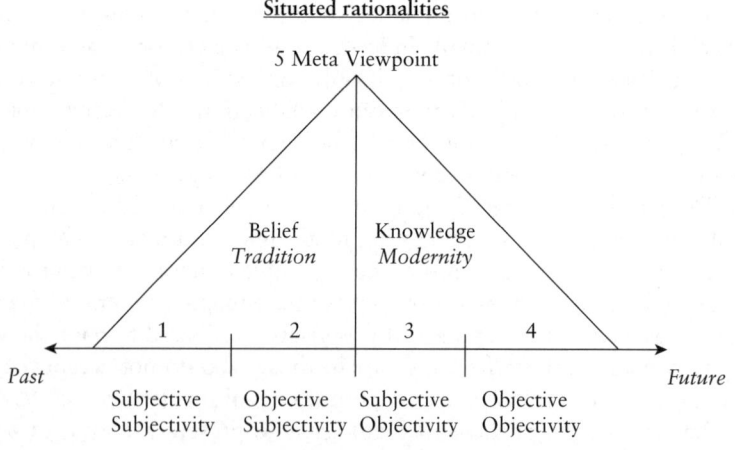

---

[25] For another view of the different kinds and degrees of objectivity as put forward by Andrei Marmor and John Rawls, see M Niemi, 'Objective Legal Reasoning—Objectivity Without Objects' ch 4 in this volume.

stages. This is not a causal relationship, but rather one of 'elective affinities', as Weber would put it. A hypothesis can be formulated that inclusive modernity, which constitutes the cultural background of American society, presents elective affinities with subjective objectivity as a means to relate to truth as these are described in social sciences and legal sciences in the United States. We will come back to this point.

(ii) Culturally Determined Rationalities and 'Subjective Objectivity'

These culturally varying rationalities, which determine 'subjective objectivity' through the respective paradigms can be illustrated by debates in legal theory. The conflict between positivism and jusnaturalism is undoubtedly one of the most fundamental to be suppressed in the history of legal theory. In Europe, it structured many of the main debates during the nineteenth century and part of the twentieth century.[26]

These two paradigms have been the subject of many different developments. According to Bobbio, these two opposing paradigms can be approached from three different angles, namely a (positive) legal approach, a theory of law, or an ideology.

From the first angle, positivism stands out for its effort to limit its object to existing law imposed by the legal system. On the other hand, jusnaturalism integrates existing law (law as it is), as well as ideal law, namely law as it should be, into its aim. In this context, legal science is a normative discipline, which furnishes precepts indicating what law should be.

In the second aspect, positivism generally regards the rules of law as acts of will, with commandments issued by human beings, while natural law sees just relationships based on the nature of things, the laws of reason.[27] Positivism gives further standing to the idea of positive law, which is characterised by formal perfection. In this context, a judge engages in a purely deductive activity. In contrast with positive law, the activity of a judge consists of adopting and improving existing law.[28]

In the third aspect, ideology, Bobbio sees positivism as a 'legalistic ethic' according to which laws must be obeyed, while natural law is an ethic, which prescribes compliance with the law as long as it is just.[29]

These comparisons and distinctions are undoubtedly helpful, but the ideological function does not appear to us to be correctly situated on the most determinant level, that is, its anthropological function. What is actually the case?

---

[26] L François, *Le problème de la définition du droit* (Faculté de Droit, d'Economie et Sciences Sociales de Liège, 1978) 35.
[27] Ost and Van de Kerchove, *De la bipolarité des erreurs* (n 21) 183.
[28] Ibid.
[29] N Bobbio, as summarised by Ost and Van de Kerchove, ibid 183–84.

Actually, the ideological function of positivism is much more fundamental. It is at the very core of the modern conception of law and represents its 'central core'. From the point of view of modern democracy, based on the principles of sovereignty of the people and separation of powers, only formalistic positivism can meet the requirements of these basic principles. In fact, the only valid law is that which is formulated by the legislature and the bodies empowered by it. A judge is restricted to his role as a neutral and impartial legal specialist, responsible for applying law as drafted by the legislature. He is, in the words of Montesquieu, the mouth by which law is expressed and is therefore its simple executor. This is the core of the modern conception of law and of its legitimacy. All other conceptions of law, which diverge from this definition, are at odds with one or more of the foregoing principles. Legal realism, for example, describes the judge's activity as diverging from this role as a neutral and impartial executor of law, since he is regarded as being influenced by a number of extra-legal considerations.

Positivism occupies a central place not only in the area of legitimation of law within modern society, but also in the more general universe in which it acts as an assumed vector of progress of the human condition. It could be said that 'one could perceive Kelsen as the "legal telos of the West"', who took the 18th century legal revolution to its highest point, culminating in the *'new legal order'* that has been installed or recommended since that period'.[30]

In fact, legal positivism goes together with the philosophical positivism fashionable in the nineteenth century. According to the concept developed by Auguste Comte, the development of the human mind corresponds to the famous *'law of three stages'*. After passing through the *theological* stage and the *metaphysical* stage, the mind has reached the *positive* stage. For him, the metaphysical stage is basically only a modification of the theological one.[31]

A parallel can be drawn between these three stages and the concept of law, which also developed following the three stages, namely, *religious* or *sacred* law, *natural* law, and *positive* law. This is neither a coincidence nor a demonstration of the truth of Comte's postulates, but rather an interpretation of a cultural programme, which shaped a certain conception of the legitimacy of law. This programme combines scientism, evolutionism and the will to break with the pre-modern past, which is assimilated with obscurantism. This breach is made according to the stages of evolution. Auguste Comte crystallised philosophical positivism in his law of the three stages, namely in a representation of the world that draws on the ideas of

---

[30] P Dubouchet, *Sémiotique juridique, introduction à une science du droit* (Paris, PUF, 1990) 182.

[31] *Cf Cours de philosophie positive*, original edn (Paris, Bachelier, 1830–42) 15, quoted in P Arbousse-Bastide, *A Comte*, (Paris, PUF, 1968) 70.

the European Enlightenment, which was the basis for the French revolution. This new conception of the world is found in the way progress of the human condition is expressed in law. The modernity paradigm has imposed a conception of things that has overtaken our perception/construction of reality. Competing or dissident conceptions have lost their legitimacy. This is an illustration of the fact that it is culture (via paradigms) which moulds our conception of law and not our conception of law which moulds our culture.

The following diagram shows in a very simplified way that each cultural macroparadigm puts the system of representation of the world, and particularly the law, in the centre.[32]

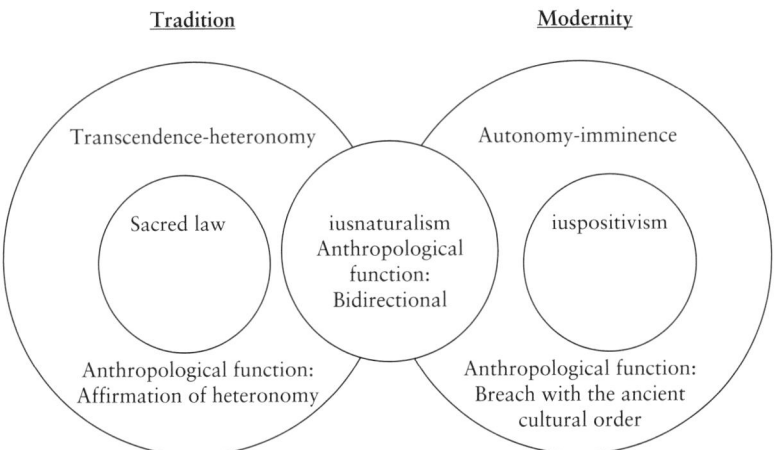

Tradition places at its centre a sacred concept of law, whose anthropological function lies in affirming the heteronomy and regulating the transcendence of a system. From an axiological standpoint,[33] this system is mainly turned to the past. Modernity, on the other hand, gives positivism a central place in its representation of law. Its anthropological function consists of affirming the independence of the legal system from other social systems and representations of the past. This system is essentially turned to the future and it aims at a breach with the former cultural order. Natural law lies between these two models and is bidirectional. So, it was able to

---

[32] Actually, an approach that tries to respect the complexity of phenomena should use a recursive, retroactive reasoning when applied to a conception of law and culture, rather than in terms of linear causality.

[33] When referring to tradition, I am referring to any cultural system where the reference to the past, by means of a founding theory of respect of the authority of the elders, constitutes the ultimate criterion of legitimacy.

uphold the principles of the Christian conception of the world explicitly in the framework of classical natural law illustrated by the Thomist doctrine. With the advent of modern natural law since Grotius, law has become secular and is now based on reason. It claims to be universal and unchangeable. From then on, it can serve equally well as the foundation of the Universal Declaration of Human Rights, as a conservative image of the social order or as law implicitly associated with some religious conception. Natural law was the means for gaining access to the law of modernity. Nevertheless, it deploys an a-historical, rigid, 'fixist' concept of law.[34] This ambivalent character makes it an anthropological vehicle with insufficient legitimacy for the tenets of pure modernity. Hence, we could conclude that Bobbio's analysis is not inaccurate in itself, but it seems to confuse the function of positivism with its consequences.

However, these (micro and meso) paradigms need not be overly reified. The anthropological function that they fulfil can change with the context. Jusnaturalism was a means of gaining access to legal modernity and was then (almost) entirely cut off from tradition. It is making a comeback, so to speak, in the form of human rights, which tend to become the law on which all law is based. This is a further indication that the most fundamental

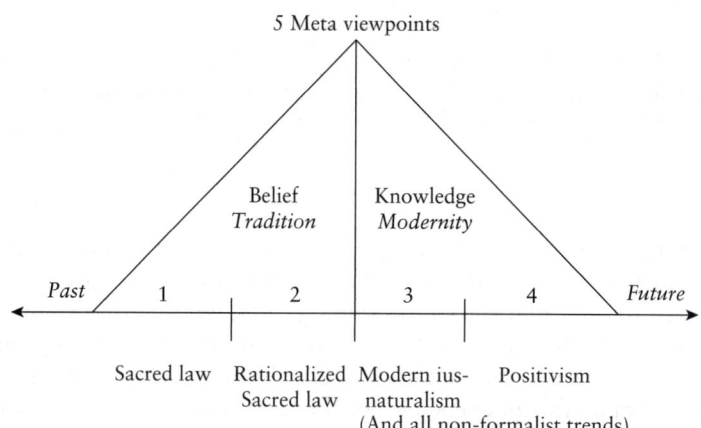

[34] It should be noted that there are different trends that claim to stem from natural law. Alf Ross identifies four: theological natural law, historical natural law, sociological natural law and rational and anthropocentric natural law. The objective here is not to analyse the various trends of jusnaturalism or of juspositivism, but to identify the highest possible level of its anthropological functions. (A Ross, 'Validity and the Conflict between Legal Postivism and Natural Law' in *Revista Juridica de Buenos Aires*, IV, 1961, 49–93).

determination of the paradigms of science (of law) is done at a higher level, that of cultural macro-paradigms.

At this point, the conceptions of law can be placed on our situated rationality triangle. We see that classical jusnaturalism is placed as a form of objectified belief (objective subjectivity). Modern jusnaturalism, and more fundamentally, all non-formalist (non-positive) tendencies fall preferentially into a framework of inclusive modernity (which shows elective affinities with subjective objectivity), whereas positivism and its claim to objective objectivity belong preferentially to the context of exclusive modernity.

(iii) Legal Theory, Anthropology of Law and Anthropology of Knowledge

'Continental legal theory is uncannily "other" for an American, perhaps because just about everything in our legal culture is present in theirs, often translated word for word, but nothing seems to have the same meaning' (Duncan Kennedy).[35]

(a) A Reversal of Perspectives for a Global Theory of Law

In any field of knowledge, it is usual to underline the influence of great authors, of paradigms or of certain current theories stemming from them. Generally, it is considered that the intrinsic qualities of these works and these theories have made them influential in the field of ideas and our understanding of reality. This is no doubt true, but an additional dimension could be added—the importance of these works is in part due to an external factor: the correspondence (or elective affinities) between these works and the social-cultural context in which they were developed. This would thus be another example of the influence of (cultural) paradigms. They influence to some degree the reception that may be given to a theory, or a construction of the mind.

How can it otherwise be explained that the works of Kelsen, which were undoubtedly the most widely commented on works by a legal theorist in continental Europe during the twentieth century, were received with much greater reserve in the United States despite the fact that Kelsen taught there and tried to develop an objective, universal theory of law?[36] Conversely, the Law and Economics movement could not gain ground in France although it has been institutionalised in the United States for about five decades.[37]

---

[35] D Kennedy, *A Critique of Adjudication (fin de siècle)* (Cambridge, Harvard University Press, 1997) 92.

[36] H Kelsen, 'Judicial Review of Legislation: A Comparative Study of the Austrian and American Constitution' (1942) *The Journal of Politics* 183–200.

[37] D Terré, *Les questions morales du droit* (Paris, PUF, 2007) 323–41.

Many more examples can be found when considering all the trends in continental and American schools of legal theory.

The same comment could be made for those who are commonly referred to as post-modern philosophers like Lyotard or Deleuze, who enjoyed a much more favourable reception in the United States than in their own country, where they were hardly thought of as convincing. How else can one explain that socialism has made so little headway in the United States, whilst according to Marx' analyses, the structure of American capitalism should make it the country where socialism would most naturally take root?

In other words, it would be appropriate to develop an angle of analysis based on a meta point of view, which implies a shift in perspective: the reply to the classical question of what is the added value of a research project, or a paradigm, must be seen in the light of the ideas they reflect. These (meso and micro) paradigms act here as anthropological catalysts. This approach entails a reversal of perspective that stresses the background of (legal) science. The idea is to look for the causes of the success of a given author, or school of thought, and to see them in relation to a given system of representation. By doing so, one may conclude that a certain context is more or less receptive to this type of thought, or that the type of thought can hope for a certain reception and interpretation in a given cultural context.

This reversal of perspective does not question the classical approach, it completes it, by bringing this theory of law to another level which both precedes and overrides the others. It precedes them because it establishes what constitutes the cognitive (theoretical) framework within which legal science is deployed and the normative (empirical) framework within which law applies. It overrides them because this is a reflective meta viewpoint that in principle falls under anthropology of law, and more importantly, anthropology of knowledge.[38] This approach may be located in one of the major fields of legal theory: the analysis of the ideological content of law or, in other words, the values and ideologies that are not explicitly stated that are found in legislation, case law and legal doctrine.[39]

(b) Weber and Cultural Paradigms: Understanding Weber's Comprehension

This concept of knowledge in terms of cultural paradigms could be linked to Weber's approach. First of all, Max Weber adopted a macro-scale approach in his comprehensive sociology. Moreover, he tried to place human actions

---

[38] Here, I am referring to anthropology understood in its fundamental sense and not in the restrictive sense that is traditionally used. In the same way as Max Weber 'broadened' his sociology by a form of anthropology, anthropology should be '« broadened' by a form of sociology. This would result in anthropology being applied with the same intensity to the study of traditional contexts and to that of modern contexts.

[39] M Van Hoecke, *verbo* 'Théorie générale du droit' in A-J Arnaud (ed), *Dictionnaire encyclopédique de théorie et de socioloige du droit*, 2nd edn (Paris, LGDJ, 1993) 611.

in a context of broader meaning and representations. So Max Weber tried to show that capitalism took meaning from the theology of Luther and his successors. He proceeded in the same way with legal phenomena. For Weber's sociology, for example, 'charisma is the key to archaic Roman law, primitive French law and Nordic law. A theocratic attitude explains the characteristics of Hindu, Islamic and Jewish law. The concept of material rationalisation is closer to Justinian legislation and eighteenth century princely law. The interests of the bourgeoisie and university training of contemporary legal specialists explain the current systematisation of law.'[40] Weber maintained with regard to legal enunciations that legal sociology must take account of the representations that men give to the meaning and the validity of these enunciations.[41] However, Max Weber developed a point of view that in itself appears to be culturally situated in the paradigm of exclusive (continental) modernity, although he did so subtly.[42] Notwithstanding the originality of his approach, Weber does not break with the presuppositions of sociology, which are those of modernity.[43]

The paradigm within which Weber's view can be situated is found particularly in his argument on the disenchantment of the world, which does not take into account the American religious exception that Alexis de Toqueville had described before him. More fundamentally for our topic, this can be seen in his study of legal phenomena via the famous 'English problem'. Weber makes foreseeability of law one of the prerequisites for the development of modern capitalism. This characteristic corresponds to formally rational law or, in other words systematic law stemming from a logical interpretation of the meaning of predefined legal norms. Continental European law corresponds for Weber to the ideal type of formal legal rationality. But historically, modern capitalism took shape in England, notwithstanding the characteristics of Common Law.[44]

The influence of the exclusive modernity macro-paradigm on Max Weber's thinking seems to be so strong that it caused him to make a surprising 'mistake', despite his exceptional sense of observation, when he

---

[40] J Grosclaude, 'Introduction' in Max Weber, *Sociologie du droit* (Paris, Quadrige/PUF, 2007) 23.

[41] M Weber, *Essai sur quelques catégories de la sociologie compréhensive*, (trans J Freund) (Pztid, Plon, 1965) 346.

[42] In our triangle (see Figure 3 and Figure 5) Weber would be in sector 4.

[43] As emphasised by Bourdon, Habermas considers that sociology cannot be conceived of as a neutral science, whose first concern would be to improve our understanding of social phenomena. On the contrary, its main principle is normative. Sociology must help societies move in the right direction (R Boudon, *L'idéologie ou l'origine des idées reçues* (Paris, Fayard, 1986) 118).

[44] M Coutu, *Max Weber et les rationalités du droit*, (Paris, LGDJ, 1995) 124ff. See also DM Trubek, 'Max Weber on Law and the Rise of Capitalism' in AJ Trevino (ed), *The Sociology of Law* (New Brunswick and London, Transaction Publishers, 2008) 220–31 and more particularly 229–31 (ch 4: 'A Deviant Case and the Problems of Historical Verification: Legalism and Capitalism in England').

refers to the West in terms that clearly concern only the European continent. For example, he maintains that: 'For its economic activity, only the West had a legal system and an administration that had reached such a degree of legal and formal perfection.'[45] And again when he specifies that 'the strictly systematic forms of thought in any rational legal doctrine typical for Roman law and its offshoot, Occidental law, are not found anywhere else'.[46] While Weber can be considered to show the axiological neutrality that he so stresses, he uses it in a paradigm-related and culturally restricted cognitive space.

(c) Cultural Paradigms and Interpretation Theory

Applied to various themes in legal theory, such as the theory of interpretation, this cultural paradigms approach, culturally determined rationality and subjective objectivity should offer a view on the issues from a different standpoint. Legal positivism considers that law is reduced to legal standards. How, then, is it possible to explain that the same legal standard covers interpretations that differ so much in time and space? It suffices to look at a legal standard as fundamental as the principle of equality. No one challenges that a revolution in representations has taken place between the nineteenth century, when it did not even include the right to vote for women in many systems, and the present day at the beginning of the twenty-first century where, in a growing number of systems it includes an obligation to maintain electoral parity. The objective standard (equality is a mathematical sign) has not changed, but it has been interpreted differently, and significantly so, without upsetting public opinion (external legal culture) or the community of legal professionals (internal legal culture). This is an example of objective objectivity (the concept of 'equality') which has taken the form of subjective objectivity (the interpretation of the concept of 'equality'). This also holds for all changes in case law inspired, for example, by the European Court of Human Rights. Even the court itself refers to evolutive case law.

It appears that the positivist approach is insufficient to apprehend the complexity of law. In reaction, American legal realism maintains that law is what the judge says. This theory could, in its extreme version, be presented in the form of the following equation:

D (judicial decision) = S (Stimulus received by the judge) × J (judge's personality).

---

[45] M Weber, 'Vorbemerkung' in *Gesammelte Aufzätze zur Religionssoziologie* (Tübingen, JCB Mohr, 1988) 11.
[46] Ibid 2.

This is another form of reductionism since the legal norm disappears from the explanation.[47]

In our approach, we propose the following equation:

D (judicial decision) = CM (Cultural Model) × LN (Legal Norms) + J (Judge's personality)

A legal decision is the result of the relationship between the legal norm (positivism, law in books) and the judge, who gives it its concrete content (legal realism, law in action), in the context of a cultural model that will exacerbate, restrict or neutralise its effects. Take, for example, the claims of certain movements that prohibition of marriage between same-sex partners is a breach of equality. The legal response to this type of claim is not found exclusively in a careful reading of the legal standards that guarantee equality. It is also found in the interaction of each element of the equation that gives us a very rough idea of the basic parameters of subjective objectivity in judicial activity.

III. CONCLUSIONS

The developments described above cannot claim to be a conclusive demonstration of the validity of the hypotheses in their own right. To achieve this, the same approach would have to be applied to all the paradigms and theories on legal science in order to map all the theoretical options and practices in connection with a given cultural model and to reproduce it in the cultural macroparadigms. This would verify whether a reasonably consistent and coherent table could be established where the final test would lie in the clearly identified cultural models and paradigms. In a second stage, the validity of the theoretical tenets would have to be tested with an application to all themes in legal theory.

We can already stress that, if this approach is validated, it should apply *mutatis mutandis*, both to legal science and to adjudication, which both respond to the need for objectivity.

This paradigm approach to culture situated on the broadest possible scale of observation, gives us a glimpse of paradoxes. The most important is undoubtedly the one that relates to objectivity, which the classical conception shows as an objectivity/subjectivity dichotomy. The paradigm approach refers us to the constructed dimension of knowledge and places us in what we call 'subjective objectivity'. This approach has fundamental consequences. It

---

[47] J Frank, 'What courts do in Fact' reproduced in J Hall (ed), *Readings in Jurisprudence* (Indianapolis, The Bobbs Merrill Company, 1938) 1107. The realist school is of course a much richer and subtler school of thought, going beyond this equation. See, eg F Michaut, *L'école de la sociological jurisprudence et le mouvement réaliste américain* (Lille, Atelier national de reproduction des thèses, 1985).

obliges us to locate sources of subjectivities in the context of a scientific process, in order to explain them. In fact, it forms the anthropological prerequisites of legal science. If these sources of subjectivity are not neutralised, a meta point of view must allow them to be described and situated. This is what we have done, briefly, with the distinction between exclusive and inclusive modernity. This distinction makes it possible to draw correlations based on elective affinities between a given paradigm of legal science and a conception of modernity (at paradigm level). An attempt could be made to establish similar correlations using a given traditional conception of law and a conception of tradition.

This is not a relativist approach. Relativism itself is a form of subjectivity, since it postulates a priori that everything has the same value. Rather, it is a principle of relativity in the basic meaning of the expression—establishing a relationship between some elements and others. We can call this *relationism*. We stressed the parallel between the axiological/metaphysical/cultural dimension of paradigms in the exact sciences and in particular physics, as Kuhn has described it. We have argued that a fortiori, this dimension would necessarily be found in human and social sciences and in the general system of representations of a society. In the twentieth century, Einstein brought about a revolution in quantum physics, in which he established that the very core of science was affected by relativity (theory of limited and general relativity). *Mutatis mutandis*, this relativity must a fortiori be found in the field of human and social sciences and representations of society in general.

Further analysis should make it possible to show that this particular, invisible form of subjectivity is apparent when comparing the 'scientific' representations in France and in the United States. This has already been noticed for the integration of the cultural dimension into the field of knowledge. In European legal doctrine and its underlying theories, formalistic positivism always remains the dominant paradigm, whereas in the United States it was quite rapidly 'overtaken' by legal realism that is shifting to a 'balkanisation' of legal theory today.[48] In other words, it appears that France, which is the heir to the French revolution and, hence, historically the central country of (politico-legal) modernity, still functions in the context of legitimisation of the (self referential) modern project, while in the United States the cultural framework is one of inclusive modernity, which may be misleading from a continental European point of view. In the context of our hypothesis, it explains the permeability of the American context to pre-modern, 'amodern' and post-modern conceptions.

These considerations lead to the development of a new 'stage' in the theory of law. It will be supplied by anthropology of knowledge and will

---

[48] D Kennedy, *Sexy dressing, Violences sexuelles et érotisation de la domination*, (Paris, Flammarion, 2008) 49–51 (introductive part in the form of an interview with Duncan Kennedy).

provide the cultural conditions (in a wider sense and, therefore, including the social dimension) for the production of legal knowledge. The idea is to bring out the cultural dimension, which positivism has concealed, by means of a systematic approach establishing the links between legal theory and its cultural universe.

From this point of view, the core of formalistic positivism could be explained in a more correct way as follows. It constitutes the most powerful framework for legitimatising the rule of law and modern democracy. For this, its contribution is indispensable. But from the point of view of pure knowledge, it does not take account of the legal phenomenon in all its complexity. Hence, positivism appears as an indispensable 'ought to be' and realism (in a wider sense, namely, one that groups all tendencies that are not strictly formalist) as an unavoidable 'being'.

Index

Aarnio, Aulis, 86, 94, 96–7, 100, 102–3, 139
'Aboutness'
  common sense, 65
  experience of problems, 65
  required standpoint, 65
Acceptability
  criteria of acceptability, 75–6, 97, 99
  judicial decisions, 15, 97
  legal certainty, 85–6, 88, 91, 96–8, 100–1
  moral acceptability, 98
  social acceptability, 98
  substantive acceptability, 99
  validity of law, 100
Access to justice
  legal certainty, 94
  popular expectation, 94
Adjudication
  binding force, 60
  evaluation of facts, 6
  external elements, 6
  fair solution, 60
  interpretation, 6
    see also **Interpretation**
  judicial decisions, 92
  legal rules, 77–8, 82–3
  neutrality, 6
  objectivity, 247
  reasons, 60
  reservoir of instruments, 60
  valid instruments, 60
Argumentation
  arguing as a practice, 113–4, 118
  argumentation theory, 112–3
  categorisation, 141
  changing communicative practices, 116
  concept of argumentation, 110, 121
  cooperative contest, 114
  deliberative democratic practices, 15
  dissensus, 114
  exchange of reasons, 114–5
  formal setting, 117
  game-like activity, 112–3, 115–7, 120–1, 129–30
  general notion, 16
  hard cases, 144, 150
  in-between cases, 148, 150
  informal setting, 117
  legal logic, 27, 30
    see also **Legal logic**
  parliamentary argumentation
    constructive politics, 120
    Discourse Quality Index, 119–20
    parliamentary meetings, 109, 111–2, 116–9
    rules of order, 123–5, 127
    top-down approach, 119
    yielding to better arguments, 120
  patterns of argumentation, 106
  political communication, 117
  presuppositions, 15, 115–9, 130
  reflexive communicative action, 114
  rules of argumentation
    acceptance of same position, 115
    arguing with others, 109–10
    basic rules, 110, 122, 129–30
    controversy, 121
    deviations, 116
    equal opportunity to contribute, 123, 125–6, 129
    equality, 114–5, 118
    exclusion of relevant contributors, 114, 123–4, 129
    factual/counterfactual, 116
    fixed rules, 110, 121
    freedom, 114, 118
    inclusion, 114, 118
    interpretation, 110
    interruptions, 125–6
    modification, 110, 119
    non-domination, 114, 118
    objectivity, 15, 20, 110, 117–8, 121, 130
    problematisations, 122–3
    relevant contributions, 115, 123
    rule-governed activity, 109–10
    rules of order, 123–5, 127
    sincerity, 114, 118
    specific games, 15–16
    specific practices, 15
    superior line of reasoning, 114–5
    tactics, 15–16, 123, 126, 130
    tone of discussion, 127–9
    transformation, 119
    withdrawal of argumentation, 126
  testing of reasons, 114
Assumptions
  see **Law's assumptions**

Bentham, Jeremy, 179
Bobbio, Norberto, 239, 242

252 Index

Capitalism
  development, 245
  theological influences, 245
Causation
  causal maximalists, 185
  causal minimalism, 184–5
  causal principles, 179
  law's assumptions, 176–7
    see also **Law's assumptions**
  legal responsibility, 180–5
Certainty
  see also **Legal certainty**
  avoiding chaos, 3–4
  collective rituals, 3
  conventions, 26
  epistemological viewpoint 3–4
    see also **Legal epistemology**
  legal dimension, 3
    see also **Legal certainty**
  moral needs, 3
  religious dimension, 3
Coherence
  criterion of rightness, 107
  legal argumentation, 107
  legal rulings, 107–8
  netting of arguments, 108
  notion of coherence, 107–8
Comparative law
  common function, 10
  common goals, 10
  comparative analysis, 53
  cultural differences, 10–11, 218
    see also **Cultural paradigms; Legal cultures**
  cultural pluralism, 18
  independent comparisons, 220
  inter-subjectivity, 10
  legal scholarship, 176
  legal terminology, 220
  legal translators, 220
  lingusitics
    linguistic and translation studies, 213, 220–1, 223
    linguistic disciplines, 213
  methodologies
    art of interpretation, 222
    comparison as process, 221
    cross-fertilisation, 222
    functionalism, 222
    inter-disciplinarity, 221
    law as subject, 221
    methodological pluralism, 221
    representation/re-presentation, 222
    scheme of intelligibility, 221–2
    selection/presentation of facts, 222
    social science, 221
  tertium comparationis, 10, 220, 222, 227
  umbrella concept, 221

  neutral viewpoint, 9
  objective viewpoint, 9
  objectives, 53
  objectivity of facts, 10
  similarities, 10
  universal law. 10–11
Competence
  administrative decisions, 35–6
  concept of competence, 24, 33, 35
  contractual competence, 34–5
  demand of competence, 34–5
  judicial competence, 34
  juridical acts, 34–6, 40
    see also **Juridical acts**
  legal powers, 36–8, 40
    see also **Legal powers**
  legal theory, 38, 61
    see also **Legal theory**
  legislative competence, 34
  limited by special rules, 35
  neutrality, 24, 37
  public officers, 34
  relevant competence, 35–6
  special legal status, 36
Concepts
  see also **Legal concepts**
  coloured concepts
    common concerns, 62
    judicial concerns, 62
    legislators' concerns, 62
    normative element, 62–3
    social practices, 62–3
  common understandings, 57–8
  criterial concepts, 58
  differences in orientation, 60
  disagreement on criteria, 57–8
  diversity, 65
  fairness, 92–3
  intension of a concept, 45, 55
  intension of neighbouring concepts, 59
  interpretive concepts, 58
  knowledge, 244
  level of abstraction, 58
  moral concepts, 92
  shared social practice, 58
  stipulated conditions, 64
  syndromes, 55
  trunk concepts, 58–9
Conditions
  disagreements, 56–7
  level of abstraction 55–6
  level of concreteness, 59
  membership of categories, 55–6
  nature of agreement, 57
  number of conditions, 55–6, 65
  specified conditions, 55
  status of conditions, 55–6, 65
  weight of conditions, 55–6, 65

Consent
    law's assumptions, 176–7
    see also Law's assumptions
    right to do wrong, 166–7
Conventions
    categorisation by convention, 30
    certainty, 26
    consequences, 32, 40
    nature of reality, 43
    new knowledge, 40
    non-legal example
        certainty by conventions, 26
        classification systems, 25–6
        nature of planets, 25–6, 39
        whales as mammals, 24–5, 39, 55
    objectivity, 24, 26, 32, 41–4, 198
    purpose, 41
    truth by convention, 39–40, 43
Cotterrell, Roger, 203
Cultural paradigms
    see also Paradigms
    cognitive frame, 235
    concept of knowledge, 244
    cultural and social representations, 234
    culturally determined rationality, 246
    epistemological consequences, 234–6
    influence, 243
    interpretation theory, 246
    legal science, 235–6, 248
    legal theory, 234–5
        see also Legal theory
    macro paradigms, 234, 241, 243
    meta-viewpoints, 238, 242, 244
    modernity, 234, 241
        see also Modernity
    rationality, 236, 246
    social sciences, 234, 248
    soft sciences, 234
    structure of thought, 234
    subjective objectivity, 246
    system of representation, 235–6, 241
    tradition, 241
Culture
    see also Legal cultures
    broad definition, 231
    constitutive elements, 218
    environment of beliefs, ideas and practices, 217–8
    ethno-linguistic culture, 230
    levels of culture, 230
    minority cultures, 231
    modernity
        see Modernity
    national cultures, 217
    polysemic nature, 230
    religious cultures, 19, 230
    social identity, 231
    state of mind and ideas, 217–8

Democracy
    deliberative democratic practices, 15
    democratic institutions, 93
    legal certainty, 85–6
    Nordic nation state, 85
    openness, 86
Discourse Quality Index
    consensus, 15
    parliamentary argumentation, 119–20
Dutch parliament
    approval of illegal actions, 124
    Communist Party, 123–4
    conduct of business, 126–7
    equal opportunity to contribute, 125–6, 129
    equality issues, 115
    exclusion of relevant contributors, 123–4, 129
    freedom of discussion, 128
    Freedom Party (PVV), 110–1
    historical controversies, 121
    immigration, 110
    interruption of speakers, 125–6
    Islamaphobia, 110
    loyalty issues, 111, 124
    nationality issues, 111, 115, 124
    non-procedural motion, 129
    parliamentary powers, 126–7
    post WWI period, 123–4
    problematisations, 123
    rules of argumentation, 109, 111–2
        see also Argumentation
    rules of order, 123–4, 127
    Socialist Party, 123–4
    tone of discussion, 127–9
    withdrawal from argumentation, 114, 126
Dworkin, Ronald, 3, 13, 46–7, 57–60, 83, 86, 90–3, 97, 103, 135, 139, 154, 198

Elster, Jon, 112–3, 115
Equality principle
    discrimination, 5
    distinctions within groups, 5
    formal equality 5
    legal certainty, 96
    legal standards, 246
    substantive equality, 5
    unequal treatment of children, 5–6
Ethical subjectivism
    philosophical background, 72
    positivism, 73
        see also Positivism
EU citizenship
    legal reasoning, 90
EU law
    competition law, 99
    customs duties, 104, 106

254   *Index*

democratic government, 85
direct effect, 106
ECJ decisions, 86–8, 104–6
efficiency, 88
equality, 88
European values, 86
free movement of goods
  customs duties, 104
  measures having equivalent effect, 88
  quantitative restrictions, 88
free movement of services, 88
human rights, 86
indeterminacy, 89–9
legal certainty, 102, 107
legality, 88
levels of justification, 88
literal interpretation, 108
moral considerations, 88
subsidiarity principle, 88
European Court of Human Rights
evolutive case law, 246

Feyerabend, Paul, 197
Finish water law
see also **Objective interpretation**
economic interests, 145–7, 149
environmental concerns, 147–8
legal interpretation
  easy cases, 146–7
  factual premise, 146–7
  hard cases, 146–50
  in-between cases, 147–50
  no relevant harm, 146–7
  lack of interpretive choice, 147
  normative premise, 146–7
  objective interpretation, 146, 150
regulation, 145
water permits, 145, 150
Foucault, Michel, 16, 110, 121–2, 129
Free movement of goods
customs duties, 104
measures having equivalent effect, 88
quantitative restrictions, 88
Free movement of services
moral considerations, 88
Friedman, Lawrence, 217–8, 230
Fuller, Lon, 13, 46–7, 56, 137, 186–7

Galilei, Galileo, 72
Gardner, John, 7
Glenn, Patrick H, 210
Grosswald Curran, Vivian, 11

Habermas, Jürgen, 15–16, 99, 110, 113–23, 129–30
Hage, Jaap, 12–14, 20, 23–4, 55, 132–5, 137, 149, 198, 212
Halliday, Michael, 214–5

Hart, Herbert LA, 13, 16–17, 23, 42, 46, 56, 73, 76–7, 137, 157–62, 164–5, 168, 175, 178–88, 190, 192, 198, 203, 206, 211
History
history of ideas, 121–2
history of individual practices, 122
history of thought, 121–2, 129
problematisations, 122
Hobbes, Thomas, 3, 205
Hohfeld, Wesley Newcomb, 160–2
Holmes, Oliver Wendell, 26–7, 197, 207–8
Honoré, Tony, 17, 179–80, 182–8
Human behaviour
cultural practices, 153
cultural relativism, 16
empirical research, 190–3
ethical relativism, 153
fundamental prohibitions, 153
human nature, 187
inalienable rights, 16–17
  see also **Inalienable rights**
individual freedom, 187
individual's rights, 154
inner morality of law, 186
law's assumptions
  see **Law's assumptions**
legal design, 190–3
moral duties, 17. 157–8, 168
morality and law, 153–5
motivational attitudes, 192
natural law, 186
  see also **Natural law**
natural rights, 153
presumed rationality, 17
regulation, 185–7, 191
responsibility, 186, 188
  see also **Legal responsibility**
social control, 188
tolerance, 153
understanding of reality, 17
universal human rights, 153
Human rights
basic human rights, 154, 167
European Court of Human Rights, 246
fundamental rights, 104
importance, 86
inalienable rights, 16
  see also **Inalienable rights**
Universal Declaration of Human Rights, 154
universal human rights, 153
universal validity, 16
Hume, John, 72, 74, 177

Inalienable rights
duty-based ethics, 169
element of 'right', 156–7
elementary truths, 168

essence of things, 155
fundamental prohibitions, 17
human dignity, 156
humanity
  duty to respect, 157
  essential features, 156
  treatment as human being, 157
inherent dignity, 154
logical inalienability, 155–6
meaning, 154–6
moral demand, 169
moral duties, 17, 157–8, 168
moral rights, 157
  see also **Moral rights**
morality and law, 153–5, 166, 168–9
principle of deceit, 168–9
prohibitions, 168–9
respect for humanity, 17
understanding, 155
Universal Declaration of Human Rights, 154
universally recognised principles of conduct, 168
US Declaration of Independence, 154
will theory, 154
  see also **Will theory**
Individual rights
  fundamental rights, 91
  human behaviour 154
  principles as norms, 91
  see also **Principles as norms**
Inside-outside dichotomy
  see also **Law as a house metaphor**
  insiders
    comparative lawyers, 52–3
    normative insiders, 50, 52
    practice-orientated, 50
  outsiders
    comparative lawyers, 52–3
    detached, 50
    neutral, 50
    objectivity, 52
    social scientists, 51–2
Interest theory of rights
  exercise of rights, 164–5
  incapacity to make choices, 164
  interests generating rights, 163
  protection of interests, 165
  rights on the basis of interests, 163
Interpretation
  context-bound, 106–7, 138
  EU law, 108
  hermeneutic circle, 137–8
  indeterminacy, 89–90
  internal logic, 105
  interpretation models
    authoritative model, 105
    defining concepts, 105
    dialectic model, 105
    discursive alternative justification, 105–6
    linguistic interpretation, 105
    subsumption model, 105
  legal rules, 16, 82–4
  literal meaning, 87, 89, 107–8
  objective interpretation
    see **Objective interpretation**
  patterns of argumentation, 106
  practical reasoning, 106
  predicate logic, 105
  prerequisite for understanding, 138
  principles as norms, 91
    see also **Principles as norms**
  subjectivists, 138–9
  systemic interpretation, 107
  teleological approach, 87, 105–7

Judges
  activism, 93
  deference, 92–3
  discretion, 92
  neutrality, 6
Judicial decisions
  acceptability, 15, 97, 99
  adjudication, 92
  casuism, 107
  conceptual definition argument, 104
  context-bound, 15
  ECJ decisions, 86–8, 104–6
  human rights protection, 104
  interpretation
    appeal to sources of law, 103–5
    literal meaning, 87, 89
    proto-norms, 103–4
    rational interpretation, 97
    relevant norm, 94–5
    systemic interpretation, 107
    teleological approach, 87
  judicial activism, 93
  judicial deference, 92–3
  judicial discretion, 92
  justification
    correct reasoning, 94
    easy cases, 141–2, 144
    hard cases, 144
    in-between cases, 143–4
    justified legal decisions, 94
    levels of justification, 86–9, 96–7, 103–5, 108, 141–4
    moral or social values, 15, 87–8, 94
    statutory support, 94
  legal certainty, 15, 85–6, 95–6, 100
  legal principles and policies, 103–4
  legal realism, 246–7
  legal theory, 92
  legality, 99
  legitimacy, 88

256 *Index*

locally varying criteria, 15
political morality, 86
precedents, 81–2, 87, 92
predictability, 95, 99
principles and policies, 91
qualification, 94–5
Juridical acts
administrative decisions, 35–7
capacity, 34
competence, 34–6, 40
conditions, 33–4
intended effects, 33–4
intentional changes, 34
legal effects, 33, 35–6, 38
legal powers, 37–8
see also **Legal powers**
performance, 33–4, 39
recognition, 38
validity, 33–5, 39
Juridiversity
legal cultures, 18, 210
Jurisprudence
common scholarly community, 12
cultural differences, 11–12
inter-subjectivity, 11–12
transcending legal systems, 11
varying approaches, 11
Western values, 11–12

Kaleidoscope approach
concept of kaleidoscope, 201
kaleidoscopic view of law
cultural context, 202
cultural variety, 201–2
different theoretical approaches, 200–1
diversity, 202
global legal pluralism, 199, 201–2
heuristic benefits, 209, 212
no single right, 201
kaleidoscopic view to legal theory
adaptability, 211
constant conceptual framework, 211
explicit epistemic base, 209
flexibility, 211
God's eye view of law, 209–10, 212
heuristic benefits, 209
images of the same thing, 211
inter-subjective consensus, 210
jurisdiversity, 210
lack of theoretical pretentiousness, 212
law-in-context, 210
legal-cultural embedding, 210
legal-cultural epistemological limits, 209
legal-cultural shape, 212
no reliance on conceptual similarities, 210
predictability, 211
relativism, 209, 212
stability, 211

theoretical background, 210
varying/changing images of law, 210
Kant, Immanuel, 82, 156, 168, 236
Kelsen, Hans, 13, 19, 46, 73–7, 79, 81, 189, 198, 203, 205–8, 211, 236, 240, 243
Klami, Hannu T, 90, 102
Knowledge
anthropology of knowledge, 249
concept of knowledge, 244
constructed dimension of knowledge, 247
general knowledge, 40
knowledge of law, 24, 78, 83
objective knowledge, 41–2
particular knowledge, 40
pure knowledge, 249
scientific knowledge, 40
truth by convention, 39–40, 43
universal knowledge, 40–1
Kramer, Matthew H, 173
Kuhn, Thomas, 229, 233–4, 237–8, 248

Language
see also **Linguistic disciplines**
act of communication
cultural context, 215–7
essence of language, 223
experimental function, 215–6
ideational meta-function, 215–6
interpersonal meta-function, 215–6
linguistic anthropology, 214
meanings, 215, 215–7
pragmatic view, 214
situational context, 216–7
situational differences, 216–7
social function, 214
socio-linguistics, 214
surrounding contexts, 215
systemic functional linguistics, 214–5, 217
texts, 215
textual meta-function, 215–7
indeterminacy, 89
language/law link
conceptual level, 219
cross-border influences, 219
dynamic interaction, 219
international/inter-cultural interaction, 219
intrinsic link, 219–20, 223, 226
Latin as lingua franca, 219
Law French, 219
legal terminology, 219
significance, 213
use of language, 214
meanings
act of communication, 215
experimental, 215–6
general concept of language, 213

Index

inter-personal, 215–6
specific linguistic system, 213
textual, 215–7
mental faculty, 213
situational differences
field, 216–7
mode, 216–7
tenor, 216–7
system of signals, 214

Law
see also **Law as a house metaphor**
acceptability, 15, 85–6, 88, 91, 100
adjudication, 229
see also **Adjudication**
binding force, 60
coherent system, 217
commitment to official sources, 81
compliance, 60, 63
conceptualisation, 65
conditions and criteria, 65
control, 60, 186
cultural concept/context, 217
see also **Legal cultures**
cultural influences, 229
definite entity, 64
definition of law, 204
developmental stages, 240–1
different legal traditions, 23
differing legal tasks, 65
distinct form of control, 186, 206
diversity of law, 23–4
effectiveness, 60–1, 63
enforcement, 60
equality principle, 65
see also **Equality principle**
foreseeability, 245
general values, 218
historical context, 217
ideological content, 244
institutionalised discourse, 219
knowledge of law, 24, 78, 83
legal phenomena, 23
legal positivism
see **Positivism**
legal scholarship, 229
legal science, 229, 235–6, 248
legitimacy, 60, 229, 240
multitude of concepts, 59
natural law
see **Natural law**
nature of law, 81, 84
normative concept, 81
over-regulation, 65
political and axiological choices, 229
real law, 101
relations between persons, 81
religious law, 19, 230, 240–1
social control, 61

socio-legal image
behaviour in courts, 207
law in action, 207
law in books, 207
socio-political context, 217
subjective objectivity, 19, 229, 236–9, 243, 246
systemisation of law, 245
unchangeability, 242
universality, 242
validity of law
axiological validity, 100–1, 103
factual validity, 100–3
naturalist, 100
positivist, 100
sociological, 100
systemic, 100–1, 103
valid legislation, 94
values, 218

Law as a house metaphor
autonomy, 48
continuity, 48
foundations, 48–9
inhabitants
comparative lawyers, 52–3
legal historians, 51
legal scholars, 50–1
philosophers, 51
social scientists, 51–2
insiders
comparative lawyers, 52–3
normative insiders, 50, 52
practice-orientated, 50
metaphor of law, 45–7, 49
outsiders
comparative lawyers, 52–3
detached, 50
neutral, 50
objectivity, 52
social scientists, 51–2
solidity, 47
spatial metaphor, 45, 47
state-centredness, 48
systematicity, 48
unity, 47
universality, 48

Law's assumptions
causation, 176–7, 179–85
common sense beliefs, 173–5
comparative legal scholarship, 176
consent, 176–7
doctrinal constructs, 173–4, 176, 178, 180, 186
domain-specific, 17, 176–7, 191–2
dominant theory, 17
earlier philosophical ideas, 173, 175, 192
epistemic nature, 174, 192
see also **Legal epistemology**

explicit assumptions, 172
factual and normative features, 171
false assumptions, 17, 172
implicit assumptions, 172, 190
incorrect assumptions, 190
institutional constraints, 192–3
instrumental perspective, 190–1
legal cultures, 176–7
  see also **Legal cultures**
legal domains, 176
legal families, 176
legal policy, 172
  see also **Legal policy**
legal reforms, 190–1
legal rules, 171–2
  see also **Legal rules**
legal systems, 176–7
methodological character, 174, 192
moral intuition, 175, 189
moral principles, 175
objectivity
  epistemic objectivity, 172–3
  ontological objectivity, 172–3
  semantic objectivity, 172–3
personhood, 185, 188–9
presuppositions, 171
reconstruction and confrontation
  legal epistemology, 175, 177
  legal policy, 175
  legal practice, 175
  legal theory, 175
  requirement, 175
  theoretical reconstruction, 176, 178
regulatory design, 172
responsibility, 185, 189
  see also **Legal responsibility**
system specific, 17, 176–7, 192
technological possibility, 187
theoretical indeterminacy, 192
theoretical status, 173, 178
true assumptions, 192
true or adequate assumptions, 172–3
truth-aptitude, 173
understanding reality, 17
wrong interpretations, 17
Legal certainty
acceptability, 15, 85–6, 88, 91, 96–8, 100–1
access to justice, 94
arbitrariness, 93–4, 96
context-bound, 86
definition, 85
democracy, 15, 85–6
efficiency, 98
EU law, 102, 107
expectation, 96
factual legal certainty, 15, 98, 101–3
formal legal certainty, 15, 96–8, 100, 103

importance, 15
interpretive choice, 99
judicial decisions, 15, 85–6, 95–6
  see also **Judicial decisions**
judicial protection, 102
legal positivism, 98
  see also **Positivism**
legal protection, 94
legal realism, 98
  see also **Legal realism**
legal rules, 91
  see also **Legal rules**
legitimacy, 85
levels of formality, 103
linguistic interpretation, 90
  see also **Linguistic disciplines**
moral evaluation, 102
moral norms, 96
natural law theories, 98
  see also **Natural law**
Nordic legal theory, 85, 93–4, 97–9, 101–2
obsolete laws, 98
openness, 86
political examples, 96–7
predictability, 15, 85–6, 90–1, 96, 98–9, 99–102, 211
principle of equality, 96
principles as norms, 91
  see also **Principles as norms**
proven facts, 94
rationality, 15, 96–7
reasonableness, 15
stability, 98
substantive legal certainty, 15, 96–9, 100–1, 103, 107
threefold conception, 103
validity of law
  axiological validity, 100–1, 103
  factual validity, 100–3
  naturalist, 100
  positivist, 100
  sociological, 100
  systemic, 100–1, 103
  valid legislation, 94
Legal concepts
analysis, 33, 37
characterising legal systems, 36
classification of legal material, 60
competence, 24, 33–8
  see also **Competence**
concept of power, 36
core concepts, 137
differing concepts, 13
doctrinal concepts, 12, 36
freedom of contract, 36
human rights, 36
internal legal concepts, 12, 36, 38

interpretation, 137
juridical acts, 33–6
  see also **Juridical acts**
legal powers, 33, 36–9
  see also **legal powers**
neutrality, 33, 37
objective legal theory, 33
penumbra, 137
reorganising, 50
restructuring, 50
sovereignty, 36
universality, 12
Legal cultures
comparative studies, 199–203, 218
concept, 202
constitutive elements, 218
cultural differences, 203
cultural framework, 19
cultural influences, 229–30
cultural paradigms, 19, 229, 232
  see also **Cultural paradigms**
cultural pluralism, 18
cultural relativism, 16, 18
cultural views
  influence, 199
  primary epistemology of law, 199–200, 203
culturally determined assumptions, 17–18
definition, 230
differing concepts of law, 203
differing legal systems, 200, 203
empirical basis, 218
images of law
  natural image, 18
  positivistic image, 18
  socio-legal image, 18
juridiversity, 18
kaleidoscope approach, 18, 200–202
  see also **Kaleidoscope approach**
language
  see **Language**
law and economics, 19
law-in-context, 18
legal-cultural differences, 199–200, 203
legal reasoning, 33
  see also **Legal reasoning**
legal scholarship, 19
legal sociology, 218
levels of culture, 230
multiplicity of contexts, 203
natural law, 18–19
  see also **Natural law**
objectivity
  absolute objectivity, 19–20, 236–8, 243
  objective objectivity, 19, 236–8, 243, 246
  objective subjectivity, 19, 237–8, 243

subjective objectivity, 19, 229, 236–9, 243, 246
subjective subjectivity, 19, 237–8
pluralism
  inherent pluralism, 204
  plurality of law, 203
positivism, 18–19, 206
  see also **Positivism**
religious law, 19, 230, 240–1
scale of observation
  broad definition of culture, 231, 247
  fundamental question, 230–1
  macro-cultural scale, 231
  mesocultural scale, 231
  microcultural scale, 231
  societal and historical context, 202
  universally neutral legal theory, 18
Legal doctrine
community of interpreters 8–9
competing paradigms, 9
cross-border harmonisation, 9
democracy, 9
  see also **Democracy**
human rights, 9
  see also **Human rights**
international law, 9
interpretation of legal texts, 8–9
inter-subjectivity, 9
rule of law, 9
Legal dogmatics
legal rules, 74–5, 77–8, 82–4
objectivity, 71
Legal epistemology
appropriateness, 183
autonomy, 178
causal minimalism, 184–5
causal principles, 179
causation, 179–85
censorial jurisprudence, 179
common moral sensibility, 181, 185,
conceptual analysis, 179
demystifying the role of legal philosophy, 179–80, 182, 184, 193
enlightenment, 183–4, 193
expository reconstruction of legal doctrine, 179
fortunate cases, 183–4, 190
hard-headed empiricism, 184
how the law thinks, 175, 177
law as form of control, 186
moral common sense, 183, 186, 192
moral intuition, 189
moral issues, 180, 185, 189
natural law theory, 186
  see also **Natural law**
obscuring metaphors, 183
ordinary language philosophy, 179–80, 186, 192

personhood, 185, 188–9
perspectives
  constructivist, 190
  instrumental, 190–1
  naturalistic, 189
  phenomenological, 189
primary epistemology of law
  cultural influences, 199
  implicit mono-epistemology, 199
  lack of objectivity, 199
  legal-cultural differences, 199–200, 203
  subconscious effect, 199
progressive idealism, 184
relationships
  description/evaluation, 180
  description/therapy, 180
responsibility
  attribution of responsibility, 180
  nature of responsibility, 185
theoretical perspectives
  Aristotelian perspective, 185
  doctrinal constructs, 178, 180, 186
  legal anthropology, 177
  modern social sciences, 178
  social constructivism, 178
  systematicity, 178
  systems theory, 178
  theoretical reconstruction, 178
  Western jurisprudence, 177–8
translation into factual terms, 180
unfortunate cases, 183–4, 189–90

Legal interpretation
see **Interpretation**

Legal logic
argumentation, 27, 30
  see also **Argumentation**
civil law tradition, 27
common law tradition, 27
declarative sentences, 30
immutability, 30
legal reasoning, 26–8, 33
  see also **Legal reasoning**
rejection, 208
rules
  exceptions, 30–2
  formulations, 30, 32
  validity, 30

Legal philosophy
Aristotelian perspective, 185
demystifying the role of legal philosophy, 179–80, 182, 184, 193
legal reasoning
  philosophical naturalism, 14
  philosophical questions, 53–4
objectivism, 71–2
philosophical realism, 70–1

positivist approach, 70, 72
  see also **Positivism**
subjectivism, 72

Legal policy
behavioural law and economics, 174
empirical research, 174
law's assumptions, 172
  see also **Law's assumptions**
libertarian paternalism, 174
neuro-law, 174
nudging, 174
regulatory reforms, 174
smart regulation, 174

Legal positivism
see **Positivism**

Legal powers
applicability, 38
capacity, 37
competence, 36, 38, 40
different legal jurisdictions, 38
doctrinal concepts, 36
juridical acts, 37–8
  see also **Juridical acts**
legal effects, 37–9
legal rules, 38
legal status, 37
notion of power, 38–9

Legal realism
American legal realism, 207–8, 246, 248
judicial decisions, 246–7
legal certainty, 98
legal theory, 74, 98, 207–8, 246–9
Scandinavian legal realism, 208

Legal reasoning
advanced legal reasoning, 84
argumentation, 15–16
  see also **Argumentation**
constructive conception, 14
correct reasoning, 82
correspondence between statement and object, 14
criteria of criticism, 81
EU citizenship, 90
formal logic, 16
ideal epistemic conditions, 81
impartiality, 82–3
legal certainty 15
  see also **Legal certainty**
legal cultures, 33
  see also **Legal cultures**
legal interpretation, 16
  see also **Interpretation**
legal logic, 26–8, 33
logical conception, 14
metaphysical conception, 14
neutrality, 33
perspective
  all things considered, 52–4

Index   261

legal point of view, 52–3
philosophical naturalism, 14
philosophical questions, 53–4
positivism, 89
  see also Positivism
rationality
  logical rationality, 89
  substantive rationality, 89
semantic conception, 14
statements with determinative truth
  value, 14
valid reasoning, 26–7
Legal responsibility
  attribution, 180
  causation, 180–5
  elimination of fault, 185
  justification, 185
  law as distinct form of control, 186
  minimising harm, 185
  moral principles, 185
  nature of responsibility, 185
  personal responsibility, 188
  personhood, 188
  regulating human conduct, 185–7
  self-respect, 188
  sense of self, 188
  social control, 188
Legal rules
  activist approach, 29
  adjudication, 77–8, 82–3
    see also Adjudication
  application, 24, 31–2, 36
  concept of law, 76–7
  constitutive elements
    conclusion, 27
    condition, 27
    consequence, 27
  contingent rules, 77
  correct reasoning, 82
  deviant logic approach, 29–31
  dynamic rules, 76
  exceptions, 30–2
  existence, 76
  expressions of law, 83–4
  facts, 36
  formulation, 30, 32
  foundation for objectivity, 82
  impartiality, 82–3
  impersonal demands, 83
  internal legal concepts, 36
  interpretation, 28, 77, 82–4
    see also Objective interpretation
  knowledge of law, 78, 83
  law's assumptions, 171–2
    see also Law's assumptions
  legal certainty, 91
    see also Legal certainty
  legal dogmatics, 74–5, 77–8, 82–4

legal powers, 38
legalistic approach, 27–8
lessons learned, 31–2
over-inclusive rules, 32
precedents, 81–2
principles of justice, 77, 80
rule of recognition, 76–7
separated from evaluative judgments, 77
separated from moral evaluations, 77
state-centred rules, 48, 204
statutes, 81–2
unattractive outcomes, 31–2
validity, 30, 76–8, 80
Legal scholarship
  classification of legal material, 60
  comparative law, 176
  legal cultures, 19
  legal methodology, 50
Legal science
  anthropological prerequisites, 248
  cultural dimension, 229–30
  cultural paradigms, 235–6, 248
  objectivity, 247
  socio-legal image of law, 207, 209
Legal systems
  characterising legal systems, 36
  comparability, 12
  differing legal systems, 200, 203
  diversity, 12
  law's assumptions, 176–7
  structure of legal system, 198
Legal theory
  anthropology of knowledge, 249
  application of legal rules, 24, 31–2
  archetypes of legal theory
    empirical reality, 204
    state-centred rules, 204
    values, 204
  axiological neutrality, 246
  characteristics of law, 23
  classification changes, 12
  classification systems, 25
  comparative law, 211
    see also Comparative law
  competence, 38, 61
  conceptual coherence, 204
  consequences of choices, 39–40
  continental legal theory, 243
  conventions, 12, 24, 26, 32, 41–4, 198
    see also Conventions
  cultural context, 202
    see also Legal cultures
  cultural images
    natural image, 204–5, 211
    positivist image, 205–7, 211
    socio-legal image, 207–9, 211
  definition of law, 204
  degree of reception, 243–4

differentiating between perspectives, 46
differing legal traditions, 23
differing social practices, 13–14
diversity of law, 23–4
dividing lines
  actors and activities, 45
  effectiveness and efficacy, 51
  generality and equality, 46–7
  insiders and outsiders, 46–7
  insiders and validity, 46
  internal and external virtues, 46
  lawyers and notaries, 51
  legal certainty and equality, 51
  legal officials and lay citizens, 46
  legal positivism, 45
  legislators and judges, 45, 51
  outsiders and efficacy, 46
  principles and perspectives, 45
  relevant moral criteria, 46
  values and views, 45
elimination of subjectivity, 235
epistemology, 203
  see also **Legal epistemology**
external morality, 46
external perspective, 13
foreseeability of law, 245
global legal pluralism, 199, 201–2
implications of choice, 33
inconsistencies, 45
inside-outside dichotomy
  see **Inside-outside dichotomy**
instrumentalisation of rules, 14, 50
internal morality, 46
internal perspective, 13
interpretation theory, 246
judge-centred law, 60
kaleidoscope approach, 209–12
  see also **Kaleidoscope approach**
knowledge of law, 24
language
  see **Language**
law's origin, use and study, 203
leading works, 243
legal concepts
  competence, 24
  content, 198
  differing concepts, 13
  doctrinal concepts, 12, 36
  internal legal concepts, 12, 36, 38
  reorganising, 50
  restructuring, 50
  universality, 12
legal logic
  see **Legal logic**
legal phenomena, 23, 245
legal positivism
  see **Positivism**
legal realism, 74, 98, 207–8, 246–9

legal sociology, 245
legal systems
  comparability, 12
  diversity, 12
lessons learned, 39
limits, 207
loss of certainty, 14, 51
material rationalisation, 245
metaphors
  law as a house, 45, 47–9
  metaphors as syndromes, 48–50
  metaphor of law, 46–7, 49–50
  spatial metaphor, 46–7
method informed by object, 52
methodology of law, 203
natural law
  see **Natural law**
nature of law, 198
neutral terminology, 12
non-legal example
  certainty by conventions, 26
  classification systems, 25–6
  nature of planets, 25–6, 39
  whales as mammals, 24–5, 39, 55
non-monotonic logics, 24, 30–1
objectivity
  legal theory
  classification changes, 12
  comparable legal systems, 12
  conventions, 12
  diverse legal systems, 12
  doctrinal concepts, 12
  external perspective, 13
  freedom from personal feelings, 198
  implicit prejudices, 198–9
  influence of legal culture, 199
  instrumentalisation of rules, 14, 50
  internal legal concepts, 12
  internal perspective, 13
  lack of objectivity, 199
  legal positivism, 13
  legal practice, 13
  loss of certainty, 14
  meta-ideas, 198
  neutral terminology, 12
  objectivity by convention, 24, 26, 32, 41–4, 198
  rational arguments, 198
  scientific approach, 13
  social practices, 13–14
  undisputed facts, 198
  universal legal concepts, 12
ontology, 203
particular jurisdictions, 33, 39
philosophy, 53–4
  see also **Legal philosophy**
pluralism
  inherent pluralism, 204

Index 263

legal pluralism, 203–6, 208–9, 211
positivism
   see **Positivism**
post-modern philosophers, 244
predefined legal norms, 245
relativism, 198, 202, 248
scientific approach, 13
shift in perspective, 244
social control, 61
social practices, 45, 59–60. 63–4
socio-cultural context, 243
socio-legal theory, 207–9, 211
   see also **Socio-legal theory**
structure of legal system, 198
syndromes, 45, 48–50
theocratic attitudes, 245
universality, 197–8, 202
Legislation
   compliance, 60
   development, 224
   effectiveness, 60–1, 63
   enforcement, 60
   equality principle 4–5
   forms of legislation, 50
   'generality', 4–5
   legitimacy, 60
   regulation, 60
   statutory rules, 4–5
   validity, 94
Levels of justification
   easy cases, 141–2, 144
   EU law, 88
   hard cases, 144
   in-between cases, 143–4
   indeterminacy of language, 89
   judicial decisions, 86–9, 96–7, 103–5, 108
   literal interpretation, 89
Linguistic and translation studies
   see also **Language**; **Linguistic disciplines**
   comparative law, 213, 220–1, 223
   contrastive linguistics, 18, 218
   contribution, 218–9
   corpus linguistics, 19, 218, 220–1, 227
   hermeneutical approach, 220
   legal translators, 220
   mediating role of translation
      cultural influences, 224–5
      development of legislation, 224
      intellectual conservatism, 224
      legal culture, 224–5
   methodologies
      difference theorists, 223
      dominant/peripheral tendencies, 225
      elements of bias, 223
      epistemology of authority, 223–4
      epistemology of inquiry, 223
      legal functionalists, 223
      legally relevant elements, 224
      re-presentation, 223
      retrieving meanings, 224
      terminological configurations, 225
      text analysis, 223–4
      text selection, 223
   parallel/divergent priorities in discourse, 225
   prior legal-discursive traditions, 222, 224, 227
   systemic functional grammar, 19, 214–5, 217–8, 227
   translational features
      acceptability, 226
      adequacy in translation, 226
      analysis, 226
      corpus-based research, 226
      explication, 225–6
      legal discourse, 226
      normalisation, 225–6
      simplification, 225–6
      specific features, 225
Linguistic disciplines
   see also **Language**
   comparative law, 213
   cultural contexts, 18
   empirical basis for research, 219–20, 226
   encoded meanings, 18
   law as institutionalised discourse, 19
   methodologies
      contrastive linguistics, 19, 218
      corpus linguistics, 19, 218, 220–1, 227
      discourse analysis, 19, 218, 220, 227
      socio-linguistics, 19, 218
      systemic functional grammar, 19, 214–5, 217–8, 227
   objective basis for research, 18
   situational contexts, 18
   translation studies, 18–19
   see also **Linguistic and translation studies**
Locke, John, 72, 153, 156
Logic
   see **Legal logic**
Luhmann, Niklas, 13, 46, 61

MacCormick, Neil, 142–3
Marmor, Andrei, 14, 73, 75, 78
McCrudden, Christopher, 51
Metaphors
   comparison with syndromes, 45, 54
   expansive nature, 50
   function, 48–9, 54–5
   generative power, 49
   heuristic potential, 49–50
   law as a house, 45, 47–9, 51
   see also **Law as a house metaphor**
   meaning, 49
   metaphors as syndromes, 48–50
   metaphor of law, 46–7, 49–50

264 *Index*

obscuring metaphors, 183
similarities, 48–9
spatial metaphor, 46–7
Modernity
  access to modernity, 242
  cultural paradigms, 234, 241
  exclusive modernity, 232, 242–3, 245
  ideal type, 232
  inclusive modernity, 232, 239, 242–3, 248
  legal positivism, 241
    see also **Positivism**
  legitimacy/illegitimacy of cultures, 231
  legitimate representation, 231
  macro paradigm, 234, 245
  meta-culture of legitimisation, 231–2
  natural law, 242
    see also **Natural law**
  orthodox modernity, 232
Moral rights
  alienability, 162
  fundamental human freedom, 157
  inalienable rights, 157
    see also **Inalienable rights**
  moral duties, 17, 157–8, 168
  moral rights/immoral things, 158, 166
  morally problematic situations, 159
  restriction of freedom, 158
  right-duty relationship, 158–9, 162, 166–7
  voluntary transactions, 158, 162, 166
  waiver, 162
Moral rules
  conduct and obligations, 76
Morality
  external, 46
  internal, 46
  law and morality 16–17, 153–5, 166, 168–9

Nagel, Thomas, 69
Natural law
  access to modernity, 242
  bi-directional nature, 241–2
  compliance with just laws, 239
  development, 240–1
  fixist concept of law, 242
  human behaviour, 186
    see also **Human behaviour**
  ideal law, 239
  integrating existing law, 239
  laws of reason, 239
  legal certainty, 98
  legal cultures, 18–19
  legal pluralism, 205
  minimum content, 76–7, 186
  moral principles, 205
  non-positive source, 204–5
  objective subjectivity, 243
  rational theories, 204–5
  rule of law, 89
  universalism, 204–5
  validity of law, 100
Nordic legal theory
  legal certainty, 85, 93–4, 97–9, 101–2

Objective interpretation
  case differentiation, 132–3, 136–8
  categorisation
    easy cases, 132–3, 149
    hard cases, 1322, 136–7, 149
    in-between cases, 132, 136–7, 149
  correctness, 131–2
  easy cases
    administrative permits, 137
    affirmation of legal act, 139
    clear rule adopted, 133, 144
    conceptual problems, 133
    conflicting interpretations of facts, 135
    constant legal application, 133
    deductive logic, 140, 142–3
    definition, 134
    economic benefit, 146–7
    evidence, 138
    factual premise, 135, 138, 140, 143, 146–7
    formal logic, 142
    frequency of similar cases, 133–5
    interpretational reference point, 135
    interpretive arguments, 134–5
    judicial application procedures, 137, 149–50
    lack of interpretive choice, 139–41, 147
    legal discretion, 135
    legal inference, 135, 140, 142–3
    levels of justification, 141–2, 144
    levels of law, 144
    logical syllogism, 140, 142, 146
    no relevant harm, 146–7
    normative premise, 134–5, 138, 140, 142–3, 146–7
    objectivity, 139–41, 146, 150
    prerequisite for application of the law, 139
    right solution, 135, 139–41, 144, 146
    single interpretation justified, 134–5
    sources of law, 134
    technical legal decisions, 136
    validity of rule not questioned, 133
  formal logic, 132
  hard cases
    absence of probabilities, 136, 150
    economic benefits, 149
    environmental harm, 148
    evaluation of evidence, 138
    levels of law, 144–5
    increased demand for argumentation, 144

Index 265

interpretive choices, 144, 146–7
legal argumentation, 150
level of legal culture, 145
major ambiguities in interpretation, 148–9
margin of discretion, 136
multiple interpretations, 136–7, 144, 149
no right answer, 149
normative choices, 149
semantic arguments, 143
hermeneutic circle, 137–8
in-between cases
  benefits to different interests, 147–8
  easy cases differentiated, 149
  environmental concerns, 147–8
  legal argumentation, 150
  legal discretion, 136
  lex posterior, 136
  lex specialis, 136
  lex superior, 136
  margin for discretion, 143
  minor ambiguities in interpretation, 147–8
  multiple conflicting syllogisms, 148
  multiple interpretations, 136–7, 148–9
  no right answer, 136, 147–9
  persuasive legal argumentation, 148
  probabilities, 136, 150
  risk of harm, 147
  semantic arguments, 143
  subjectivity, 140
interpretation of rules, 131–2
lack of choice, 132, 139–41
legal inference, 132, 135, 140, 142–3
Objectivism
minimal objectivism, 42
modest objectivism, 42
objective judgments, 71
philosophical background, 71–2
projectivism contrasted, 72
strong objectivism, 42
subjectivist critique, 138
Objectivity
see also Objective interpretation; Objectivity of values
adjudication 6
  see also **Adjudication**
argumentative power 7–8
  see also **Argumentation**
aspiration, 83
cognitive dimension, 70
comparative law, 9–11
  see also **Comparative law**
concept of truth, 69–70, 78–9
consistent descriptions, 43
cultural relativism, 20

dimensions of objectivity
  correct reasoning, 82
  impartiality, 82–3
  impersonal demands, 83
  inter-subjectivity, 81
  legal interpretations, 82
  objective intentions, 83
  official sources of law, 81–2
epistemology of law, 108, 172–3
good decisions, 7, 9
importance, 20
inter-changeability with other concepts, 8
inter-subjectivity 7–8
jurisprudence, 4, 11–12
  see also **Jurisprudence**
legal actors, 4
legal certainty, 20
  see also **Legal certainty**
legal cultures
  absolute objectivity, 19–20
  influence, 20
  objective objectivity, 19, 236–8, 243, 246
  objective subjectivity, 19, 237–8, 243
  subjective objectivity, 19, 229, 236–9, 243, 246
  subjective subjectivity, 19, 237–8
legal doctrine, 4, 8–9
  see also **Legal doctrine**
legal dogmatics, 71
legal education, 20
legal realism, 74, 98, 207–8, 246–9
legal reasoning, 14–16, 71, 84
  see also **Legal reasoning**
legal theory
  classification changes, 12
  comparable legal systems, 12
  conventions, 12
  doctrinal concepts, 12
  diverse legal systems, 12
  external perspective, 13
  freedom from personal feelings, 198
  implicit prejudices, 198–9
  influence of legal culture, 199
  instrumentalisation of rules, 14
  internal legal concepts, 12
  internal perspective, 13
  lack of objectivity, 199
  legal positivism, 13
  legal practice, 13
  loss of certainty, 14
  meta-ideas, 198
  neutral terminology, 12
  objectivity by convention, 24, 26, 32, 41–4, 198
  rational arguments, 198
  scientific approach, 13
  social practices, 13–14

undisputed facts, 198
universal legal concepts, 12
legislation, 4–5
see also **Legislation**
meaningfulness, 69
meta viewpoint, 238
mind-independent, 70, 76
normative concept, 69
objective-subjective dichotomy
　ethical dimension, 69–70
　paradigm, 247
　paradox, 247
　philosophical dimension, 69–71
ontology of law, 108, 172–3
perspective-bound, 41–4
philosophical realism, 74–5
quality of reasoning, 71
rationality, 69–70
reasonableness 7, 9
reality described, 41–3
relationships
　statement/defined object, 70, 74–5
　subject/person speaking about it, 69
semantic objectivity, 172–3
situated rationalities, 238
strong conceptions, 73–8
see also **Strong conceptions**
theory of truth, 74–5
'toothless' objectivity, 40–1
typology
　minimal objectivism, 42
　modest objectivism, 42
　strong objectivism, 42
　subjectivism, 42–3
vagueness 8
weak conceptions, 78–9
see also **Weak conceptions**
Objectivity of values
adoption, 80
ethical relativism, 80
existence, 79–80
forbidden actions, 79
justice, 80
objective moral values, 79–80
particular society's values, 80–1
subjective values distinguished, 80
universal values, 80
O'Neill, Onora, 166, 168

Paradigms
see also **Cultural paradigms**
axiological dimension, 248
change of paradigm, 233
conceptual context, 233
constructed dimension of knowledge, 247
context of reference, 233
knowledge of reality, 233
legal science, 248
mesoparadigms, 244
metaphysical paradigms, 233, 248
microparadigms, 244
pure objectivity, 236–7
rationality, 236
recognised values, 233
reversal of perspective, 244
scientific paradigms, 233
set of beliefs, 233
social sciences, 234, 248
subjective objectivity, 19, 229, 236–9, 243, 246
Parliamentary meetings
see also **Dutch parliament**
communication, 109
populist politicians, 109–10, 130
rules of argumentation, 109, 111–2, 116–9
see also **Argumentation**
rules of order, 123–5, 127
Paunio, Elina, 89, 99, 107
Peczenik, Alexander, 94, 96–7, 100, 102–3
Pluralism
global legal pluralism, 199, 201–2
inherent pluralism, 204
legal pluralism, 203–6, 208–9, 211
Positivism
acts of will, 239
common elements/general methods, 206–7
complexity of law, 246
cultural dimension, 249
development, 240–1
distinct nature of law, 206
ethical subjectivism, 73
formalistic positivism, 240, 248–9
grundnorm, 205–6
ideological function, 240
judicial role, 240
legal certainty, 98
see also **Legal certainty**
legal cultures, 18–19, 206
see also **Legal cultures**
legal pluralism, 206
legal reasoning, 89
see also **Legal reasoning**
legal rules, 239
see also **Legal rules**
legal standards, 246
legalistic ethic, 239
legitimation of law, 240
limiting object to existing law, 239
modernity, 241
see also **Modernity**
moral values, 73, 205
non-universal context, 206
objective objectivity, 243
philosophical positivism, 240–1
positive law, 239

role of man, 206
rule of law, 89
separability thesis, 72
social thesis, 72–3
strict objectivity, 205
validity of law, 100
Principles as norms
acceptability, 91
concepts of fairness, 92–3
constitutional rights, 92–3
equal pay, 91
legal certainty, 91
see also **Legal certainty**
literal interpretation, 91
moral concepts, 92
predictability, 91
relevance, 91
rights of individuals, 91
scope of application, 91
sex discrimination, 91
weighing up and balancing, 90
Public law
privatisation, 53

Rawls, John, 14, 78
Reasonableness
inter-subjective consensus 7, 9
'justified', 7, 9
'rational', 7
Relationism
principle of relativity, 248
Religious law
development, 240–1
legal cultures, 19, 230
Responsibility
see **Legal responsibility**
Ross, Alf, 198, 208
Rule of law
legal doctrine, 9
legal positivism, 89
natural law, 89
Rules of argumentation
see **Argumentation**

Searle, Johan, 48, 97
Sexual behaviour
appropriateness, 88
limits of tolerance, 88
public morality, 88
Siltala, Raimo, 100, 103, 135, 143
Simmonds, Nigel, 161–2
Social practices
importance, 59–60, 62–3
Socio-legal theory
actual behaviour in courts, 207
American legal realism, 207–8, 246, 248
demystification of doctrinal rhetoric, 207
law in action, 207

law in books, 207
legal cultures, 18
legal instrumentation, 207
legal pluralism, 208–9
legal science, 207, 209
limits of legal theory, 207
objectivism, 211
realistic/sociological jurisprudence, 207
Scandinavian legal realism, 208
socially binding norms, 208–9
use of logic rejected, 208
validity of law, 100
Soriano, Leonor Moral, 107–8
Strong conceptions
correctness of statements, 75
criteria of acceptability, 75–6, 97, 99
interpretation, 73–5
logical conception, 78
metaphysical conception, 74
ontological conception, 74
semantic objectivity, 75–6
Subjectivism
ethical subjectivism, 72
moral judgments, 72
Subjectivity
inter-subjectivity, 7–9, 11–12, 81
invisible form, 248
level of representations, 237
meta viewpoint, 238
monotheistic religions, 237
objectifying beliefs, 237–8
objective subjectivity, 19, 237–8, 243
relativism, 248
situated rationalities, 238
sources of subjectivity, 248
subjective objectivity, 19, 229, 236–9, 243, 246
subjective subjectivity, 19, 237–8
Syndromes
comparison with metaphors, 45, 54
concepts, 55
conditions, 62
function, 54–5
intension of a concept, 45, 55
metaphors as syndromes, 48–50

Translation studies
see **Linguistic and translation studies**
Tully, James, 118–20

Van Hoecke, Mark, 3, 41, 210, 218, 235

Weak conceptions
arguments and conclusions, 78
constructive conception, 78
criteria of objective reasoning, 78–9
different degrees of objectivity, 79
Weber, Max, 232, 239, 244–6

Will theory
    advantages, 154, 160, 163–5
    defenders, 161
    discretionary power, 163
    expression of choice, 154
    inalienable rights, 154
    law and morality, 16–17, 166
    legal rights
        breach of duty, 159
        civil law, 159–60
        claim rights, 160
        control over another's duty, 159
        criminal law, 159–60, 162–3
        fundamental rights, 161
        immunity rights, 160–3
        jural relations, 160–3
        legally respected choice, 160–1
        nature of legal rights, 159, 161
        non-waiver, 160–3
        powers, 160
        privileges, 160
        theory of legal rights, 157
    moral rights, 157–9, 162, 166
        see also **Moral rights**
    ordinary citizens, 162–3
    paternalism, 164–5
    right-holders
        benefit, 162–3
        choice, 161, 165
        protection, 165
    right to do wrong
        consent, 166–7
        immoral activity, 166
        individual's free choices, 166
        lack of clarity, 166
        medical procedures, 166–7
        moral rights, 166
        morality and law, 166
        partial understandings, 166
        rights-duty relationship, 166–7
        voluntary harm, 167
    rights
        arising out of provisions, 158
        demarcation, 163
        forming part of morality, 159
        interest theory of rights, 163–4
        interference with freedom and privacy, 158
        nature of rights, 154
        peremptory rights, 167
    separation for civil/criminal law, 160
Wittgenstein, Ludwig, 16, 59, 76, 112, 131–2, 140
Wróblewski, Jerzy, 15, 98, 100–2, 106